Minds in the Making

Minds in the Making

*Essays in Honor of
David R. Olson*

Edited by
Janet Wilde Astington

BLACKWELL
Publishers

Copyright © Blackwell Publishers 2000
Editorial selection and arrangement copyright © Janet W. Astington 2000

First published 2000

2 4 6 8 10 9 7 5 3 1

Blackwell Publishers Ltd
108 Cowley Road
Oxford OX4 1JF
UK

Blackwell Publishers Inc.
350 Main Street
Malden, Massachusetts 02148
USA

British Library Cataloguing in Publication Data

A CIP catalogue record for this book is available from the British Library.

Library of Congress Cataloging-in-Publication Data

[copy to come]

ISBN 0-631-21805 X (hbk); 0-631-21806 8 (pbk)

Typeset in 10 on 13 pt Galliard
by Ace Filmsetting Ltd, Frome, Somerset
Printed in Great Britain by MPG Books Ltd, Bodmin, Cornwall

This book is printed on acid-free paper.

For David R. Olson
mentor, colleague, and friend

Contents

List of Figures

List of Tables

List of Contributors

Janet Wilde Astington, Institute of Child Study, OISE/University of Toronto
Jens Brockmeier, Free University Berlin and OISE/University of Toronto
Jerome Bruner, New York University
Robin N. Campbell, Department of Psychology, University of Stirling
Carol Fleisher Feldman, Department of Psychology, New York University
Angela Hildyard, Woodsworth College, University of Toronto
Bruce D. Homer, Centre for Applied Cognitive Science, OISE/University of Toronto
Deepthi Kamawar, Centre for Applied Cognitive Science, OISE/University of Toronto
Thomas Keenan, Department of Psychology, University of Canterbury
Kang Lee, Department of Psychology, Queen's University
Anne McKeough, Department of Educational Psychology, University of Calgary
Josef Perner, Department of Psychology, University of Salzburg
Joan Peskin, Institute of Child Study, OISE/University of Toronto
Ted Ruffman, Experimental Psychology, University of Sussex
Nancy Torrance, Centre for Applied Cognitive Science, OISE/University of Toronto
Penelope G. Vinden, Department of Psychology, Clark University
Rita Watson, School of Education, The Hebrew University of Jerusalem
Gordon Wells, Department of Curriculum, Teaching and Learning, OISE/University of Toronto
Philip David Zelazo, Department of Psychology, University of Toronto

Acknowledgments

When I was first planning a volume in honor of David R. Olson, I wrote to some of his many colleagues, friends, and former students, asking if they would like to contribute to it. I am very grateful for the enthusiastic and generous responses that I received. Obviously the volume would not exist without them. It could indeed have been much longer than it is, even though I limited the invitation to people who had spent some time teaching, talking, or studying with David at the Ontario Institute for Studies in Education during his tenure from 1966 to the present.

As the project got under way, two local participants, Philip David Zelazo and Joan Peskin, were helpful in reading drafts and discussing the issues involved. At the end of the project my postdoctoral fellow Jodie Baird provided invaluable help with the compilation of the index. I thank them all sincerely for their assistance. I am also grateful for the cheerful administrative assistance provided by Audrey Goba, Susan Murphy, and Cheryl Zimmerman in the Dr. R. G. N. Laidlaw Research Centre at the Institute of Child Study, OISE/UT. And I thank Rick Volpe, Director of the Centre, for the photograph of David R. Olson that forms the frontispiece to the volume.

Martin Davies, Commissioning Editor at Blackwell Publishers, was helpful and enthusiastic right from the beginning. When he first heard about my idea for the volume he encouraged me to submit a proposal to him and expedited its acceptance. Alison Dunnett, Editorial Manager, provided timely advice and guidance throughout the project, and Maggie Walsh, Lisa Eaton, and Tessa Hanford, Project Manager, were most helpful too. I am very grateful to them all.

I also thank my family – John, Susan, Kevin, Meg, and Gethin – for keeping me happy and well fed, and not complaining even when drafts and laptop occupied the picnic table by the lake.

Janet Wilde Astington
Toronto
January 2000

Foreword

Jerome Bruner

Never mind Isaiah Berlin's famous oversimplification about hedgehogs and foxes, how "The fox knows many things; the hedgehog knows one big thing." David Olson is proof contrary to this preclusive dichotomy. He has always known one *very* big thing – that the reality we experience is constructed, not just "there" to be found or stumbled upon. But beyond and despite that, when it comes to *how* we human beings go about constructing our realities, he has been the Compleat Fox, recognizing, even being somewhat bemused by the myriad ways we justify our claims about what is *really* Real. So while David Olson has been a steadfastly constructivist hedgehog from the start, his approach to how reality construction is accomplished has been foxlike, canny, open.

He even has a way of keeping his mind unsettled on how we accomplish our construction of the Real – a way of finding and reading the book most likely to protect him from dogmatism. I recall our first talks together. It was in the 1960s, and David had just arrived as a grown-up post-doc at our still new Harvard Center for Cognitive Studies. There was a lot of corridor chat in those days, all of us wanting to make plain to each other just what we each were rebelling against and how we each proposed to go about saving psychology from its mindlessness. David, like most of us, had also been brought up in hard-knuckled North American "learning theory." During our first chat he quickly and enthusiastically turned from standard psychology to what he was presently reading. It was Ernst Cassirer's *Essay on Man* – "fascinating, really mind opening." He was smitten by that neo-Kantian two-volume classic, a book to humble psychology's antimentalist pretensions.

Cassirer was David's first epiphany in continental constructivist philosophy. He rode on its high-arc trajectory for weeks afterwards. But I realize now in retrospect that he was not being "carried away" by it. The epiphany sparked by Cassirer had inspired him to undertake a little experiment with ordinary subjects; it even involved a clever bit of laboratory apparatus! It had to do, of all things, with the representation (as we would now say) of "diagonality." Can a child reproduce a diagonal line of lights displayed kitty-corner across a board of discrete individual lights laid out in Cartesian horizontal-and-vertical rows and columns? Why do young children have such a devil of a time matching such diagonal displays on an identical light board under their own control? What's so special about diagonality, for Pete's sake? It seems phenomenologically simple enough. It only requires an "imaginary slanting line," say, from the upper left to the lower right corner? Or does it?

Before he was done with it (some years later), David wrote an intriguing book about diagonality, or was it really about diagonality? In fact, I think it was David's first go at the problem of representation. His first hypothesis about the matter seemed reasonable enough, even a bit Piagetian. To trace a diagonal on a rectilinear, Cartesian array of lights, he reasoned, required keeping in mind *two* rule specifications at once: for example, move-one-*across* and move-one-*down*. This two-element procedure was beyond the young child's capacities. The young child's perception of diagonality was simply not representable in terms of positions on a Cartesian grid (Olson, 1970). That was the heart of the matter – but it provided the goad to much of David's later thinking about the relations between input, perception, and representation, the key problem of constructivist theories of reality construction.

It took him directly to the issue of how *modes* of *representation* play a key role in determining what we see, what we can think about, how we construct our knowledge. If you can't carry out the twofold mental operations needed for *copying* a diagonal on a Cartesian array, how in the devil do you manage to *see* diagonals so easily? What's so different about moving slantwise from Column 1/Row 1, to Column 2/Row 2, etc. and just plain *drawing* a diagonal? That was the kind of constructivist puzzle that was gnawing away at David, even in those distant days – not so different from his later preoccupation with the question of what makes the "world in print" so different from the "world of immediate experience" and the "world of spoken dialogue." Questions like these were lurking in David's intellectual unconscious from the very start. They kept recurring in his letters, in our conversations in Cambridge and Toronto (where he had moved), and especially in our phone calls (to which we are both extravagantly addicted). And he kept them reactivated by his irrepressible habit of reading speculative books that convinced him that he hadn't yet got the story right!

His reading and research invariably led him into uncomfortable (and often unpopular) epistemological stances, always at war with the fundamental postulate of positivism which accounts for experienced reality by reference to what is "out there" in the world, to some sort of frontal ontology. David's questions were principally epistemological, questions usually taken as pure mischief by committed positivists. Is "reality" exclusively constructed by one's system for representing it? If it were that "autistic," how do we manage to "get on" so well either in the natural world or in the shared world of social realities? With regard to the latter, how do we succeed in creating a culture dependent upon shared and sharable "realities"? The positivist's "verificationist" epistemology simply can't get hold of such cultural matters, and chooses to ignore them.

David was soon launched into an interpretivist view of meaning making and/or reality construction, but he wanted to develop a view that was sufficiently "steady" to account both for our representations of the natural world, yet socially labile enough to allow for the forming of like-minded communities of interpretation.

Not surprising that speech act theory soon enlisted David's enthusiasm. It was just right for his dilemma. For meaning making in such theory involves a hearer recognizing a speaker's *communicative intent*. It is highly conventionalized and depends upon the existence of an interpretive community that recognizes that the illocutionary force of the utterance "Would you be so kind as to pass the salt?" is not to inquire about the hearer's compassion but to request salt with requisite politeness. The appropriate "uptake" of a speaker's communicative intent depends heavily, of course, upon there being conventionalized preliminary, essential and (perhaps most important) felicity conditions relating to the time, place, and conditions of any utterance. A considerable part of "meaning making," then, depends upon grasping the conventions governing the making of an utterance – even the conventions for violating these in particular ways in order to create "implicatures" (Grice, 1975).

Both meaning making and "reality construction," are, when viewed in this way, transformed in two crucial, though related ways. For one thing, this approach rests on shared cultural conventions rather than ontological verification. For another, conventionalization implies the pre-existence of an interpretive community whose members can "understand each other's minds."

With respect to the first of these, conventionalism, David and his students and colleagues soon began a Toronto series of research studies on the ontogenesis of speech acts, how the young acquire the conventions and constraints required for communally appropriate illocutionary meaning making. One of the first of these was Janet Astington's landmark study on the ontogenesis of promising. I was the "outside examiner," as Toronto requires, and I recall not only the brilliance of her dissertation but also the dedication of the group at OISE, the Ontario Institute for Studies in Education. Even then, without it being quite explicit, David was beginning to posit a role for an "interpretive community," though, as Carol Feldman remarks in her chapter later in this volume, its importance only comes into full focus when David's interests were extended to the study of written texts and writing.

But there was an intermediate step still to be taken, and it was a somewhat curious one. Perhaps through the influence of Josef Perner or Alison Gopnik or Janet Astington, all Torontonians in the late 1970s and 1980s, or perhaps it was just by dint of David's receptivity to the *Zeitgeist*, in any case, he soon became explicitly intrigued by the problem of intersubjectivity – how we come to know Other Minds. For it is precisely this ability that makes possible an interpretive community. Given speech-act emphasis on a hearer "reading" a speaker's communicative intent, intersubjectivity had to be center stage. Not surprising that one of the earliest and most fruitful conferences on that subject was held in Toronto in 1986 under David's chairmanship.[1] It was a conference of especial note, for it focused principally on the conditions and functions of intersubjectivity rather than on narrower, previously dominant issues of intersubjective "accuracy" or on the even narrower though then much debated issue of when children come to understand others' false beliefs as false beliefs. That conference, under David's learned guidance, was a major turning point. It turned the psychological study of intersubjectivity from a rather narrow experimental specialty, dominated by an interest in the "accuracy" of interpersonal perception, into a much broader concern with conventionalized means whereby we impute crucial mental states to others under a variety of culturally specifiable conditions. From then on, intersubjectivity became recognized as central in a much wider range of phenomena, ranging from its role in the evolution of human culture, to its importance in ontogenesis generally and the ontogenesis of language particularly.

In the colloquia David arranged in Toronto in the years following, he managed to broaden the scope of these inquiries even further.[2] For by now, he was in the final phases of writing *The World on Paper* and the sharing of perspective by writer and reader was looming up as a crucial issue. In any case, the ripple effect of these colloquia was enormous, modulating the thinking of so diverse a group of participants as Michael Tomasello, Alison Gopnik, the "two Andies" (Meltzoff and Whiten, both of whom had been in my laboratory at Oxford when David had spent a visiting year there) Janet Astington, Michael Chandler, Stuart Shanker, Sue Savage-Rumbaugh, Carol Feldman, myself, and many others.

What can I say about David's latest pioneering work on the impact of printed media on individual mental processes and on the nature and role of culture? I think it was plain to all of us who participated in a Toronto colloquium on literacy in the spring of 1999[3] that he had succeeded in rescuing literacy from the historical enthusiasts who had seen it as the sole Artificer of Modernity as well as from the pedagogical enthusiasts who had seen it as a kind of Self-Improving Skill to be cultivated principally as a tool for achieving academic success. We can see literacy now for what it is, as a powerful if necessarily selective means for creating analytically explicit ways of representing reality – past, present, and possible. Its capacity for record-making (always in the light of a perspective) offers powerful new possibilities for constructing history, law, even commerce. But it is not just record-making that matters, for print also provided an undreamed of means for revisiting, rethinking, and metacognition. The glory of text is its openness to reinterpretation, its invitingness to reading in another register. Now, finally, we can indeed inquire what has been our past desire, for we know at last how much it depends on how we have read it!

What a contribution this man has made! Yet oddly, it does not come in upon you until you reflect upon it. For his name is not associated with One Big Breakthrough, nor has he thumped One Big Tin Drum. His style is to remind us by stunning demonstration how things fit together, what needs putting in, what remains conjectural.

Our phone conversations (still unabatedly extravagant!) still close with David trying to a recruit me into his self-disturbing reading game. For example: "By the way, Jerry, have you by any chance seen xxxx's book on Greek literacy. You know, you don't need the printing press for literacy to have a powerful effect. Have a look." Well, I've long since come to the conclusion that David is always reading *some* version of Ernst Cassirer's *Essay on Man*, still searching out thinkers who goad him into second thoughts. I'm flattered that he sometimes invites me along.

David Olson is an astonishing friend, and I've long believed that it was his wonderful gift for friendship that marks him as such a great teacher. I can speak with some authority, for we have been close for many years, and worked together in many places on many projects. We have walked together, sailed together, dined together, written articles together, got tipsy together, even played weekly tennis on a freezing cold, unheated Dutch indoor court. We have even been at each other in print (Bruner, 1995; Olson & Astington, 1995). All this despite the fact that we come from completely different backgrounds, David a Canadian Midwesterner, me a New Yorker.

I have also seen David with his students and younger colleagues. What makes David a great and much loved teacher is just exactly what makes him a treasured friend. For one thing, he listens – and goes on listening until he come up with a reasonable version of what you mean. Besides, he is incurably interested in the particular, however devoted he may be to Large Ideas. But what makes all this lively is that he is a devotee of the possible, interested not only in what you've been up to, but in what you *might* possibly have been up to instead. And that is his perspective toward students and colleagues. It is the same open-mindedness he brings to his scholarship. That and his wonderful loyalty – loyal friend, loyal teacher.

It is difficult to conclude this Foreword, for I do not leave David's company easily, even on the printed page. I've reached my page limit, alas, without a word about David's contribution to education, not even to Canadian education, and, at that, not even to that extraordinary institution, OISE, to which he has given so much and by which he has been so enriched. Others in this volume will speak to these and other matters. What I have tried to make plain is how much David has given to so many. That is an endless story.

Jerome Bruner
Reenogreena, Glandore, Co Cork
August 1999

Notes

1 International Conference on Developing Theories of Mind, University of Toronto, May 1986.
2 For example, Conference on Orality and Literacy, University of Toronto, June 1987; Workshop on Modes of Thought, Ontario Institute for Studies in Education, June 1993; Conference on Developing Intentions in a Social World, University of Toronto, April 1997.
3 Conference on Literacy and Conceptions of Language, OISE/University of Toronto, April 1999.

References

Bruner, J. (1995). Commentary. *Human Development, 38*, 203–213.

Grice, H. (1975). Logic and conversation. In P. Cole & J. L. Morgan (Eds.), *Syntax and semantics, Vol. 3: Speech acts* (pp. 41–58). New York: Academic Press.

Olson, D. R. (1970). *Cognitive development: The child's acquisition of diagonality.* New York: Academic Press.

Olson, D. R., & Astington, J. W. (1995). Reply. *Human Development, 38*, 214–216.

1

Constructivist to the Core: An Introduction to the Volume

Janet Wilde Astington

This volume contains a collection of essays honoring David R. Olson on the occasion of his official retirement from the Ontario Institute for Studies in Education, University of Toronto. Although some contributions range more broadly, the general theme is Olson's work on literacy and on children's theory of mind, and its influence on educational thought. The title *Minds in the Making* reflects Olson's lifelong interest in the development of children's minds, and his role in developing graduate students' minds as they wrestled with the problems of cognitive development. It also acknowledges his Presidential Address to the Canadian Psychological Association, in which he reiterated his belief that "mind" is a cultural invention (Olson, 1989). The contributors are former students, postdoctoral fellows, and colleagues, all of whom have spent some time at OISE/UT discussing these issues with David, whose own work in the area began almost 40 years ago, in the early 1960s.

The sixties hold a special place in our collective memory, even for those who don't go back so far. Times were changing fast, no less in psychology – where mind was making a comeback – than in the rest of the world. In the early 1960s Olson published his first academic papers while completing his doctorate in the Graduate School of Education at the University of Alberta. Their titles reflect the learning theories of earlier decades (e.g., "The effect of foreign language background on intelligence test performance," Olson & McArthur, 1962). By the mid-1960s, however, Olson was at the newly created Harvard Center for Cognitive Studies, joining in, indeed, helping to foment the cognitive revolution. By all accounts these were exciting times (Bruner, 1983b). It was here that Olson's constructivist views were first formed, prompted and inspired by his conversations with Jerome Bruner – I will not reiterate the story that Bruner tells in the Foreword to this volume (p. xv) but merely repeat his point that all of Olson's work has been informed by a constructivist perspective: "the reality we experience is constructed, not just 'there' to be found or stumbled upon."

Constructing the World

Olson was also prompted by George Miller, Co-director with Bruner at the Harvard Center for Cognitive Studies, and his persistent questions. For example, when Olson presented his findings – that young children cannot copy diagonal patterns – to a Center research group, Miller was not content with data showing that children got better at the task as they became older. His concern was with the younger children's performance – *why* they did what they did and what they *thought* they were doing. As Olson (1995, p. 281) tells it, he gradually came to realize that Miller's question is the vital one, and the one that has dogged him ever since – not "what is the child doing?" but "what does the child think he or she is doing?" That is, the critical issue is how the child represents a problem to him or herself. The world is not given to the child but is constructed by the child's representational system and his or her understanding of the world changes as representational abilities develop. It is easy to see the sea change from learning theories' considerations of input–output conditions, and revealingly, by the late 1960s Olson's papers have titles like "Tapping the mind of the child" (Olson, 1967).

During the following decade, Olson started to grapple with the topic that has dominated his career, that is, literacy and in particular, the cognitive consequences of literacy. I think there are (at least) two reasons for his move into this area. In addressing the question of how children represent the problem of the diagonal, Olson (1970a) argued for the Vygotskian idea that children's mental representations of a problem are verbal representations. Yet he was aware that the ability to represent diagonals came at the age when children enter school and learn to read and write, not at the age when they learn to talk, and so there was something more involved than the influence of speech on thought. Spurred on by McLuhan's (1962) claims that more sophisticated cognitive abilities result from exposure to written text, he became convinced that the ability to represent diagonals was a consequence of literacy, without being clear why this effect occurred. Perhaps it was due to the acquisition of specific semantic terms that literacy provided. Whatever the reason for the effect, Olson continued to puzzle over the relations between language and thought, words and intentions, semantic and pragmatic meaning, eventually claiming that meaning resides in intentions, not in words (Olson, 1970b). However, the problems encountered here (see Astington, Chapter 16) led him to distinguish between meaning in speech and in writing (Olson, 1977), arguing that in speech, meaning resides in the speaker's intentions, while in writing, meaning resides in the words. That is, pragmatic meaning is primary in speech and semantic meaning is primary in written text. Although in oral communication what is actually meant may be implied by, for example, the speaker's tone of voice, in writing, meaning has to be made explicit in the text. For example, "The chair's been moved," shouted exasperatedly, may well mean "Put it back," but in writing it is a statement about a rearrangement of the furniture.

Constructing Textual Meaning

Thus, according to Olson in the 1970s, meaning is in the text, which means what it says, so that authors and readers can treat texts as autonomous representations of meaning. Explaining, defending, and justifying this large claim has occupied much of Olson's subsequent career. Indeed, he never intended to imply that meaning is there for the taking, because his constructivist outlook precludes the notion that anything can be provided gratis. Textual meaning is constructed by the reader, just as the natural world is constructed by the observer (Olson, 1994). The question is: what is there to inform the construction? Olson's point is that, in constructing textual meaning, all that is available is the text itself. Writing excludes the prosodic features of utterance (stress, pitch, timing, rhythm, melodic tone) and extralinguistic features (eye contact, gesture, and surrounding context) that together convey information regarding intended meaning in speech. Written text has none of these and is interpreted by readers who may be remote from authors in time and space. Texts can be understood because they are interpreted within a community in which authors and readers assume a shared background (see Feldman, Chapter 2).

The crucial point is that textual meaning is constructed. Just as we construct representations – mental models – of the world, so we construct representations – textual models – of written language. The meaning is not really in the text, rather, Olson's point is that writing is based on the assumption that meaning is in the text, that is to say, that texts can be written and read as if they were independent and self contained. His interest is and always has been (Olson, 1977) what effect this has on the mind. That is, what are the cognitive consequences of reading and writing texts that are assumed to be autonomous representations of meaning?

Over the past two decades, Olson has modified his claims about the effects of literacy on the mind (see Brockmeier, Chapter 4), focusing more recently on its metalinguistic effects (Olson, 1991; 1994), that is, its effects on language awareness. He has shifted toward a more cultural view, that the effects of literacy are less due to individual cognitive consequences of learning to read and write, and more due to growing up in a literate culture which highlights the metalinguistic aspects of language use (Olson, 1991). Western children acquire a literate mind and a consciousness of language because they are immersed in a literate culture (Brockmeier, Chapter 4; Vinden, Chapter 3).

One of the main features of this culture is its focus on the life of the mind, on the beliefs, desires, intentions, and so on that govern our interactions with one another. Why might this be? Why such consciousness of mental life and what is its link with literacy? Writing can easily reproduce the form of what someone said, or the form an author wants to express; by "form" I mean vocabulary and syntax. However, writing can less easily reproduce the "force," that is, how it was said, or how the author wants it to be taken – is "the chair's been moved," a request for it to be returned to its original position or a comment on the new arrangement?

We know well what a text says; indeed, better than we do for speech, because writing fixes what is said – the words are held for all time. But we may know less well what the author meant by them, that is, how he or she intended the text to be taken. In informal writing, such as letters to a friend, we may use exclamation marks, capital letters, and underlining to indicate prosody, to put our voice into the text. Indeed, in reading such a letter we often hear the friend's voice in our mind's ear. E-mail provides an interesting recent example. The message is hardly a text, it is more like a phone message, but it is written and so the voice is absent. Devout e-mailers have developed an elaborate system of marks, called *emoticons,* in order to convey the missing aspects of the message (e.g., '-) means "wink"; :-I means "hmmm . . ."; :-& means "tongue-tied"; :-/ means "skeptical" etc.; Ahmad, 1996).

However, there is a limit to how far one can go with punctuation and emoticons. One cannot capture the subtleties and nuances of intended meaning, which can so easily be expressed para- and extralinguistically in oral language. In written text the words are all that one has and so one is forced to elaborate the words. That is to say, a consequence of literacy is the development of lexical terms to indicate intended meaning (Olson & Astington, 1990). And a cognitive consequence of this is a heightened awareness of intentions and of beliefs, desires, and other mental atti-tudes underlying our intentions. In attempting to compensate for what writing lacks that speech possesses – intention behind the utterance, the force of what is expressed, our attitude toward it – we become more aware of these things. They are implicit in speech, that is, implied by tone and gesture, but in writing they are made explicit using lexical terms, and this makes us conscious of them. As Olson (1995, p. 290) puts it: "Ironically, much of the intellectual impact of writing comes from the attempt to compensate for what was lost in the act of transcription!"

Constructing Minds

The terms that we use to explicate meaning in text draw attention to mental states. It is this aspect of his theorizing that led Olson in the 1980s into the newly develop-ing field of children's theory of mind (see Astington, Chapter 16), and it is within this field that he has put forward the most original and daring of his constructivist ideas. Olson is a constructivist through and through – not only is the world con-structed, not only is textual meaning constructed, but also the mind itself is con-structed.

This proposal is developed in a series of papers (Olson, 1988b; 1989; 1993; see also Campbell & Olson, 1990; Olson & Campbell, 1993; 1994; Campbell, Chap-ter 10) which all contain the paradoxical idea that mind is constructed. From a constructivist perspective, nothing is given but only taken as given; our models of the world and of text are constructed through our perceptual and conceptual activi-ties, that is, our mental activities – our mind. The paradox is this: if the mind too is constructed, what is doing the constructing? The brain, of course. But perceiving and conceiving are not brain functions, rather they are mental processes. They are constructions, like their folk-psychological counterparts, seeing and thinking, which are part of the construction we create to represent human action and interaction. Mind is not there, any more than the "real" world is there; they are both constructions.

Here Olson provides his response to the perplexing question of how a physical, biological system, the brain, can be a mental system that operates on the basis of beliefs and meaning, that is, how a causal system can be an intentional one. He rejects the view that mind is just a folk-psychological notion and human behavior is a direct causal response to states in the world (e.g., Churchland, 1986; Stich, 1983), and aligns himself with the view that behavior has to be explained by appeal to representational states (e.g., Fodor, 1987; Pylyshyn, 1984) but insists on taking a developmental stance on this issue. The infant has no representational states; the perceptual system of the infant brain allows for causal connections between child and world, but the infant child has no symbols, which are later constructions.

Olson (1989, 1993) highlights three stages in the construction of mind. First, the sensory-motor stage of infancy when the infant can perceive and think about objects in the world. Second, a symbolic-propositional stage, which develops in the second year of life and allows the child to represent propositions and to think about properties of objects in the world. And third, a representational-belief stage, around four years of age when metarepresentational abilities develop, allowing the child to think about propositions, that is, not just to represent a proposition but to relate a proposition to some aspect of the perceived world, which is needed to represent false beliefs. Olson postulates that this sequence of development comes about because of increasing resources to hold something in mind while relating it to something in the world (Keenan, Chapter 14). Thus:

> "Making up your mind" in this sense implies that mind is not an object in the world which is there to be discovered, but rather something which has evolved along with human culture and which each of us invents for ourselves, in the course of cognitive and social development. (Olson, 1989, p. 617)

The outcome of this claim is that "mind" may not be universal (Vinden, Chapter 3) and may not be there in infancy (but see Zelazo, Chapter 9, who disagrees with Olson on this point).

One might argue that Olson's theory is essentially Piagetian constructivism, although Olson gives more role to language and culture than did Piaget, and might wonder why I referred to it as the most original and daring of Olson's constructivist ideas. Perhaps in this post-Piagetian era, where many would agree that mind develops at least in part according to constructivist principles, what is daring in Olson's version is his holding fast to Piaget's idea that "mind" is constructed out of "no mind" (Zelazo, pers. comm. 19 November 1999). One might also argue that Olson's theory lacks much empirical support, and probably he would not disagree; his concern is the theoretical scheme, not the mechanisms involved. As he himself says, in writing about the development of the representational-belief stage (Olson, 1993, p. 300) "precisely *how* this is done, again, is not my major concern. Rather it is with *what* is done" (emphasis in the original). Olson is more concerned with the ideas than the processes of constructivism. I am reminded of the charming title he gave to his invited address when receiving an honorary degree from his alma mater, the University of Saskatchewan: "Writing and the mind: Extravagant theories and modest facts" (Olson, 1997).

Constructivism, Conversing, and Teaching

I intended the volume title *Minds in the Making* not only to evoke Olson's interest in children's cognitive development and his argument that mind is constructed in the course of development, but also to acknowledge his role in the development of graduate students' minds. A vital part of the making of minds is the contribution from the social world, where children's development is scaffolded by parents and teachers. Parents treat infants as having intentions and beliefs, and so they come to see themselves as intentional beings and as holders of beliefs (Bruner, 1983a). As children start to talk, at home and school, they participate in conversations without full understanding of all the words – and thus come to understand the words (Nelson, 1996). The child extracts the meaning of a word from its use in discourse by identifying the relevance of the word within the context. The discourse provides clues, not explicit meanings, which are gradually derived. "The process of *use before meaning* . . . may be engaged by the child, from which *meaning from use* gradually accrues" (Nelson, 1996, p. 145, emphasis in original).

Not just in childhood. Olson remembers Bruner, at the Harvard Center for Cognitive Studies, as having ". . . the gift of treating beginners like myself as if we were knowledgeable colleagues. The mere fact that we were treated as knowledgeable assured that, so far as possible, we became so" (Olson, 1995, p. 280). Perhaps this gift was passed on from Bruner to Olson or perhaps it is a characteristic they share. Whatever the source, it is obvious in reading the chapters in this volume that David Olson's students remember him as a teacher like Bruner, who made them full participants in any seminar conversation, who assumed they understood and had ideas and opinions that counted and mattered. Olson was always open to new ideas, treating even the wildest ones with a seriousness they perhaps didn't deserve.

Thus, Olson carries his constructivism into conversations: "He listens – and goes on listening until he comes up with a reasonable version of what you mean" (Bruner, Foreword, p. xix). Never mind if the meaning he comes up with is not the one you intended. Perhaps sometimes it is better than you intended, and if it is not, there is always chance for another round of debate and disagreement. Indeed, the chapters of this volume are inspired as much by disagreement with Olson as by agreement, and this is real constructivism. As his colleagues put it: "I have benefited enormously from his provocative observations, even when I don't agree with them. Indeed, there is nothing so stimulating for one's own thinking as the attempt to construct arguments to counter the opposition" (Wells, Chapter 8, p. 115), and

". . . nothing is more supportive and growth promoting than to have the good luck to be in a small band of closely focused scientists, each with a divergent view" (Feldman, Chapter 2, p. 20).

Structure of the Volume

The chapters are divided into two sections, which correspond roughly with the two areas of Olson's work discussed above, that is, literacy and its cognitive consequences, and children's theory of mind. The first section covers a broad range of issues, all essentially concerned with the construction of meaning in various ways and forms.

Meaning making, literacy, and culture

In Chapter 2 Carol Fleisher Feldman gets to the heart of the problem of meaning making – how on earth do we do it? Speakers and authors produce words, and listeners and readers make meaning from them. Feldman argues that what makes this possible is the fact that the language, whether oral or written, is produced within a community whose interpretive system is shared by speakers and listeners, or by authors and readers. She illustrates her argument by citing a case from 15th-century Italy where this was not so. A man who had taught himself to read but who had no theological education, was charged with heresy for creating his own interpretations of theological writings that conflicted with those accepted by the ecclesiastical authorities. The example allows us to identify and subtract out the interpretive system from the reading process, and shows us how meanings are usually socially shared within an interpretive community. Feldman adds a dynamic aspect to this model, illustrating the important role of time – short term and long term – in permitting the incorporation of new patterns, which gradually change the old pattern of interpretation and allow for the creation of new meanings. Her discussion of evolution in the shared knowledge of any active interpretive community over time sheds new light on the idea of "communities of learners," much discussed in education circles currently, and well exemplified in Wells' (Chapter 8) description of a Grade 2 science project.

Penelope Vinden (Chapter 3) explores how we enter and become part of an interpretive community by drawing parallels between the child's participation in the social world and the adult's participation in a new educational world. Throughout the chapter she sustains a parallel between the child's development in the social world and the student's progress through graduate school. She maintains that both are situations of "minds in the making" and makes a strong claim for mind making as essentially a process of enculturation. Parents and professors pass on theories of mind and world to children and students through the ways in which they use language in the context of experience. To have one's mind made up is to receive, in interaction with those who are more expert, a frame of mind, a language, and a frame of action through which to live. However, both children and students, she claims, are active collaborators in this enculturing process and to learn a culture is also to make up one's own mind.

The idea of mind making as enculturation continues in Chapter 4, where Jens Brockmeier explores a shift in Olson's thinking about the cognitive consequences of literacy. Olson (1991) moved away from strong claims about direct autonomous cognitive consequences of a child's learning to read and write, toward a view that children acquire a literate mind – essentially a consciousness of language – because they grow up in a culture of writing. Literacy, Brockmeier argues, is an ensemble of cultural practices, that is, the material, discursive, cognitive, and institutional practices of reading and writing which integrate us into a literate tradition. Its influence on the child is not primarily through the child's acquisition of reading and writing skills, but through the child's immersion in a cultural symbol system, what Brockmeier refers to as the "symbolic space of literacy." Growing up in a culture of literacy turns language in upon itself so that it becomes an object of metalinguistic reflection. Brockmeier argues that this effect is due to the whole symbolic space of literacy in which different elements overlap and interrelate, although he acknowledges that these elements might be separately explored, as is apparent in the next three chapters.

A number of factors listed by Brockmeier as influencing metalinguistic awareness are elaborated by Rita Watson in Chapter 5: orthographies, bilingualism, and the material practices and technologies of writing. Watson examines the influence of literacy on the idea of words as constituents of language, whose meanings can be separately spelt out in definitions. She argues that the development of the concept of word is independent of a particular type of script (e.g., alphabetic) and provides two pieces of evidence from pre-classical texts that support the "orthography-neutral" claim. She suggests that the concept of word may have arisen as a result of translating from one language to another. Following Olson (1994), Watson claims that the orthography in a sense gives rise to a theory of the language it represents, and argues that this applies equally to non-alphabetic orthographies. Thus, the conception of "word" emerged with other conceptions of language as a consequence of the use of orthographies. She argues, however, that awareness of words as meaning-bearing units, that can be defined, came later, with the demands of interpretation.

Poetic features of language are another dimension highlighted by Brockmeier (Chapter 4) as contributing to metalinguistic consciousness. Joan Peskin develops this idea in Chapter 6, arguing that the language of poetry draws attention to itself. Poetry is both text and art, and thus the interpretation of poetry requires attention to both rhetorical and aesthetic form. She reports a study comparing experts and novices reading difficult period poetry and suggests that poetic discourse heightens readers' awareness of rhetorical form. In searching for a poem's meaning, even the novices attended not just to the semantic content but also to authorial intention, that is, rhetorical form. However, when the poem's meaning became completely obscure, the novices worked harder at their attempt to interpret it but still focused on rhetorical form, whereas the experts switched their attention to the poem's aesthetic or artistic form, that is, how the components of the poem effect and amplify the meaning. Peskin argues that expertise leads to a heightened awareness of poetry as textual art, and pursues the educational implications of focusing on how form gives rise to meaning.

Expertise in the interpretation of text is also the topic of Chapter 7, where Anne McKeough elaborates a further dimension highlighted by Brockmeier (Chapter 4) as contributing to metalinguistic consciousness, that of story-telling and narrative practices. Her chapter also echoes Feldman (Chapter 2) and Vinden (Chapter 3) as McKeough considers how individuals gradually become enculturated into interpretive communities as they take up literacy practices. Based on Olson's (1988a, 1994, 1996) discussions of oral and literate traditions, she compares skilled literate adults' ability to compose, to recall, and to interpret stories with that of adults who are only just acquiring literate skills, and she analyses adolescents' developing skills in story production. She shows that higher levels of literacy are associated with the use of a set of literary conventions that can be thought of as cannons institutionalized in the person of editors and teachers who insist that they be used by all those who claim membership in certain interpretive communities.

Gordon Wells (Chapter 8) moves beyond a focus on meaning making in written language to examine the broad scope of ways in which meanings can be expressed. His discussion ranges widely, considering the biological bases and cultural origins of the various modes of representation that mediate understanding. He shows that, both phylogenetically and ontogenetically, action is the earliest to emerge and writing and other visuographic modes the latest. However, in most educational institutions there is a strong bias toward writing and the modes of knowing associated with technical written genres which, although valuable in itself, tends to exclude the other modes and so risks restricting the human potential for meaning making. Wells argues that, in a world in which communication is becoming progressively more multi-modal, it is important for students to learn to exploit all the modes of representation as tools for thinking and problem solving. Drawing on observations from elementary school classrooms, he shows the advantages to be gained from organizing curricular units to exploit the complementarity of the different modes of representing and knowing.

Representation, language, and theory of mind

Wells' chapter provides a bridge to the second section of the volume, where the focus is on the development of representations and more particularly, on the development of children's understanding of representation, that is to say, their metarepresentational abilities or their theory of mind. Wells speculates that "metaknowing" activities, that is, reflection on the various modes of knowing that he describes – action, language, writing, etc. – facilitate the transition from one mode of knowing to the next. A related idea is developed by Philip David Zelazo in Chapter 9. He describes a theory of representational understanding and use that draws on the hermeneutics of Paul Ricoeur and the genetic epistemology of James

Mark Baldwin. On this view, representations are intrinsically imitative but involve productive imitation not simple copying. *Pace* Olson (1993), Zelazo argues that representing occurs in infancy, but he agrees with Olson that then there are qualitative age-related changes in children's representational abilities. On Zelazo's view, increasingly complex representations are produced as the contents of consciousness are fed back into consciousness. The production and interpretation of these representations leads to reflection on them and to a conceptual understanding of representation.

Robin Campbell (Chapter 10) argues that children's understanding of representation is partly dependent on what representations are considered, and in particular, how different types of representation differ in terms of their content. He describes the ways in which beliefs and desires are said to differ, and goes on to discuss some possible ways of distinguishing beliefs from desires in terms of their typical contents, arguing that this has been ignored or, at least, that its importance has been underestimated. He relates some of the distinctions discussed to studies of children's understanding of belief and desire, justifying his claim that it is important to consider desires from the point of view of content.

Children's understanding of belief, desire, and intention allow them, among other things, to understand lying – when a speaker says something he or she does not believe, with the intention of deceiving the hearer. In Chapter 11, Kang Lee uses a speech act theory approach to provide an account of the development of children's knowledge about lying. This approach links back to issues raised in the first section of the volume. The interpretation of any speech act, that is the uptake of the speaker's communicative intent, depends on the conventions governing the speech act – conventions that are shared by the interpretive community. Lee considers children's understanding of both the intentions and the conventions that characterize lying. He compares the development of Canadian and Chinese children's concept of lying and their moral judgments of it, showing how children come to take account of the speaker's intentions and beliefs and of the social function that a false statement serves in a specific cultural context.

In Chapter 12, Deepthi Kamawar and Bruce Homer, two of David Olson's most recent doctoral students, discuss aspects of children's understanding of belief and writing. Although belief and writing might seem to be quite unrelated concepts, Kamawar and Homer argue that they are linked because understanding in both cases requires metarepresentational ability. Kamawar's work focuses on the referential opacity of belief. Understanding opacity, Kamawar shows, is more difficult than understanding false belief, because to understand opacity the child has to be able to deal appropriately with partial knowledge. But like false belief tasks, opacity tasks require an understanding of the representational nature of belief, that is, they require metarepresentational ability. Writing, by its very nature, is metarepresentational; it is a representational system that is used to represent another representational system, that is, language. Homer examines the ways in which the metarepresentational nature of writing affects children's literacy acquisition, and subsequently, their conception of language.

Children's metarepresentational abilities are also the focus of Chapter 13. Here, Josef Perner discusses the strong correlations found between children's understanding of false belief and their understanding of synonyms (Doherty & Perner, 1998). The original explanation for this finding was that both require metarepresentation – in the false belief task the child has to think of beliefs as representations, monitoring content and reference, and in the synonyms task the child has to think of words as representations, monitoring form and meaning. However, more recent work has shown similar correlations with new tasks requiring children to say something different about an object, as in the synonyms task, but the new tasks use sortals, such as superordinate-basic terms, and form/meaning monitoring is not required. The use of different sortals requires an understanding of perspective because it involves two different ways of looking at the same reality, as do the false belief and synonyms problems. Thus, the ability to represent two different perspectives explains children's performance on all of the tasks. Perner argues that the hypothesis of a perspectival understanding of mind is more comprehensive than the hypothesis of a representational understanding of mind. None the less, both understandings are tightly linked and probably develop at the same time.

In Chapter 14, Thomas Keenan discusses the computational resources that metarepresentation requires. He examines the relation of domain general developments in working memory, language competence, and inhibitory control, to the development of false belief understanding, and argues that, in line with Olson's (1989, 1993) theory, there is increasing evidence that the growth of working memory capacity allows children to construct representations of false belief. Keenan acknowledges that although the working memory hypothesis may help explain why the changes in performance come when they do, the hypothesis does not explain what brings about the change. He suggests that a comprehensive account of theory-of-mind development needs to consider the role played by social and linguistic interaction – issues picked up in the final two chapters.

In Chapter 15, Ted Ruffman moves beyond a focus on metarepresentation and false belief understanding to consider theory-of-mind development more broadly as the development of general social understanding. He argues that tasks which employ behavioral measures of theory of mind are likely to be central to real-world social abilities, indeed, more central than tasks which tap explicit theoretical knowledge. He shows that in a false belief task, eye gaze towards the correct location precedes correct verbal answers and is indicative of unconscious social knowledge, which becomes increasingly theoretical, explicit, and verbally mediated as children's metarepresentational abilities develop. He has found that children with autism do not show appropriate eye gaze on tasks of social understanding, even when they can show correct performance on explicit verbal measures. He argues that autistic children's key deficit may be in implicitly grasping social insights rather than in explicit theorizing, and that general language ability may not correlate with core social insights, but rather with explicit theoretical understanding.

In the final chapter (Astington, Chapter 16) I draw on many conversations and arguments that I have had with David Olson regarding the role of language in the development of children's metarepresentational abilities, or their theory of mind. Olson's position is that the acquisition of metacognitive language is central to the development of a theory of mind, whereas I argue that language promotes children's theory-of-mind development because of their increasing general linguistic abilities, not because of specific vocabulary items. I review the literature supporting these two positions, and present some data of my own. I conclude that language and metalanguage are both involved in theory-of-mind development in western children. Language is a biological universal that underlies metarepresentational ability by allowing for representation of a false belief, for example, in contradistinction to the perceptual representation of the actual situation in the world. Metalanguage provides children with our culture's way of explicating this distinction.

In the Afterword to the volume, Angela Hildyard and Nancy Torrance, Olson's longtime colleagues and collaborators, reflect on what he has given to his students, his colleagues, and to the field. They say that one thing he gave to students was the urge to look, and to look again, at a problem or a piece of data, not only in fine detail but always as part of the larger picture. The chapters collected in this volume stand in testament to this assertion. The ideas discussed, the research findings described, the new directions proposed, form a richly detailed collection, that together create a broad view. The authors take complementary externalist and internalist perspectives on minds in the making, showing the role of culture and language in the construction of the mind, and also showing how the mind constructs itself during the course of cognitive growth. Each author acknowledges a debt to David Olson and we hope that, in Zelazo's (Chapter 9) words, this collection serves as partial requital.

Acknowledgments

I am grateful to Philip D. Zelazo, Joan Peskin, and Terri Barriault for their helpful comments on this chapter.

References

Ahmad, N. (1996). *Cybersurfer: The Owl internet guide for kids*. Toronto, Canada: Owl Books.

Bruner, J. (1983a). *Child's talk: Learning to use language*. Oxford, UK: Oxford University Press.

Bruner, J. (1983b). *In search of mind: Essays in autobiography*. New York: Harper & Row.

Campbell, R. N., & Olson, D. R. (1990). Children's thinking. In R. Grieve & M. Hughes (Eds.), *Understanding children: Essays in honour of Margaret Donaldson* (pp. 189–209). Oxford, UK: Blackwell.

Churchland, P. (1986). *Neurophilosophy: Toward a unified understanding of the mind/brain*. Cambridge, MA: MIT Press.

Doherty, M., & Perner, J. (1998). Metalinguistic awareness and theory of mind: Just two words for the same thing? *Cognitive Development, 13*, 279–305.

Fodor, J. A. (1987). *Psychosemantics: The problem of meaning in the philosophy of mind.* Cambridge, MA: MIT Press.

McLuhan, M. (1962). *The Gutenberg galaxy.* Toronto, Canada: University of Toronto Press.

Nelson, K. (1996). *Language in cognitive development.* New York: Cambridge University Press.

Olson, D. R. (1967). Tapping the mind of the child. *The Manitoba Teacher, 45,* 26–8.

Olson, D. R. (1970a). *Cognitive development: The child's acquisition of diagonality.* New York: Academic Press. (Second edition: L. E. Erlbaum and Associates, 1996)

Olson, D. R. (1970b). Language and thought: Aspects of a cognitive theory of semantics. *Psychological Review, 77,* 257–73.

Olson, D. R. (1977). From utterance to text: The bias of language in speech and writing. *Harvard Educational Review, 47,* 257–81.

Olson, D. R. (1988a). Mind and media: The epistemic functions of literacy. *Journal of Communication, 38,* 27-36.

Olson, D. R. (1988b). On the origins of beliefs and other intentional states in children. In J. W. Astington, P. L. Harris, & D. R. Olson (Eds.), *Developing theories of mind* (pp. 414–26). New York: Cambridge University Press.

Olson, D. R. (1989). Making up your mind. *Canadian Psychology, 30,* 617–27.

Olson, D. R. (1991). Literacy as metalinguistic activity. In D. R. Olson & N. Torrance (Eds.), *Literacy and orality* (pp. 251–70). Cambridge, UK: Cambridge University Press.

Olson, D. R. (1993). The development of representations: The origins of mental life. *Canadian Psychology, 34,* 293–306.

Olson, D. R. (1994). *The world on paper: The conceptual and cognitive implications of writing and reading.* Cambridge, UK: Cambridge University Press.

Olson, D. R. (1995). Conceptualizing the written word: An intellectual autobiography. *Written Communication, 12,* 277–97.

Olson, D. R. (1996). Toward a psychology of literacy: On the relations between speech and writing. *Cognition, 60,* 83–104.

Olson, D. R. (April, 1997). *Writing and the mind: Extravagant theories and modest facts.* Invited address to the Education Faculty, University of Saskatchewan.

Olson, D. R., & Astington, J. W. (1990). Talking about text: How literacy contributes to thought. *Journal of Pragmatics, 14,* 557-73.

Olson, D. R., & Campbell, R. N. (1993). Constructing representations. In C. Pratt & A. F. Garton (Eds.), *Systems of representation in children: Development and use* (pp. 11–26). Chichester, UK: Wiley.

Olson, D. R., & Campbell, R. N. (1994). Representation and misrepresentation: On the beginnings of symbolization in young children. In D. Tirosh (Ed.), *Implicit and explicit knowledge: An educational approach* (pp. 83–95). Norwood, NJ: Ablex.

Olson, D. R., & McArthur, R. S. (1962). The effect of foreign language background on intelligence test performance. *The Alberta Journal of Educational Research, 8,* 157–67.

Pylyshyn, Z. (1984). *Computation and cognition.* Cambridge, MA: Bradford Books/MIT Press.

Stich, S. (1983). *From folk psychology to cognitive science.* Cambridge, MA: Bradford Books/ MIT Press.

Part I
Meaning Making, Literacy, and Culture

2

The Sociability of Meaning: Olson's Interpretive Community

Carol Fleisher Feldman

We have come a long way since those innocent times in the 1960s when the expression of meaning could be found fully exemplified in these three famous texts: (1) The cat is on the mat; (2) Flying planes can be dangerous; and (3) Colorless ideas sleep furiously. Innocent because only the syntactic ambiguities of (2) above, and the semantic ambiguities of (3) lurked as complications for the prototype (1). And what a prototype it was. Its pretensions to universality were counter intuitive, and yet comforting. This seductive claim pulled along an army, with, at first only a few uncomfortable bystanders, chief among them Olson, wondering what on earth was missing in that sentence. It took years to "identify" from their absence all the many obligatory features that should have been there with the cat, the mat, and the declarative structure. The first among them was the missing speaker, then a missing mental attitude toward the cat/mat relationship, and finally the missing communicational attitude toward the listener. Eventually, figuring out what had been left out led to the discovery of linguistic systems that subsumed the missing matter under theoretical notions such as language use, *parole*, linguistic function and pragmatics, and to their further development.

Those were lonely times for the functionalists, for functionalism was messy. The optimistic hope that linguistics could be reduced to the circumscribed and tidy world of the cat on the mat promised that some day machines operating under algorithms would be able to do their work in natural language, and what a boon that would have been. So it was pessimistic and unmodern, unenlightenment, unpositivistic, even unscientific to emphasize those messy missing pieces. In fact, it was brave.

The Olson I have Known

That this general line of criticism was true now seems to be widely recognized. But within it, Olson was a real pathbreaker, and a singular voice, for he alone among the pragmatists focused on written language. Perhaps this was due to his lifelong inter-

est in literacy and what literacy brought to cognition. He took as the pure exempli-
fying case the historical turn in the 16th century. Widespread literacy occurred with
the simultaneous appearance of printing, the Protestant Reformation, and a written
vernacular. The result was that everyman became for the first time his own reader
and interpreter, freed of dependence on a sacred authority for access to the "word
of God." The upshot is that Olson has had a distinctive orientation to linguistic
functionalism as a feature of written language.

In the 1970s, Olson joined a wave of interest in importing notions from British
ordinary language philosophy, with its ideas about meaning as use, into psychology. This framework took the speaker and hearer in an ordinary communicative
situation as the basic one for meaning. And as a result, its basic picture of language
use was of oral language – conversation, speechmaking, and the like. What was
singular in Olson's approach was that he turned the apparatus of ordinary language
analysis, and especially its tripartite distinction between locution, illocution, and
perlocution, to the analysis of written text.

How was this possible? In Austin's (1962) original enunciation, *locution* was the
words themselves, and the *illocution*, or illocutionary force, was how the speaker
intended his message to be taken by the listener, whether such a naked expression
as "John will marry Mary" should be taken as an offer, a prediction, a bet, a threat.
The illocution could be made explicit by lexicalizing it as in "I *bet* John will marry
Mary," but in general it was not lexicalized for it was not necessary. In ordinary
conversation, context and such paralinguistic features as intonation and stress could
usually be relied on to fill in the blank. But in written text, it was not usually lexicalized
either, and there lexicalization would have seemed necessary if the force of utterances was to be part of the picture, if the speaker was to guide the listener in how he
intended the listener to take them. Perhaps then such use-based aspects of meaning
were confined to oral language, and it, in turn, was a degenerate case of language.
The central case, it seemed to the Chomskyans (Chomsky, 1965), was of meaning
independent of use, and especially of context of use. And the central case was of
written language.

Context posed a problem not just for a universal grammar, but also troubled
positivist scientists by seeming to require mind reading, a mind reading different in
each situation that must depend on great pools of background knowledge, which
would preclude there being a set of general, much less universal, rules. Use-based
notions of meaning seemed to yield a disturbingly idiosyncratic series of cases with
no general pattern. But, on the other side, a universal, positive account of meaning
had been bought at a very high price. In this picture, generality was achieved by
concocting a vitiated notion of meaning that required no context of use at all, and
so, for starters, could not begin to explain the processes through which a speaker's
illocutionary intentions worked in the listener's construction of a meaning even in
the case of ordinary conversation where it seemed to have such a central role.

Conversely, from the use-based point of view the universal meanings of text were
a mystery. And language, most implausibly, had been divided into two seemingly
unconnected systems of talk and text. Thus Olson's application of Austin's notions

about illocutionary force to written texts was pure genius. In one fell swoop he took a first step on a path that would put *langue* and *parole* back together, adopt the richer use-based account of meaning, and provide a general theory. For if illocutionary force could be explained in text, its context-dependent idiosyncrasy would be addressed: the context-independent language of written text that had been basic to the competing model would be taken as basic for it, too. For the Chomskian "cat is on the mat" had been, first and foremost, a sentence inscribed somewhere, say on a blackboard, rather than an utterance.

Olson eventually solved the problem by means of a wholly original idea, the notion of the *interpretive community*. It could serve as a surrogate for local contextual information in conversation by supplying a generalized context that allowed the unpacking of illocutionary force even when it had to be recovered in texts at a distance from the speaker.

But finding a solution for the problem of illocutions, and use-dependent meaning more generally, in writing was a tall order, and it has taken him down a long and winding path. It led him to a universe of language forms longer than the sentence, and back to conversations again. It led him to the natural experiments provided by historical and cultural variations, and back to the bible again. And these linguistic considerations in turn opened a new understanding of cognitive development and cognition, of what the thinker would have to know to manage them. Here, too, Olson led the way, discovering interesting questions about illocutionary meaning in the new work in theory of mind, and a much broader view of cognitive processes of literacy that pointed to interpretation. As I'll discuss more below, the real reward for this broadened functionalism was not just that it solved certain problems in the theory of meaning, but the way that it opened up new and wider worlds further down the road, and especially an interest in interpretation.

As I indicated above, I think the notion of the interpretive community was a key conceptual breakthrough in all this, and I want to take some credit for it, not because it was mine – indeed far from it, but because I think I drove him to it in pure exasperation with an argument I was making in defense of the full universality of oral language. It was in the course of a very amusing argument we had at one of his conferences. Olson was saluting literacy and the written text as unique opportunities for metacognition. I, citing anthropological evidence that oral forms could provide the same opportunities to fix a text for further interpretation by formal patterns of recitation, claimed that therefore such metacognition was not unique to written text. As I went on and on with my explanation, that both had a genre pattern that permitted interpretation, Olson finally said, exasperated, "what's important is that they both take place within an interpretive community" that allows the speaker to indicate to the listener how things should be taken. He was, of course, right, indeed more than right, for if I had been early in noticing the importance of the speaker, I had never really taken the listener seriously before that moment of truth. It led me much further downstream to study interpretation, the listener twin of speaker intention. And we continued our good-natured brawling in the literature.

I have been so much a beneficiary of these discussions that I think I would have had a completely different intellectual course without them, and a good deal less travel altogether. I didn't deserve them and, of course, I was very lucky. Nothing is more supportive and growth promoting than to have the good luck to be in a small band of closely focused scientists, each with a divergent view. It's one of the best of the interpretive communities.

In the rest of this paper, I plan to explore Olson's (1994) notion of the interpretive community, a notion I think is essential for understanding ways that meaning works. What the interpretive community allows is for a speaker to intend a certain meaning, for the hearer to understand a meaning, and for the two meanings to be more or less the same. Even at a remove, even for written text. It includes the listener as essential to the meaning process, and gives the listener the means for the listener to get it right. To see how this is possible, we are forced to reconsider the role of the speaker, too, in light of this new picture. For the speaker has to do what is necessary at their end to make this whole picture come together, principally by formulating their intended meaning within the rule-structured framework of the interpretive community of which the speaker's putative listener is a member.

The role of interpretive community in this picture is that it gives the speaker a new method by means of which speakers take their intended audiences into account, a means that does not depend on knowing exactly who the listener is, nor therefore on being at close conversational range. The notion is that speakers orient to the interpretive system they expect their listeners to orient to, rather than to the listeners themselves. Thus, it presents a solution to the otherwise baffling problems of how writing could ever bear meaning within a pragmatist, use-based account, and, at the same time, explains how use-based meaning can have a general form.

The interpretive community, by first answering the question of how meaning in texts could be use-based, at the same time allowed a reconstrual of how meaning in discourse worked in the same terms. But I get ahead of my story. For now, I want to consider how the meaning of written text can be understood as use dependent on an interpretive community.

In the Absence of an Interpretive Community: Early Reading

I begin with an exemplification, and a negative one at that. It is the story of Menocchio, Carlo Ginzburg's (1982) protagonist in *The Cheese and the Worms*. Menocchio's story can be seen as an example of what happens when texts are read by someone from outside the interpretive community to which they are addressed, someone outside the literate community altogether. Obviously, this is a rare disjunction in the normal course of human affairs, for simply to read is perhaps the essential step for becoming a member of the interpretive community, and in general it is sufficient as well. But Menocchio lived at a moment in history that was the cusp of literacy for ordinary people, when printing first created books directed to them in the vernacular, and enough copies were produced so that they became commodities of the markets owned by ordinary people.

At that strange moment, there were people who did read, having more or less taught themselves to read, but who did not know the canons of interpretation. This suddenly numerous group of the unschooled literates coexisted at that moment with the highly schooled group of clerics who had previously done their reading for them, and who had well-worked out canons of interpretation that were the ones taken as given by the writers of the period, even by writers writing in the vernacular. This created a disjunction for ordinary people like Menocchio between reading and membership in an interpretive community that is very rare, but helpful for our purposes. For it allows us to identify and subtract out the interpretive system from the reading process. Indeed, in general, the background condition of an interpretive community in the reading process is so ubiquitous that it can be hard even to see that it is there.

If we have the luxury of examining Menocchio's story for the breakdown of these background conditions for meaning, it is due to the strange aberration that he was interviewed for hours about his interpretations of what he'd read, and these interviews recorded verbatim. Why would anyone have cared enough about the interpretations of a self-taught reader to bother discussing and recording them? The answer lies precisely in his departure from the canons of the then-entrenched interpretive community. This created a situation of puns, of idiosyncrasy taken as heresy.

Menocchio was a miller in 15th-century Italy, from a small town in the Friuli region, a poor and hilly, and we suppose therefore isolated, area in the northeast of Italy. We learn from Ginzburg that millers were a sort of Corporal class; they were of the peasantry but at its apex. They negotiated their leases with the gentry who controlled licenses to mill, they had to be able to keep records requiring basic literacy and numeracy, and perhaps Menocchio is not atypical in serving as mayor and church bookkeeper, or even in his heresy, for we hear about another miller who ran into the same difficulties with the court, who had even owned the very same book that Menocchio owned.

The book, *Fioretto della Bibbia*, was a collection of theological readings culled from here and there. One important first step for vernacular print was to translate other written matter, and nearly all of this was theological (though of course there were a good many other genres around, they had historically been oral, and it took a bit longer till they or their written devolutions were turned into popular books, and for new genres of text to appear such as the cookbooks of Florence that appeared over the next decades). But until this moment theological writing had always been entirely in the hands of priests and philosophers, and the handful of upper classes educated by them. Still, printing apparently came on with breathtaking speed. As we know, Martin Luther's Protestant Reformation was very much tied up with it, and at this moment his position, not yet established, was itself seen as heretical. The authority of the church in Rome had been very tied up with the control of literacy, and it was enormously undermined by literature's popular dissemination; hence this Italian inquisition and the unusual transcript. Menocchio, indeed, is a microcosm of the times, and a part of them – he said he expected some

Lutherans to come for his body after his death, whatever he may have meant by that.

So how did Menocchio the Medieval miller read when he read the *Fioretto della Bibbia*? First, he read looking for evidence or confirmation of ideas he already had. Without the rules of an interpretive community, he wouldn't have had the means to unpack a writer's views that differed from his own, to recover the illocutionary force of utterances. This may be part of the reason why second, he tended not to distinguish accurately the background and foreground of what he read. Ginzburg notes that he often took the wrong thing as the point of a passage, taking as the point any utterance that confirmed his own belief, whether asserted or merely mentioned by the writer. These two tendencies led him to wrong readings, some of which happened to coincide with heresies worrying to the church, others merely strange and idiosyncratic: life came out of matter as a kind of spontaneous generation in the way that worms come from cheese. Even here though, he pointed out the trope: it was a metaphor.

Menocchio became through reading, or through talk about reading, conscious of such "ways of taking" as metaphor. Furthermore, he became an epistemic agent. He distinguished between his own notions, as reactions to the book, from what the book said. The text as object of thought created an inviting epistemic space for the reader that Menocchio was enormously attracted by. He wanted to hear himself think. And he wanted to have a conversation to share those thoughts with other epistemic readers who had read the same book, to enter a live interpretive community. Indeed, as he noted with apparent pleasure, his interlocutors had read many more books than he had. He was apparently drawn to the court, or to the conversation with the court, like a moth to a candle.

Menocchio's time was a particular moment of disjunction between the new lay readers and the older, literate-interpretive community of priests, but such disjunctions do occur under a variety of conditions. One that is structural and recurrent is when there is so much passage of time between the time of writing and the time of reading that readers from a new interpretive community cannot imagine the interpretive rules the writer intended to appeal to for the putative reader of their own time. This happens when interpretation is at the two times oriented by entirely different, non-orthogonal axes. It is a problem endemic to doing historical scholarship of remote times, which when it is solved by attributing to them membership in something like our own interpretive community amounts to the error now called "presentism."

Olson's Interpretive Community

What does the appeal to a shared interpretive community for text understanding tell us about ordinary conversational exchanges, and oral language forms generally? In face-to-face contexts of language exchange, Olson notes that more information is available in paralanguage about how the speaker wants the listener to take what is said, and there is less work altogether for the listener to do. Meaning is less underspecified. Still, illocutionary force and other instructions for taking, and speaker's attitudes, are still typically not made fully explicit. I think this is a way we protect ourselves from being too well understood by an unsympathetic interlocutor, and have written about it elsewhere (Feldman & Kalmar, 1996).

So long as the speaker's stance has to be recovered by appeal to the rules of an interpretive community, there is still the same possibility of misunderstanding – even when the listener, as in ordinary conversation, also has contextual knowledge. The process of interpretation, though perhaps aided by contextual information, is still subject to the usual vagaries of the interpretive process. Thus in oral contexts, there can for example be a misunderstanding due to different terms of interpretation in cultures too different from our own, a worry never far from the minds of anthropologists. And there may even be a sense in which children and adults make up two such incommensurate interpretive communities, for as Paley (1988) and others have noted, young children seem to invent the same genres in generation after generation, and they are not genres of their parents. Not to mention the powerful and the unempowered, the poor and the rich, and, if we are to believe such feminists as Carol Gilligan (1982), men and women.

In fact, written text would seem to have a certain advantage here, because writers, in contrast with speakers, are actively trying to trigger understanding in an unknown, distant, generalized other. To serve this goal, they can and often do make use of widely available explicit formulations of their intended meanings, the lexicalized expressions of mental state for example. This can have the effect of leveling the playing field, of broadening the reach of a text to a wider group of readers, of creating a shared interpretive community out of readers who might otherwise not be joined together. As can reducing the amount of such meaning altogether, as in scientific writing. Or, writers can make use of genre signals, say by adopting the formulas of the 19th-century English novel, and in this way invite all members of the interpretive community familiar with this genre to be able to share the meaning, something entirely possible even if, for example, they hate the class-consciousness of the characters or the narrator.

The appeal to a known genre is one of the powerful elements of the writer's ability to reach a putative reader. Genres have patterns known to the readers within an interpretive community and so permit the triggering of intended interpretation. The skillful writer does this by honoring the canonical generic rules, which is to say, breaching them only by design and with a purpose, only where the genre allows for breach and free variation. Occasionally, such breaches occur in the wrong place, or by mistake. When they take place within an interpretive community, their predictable effect on the reader is to try to make the genre whole again, to reject the error, to refuse to accept it as an interpretive trigger within the genre.

The widespread revulsion of the American people at the actions of the Starr investigation (1998) had to do with a mismatch that they saw between the rather majestic civic nature of an impeachment investigation, and the private acts being investigated. Starr had not wanted to trigger that revulsion, and so reiterated endlessly that this was not about those private acts, but about civic acts (namely of perjury and obstruction of justice). But these civic acts were seen as being the result of intrusion into private acts, and so they did not wash as providing a suitable civic content for the impeachment process. The majority of people shared an interpretation triggered by a perceived violation of the rules of such an investigation, one that closely aligned with the legal defense that such acts did not constitute an offense sufficiently grave to impeach in constitutional law.

To sum up to this point, when it is skillfully done, the common appeal of writer and reader to the shared interpretive community of which both are members, allows writers to write for a putative or remote reader, and for the speaker's intended meaning to be unpacked by such a reader in a manner consistent with the writer's writerly intentions. Generic patterns are one important constituent of the knowledge shared by members of an interpretive community. Another is the not fully explicit signals in text for the recovery of intended illocutionary force. Still a third are the markers for tropes such as irony, metaphor, and the like. A fourth are the text-forming discourse devices that connect sections of longer discourse, the *but*, *so*, *because*, and *therefore* that give a shape to the sequence of events in text. And one could go on.

The funny thing about people, though, is that, like Menocchio, we are all fighting to hear ourselves think, to find our own singular view, our own distinctive voice. How does our membership in an interpretive community jibe with that desire? I said of Menocchio, I think fairly, that he simply got the meaning wrong from the clerics' point of view, being too unschooled in the machinery of interpretation in that community. Is that what schooledness in these matters buys us? Do we learn only how to get it right? If so, how do we readers find our own voice, express our own ideas, disagree with the text? At least as important a linguistic function as the comprehension of meaning is the creation of new meaning. How can membership in an interpretive community help us with that? How can it avoid, indeed, defeating our efforts to create new meaning?

If our answer is that we do this by reworking the message into the framework of our own point of view, we find that we now face the Charybdis of relativism. If a reader's correct understanding of a writer depends on their sharing a system of interpretation, and each reader within that coming up with an individual creative interpretation, how does anyone ever get anything really right? Why are we not locked into the terrifying relativism Nagel (1997) worries about?

Many philosophers of meaning would like to eliminate the interpretant altogether from accounts of meaning, to go back from triadic accounts generally, of which Olson's is one, to a meaning dyad that contains only a term and the thing it "represents" (all by itself, without any action of mind). For them, the rightness of members of a shared interpretive community is not right enough; it is relative to point of view (or, now with Olson's interpretive community added) to a shared perspective, and so never rises to the level of real truth. This is surely not the place to go into the deep reasons why all viable models of meaning must in Peirce's (1931–35) sense be triads that contain one term for the interpreter. I'll just say here that that is my, and

I think Olson's, view. But what I will discuss is whether it is any longer reasonable to worry about losing ourselves in relativism once we have the notion of an interpretive community.

Creativity and Relativism: Flaws in the Glass?

I want to turn now to these two worries – the one about creativity and the one about relativism. To address them, we need a more detailed picture of how the writer's meaning is discovered by readers within the interpretive community of the writer's intended putative reader. How does this interpretive process actually work when everything goes right?

One important part of the answer here lies in the essential sociability of language. As readers we read because we want, in some sense, to know the writer. But as writers, too, we crave the reader who will understand us. Indeed, it often seems to me that there is no real sense to be made of a notion of meaning that is not essentially bound up with communication, even if, as is the case in so much of what passes for "speech for the self," it is to communicate with oneself at some later time, or as a dialogic other. Of course, it is the case that as readers there is no hope that the writer can come to know us, or how clever and original our interpretations of their book were. This puts an essential asymmetry into the picture, and suggests that it is the writer's privileged position to create new meanings, which the reader must try to discover. Asymmetry apart, the ultimate fact of sociability of language places a hard brake on idiosyncrasy; we cannot mean just what we like if we are to mean something anyone else will understand. Whenever everything goes right in interpretation, meaning is socially shared or sharable. This is, I think, a partial answer to some of the worries about relativism. It won't get us to absolute truth, but it places sharp limits on how idiosyncratic our world-making activities can be.

The answer to the question then of how meaning works when everything goes right must, therefore, lie in the manner in which the writer states or indicates a new meaning, doing so in such a way that will be possible for the reader to discover it. The common knowledge of the interpretive community provides the means for writers to create meanings that readers understand, even new meanings that surprise and shock.

Sometimes this is accomplished by playing with the rules of genre, or with the slot fillers or even the slots of certain well-known plots – the cowboy movie in which the good guys don't win, the hero who isn't brave, the hero who isn't good. At the extreme, these can lead to such a deep blurring of genre that the story is finally understood as a new subgenre, or even the first example of a new genre. But genres are constantly evolving if they are in active use, and new ones do come on the scene. Although the spaghetti western may seem a trivial innovation, the psychological novel was plainly not. At other times, remaining strictly within the rules can also lead to new meanings as when a genre, say the picaresque, is applied to a subject matter well known but under very different generic frameworks, say the story of life in a concentration camp (Benigni, 1998).

Other methods for creating new meanings are truer to known genres, but allow for new meaning by permitting the characters to have hitherto unfamiliar reactions to well-known events that normally in our literature evoke a different, standard response. Or, for the author to have different attitudes than usual to certain well-known characters. Then there is the invention of a new kind of character, immediately recognizable in some sense, but hitherto unknown.

In general, the framework of the interpretive community seems to allow us room to innovate just so we do not innovate too much all at once; that is, so that there is enough familiar pattern in place to help us interpret the part that is not familiar. But at the same time, and it is important to emphasize this, the framework of the interpretive community does not merely permit, but also requires us to be creative. We cannot keep telling the same story over and over again. If Propp (1968) is right about the folk tale, perhaps there was a simpler time when readers did not require so much that was new, for in his analysis of the folk tale it seems the great preponderance of meaning is conserved from one exemplar to the next. One would have thought the readers would rebel. Or, perhaps they didn't because in the main they were children, and as we all know children, on their way to mastering the rules of the interpretive community, do like to hear the same story over and over again. But that is really the exception. To go back to Ken Starr, Americans were particularly annoyed at having to hear his story over and over again.

Time and Change in the Interpretive Community

The crux of the matter of how possibilities for new meaning are created within an interpretive community is the fact of constant change: new patterns are introduced on old, then incorporated in the shared knowledge of the community, and inviting further variation. It depends on community then, too, to serve as a(n evolving) memory of the traditions of the past. And it depends on individual effort of all the members to stay abreast of the evolving patterns of the interpretive community. And on an educational system that gives the young an entry into culture.

The realization of creative meanings in a socially communicable form is mediated, then, not just by the shared interpretive system of the community, but also by time. The interpretive system is in a constant state of evolution with time, and the tracking of these changes, and trajectories of change are, I would argue, an essential part of the knowledge of the members of an interpretive community.

In the small, changes take place from the beginning to the end of conversations in which new comments on old topics are gradually incorporated into the given in a fashion that opens a new set of possibilities of creative meaning within the shared interpretive framework of that particular conversation. Time changes in the middle range are seen in the way that small work groups continually recreate their shared pattern of interpretation over the months and years of their association together. A similar time scale is found in the way that a national group recreates its interpretive system for national events rapidly over a short period only several months long at a time of crisis. More glacial and lengthy changes occur in the interpretive system for important and enduring learned literatures, say the meaning of *Magna Carta* in the British common law. The main point is that an interpretive community shares not just a rule system but also a sense of its evolved position on a time line.

Interpretive communities have a kind of organic growth of their own, a growth that seems to arise inevitably from the nature of the communicative processes that take place within them. If in ordinary conversation every new utterance contains something new and that becomes part of the old once it is uttered, something analogous happens on a larger scale across the successive productions of, say, the 19th-century novel. And sometimes a completely new interpretive community can be born. Menocchio's interesting historical moment was on the cusp of the historical formation of a completely new lay interpretive community of religion. It eventually became the vast interpretive community of Protestant churchgoers, with its own interpretive canon.

Interpretive communities rely on a canon for communication and intersubjectivity. By definition, at any moment, the canon is composed of old meanings, but at every subsequent moment it will permit and invite new meanings to appear, new meanings that will be made intersubjective and communicable by their connection to the canon. The canon gives a set of rules from the past to which speakers can refer in their indications to their listeners, and writers to their readers. In giving these indications writers and speakers anticipate listener or reader's need for guidance about how to unpack the new meaning. The speaker or writer's allusions to the old canon tell the listener or reader, roughly, where to look in the relevant interpretive system for the relevant rules, the rules that will unpack this particular new meaning. In this way the interpretive community makes use of canon and convention to support the original and the new. In this sense, the interpretive community is essentially a conservative force, or a conservator of interpretive rules, though these be constantly evolving over time.

Conclusions

Olson began by being puzzled about two issues that no one but he would have thought could be put together, and then in fact did put them together in what I think is one of the landmark discoveries of our period. The two issues were (1) How speakers communicated their use-dependent meanings to interlocutors in everyday life, and (2) What were the cognitive advantages of literacy. The bold first step was to ask how use-dependent meaning can be conveyed in text. The problem was that the text distanced the speaker and listener of ordinary discourse: speakers were unavailable for interpretation, listeners were "putative."

The solution was to have listeners read the meaning not from utterance and speaker but from utterance and, roughly, the interpretive system shared by the two of them in their interpretive community. Similarly, writer need not orient to the particular knowledge of reader but could instead orient to the interpretive community of which the reader was a presumed member. The interpretive community joined them with a *tertium*: the shared interpretive system. It is something like Peirce's interpretant, but as it is not for the interpretation of single words, but of larger texts, it has a much more elaborate patterning.

The notion of the interpretive community has proved to be a rich one that has helped to explain other fundamental problems. Chief among these is a better understanding of how creative meaning is possible. Olson points to the way a shared canonical knowledge is recruited by writers for a putative reader in the same community, pointed to, and then reacted to. Along with Olson's answer, I have added a suggestion that there is constant evolution in the shared knowledge of any active interpretive community over time, and that this fact is essential in supporting the creation of new meaning.

Acknowledgments

This work was supported by the Spencer Foundation, through its grant "Meaning-making in context" to Jerome Bruner, P.I. Support is gratefully acknowledged.

References

Austin, J. L. (1962). *How to do things with words* (J. O. Urmson, Ed.). Oxford, UK: Oxford University Press.

Benigni, R. (Director). (1998). *Life is beautiful.* [Film].

Chomsky, N. (1965). *Aspects of the theory of syntax.* Cambridge, MA: MIT Press.

Feldman, C., & Kalmar, D. (1996). You can't step in the same river twice: Repair and repetition in dialogue. In C. Bazzanella (Ed.), *Repetition in dialogue* (pp. 78–89). (In the series Beitrage zur Dialogforschung.) Tubingen, Germany: Niemeyer.

Gilligan, C. (1982). *In a different voice.* Cambridge, MA: Harvard University Press.

Ginzburg, C. (1982). *The cheese and the worms.* New York: Penguin Books.

Nagel, T. (1997). *The last word.* Oxford, UK: Oxford University Press.

Olson, D. (1994). *The world on paper.* Cambridge, UK: Cambridge University Press.

Paley, V. G. (1988). *Bad guys don't have birthdays: Fantasy play at four.* Chicago: University of Chicago Press.

Peirce, C. S. (1931–1935). *The collected papers of Charles Sanders Peirce, Vol. II,* C. Hartshorne & P. Weiss (Eds.). Cambridge, MA: Harvard University Press.

Propp, V. (1968). *Morphology of the folktale* (2nd edn.). Austin: University of Texas Press.

Starr, K. (1998). *Report of the Special Prosecutor on the impeachment investigation of William Jefferson Clinton, President of the United States.* Washington, DC: US Government Printing Office.

3

Making up my Mind: Learning the Culture of Olson and OISE

Penelope G. Vinden

A meeting of minds took place in my life some years ago which changed me irrevocably. Tucked away in the back corner of a library, hunched over a microfiche reader, I discovered David's landmark article "From utterance to text" (Olson, 1977). I was in the middle of writing my MA thesis on spoken and written language, and was feeling like a stranger in a strange land. I was involved with an organization that does translation and literacy work around the world, and I was becoming more and more convinced that introducing written language into a predominately oral culture was going to have some amazing and potentially devastating consequences. Yet I knew of no one who was exploring this issue. Until I read David's article. Yes! I thought. Finally here is someone who understands, here is someone who has thought my half-formed thoughts and given them life. Now I even have a name for what I'm thinking about! – the cognitive consequences of literacy.

Several years later I was deep in the mountains of Peru, struggling to help Quechua speakers develop their own literacy program, which included writing down some of their folk tales for the first time. The opportunity arose for me to study in Toronto, and I remembered that David Olson was there. With great hesitation I wrote to him, asking about studying with him. He sent me his latest preprint, written with Janet Astington (Olson & Astington, 1990). For the second time I was wonderfully surprised. This article was also about the cognitive consequences of literacy, and how it is talk about text rather than reading and writing skills generally, that is crucial to changing the way we think. Of particular interest to me was the list of Latinate speech act and mental state verbs borrowed into English in the 16th and 17th centuries as English became the language of science, philosophy, and the government, and as the advent of the printing press led to both the standardization of language and to the rise of English literature. The very same lexical items that were borrowed into English from Latin were ones being borrowed into Quechua from Spanish as Quechua speakers came into contact more and more with the larger portions of Peruvian society. I immediately wrote to David about this discovery, and was thrilled to find that he was as excited as I.

So that was how I came to OISE as a graduate student. After arriving I soon

became swept up into theory-of-mind research and before long I was planning trips
to take theory of mind on the road, as it were, testing children in Africa, Papua New
Guinea, and Peru. I think I went through graduate school in a daze. I drank deeply
from research group meetings and classes, bedazzled by the ideas, the exchange of
thoughts, reeling from the heady wine of discussions and arguments. But in all of
this I learned and grew. What I didn't know at the time is that in the process I was
becoming literate in a new way – I was becoming enculturated into the mind of
Olson and the world of OISE.

To become literate is to be enculturated. Whether we take literacy in its narrow,
traditional sense to mean the ability to both read and write texts, or whether we
take it in its broader sense of the communicative practices, both spoken and written, of particular social groups; becoming literate is learning to "read" and "write"
culture. Reading and writing, in the narrow sense, while they do not comprise the
totality of what literacy is, are its cornerstones. They are also examples par excellence of cultural artifacts. There seems to be no literacy module that unfolds as we
mature biologically. No children of the human species spontaneously read and write
without access to the cultural artifacts, and only a few primates, with intense human
scaffolding, achieve something that is even remotely close to what humans achieve.
Primates do clearly communicate, they use gestures and may even leave signs, but I
don't know anyone (yet . . . though I may be out of touch) who is discussing literacy among the Bonobo or literate activities among chimps. Even for humans,
however, becoming literate in written language clearly is not a necessary part of
enculturation, for there are many cultures in which reading and writing, and all the
activities that surround it, play little or no part. But becoming literate is clearly a
part of what has come to be called "western" culture, and it is the foundation of the
culture of school.

Out of this literate, schooled, western culture a distinct understanding of mind
has arisen. This is the theory of mind whose development researchers have traced in
3- to 5-year-olds. To say that the way young minds are made up in the west has
something to do with literacy and schooling clearly indicates that I have been
enculturated by Olson, for he says something somewhat similar in *The World on
Paper* – "literacy contributes in particular ways to the development of distinctive
modes of thought that are conveyed through systematic education" (Olson, 1994,
p. 17).

What are the processes by which these minds are made up? In this chapter I will
illustrate the mind-making process with a description of the way in which I was
enculturated in my graduate school experience. From there I will show that these
very same processes are at work as we enculturate children, as we construct with them
what has been called a theory of mind. One conclusion will be that the making of
minds does not end in early or even middle childhood, but continues into adulthood.
This is especially true in a school setting, where we enter into a context that is specialized in mind making. I will also show that enculturation is not a one-way process, it
is not simply the imparting of a system of cultural knowledge to a passive recipient.
Rather, children are active collaborators in the enculturing process. To be sure, there

is an ebb and flow to development, with the process at times more active, at times more passive. Yet even in receiving children are never simply sponges, soaking up what is presented to them, but are always active to create a kind of match between their world and the world of others, whether that means changing their own world or the other's world. A further conclusion will be this process of learning culture is not just one way of viewing how an understanding of mind develops, it is the only way.

A Frame of Mind

The first thing that Olson offered me was a frame – a frame of mind, if you'll pardon the pun, or perhaps a frame for mind. "From utterance to text" (Olson, 1977) provided that frame when I was working on my MA thesis, struggling to make sense of what I was reading concerning the changes that new writers make in their language as they begin to put their thoughts on paper for the first time. The article on borrowing Latin terms for English (Olson & Astington, 1990) provided the frame as I entered a PhD program when I was striving to understand when and why Quechua speakers would borrow mental states terms from Spanish. The frame is a starting point. It provides both a coherence to the "blooming, buzzing confusion" of one's intellectual struggle and a stepping stone to move on from on one's own – if it doesn't one had better not be in a PhD program! The bare bones of what I started with was "there are cognitive consequences to literacy." In other words, I had taken a first step toward a rudimentary theory regarding the relationship between literacy and the mind. If we learn to read and write, I thought, we will start to think differently. In other words, if we behave in certain ways, it will have an impact on our mental life.

The frame for mind that is offered, as it were, to young children in western culture is a view of humans as intentional beings, whose inner life drives their outward behavior. It is a causal frame, one that points the child toward mental states as being the true, underlying causes of behavior. Whereas the direction of causality of my graduate student frame was from world to mind – the activities surrounding reading and writing have cognitive consequences – the child's frame moves from mind to world – cognitive states have behavioral consequences. This theory of causality is a cultural theory, one that, as I have pointed out elsewhere (e.g., Vinden, 1996, 1999) may not necessarily be shared by all people everywhere.

Of course, as Shanker (1992) has noted, and I agree (and so do Astington & Olson, 1995), our actions are not strictly speaking caused by what he calls the rules of our culture, but rather those rules arise as characterizations of our actions. But I would go on to say that there is a looping back, that once a framework has been established which characterizes or explains why we act the way we do, this frame then starts to exert a causal influence on our actions. We don't merely characterize behavior in some neutral, off-hand way. Rather, we become invested in our explanations, even a little obsessed by them – or as someone once put it, we are in the grip of our theories. This kind of looping process occurs, for example, in language which, once written down, begins to change in response to the demands of written communicative contexts which differ in important ways from face-to-face interactions. Gradually, however, the characteristics of written language start to filter back into spoken language (cf. Collins & Michaels, 1980; Lakoff, 1982). And it is certainly what seems to happen when academics talk!

The same kind of recursive process happens in the child's life. The adult provides a frame for the child, the cultural rules if you like, for the way to think about behavior and its relation to mental states. The child begins to think in similar terms, and more and more begins to explain and finally predict behavior in terms of inner states – thoughts, beliefs, emotions, and so on. And so it is that thoughts and beliefs in fact come to govern actions in some new way, that inner states in fact do become the causes of behavior that we say they are.

This is not to say that children acquire a theory of mind, after which they start to act on the basis of their thoughts, whereas before they didn't. Rather, I'm claiming that as children begin to see themselves and others as both "mind readers" (i.e., people who think about their own and others' thoughts) and "mind actors" (i.e., people who act on their thoughts), then the thoughts on the basis of which they are acting have changed, and so does their behavior. They become not just little reactors to the world, but little reflectors on the world – both the world of self and of other.

To give an illustration that falls just outside the traditional theory-of-mind realm, many people believe that individuals who view people as objects will treat them as objects. This belief is not merely some fact that is taken in and added to a list of facts. It is absorbed into a framework of explanations of behavior, and an overarching frame which connects the bits of knowledge together around the supposition that we are creatures whose behavior is governed primarily by mental states. So when we see somebody mistreating someone else, we both impute to that person a similar mentalistic framework ("She is treating him like an object, so she must think that people are objects") and we go on from there to use our framework to explain the reasons for this behavior in more detail. For example, we might extrapolate to what her childhood was like, or suggest some current psychological cause for her behavior.

Whatever our explanation, we will also start treating her differently. We might withdraw from any close relationship with her, or put up walls so that we are not hurt by her treatment of us, or reach out with the intention of helping her change, and so on. And how we treat her will in turn impact how she treats us in the future. In the same way, a young child, once he learns the culturally acceptable way of explaining behavior, will increasingly see people as driven, as it were, by inner motivations. He will then in turn come to treat people differently, working to change people's minds rather than just their actions.

The Language of Mind

The second thing I got from both Olson and OISE was a language to hang on the frame. Of course, the words were ones I already knew – belief, intention, theory, desire, emotion – but in the context of the frame these words took on a new life, they pointed to a certain way of construing the child's world. The mere words of language, when hung on a frame, become concepts.

Of course, talk is not neutral. The way the words are hung on the frame depends both on the frame itself, and on what the "hanger" wishes to do with the frame. Let me give an example to illustrate. Dennett takes the word *intentional*, which the average person knows means something like *purposeful*, and the non-average person with a modicum of philosophical training knows has another meaning, namely *aboutness*. He then couples it with the word *stance*, which we also know means a viewpoint or a position. So we have the phrase, *intentional stance*. Now the frame on which he hangs this phrase is one which has a strong evolutionary base – his view is that we and all other living things, from bacteria to grass to chimps, are descended from macromolecules (Dennett, 1996). This frame brings with it certain implications, for example that there is simply no way to get a real mind into the system, no way to get a real agent. Of course, there is one agent – good old Mother Nature – though how she got to be an agent in any real sense remains a mystery. Be that as it may, my point here is that one really doesn't need to know what Dennett's frame is, or even to consciously share his frame, to have one's own frame shaped by the language he gives us. For the very words he chooses – intentional stance – carry with them the shape of his frame and realign our frame to be more like his. We may have lived our lives fully convinced that beliefs as abstract entities are in some sense really real, that I can really change my mind and that my desires are distinctly my own. But as soon as we encounter Dennett using the word *stance* in relation to the realm of intentionality, our belief in belief starts to waver, and we find our frame changing to accommodate *his* belief that this is all just merely a strategy, a perspective, a standpoint that we adopt to help explain the cold hard facts of behavior.

The Dennett of the child's world is the primary caregiver first and foremost, and the others among whom she spends her first years. As the graduate student receives a language to hang on his or her frame, so young children receive a language with which to construe their own and others' behavior. The language children receive is a kind of concrete instantiation of the language I received as a graduate student for my frame – *think, want, know*. Children acquire first the language of desire, giving flesh to the bones of their basic drive for food, touch, sleep. Next comes the language of thought – first as a vague marker of intention ("I think I'll go to the store"), then as marking distinct thought processes. The chronology of the acquisition of mental state language has been studied by Wellman and others and is well documented (e.g., Bartsch & Wellman, 1995; Bretherton & Beeghly, 1982; Shatz, Wellman, & Silber, 1983).

But the development of theory of mind is more than the acquisition of certain lexical items in a certain order. And children (and graduate students) are more than passive recipients. (Or at least the good graduate students resist our efforts to make them just recipients of our brilliant ideas!) Children actively participate in the language learning process, and as Budwig (in press) has documented, learn and use language in quite different ways than their caregivers. In this process there is always the guiding of the caregiver, the subtle shaping processes which implicitly tell the child how to use language in our culture. An example of this would be the different uses of the language of desire. The child first uses "want" as a means of getting the caregiver to fulfill his desires – "wanna cookie" is not simply an expression of a desire but a request that the caregiver supply a cookie. The caregiver, because she is in control of fulfilling both her own and the child's desires, uses "want" in a different way, a way which, with no formal instruction, guides the child on to new uses of the word as a communicative device, to signal an inner state just for the sake of signaling inner states. Thus the child discovers that "want" can be used not just as a request, but as a means of maintaining social contact by informing the other what one intends to do next – for example, "I wanna get the block" which is said as the child begins to open the box to get it. The mother's use continues to differ from the child's – for example "do you wanna eat something now" being not a reference to the child's desires at all, but an attempt to implant, as it were, her own desire in the child (cf. Budwig, in press, for further elaboration on this example). Note, however, that there is nothing about the English language per se that requires this use of the word *want*. *Want* could be used strictly to announce desire, and other nonmentalistic language could be used to accomplish the pragmatic function of announcing what one is doing (e.g., "I'm opening the box and getting the block now) or to elicit behavior (e.g., "Come and eat lunch now"). It is our notion of the relationship between thought and behavior that drives our language use as adults. As caregivers we have been enculturated into a certain theory of mind, and we in turn pass it on to the children under our care through the way in which we use language with them.

The study of how language functions in social interactions and its relation to the making of minds has been understudied, although some have looked in this direction. Hughes and Dunn (1998), while they focus on the frequency of usage of mental state talk, note that different types of social contexts might influence the frequency. Furrow, Moore, Davidge, and Chiasson (1992) focus more on how mental state language functions in mother–child interactions. Not only should the function of the so-called genuine uses of mental state terms be studied, but also those uses which do not conform to the standard, adult patterns of use, for it is there that we will gain access to the child's view of the world. For, though I have said that we hang language on our frame, that is not all of the picture. How language functions in various social interactions, how it is used in communicative practices, at once both illuminates and changes our frame.

The Social/Cultural Act of Mind Making

The making of a mind is not a solitary activity, but a social one. As a graduate student struggling to make up my mind, I had a support system. My mind was made up, not through solitary contemplations, not through any Cartesian meditations, but through my interactions with the students and faculty of OISE, through classes, one-on-one meetings with professors, research groups, endless cups of coffee with other students, and so on. Though there were also hours alone composing papers, the entire process was more social than it was individual. Even the papers were written for an audience and were thus also social events – rarely did I sit alone and think just for my own sake. My understanding arose out of those contexts, but was also most clearly displayed in those contexts.

The development of an understanding of minds in the young child is likewise rooted in social interaction. While some of the building blocks of the frame, such as the distinction between animate and inanimate, and some basic laws of motion, (e.g., Spelke, 1985) may be innate, minds are formed through interactions with other children and adults. The frame is passed on from older to younger, language arises in social interaction, indeed the very need for an understanding of minds is rooted in social interaction, for it is primarily the behavior of others that needs explaining and predicting, not one's own. The process is not just one way, with the cultural expert imparting appropriate knowledge to the novice, but the child participates in construction of mind as he interacts with and reflects on the world and its inhabitants around him, adapting the frame and the language for his own purposes.

How this dual process of enculturating and being enculturated works is something that needs more investigation. Some would say that the strict experimental approach is not going to give us all the answers for it pulls the child out of the very context in which development occurs. Yet others (e.g., Astington & Olson, 1995) have suggested that these experimental procedures allow us to find out the child's true ability – some sort of underlying competence that is at the basis of the child's everyday performance. There are problems with this latter view, however. In the first place, one's true competence can be masked in many ways. In this sense, competence is analogous to the statistical notion of true score. Foundational to classical reliability theory is the notion that any individual's performance is a combination of one's true ability and random error. Various factors such as chance, individual and environmental fluctuations affect performance so that one's true ability is covered up, as it were, by "error." The experimental method attempts to reduce this noisesome error and arrive at as accurate a measurement of the true ability as possible. However, one's true competence, I would maintain, is not more clearly demonstrated in a decontextualized experimental situation. We are creatures of context – familial, societal, historical – and it is only within these contexts that our true competence shines forth. Experimental methods as they are presently viewed may be able to show us that there is some relationship between number of siblings, or parenting style or language development and the child's understanding of mind, but so far they do not appear to show us much about what the nature of that relationship is. For that we need to watch development in progress.

Yet I do not want to suggest, as some such as Raver and Leadbeater (1993) have, that the answer is simply to abandon experimental methods in favor of more naturalistic methodology. To see these two methods as arising from two different views of the child may have historical validity, but ultimately leads us in the wrong direction. Raver and Leadbeater put experimental methods in one camp with a view of the child as an isolated entity who understands others through intrapsychic mental activity, and naturalistic methods in an opposing camp that views the child as a social entity who understands others through interpersonal communicative activities. This contrast of Raver and Leadbeater assumes first, that an understanding of mental states must underlie competent social interaction and second, that experimental methodology is somehow free from sociocultural influence.

With regard to the first assumption, social interaction may be possible without a complete understanding of mental states. Those who favor an early competence include researchers in social cognition who claim to find evidence both in traditional experimental situations and in more naturalistic social interactions of an understanding of minds prior to the age at which children pass theory-of-mind tasks (e.g., Clements & Perner, 1994; Dunn, 1991; Ruffman, this volume, Chapter 15). Those against an early onset of theory of mind could explain the evidence as the child behaving in certain culturally appropriate ways without having the concepts to really understand what they are doing. It looks like a duck, it quacks like a duck, but, say the scoffers, . . . it's not a duck, or at least it doesn't understand what a duck is! Yet this apparently anti-commonsense view may seem more plausible to those of us who have spent time in other cultures. We know that it is quite possible to "go through the motions" – to say or do the right thing at the right time – without having a clue as to what's going on. We are something like the child who stands next to the open cookie jar with crumbs on his mouth and a cookie in hand staunchly denying having taken a cookie. Is the child lying? Either he is a terribly poor liar, or he doesn't really understand the concept of lying. But he certainly knows what to say in order to avoid punishment.

An argument against an early theory-of-mind onset would be to say that key to understanding lying is understanding what it means to create a false belief in the other person, and the child clearly demonstrates a deficit in this area. An argument in favor of an early onset would be that the child understands a key part of what is required in lying, namely that you deny whatever it is that you are being accused of. Clearly both the child and a certain US president have mastered the ability to deny one's actions, but one wonders whether either should really be said to understand lying. The case of the president is slightly more complex than the child's. Surely he does really understand lying, but is suffering from what we might be kind enough to call "temporary theory-of-mind loss." We have perhaps all experienced this on occasion – times when we fail to understand or we ignore the other's perspective. Often we become mind-blind, I suspect, because we have some deep emotion such as fear or love or anger that is interfering with our rational thought processes.

Does this also happen to the child? In my recent research on parental influences on the development of an understanding of mind I videotape a task embedded in a mealtime context. We replace the contents of a cookie box with a plastic mouse while the mother is out of the room. One young girl who is almost seven was so fixated on her thought that her mother would be mad when she returned, that she failed to answer any of the questions correctly. But it is not only emotion that gets in the way of our using a theory of mind. De Villiers (2000) finds that socially competent deaf children routinely fail all sorts of tasks, both verbal and nonverbal, that require an understanding of false belief. Whether in child or adult, then, it seems as if a distinction must be made between how something such as a lying functions in real life and how it is conceptualized. What one does, how one participates is not just a matter of having concepts. But neither is the existence of concepts all that is required to say that social understanding exists. How the child comes to both act in culturally appropriate ways and understand what she is doing, and how the doing and the understanding interact, is what developmental research is all about.

In contrast to Raver and Leadbeater's second assumption, I suggest that experimental methods are not culture-free. An experiment is a sociocultural event just as much as a naturally occurring parent–child interaction over a meal at home. We simply fail to treat experiments as cultural events, parsing children's behavior as either right or wrong, passing or failing. In doing so we miss out on vital information about the child's understanding of the situation they are in and also the concepts which they bring to the situation, if you will. Clement and Perner's (1994) study in which they videotaped which location children look at in a false belief task involving the moving of cheese by a mouse was one of the first experimental tasks to show that much more was happening than is revealed by mere verbal response. While the interpretation of where a child looks before he or she answers questions is fraught with difficulty, it is a necessary part of the analysis. Also the precise language that is used by the child in response to our questions deserves further attention. In pilot studies by Quinn (personal communication, April 1999), for example, one child consistently answered questions about the past with the present tense of the verb "think." What does this mean? Is the child really answering the question we are asking, or some other question? If we were collecting naturalistic data these are all questions we would struggle to answer. But they are also questions which we should be answering about the sociocultural interaction between experimenter and child.

The standard theory-of-mind tasks take our adult explanations of behavior, explanations in terms of mental states, and test how well children have learned to think like us. Admittedly, this may be an important thing to know – but I do not agree with Astington and Olson (1995) that this kind of research method is one that is tied to the theory theory, as opposed to more naturalistic methods which reflect an orientation toward an enculturation theory. The standard tasks are quite simply tests of enculturation, when enculturation is viewed as a one-way process from expert to novice – how well do kids think like us adults. What is needed, and what more naturalistic tasks show promise to provide, is how kids think when left to think like kids in everyday contexts. Of course, this is not to say that kids are not affected by the adults around them – so in that sense they never really think like kids. But what experimental tasks do is adopt a kind of cross-cultural approach – if we can think of childhood and adulthood as two different cultures for a moment. The cross-cultural approach, which traditionally has taken tasks and measures constructed for one culture and attempted to adapt them to another culture, has been widely criticized for attempting to make other cultures do our tricks. In a sense that is what the theory-of-mind tasks are doing – attempting to make children do our adult tricks. Of course, children eventually do come to be able to do our tricks – we scaffold them well to become fully functioning members of our culture.

Rather than the problem being a conflict of methodologies, I think the differences in what appear to be two camps in theory-of-mind research are better described as differences in implicit views of culture. Rohner (1984) suggests that there are two main theories of culture – behavioral and ideational. A behavioral theory defines culture as systems of socially transmitted patterns of behavior, often including the artifacts produced by those behaviors. This view has much in common with the current activity theorists who maintain that it is practical activity as socially organized that gives rise to psychological phenomena. An ideational theory defines culture in terms of ideas and beliefs, of shared concepts about the meanings of things. We might want to say, therefore, that those who wish to study the concepts acquired as minds are made up have an ideational view of culture. They are simply interested in the ideas and beliefs acquired, and how concepts related to mind fit together to form a coherent whole with predictive power. It's a small step from there to coining the term theory of mind, though some might want to argue it is not a necessary step. Those who choose to study how children act in social situations seem to take a more behavioral view of culture – they are interested in children's ability to learn how to behave in culturally appropriate ways, in everyday practical activities.

What Astington and Olson (1995) claim needs to be explained is "the beginning of children's efforts at interpretation of their own and others' talk and action" (p. 187). They are very clear about where this true beginning lies – not in participation but in concepts – "understanding presupposes concepts" (p. 187). Their very phrasing of the enterprise implies a specific view of culture and the relationship between the social and the psychological. What they seem to be searching for are some psychological primitives, some indication of what the child can do/think alone, unaided by any social interaction. In seeking this beginning point, they seem to be opposing Vygotsky who clearly prioritized the social – "Every function in the child's cultural development appears twice, or on two planes. First it appears on the social level, and then on the individual level" (1978, p. 57). What Vygotsky, and others who follow him seem to be saying, is that the psychological cannot be explained without regard to the social. What Astington and Olson seem to be saying, which surprised me, is that the psychological precedes the social, that concepts arise in the midst of a sociocultural milieu, but that true understanding occurs only if there is first this personal, conceptual understanding.

Perhaps part of the problem here is a difference in opinion as to what constitutes understanding. Is it the old declarative and procedural knowledge revisited – are we asking whether understanding is thinking or doing? Astington and Olson seem to say it is thinking, so that inasmuch as an understanding of minds is culturally constituted it is so from the perspective of culture as groups of ideas. The social cognition group appears to say that understanding is doing, so that inasmuch as an understanding of minds is culturally constituted it is so from the perspective of culture as patterns of behaviors.

I would maintain, however, that culture is not either ideational or behavioral, but both. Behaviors are not interpretable if they have no meaning. Ideas and concepts are also not interpretable without reference to experience. Thus a child's understanding of mind is not only acquired in a sociocultural context, but also has no meaning apart from that context. It is not a question of two sides of a coin. Rather, there is only one game in town, and the game is culture. Social interaction is not some "added on" variable that we can chose to include or not to include. The experimental situation is just as much a social situation as any other part of the child's life, albeit not one with which most children are very familiar. It is not the case that we must supplement experimental methods with naturalistic methods (or vice versa), nor that one method is scientific and the other interpretive. Nor is it the case that children acquire concepts which are organized in a theory-like manner and which we can study apart from the cultural interactions from which they arise. The child's understanding of mind is cultural through and through.

Conclusion

To learn a culture, to become enculturated, is to have one's mind made up. It is to receive, in interaction with those who are more expert in the culture, a frame of mind, a language, and a frame of action through which to live and create culture. But to learn a culture is also to make up one's mind, to actively participate, with mind and body, in a world of concept making. It is not just being a passive recipient of what those who are further along the path have to offer you, but joining in the process of enculturation. Thus mind making is not something that ends at the magic age of five with the acquisition of a theory of mind, any more than the enculturation process ends there. At times one can even choose one culture over another, which is what ones does, consciously or unconsciously, when one goes to graduate school.

My mind continues to be "made up." Moving on from the culture of Olson and OISE, I take with me guidelines for enduring questions that continue to be part of the making of my mind.

First, don't be afraid to try out your ideas, no matter how silly they might seem at first. Surely this is how the young child's mind develops, through trial and error. Fortunately children's relatively naive state protects them from the feelings of foolishness that we adults have to endure as we experience the error side of the process. Imagine if the child attempting his first lie while standing at open cookie jar realized how foolish he looked – would that inhibit or encourage rapid learning? The research group with David provided this kind of relatively safe haven for half-formed (though not half-baked) ideas. I learned to respect his willingness to throw his half-formed ideas into the ring and let us young lions tear into them. At times the play among us graduate students was rough – and yes, the boys did seem to hit harder than the girls, but most of us got used to that. It was all a part of playing with our new ideas, and as all theory-of-mind researchers know, play is a crucial part in the process of making up minds.

I also learned that if you are going to produce some truly great ideas, you are likely going to also produce a few not-so-great ones along the way, but that's okay. I also learned that weak ideas, the not-so-great ones, get stronger as they take on the lions, whereas if you are afraid to let your ideas enter the ring of debate, they just shrivel and die. If you think you have a good idea, don't give up on it too easily. Experiment, work at it from different angles, don't take rejection personally, but as an opportunity to fine tune. Easier said than done. Easier done when you are well along in your career than when you are first starting out. But isn't this just the process of mind making at any age?

Finally, I learned that the major question of cognitive psychology is still "How does anything out there get in here?" This question, so simply stated by David (or at least that is my memory of how he stated it!) has been asked by others in a variety of ways, and with a variety of twists and turns, but it all amounts to the same thing. To ask the question in Vygotskian (1978, p. 57) terms, how do interpsychological categories become intrapsychological categories? This question need not set up an antimony between the world and the child, between culture and cognition (cf. Cole, 1985). Rather, it speaks to me of the embeddedness of the child in culture, the entanglement of what's out there with what's in here. We can talk about internalization and zones of proximal development, we can talk about stages or scripts or modules, we can take a stand at any level of explanation from neurons to beliefs. But whether or not we chose a micro- or a macro-level as our base camp in our assault on understanding what goes on "in here," whether or not we chose to call our work explanation or description, it seems there always remains a mystery, that we never quite get to the answer to that question "How does anything out there get in here?"

It is that mystery that keeps us motivated to keep on reading and writing and learning and doing research. We keep hoping we will find the definitive answer. Ultimately, I believe, we will not find the one answer, but only come to see the richness of the ways in which development takes place. The say/mean distinction, one of those intellectual bones which David has worried as long as I have known him, is relevant here. What the question says – how does anything out there get in here – is simple enough. Part of what the question means, however, is that we are studying something truly amazing, something wondrous and earthshattering. We should not lose that wonder in the flurry of publishing lest we perish, in the quest to leave our mark on the field or even in any of our more altruistic endeavors such as providing a better education for children. I think it is the same wonder that keeps young children hard at work in the making of their minds. It was into that world of wonder, and the hard thinking that goes with it, that I was enculturated by Olson and OISE, where my mind was made up anew . . . but not completely.

References

Astington, J. W., & Olson, D. R. (1995). The cognitive revolution in children's understanding of mind. *Human Development, 38*, 179–89.

Bartsch K., & Wellman, H. M. (1995). *Children talk about the mind.* New York: Oxford University Press.

Bretherton, I., & Beeghly, M. (1982). Talking about internal states: The acquisition of an explicit theory of mind. *Developmental Psychology, 18*, 906–21.

Budwig, N. (in press). A developmental-functionalist approach to mental state talk. In J. Byrnes & E. Amsel (Eds.), *Language, literacy, and cognitive development: The development and consequences of symbolic communication.* Mahwah, NJ: Erlbaum.

Clements, W., & Perner, J. (1994). Implicit understanding of belief. *Cognitive Development, 9*, 377–95.

Cole, M. (1985). The zone of proximal development: Where culture and cognition create each other. In J. Wertsch (Ed.), *Culture, communication and cognition* (pp. 146–61). Cambridge: Cambridge University Press.

Collins, J., & Michaels, S. (1980). The importance of conversational discourse in the acquisition of literacy. *Proceedings of the Sixth Annual Meeting, Berkeley Linguistics Society*, 143–56.

de Villiers, J. (2000). Language and theory of mind: What are the developmental relationships? In S. Baron-Cohen, H. Tager-Flusberg, & D. Cohen (Eds.), *Understanding other minds: Perspectives from developmental cognitive neurosciences* (2nd ed. pp. 83–123). Oxford, UK: Oxford University Press.

Dennett, D. (1996). *Kinds of minds: Toward an understanding of consciousness.* New York: Basic Books.

Dunn, J. (1991). Young children's understanding of other people: Evidence from observations within the family. In D. Frye & C. Moore (Eds.), *Children's theories of mind: Mental states and social understanding* (pp. 97–114). Hillsdale, NJ: Erlbaum.

Furrow, D., Moore, C., Davidge, J., & Chiasson, L. (1992). Mental terms in mothers' and children's speech: Similarities and relationships. *Journal of Child Language, 19*, 627–31.

Hughes, C., & Dunn, J. (1998). Understanding mind and emotion: Longitudinal associations with mental-state talk between young friends. *Developmental Psychology, 34*, 1026–37.

Lakoff, R. (1982). Some of my favorite writers are literate: The mingling of oral and literate strategies in written communication. In D. Tannen (Ed.), *Analyzing discourse: Text and talk* (pp. 239–60). Washington DC: Georgetown University Press.

Olson, D. R. (1977). From utterance to text: The bias of language in speech and writing. *Harvard Educational Review, 57*, 257–81.

Olson, D. R. (1994). *The world on paper.* Cambridge, UK: Cambridge University Press.

Olson, D. R., & Astington, J. W. (1990). Talking about text: How literacy contributes to thought. *Journal of Pragmatics, 14*, 705–21.

Raver, C., & Leadbeater, B. (1993). The problem of the other in research on theory of mind and social development. *Human Development, 36*, 350–62.

Rohner, R. (1984). Toward a conception of culture for cross-cultural psychology. *Journal of Cross-Cultural Psychology, 15*, 111–38.

Shanker, S. (1992). In search of Bruner. *Language and Communication, 12*, 53–74.

Shatz, M., Wellman, H. M., & Silber, S. (1983). The acquisition of mental verbs: A systematic investigation of the first reference to mental state. *Cognition, 14,* 301–21.

Spelke, E. S. (1985). Perception of unity, persistence, and identity: Thoughts on infants' conception of objects. In J. Mehler & R. Fox (Eds.), *Neonate cognition* (pp. 89–113). Hillsdale, NJ: Erlbaum.

Vinden, P. G. (1996). Junín Quechua children's understanding of mind. *Child Development, 67,* 1707–16.

Vinden, P. G. (1999). Children's understanding of mind and emotion: A multi-culture study. *Cognition and Emotion 13,* 19–48.

Vygotsky, L. S. (1978). *Mind in society: The development of higher psychological processes* (M. Cole, V. John-Steiner, S. Scribner, & E. Souberman, Eds.). Cambridge, MA: Harvard University Press.

4

Literacy as Symbolic Space

Jens Brockmeier

"To put it simply, writing has an impact on cognition through culture, a culture of writing."

D. R. Olson (in press)

Over the last 30 years our conception of literacy has changed fundamentally. In a sense, only during these years has literacy become a subject in its own right, an epistemic object – albeit of many different academic investigations. Today, scholars in a variety of disciplines agree that the notion of literacy refers to a broad spectrum of diverse linguistic and technological phenomena, that all these phenomena are historical formations, that they are tied to specific cultural contexts, that they are of great economic and political relevance, and that they have far-reaching educational and social consequences. However, there is less agreement about the particular psychological and the cognitive implications of literacy; indeed, it is even doubted if there are any at all.

One can be inclined to think that we are faced with this uncertainty not in spite of numerous empirical studies of diverse cultures of literacy which have been carried out over the last two decades, but rather as a consequence of this research. The more we have learnt about the complex linguistic, psychological, and cultural relations between oral and written language use, the more yesterday's groundbreaking insights have taken on the air of heroic illusions. For example, recall Eric Havelock's (1963, 1982) claim that western culture, and especially the intellectual and cultural achievements of modernity, is a consequence of the "alphabetic mind" which originated in the "literate revolution" in ancient Greece. Likewise, Goody and Watt (1968) believed that they had demonstrated that the invention of logical reasoning was a byproduct of the invention of the Greek alphabet. Walter Ong (1982), another theorist of the *great divide* between orality and literacy, presented a neat list of dichotomies attributed to the "psychodynamics" of oral thought and literate thought: additive versus subordinative, aggregative versus analytic, redundant versus linear, conservative or traditionalist versus original, close to the human lifeworld versus distant from it, empathetically and participatory versus objectively distanced, situational versus abstract. On a similar note, Claude Lévi-Strauss (1962) claimed to have discovered a primitive mode of thought, *la pensée sauvage*, which was characteristic of a genuinely preliterate mind and in sharp contrast to the rational and scientific mode of the modern western mind, that is, the literate mind. Today, this "strong literacy hypothesis," held by Havelock, Goody and Watt, Ong, Lévi-Strauss, and others, seems to have become a closed chapter in the history of ideas and, together with it, all strong claims about direct and causal relations between literacy and thought.

In hindsight, the emergence of the "strong literacy hypothesis" in the 1960s and 1970s appears more as a spectacular proclamation than the introduction of a new research paradigm. When the strong literacy hypothesis was first articulated, as David Olson (1991, p. 251) has remarked, it had some of the properties of a "ground-clearing operation, a sort of slash-and-burn quality," while "it has fallen to a second generation of scholars to clean up the debris and turn the clearing into arable land." In the same paper, Olson made a concrete suggestion how to clean up the debris. Distinguishing several possible explanations of the psychological and social relations between writing and thought, he outlined four hypotheses which each highlight one particular feature of alphabetic literacy that has been claimed to account for its particular psychological and intellectual quality: literacy as the modality, as medium, as mentality, and as metalinguistic activity. In what follows, I shall sketch briefly what, in my view, is the point of the first three hypotheses and then focus on the fourth, the metalinguistic hypothesis, which has become fundamental for much of the research on the cognitive implications of literacy, including that of Olson. I shall argue that the metalinguistic hypothesis provides a useful model to also understand literacy as an ensemble of cultural practices, that is, the material, discursive, cognitive, and institutional practices of writing and reading which integrate us into a literate tradition. Finally, I shall offer the idea of understanding these practices as interrelated within one cultural symbol system, the symbolic space of literacy.

Awareness of Language and Metalinguistic Discourse

One of the first models relating literacy and forms of thought, Olson suggests, was McLuhan's (1962) modality hypothesis, that is, the view that writing calls into play a highly specializing sensory modality, the eye, which came to substitute for the ear. Although McLuhan's formula "an eye for an ear" did not explain much and even failed to capture the different modalities of both oral and written language, it became a suggestive metaphor for the visual mode of cognition associated with written language.

The second hypothesis states that literacy is a medium, as opposed to a mere modality, which draws upon the fact that writing is not only a visual mode but also serves as a medium of communication. In this view, it is the particular properties of writing as a medium that distinguishes it from oral communication and lead to the evolution of new forms of discourse and linguistic genres, ranging from lists, ency-clopedia articles, philosophical and scientific treatises to business documents and legal texts. Authors such as Goody (1987) conceived of these forms of literate spe-cialization as the key to the particular cognitive resources that are characteristic of modern societies. In creating a new medium of communication, written texts also provide a new mode of thought, representing forms of "decontextualized," "self-referential," and "autonomous" knowledge (Olson, 1977, 1991, 1994). In other words, thought and knowledge become text-based.

The third hypothesis relating literacy to thought suggests that writing and read-ing impinge not only on the specific linguistic and cognitive skills involved in be-coming a writer and a reader but also change the entire mental outlook upon world and self. The mentality hypothesis tries to avoid the objections raised to the earlier hypotheses in that it allows that linguistic and cognitive skills transfer across differ-ent modalities and media. As Roy Harris (1989, p. 99) writes: "The essential inno-vation which writing brings is not a new mode of exchanging and storing information but a new mentality." Many studies have pointed out that there is no borderline between oral and literate forms of communication and thought. Oral thought and literate thought are, at best, analytically isolated extremes of one continuum, a con-tinuum of discourse that underlies all our communication and cognition. However, as several historians and anthropologists have argued, there might be different men-talities rooted in the cultural practices of dominantly oral and dominantly literate societies, for example, in memory practices (e.g., Carruthers, 1990; Finnegan, 1988).

The fourth hypothesis is that writing is a material, social, and cognitive practice that brings language into consciousness. Because reading and writing are opera-tions on language, they are understood as metalinguistic activities which raise aware-ness and knowledge about linguistic activities. Writing, in this view, is an intrinsically metalinguistic practice that turns language into an object of discourse and thought. In "quoting speech" (Olson, 1999), writing seems to materially fix and objectify discourse in such a way as to offer to the reflective mind a model of understanding language. Compared with the modality, medium, and mentality hypotheses, the metalinguistic hypothesis is obviously more modest and limited in its claims about the cultural implications of writing, since its primary scope is restricted to language and thought about language. Indeed, we might call it the weak or moderate literacy hypothesis.

The metalinguistic view has been suggested by several authors (e.g., Brockmeier, 1998; Ferreiro & Teberosky, 1982; Harris, 1986; 1996; Herriman, 1986; Luria, 1976; Olson, 1994; Pontecorvo, Orsolini, Burge, & Resnick, 1996; Vygotsky, 1987). They have argued that written language plays a central role in the developing con-sciousness of language, particularly in raising awareness of properties and functions of speech as well as of structures of discursive interaction. Moreover, writing high-lights not just language, but also brings into consciousness the complex relations between oral and literate discourse and the world. Writing, we might say, is a par-ticular way to "stage" the communicative and referential fabric, the "universe of discourse," as it is called in semiotics. It is within this universe of discourse that we construct our vision of the world and our selves, the "universe of the mind," to borrow Lotman's (1990) term.

However, even if there is ample evidence that metalinguistic awareness and literacy are closely intertwined constituents of the "universe of discourse," it is an open question which specific factors contribute to this effect and how these factors relate among each other. What exactly is it that turns language into an object of metalinguistic awareness, reflection, and even consciousness?

Typically, researchers have focused on *one* factor, either because they claim, for theoretical reasons, that there must be a one-causal-factor-explanation or, more often, for reasons of research methodology (since one or two "single factors" are easier to test and to measure). In contrast, I want to argue that there is no such thing as a "single factor" (or a combination of various single factors) which accounts for the relationship between literacy and metalinguistic consciousness. In today's modern societies, becoming literate is not just acquiring a skill; rather, it is growing into a literate culture, into a literate tradition which comprises many discourses, including an elaborated metalinguistic discourse. Growing into such tradition is becoming immersed into a symbolic space.

Historically, the symbolic space of literacy has developed into what could be called a cultural and historical *a priori*, using a concept suggested by Michel Foucault (1973). By "historical *a priori*," Foucault meant the semiotic conditions of the possibility of communication, thought, and imagination which define the cultural codes of a certain epoch. These cultural codes lay out the conceptual structure and range of those ideas that can become, in this very epoch, a subject of communication, thought, and imagination. In the modern world, I suggest, literacy has long become such a *cultural a priori* of our consciousness of language, a universal symbolic space that has (re-)defined our entire metalinguistic discourse. In fact, what we call writing stands for a symbolic reality, a "universe of discourse," which is difficult to separate from the reality of modern societies itself. This is the main point I want to make, and I hope it will become all the more convincing if it is viewed against the backdrop of an increasingly specialized and particularized research landscape.

What Makes Language an Object of Thought?

Emphasizing literacy as a symbolic space is, however, not to say that there are no distinct elements, aspects, and dimensions of this space which specifically affect the development of metalinguistic discourse and consciousness of language. Gombert (1992) has reminded us that since language is such a complex and differentiated system, metalinguistic activities and forms of consciousness can hardly be conceived of as one homogeneous and uniform phenomenon. But what are appropriate criteria to theoretically reflect such functional and cultural diversity? Drawing on the literature on literacy development as well as on my own studies, I suggest distinguishing the following categories of factors which have been investigated from various theoretical and empirical vantage points.

(1) *Phonemic awareness.* There is an enormous and continuously expanding literature about the mutual relations between children's development of writing and reading and their metalinguistic awareness. Although all studies unequivocally report evidence that metalinguistic awareness is crucial in children's successful literacy acquisition, there are divergent views as to the nature of the relationship between literacy and metalinguistic awareness – especially, whether metalinguistic awareness is a prerequisite to, a facilitator of, or a consequence of learning to write and read. The interactionist view, for example, suggests that a certain amount of metalinguistic awareness is a prerequisite for learning to read and write, whereas the process of literacy acquisition itself may further facilitate the development of metalinguistic consciousness. Along these lines, most research has focused on the role of phonemic or phonological awareness, but there also are numerous studies suggesting that (meta)linguistic awareness is not restricted to letter-sound relations, but also affects children's consciousness of language at graphic, lexical, syntactic, and pragmatic levels (e.g., Clark, 1992; Ferreiro, Pontecorvo, Ribeiro Moreira, & Garcia Hidalgo, 1996; Gombert, 1992; Scholes, 1993). To my mind, considering the various results of this research as a whole suggests, in contrast with the theoretical and methodological assumptions of most studies, a broad notion of (meta)linguistic consciousness – a notion that embraces any knowledge, reflection, ideas, rules of use, concerning the entire spectrum of language use in a given culture. Viewed this way, it seems to be all the more misleading to base theoretical generalizations on the investigation of isolated single factors.

(2) *Orthography* and orthographic awareness is one such single factor to which much attention has been allotted, following traditional classroom practices as well as the imperatives of "easy and clean" research methodologies.

(3) *Poetic features of language* are further elements that become the subject of oral and literate practices which refer to language as an object in its own right. From early on, children are fascinated by such poetic features as rhymes, alliterations, rhythm, and morphological, syntactical, and graphic patterns. For example, preschoolers who have difficulties with tasks that require them to isolate single phonemes show an impressive facility with rhyme games that involve the same linguistic sensitivity (Kirtley, Bryant, McLean, & Bradley, 1989). A similar metalinguistic function is served by the language of songs and sociodramatic performances each of which, in their own way, "stage" language and draw attention to particular aspects of language. The use and the interpretation of metaphors and idiomatic expressions are further sources of children's growing awareness of language as a particular, semiotically independent dimension of the world.

(4) In every culture, there is a wide spectrum of *verbal and nonverbal communicative practices* which include explicit references to language. In fact, in the literature on literacy development it has been often pointed out that it is hard to draw a line between discourse and metadiscourse (e.g., Pontecorvo et al., 1996). Metadiscourse comprises both oral metalanguage (in which, for example, we correct, make clear, and interpret the spoken word) and literate metalanguage (in which we refer to written texts). In both oral and literate metadiscourse, we use metalinguistic

categories such as say, tell, ask, lie, swear, misunderstand, comment. A similar
metalinguistic role is played by another category of children's self-referential practices of communication: corrections and self-corrections, as well as misunderstand-
ings and clarifications. From the beginning, these conversational practices are
important hinges between discourse and metadiscourse, language and metalanguage.
Soon, jokes, humor, irony, and pretense become further components of the same
linguistic and metalinguistic fabric. This fabric also can comprise verbal conflicts
among children and children and adults. Sometimes, the meaning of a single word
or expression becomes the subject of controversial interpretations among children
which may extend to many turns in an argument (Brockmeier, 1996). Likewise,
language games such as the naming of dolls, animals, and newborn babies, as well as
(known and invented) objects draw children's attention to the differences between
proper names and common nouns, raising a "nominalist" awareness of the arbitrary
and conventional character of language (Homer, Brockmeier, Kamawar, & Olson,
in press).

(5) Children's *play* is pivotal in the development of what Piaget (1951) called the
"symbolic function" and what Vygotsky (1978) called the "semiotic function." In
symbolic or pretend play children operate with meanings severed from objects and
actions; they begin to distinguish between the meaning of an object and the meaning of a word. "To a certain extent," Vygotsky (1976, p. 547) wrote, in play "meaning
is emancipated from the object with which it had been directly fused before." In
this way, the child enters in the sphere of semantic operations. The spectrum of play
particularly relevant to the development of metalinguistic consciousness ranges from
forms of symbolic play (Pellegrini, 1993, 1997) to the many kinds of plays and
games with language – for example, with letters (as in crossword puzzles), fantasy
words and names, and puns. In addition, in most forms of symbolic play, language
takes center stage, creating, supporting, and surrounding all symbolic activities.
From the point of view of developing metalinguistic awareness, especially interesting is play with different media (which usually involves different speech and discourse genres); as for example in the scenario, analyzed by the linguist Andresen
(1995), of a boy playing radio reporter and then commenting as a "normal boy" on
the formalized genre of news and public announcements, which he himself tried to
imitate.

(6) It is widely acknowledged that *story-telling and narrative practices* play a
major role in the development of children's conception of language. These practices include listening to, and telling of stories, as well as re-narrating, paraphrasing,
summarizing, interpreting, and co-narrating of stories. In various narrative games a
word or expression can become of decisive significance. In a number of stories told
by Austrian first-graders at the beginning of formal writing instruction, the favorite
letters of the children turned into agents and protagonists of fantasy stories about
letters and words which get involved in adventures (Brockmeier, 1998). It might
be the distancing function of narrative (Bruner, 1999) that makes stories about
language, its elements and properties, instrumental in children's understanding of
language as a particular mode of constructing reality.

(7) When children learn to write, they learn a set of *material practices*. Writing, not least, is creating a visible, usually tangible product, a meaningful and decipherable trace. What is particularly fascinating for small children about scratching, scribbling, drawing, and writing is "making something on the world" (McLane & McNamee, 1990). Writing as a material product is a semiotic body, the "graphic substance," as linguists call it, which makes language visible and materially concrete. Writing as an activity is to produce this semiotic body. Viewed in this way, learning to write, in its early stages, implies the discovery of language as an object of signs, a peculiar object, but also an independent object. Like a word that is scribbled on a piece of paper: a "thing" that is fixed and can be carried around; something that can become subject to thought and talk, even some days after its actual production. It is not least the physical and material presence of writing – including the forms of early literacy or emergent literacy (Sulzby & Teale, 1991) – that, in a specific way, turns language into an object, a physical object and epistemological object, so to speak. Studying the practices in which children begin to materially construct the signs of written language (Brockmeier, 1994, 1998), I have come to see that they begin, in these very activities, to explore in an elementary way some general properties of language – for example, its conventionality and arbitrariness. Such, as it were, material linguistic practices may help children to gradually overcome what Piaget and Vygotsky called "infantile realism," the confusion of word and thing, sign and signed object, signifier and signified.

(8) *Writing technologies* have always had a strong influence on our conceptions of the communicative and representational capacities of language. From the typewriter to the computer revolution with its particular forms of electronic or on-line literacy, writing technologies provide a sophisticated material and symbolic armature to "stage," and to operate on, language. To be sure, the actual technology identified as a revolutionary force has changed – from printing press to word processor, electronic mail, hypertext, and Internet as "information highway" in present days; yet "in most cases it is technology of words, a technology that changes how written language is produced, processed, transported, and used" (Haas, 1996, p. ix). Obviously, writing devices are not just technological settings; they are carriers of societal symbol systems which bind their user into a culture. Let me add two more categories of sociocultural factors whose significance for the development of metalinguistic consciousness has been extensively investigated.

(9) A large literature deals with how *bilingualism* and *multilingualism* influence children's ideas about language. This question has been extended in the literature on *biliteracy* or *multiliteracy* to "any and all instances in which communication occurs in two (or more) languages in or around writing" (Lüdi, 1997). It has often been observed that the experience of more than one linguistic system has an impact on children's consciousness of language, to the extent that degrees of bilingualism seem to correlate to levels of metalinguistic awareness (Bialystok, 1988). Furthermore, it has been argued that bilingualism and multilingualism relate to an increasing understanding of the referential and communicative function of words, expressions, and more extended speech acts. This is all the more the

case if the experiences of different linguistic systems coincide with different cultural environments (Verhoeven, 1997). Such (cor-)relations, however, become more complicated if different aspects of metalinguistic awareness are defined not only with respect to particular language features, but also to the particularities of different languages and literacy systems. Metalinguistic awareness can mean quite a different thing in Spanish, Japanese, or Chinese than in English (Nagy & Anderson, 1999).

(10) It has often been demonstrated that the *social environment* of language use accounts not only for specific forms of discourse, but also for people's ideas about language. The elementary social unit of the family is a case in point. Primary linguistic community for most children, the family is a sociolinguistic microcosm (Wells, 1985, 1990). Further societal factors such as education, economic status, neighborhood, local political institutions and policies impinge upon this most sensitive discursive system at least as much as the (meta)linguistic canon (Heath, 1983, 1990; Pellegrini, 1997; Stevenson, Lee, & Schweingruber, 1999). Equally fundamental for children's ideas about, and consciousness of, language and literacy are societal institutions of education, such as kindergarten, school, college, university, and religious institutes: all of which are built around literacy practices. Focusing on the cultural functions of these practices, a recent current of research on writing and language use in educational environments and the workplace has turned from primary attention to the language of the text to the social activities that the texts mediate and which are mediated by texts (Russell, 1997). These studies suggest that our consciousness of language depends not only on linguistic activities that refer to language as such, but also on social activities that are realized in and through language. In the end, then, there remains not much of a difference between linguistic, discursive, and social practices, as we might say in the wake of Wittgenstein.

It is exactly this Wittgensteinian point of view that allows us to summarize the factors I have listed, that is, understanding them as moments of one "cultural grammar." From this perspective, consciousness of language (at graphic, lexical, syntactic, and pragmatic levels) and the implicit poetic dimension of language do not exist as isolated features but are inextricably intermingled with the entire gamut of verbal and nonverbal communicative practices. Phenomena like play and narrative practices are good cases in point. At the same time, all language use has a material dimension, a physicality that Derrida (1974) has called *écriture*; and this becomes particularly evident if we look at writing as material activity, as a process of sign construction, mediated by writing technologies. Furthermore and overlapping with all these features and dimensions, sociocultural factors such as bilingualism or multilingualism, and biliteracy or multiliteracy come into play, as well as an even more fundamental trajectory: namely, the particular social and societal environment in which all speakers and writers of a language live – and in which their ideas and view of that very language emerge. In short, then, my point is that if language becomes an object of thought, this cannot be understood but within the whole of this interacting context.

Being Immersed into a World of Literacy

Everything that is important in the "universe of discourse" of modern societies is laid down in written language. This is particularly true for the theoretical, that is, (meta)linguistic conception of language itself. There is no particle of language that is not subject to a normative societal canon specified in dictionaries, grammars, textbooks, curricula, handbooks of style and academic publishing, and even in laws. I would like to follow this societal perspective on literacy to look more closely at how the factors just outlined are interwoven into what I have called the symbolic space of literacy.

To conceive of our societal culture as a huge organization of literacy or, to put it the other way around, to conceive of literacy as a societal and cultural space, is fundamental for the view I have suggested. No doubt, there are different ways to categorize the factors I have mentioned, as it is also possible to highlight and add other aspects. As I said earlier, almost all empirical research in this field has focused on a single factor or, at most, on a few factors. Of course, one might add, how else can empirical investigation take place if not by isolating single factors. Yet the problem arising here is not one of empirical literacy research as such, but of the underlying theoretical conception of most single-factor research (and I am thinking here especially of the research on phonological awareness, which, arguably, covers much of the research in this area). In contrast, I have argued that it is decisive for an appropriate conception of the manifold relations between literacy and thought to bear in mind that literacy first of all is a cultural organism; it is a societal synthesis that does not leave any aspect of language use untouched. In modern societies of writing, there are no islands of pristine oral speech.

That is to say, each of the factors just outlined is always already part and parcel of a historically developed system of literacy; each factor becomes effective only as an element of this cultural system with its numerous overlaps and mutual interrelations. All of them together – as well as what in system theory is called their "synergetic effect" – constitute a multilayered context of interdependence whose ultimate trajectory is the entire symbolic space of a culture.

Viewed from this societal vantage point, the meaning of literacy is closely connected to the notion of a cultural environment which, as a whole, has shaped not just our metalinguistic concepts (such as "word" and "sentence"), but our entire understanding of what language is all about. My suggestion, thus, is that children become literate and develop an explicit consciousness of language, a "literate mind," not primarily because they are taught writing and reading skills but because they grow up in a culture of writing. From the very beginning, they are immersed into a world of literacy which includes not only books and newspapers, files and e-mails, but also scribbles on the margins of wrapping paper, balance statements and shopping lists, cereal boxes on breakfast tables and ubiquitous slogans from commercials, the first love letter to mom and toys which have the form of alphabetic signs. From early on, children become familiar with a world made out of countless literacy practices and literacy events.

Hamilton, Barton and Ivanic (1994) have collected various case studies of literacy events and literacy practices which offer a panorama of the countless situations and contexts in which writing plays a role in a modern society. In their studies of the social and societal organization of literacy in Britain, Hamilton and his colleagues show that there are many distinct worlds of literacies which exist alongside each other. Yet it is not only for this reason, they point out, that we live in "multiple worlds of literacy," but also because "individual people have different experiences and different demands made upon them; and . . . different people have distinct experiences and hopes of and purposes for reading and writing. There are the separate worlds of adults and children, of people speaking different languages, of men and women. There are also various public worlds of literacy, defined by the social institutions we participate in including school, work and official bureaucracies" (Hamilton et al., 1994, p. x).[1] In my view, analyzing these concrete contexts of language use is particularly interesting because it is in such embedded discursive situations where literacy as a dimension of personal lifeworlds fuses with literacy as symbolic space of a culture.

Patently, such private-public worlds of literacy are not only about letters and words, reading and writing, paper and computer screens, but they are also – and, as I argue, first of all – about cultural practices. Growing up in the symbolic space of a literacy culture means, from early on, learning to master these practices; it means coming to terms with what underlies them: namely, the various cultural codes of interaction and thought which specify, among others, the moral appropriateness of (linguistic and nonlinguistic) behavior. In other words, it means learning how to play and understand the oral and written language games of this culture, a culture of many different worlds indeed.

Olson's Point

Against this backdrop, let me go back to my initial issue, the metalinguistic hypothesis. As far as the relations between metalinguistic discourse and consciousness of language are concerned, the argument that I have outlined is twofold. First, it suggests that within the symbolic space of writing all forms of personal and societal literacy have some impact on our consciousness of language, even if to a different degree. Second, the symbolic space of literacy does not consist only of consciousness of language (which I have concentrated on in my account); rather, literacy comes to have an effect on a broad spectrum of discourse forms, especially on theoretical, scientific, legal, and other reflective and formalized genres. It influences, if not determines, forms of argument, logical reasoning, modes of literary prose and poetry, the uses of "evidence" and the nature of what is conceived of as "proof," particularly in such specialized institutions as economics, law, science, philosophy, and education.

This influence has been emphasized by several authors (Bazerman, 1988; Geisler, 1994; Goody, 1987; Ivanic, 1997; Olson, 1994), although they have offered different explanations for it. Olson, as already pointed out, has particularly highlighted the metalinguistic potentials of writing. However, he has not always done so in the same way. It might be said that the most significant shift in Olson's study of the cognitive implications of literacy has been that he has moved away from the "strong literacy hypothesis," the claim of a fundamental intellectual and cultural divide between speech and writing, upon which he drew in his earlier work. Over the last decade he has instead oriented his work toward a more dialectical view of the mutual interdependencies of oral and written language, a view that takes into account the social and institutional contexts and cultural embeddedness of language, literacy, and thought (e.g., Olson & Torrance, 1999).

To some – perhaps even for David Olson himself – this shift has come unexpectedly, considering that his fundamentally cognitivist outlook upon the mind has never really changed. The focus of cognitive science, as he often has stated in programmatic fashion (e.g., Olson, 1993), is the individual mind; the aim of scientific psychology is to causally explain the forms and modes of mental representation. So why, then, did Olson not stick to the "strong literacy hypothesis" (as did Havelock and Ong), why did he give up on his cognitive version of a *great divide* between an "oral mind" and a "literate mind"? To be sure, Olson has always tried to explain the mind as a cognitive psychologist; however, he has never been exclusively a cognitive scientist. It seems that, over the years, he has developed too many interests, too many curiosities, too many questions which cannot be framed within the experimental and causal-explanatory epistemology of cognitive psychology. Language and thought have been said to sometimes lead a life on their own; and this also is true for intellectual interests. It is not without irony that Olson's long-standing interest in the relation between writing and thought, which was originally motivated by a cognitivist research agenda, has led him to become more and more involved with the social and cultural dimension of his subject – as contradictory as this might have been.

Although being a theorist of writing, Olson first of all is an inexhaustible reader, a reader, I might add, in the old style. He is one of those who, left alone on a transatlantic flight with nothing but the weekend editions of the *New York Times* and the *Globe and Mail*, has read upon arrival every single article in both papers, at least once. Now to read writing which is about writing and reading can easily become like a tale by Jorge Luis Borges, the great Argentine writer of the fantastic obsessions of bookishness. Olson's story, I suspect, has some Borgesian flavor. It is the story of a passionate reader who finds himself in an endless library, a library, however, in which the books do not have very much in common with the traditional scenarios of cognitive science. To read these books, draws one into the puzzling issues of writing and thought in Greek antiquity and Chinese classrooms, systems of musical notations and Inuit proper names, medieval mnemotechniques and feminist text theory – to name a few titles on a randomly chosen shelf in this Borgesian library of literacy and thought.

Olson's shift to the social and cultural trajectory of literacy and literacies has also centrally affected his version of the metalinguistic hypothesis. In recent papers (1999, in press), he repudiates the idea that the cognitive implications of written text and oral speech can be described as distinctive. If there are different cognitive styles and mentalities associated with orality and literacy, they must be spelled out in terms of their different cultural functions. Since the intellectual development of children, Olson (1995, p. 95) writes, can be seen, at least in part, as the acquisition of symbolic and representational systems of the culture, alphabetic literacy arguably is of central interest for the investigation of the interplay between culture and cognition in modern societies. In this interplay, the symbolic system of writing has developed as a special form of discourse. This discourse, Olson argues, picks up and elaborates one of the natural and universal functions of speech, the reflexive ability that makes linguistic self-reference possible. It is, in particular, the capacity of language to "mention" itself (that is, to "quote") on which writing capitalizes.

Certainly, such self-reflexive reference also is a property of speech. It has often been stated that even predominantly oral cultures have complex forms of reflexive metalanguage (Feldman, 1991). Moreover, in as far as all languages are life forms, they represent, and realize (through what Wittgenstein called their "grammar"), highly reflexive forms of cultural memory (Harré, Brockmeier, & Mühlhäusler, 1999). But, Olson specifies, while the reflexive potential of speech remains altogether limited in scope and application, it is precisely this potential that becomes the central property of written texts, especially of those texts which provide the basis for scientific, philosophical, legal, and literary discourse. All these texts, according to Olson, are systems not just of "use" but of "mention" or "quotation" of utterances. Literacy, thus, has an impact on thought because it turns language from something that is "used" into something which is "mentioned."

In this view, advanced levels of writing competence involve the mastery of a complex set of metalinguistic concepts for specifying just how the writer intended the text to be interpreted; that is, the writer must anticipate the specific discursive context. This can be, for example, the conceptual framework of the "interpretive community" (Feldman, this volume, Chapter 2), in which his or her text is meant to be read and understood. Olson and Astington (1990) showed that the mastery of such metalinguistic concepts includes verbs such as *imply, assume, conclude, infer*, and the like. Along the same line, they also demonstrated that higher levels of reading competence imply learning how to understand, that is, to interpret such metalinguistic terms. The acquisition of the metalinguistic potentials of a culture of writing, they argued, provides a learner with these new reflexive concepts and interpretative techniques, in addition to the more limited concepts of word and sentence acquired in the early stages of learning to read.

Even if neither Olson, nor Olson and Astington, have investigated other forms of (meta)linguistic practices – which, as I have argued, as a whole constitute the symbolic space of a literate culture – their findings are certainly not excluded from being located within a wider cultural context. Viewed from this perspective, the significance of Olson's metalinguistic approach to the relationship between literacy and thought is threefold. First, despite being elaborated along the lines of traditional cognitive psychology, this theory does not postulate or assume any form of autonomous human cognition, either as a prerequisite or as a direct consequence of writing and reading. Cognitive constructions, in this view, are not just innate biases of the mind. Rather, and second, this theory conceives of the cognitive implications of literacy as being bound to a specific use of language. The forms of written language, as all human language, organize human actions and interactions. They mediate communication and thought. They have cultural-historically developed with the evolution of literacy as a societal synthesis, a semiotic synthesis that I have suggested as the symbolic space of modern cultures. And third, perhaps it is less surprising that Olson, in his work as a cognitive scientist, has never been particularly interested in the discursive and social nature of literacy, than the fact that he has come to point out that, in a nutshell, "writing has an impact on cognition through culture, a culture of writing" (in press). The child's access to literacy is not through deciphering a psycholinguistic code linking written signs to phonemes but rather through mastering a cultural symbol system (Vinden, this volume, Chapter 3). I think Olson's investigations on this mastering provide an indispensable contribution to any theory that aims at explaining the discursive and social nature of human thought under conditions of the historical *a priori* of literacy.

The Metalinguistics of Writing

If the relations between writing and self-reflexive properties of language, as suggested by Olson, hold up to scrutiny, we may have been offered a general explanation for modern consciousness of language. Historically, this consciousness has become elaborated in the systems of metalinguistic concepts that we use to describe and evaluate language. We have good reasons to suspect that writing, from its very beginning, has been instrumental in this elaboration of metalinguistic concepts and theories. If writing is intrinsically metalinguistic, we also can say that the system of metalinguistic concepts, as suggested by linguistics and philosophy of language, is intrinsically a system of written language. In fact, there are various arguments put forward to view literacy as the principal *raison d'être* for systematic linguistic reflection (Brockmeier, 1999; Harris, 1986; 1996; Scholes & Willis, 1991).

In modern societies, learning to write and to read has become a highly institutionalized and formalized process. As a consequence, it has turned into a process in which, at the same time, a highly formalized metalinguistic code has to be learnt. This code is laid out in the rule systems of orthography, grammar, style, and other discursive norms, all of which aim at defining a universal metalinguistic order. It is interesting to trace back how, in the history of linguistics, philosophy of language, and language education, this order, which originated as a reflection of the grammar of written language, has been imposed upon our view of oral speech. In this sense, Harris (1989) remarked, writing has indeed "restructured" our thought about language. As a result, our entire (meta)linguistic understanding of speech, and language in general, has become identical to the conceptual space of literacy.

To explain this argument in more historical detail, it should be noted that learning to write and read, and learning a particular metalinguistic code (which defines what counts as proper writing and reading) has not always been the same process. Their fusion is the outcome of a rather recent sociocultural development that begins in the 19th century with modern formal education. This development has led to the intermingling of two orders that, for most of the history of literacy in the west, were separated: practical literacy skills on the one hand, and mastery of a normative canon of metalinguistic concepts on the other.

Jean Hébrard (1997) has pointed out that until the end of the 18th and the beginning of the 19th century, the ability to read appears to have been the only aim of Christian teaching of literacy, which for most parts of Europe and North America and in both Catholic and Protestant countries, was the only institutional form of teaching literacy. The Christian concept of literacy was the concept of a "restricted or constricted literacy, . . . not one that assumed active autonomous engagement with texts." (Venezky, 1999, p. 124). Even the teaching of writing for professional and commercial purposes was not guaranteed by schools. Examining the history of literacy teaching in France, Hébrard shows that this picture only began to change upon the introduction of a compulsory exercise book, the *cahier*, in French elementary schools in the first half of the 19th century. It was only during the period between 1860 and 1960 when the teaching of literacy skills was to include reading, writing, and metalinguistic exercises. Such metalinguistic exercises were meant to systematically familiarize pupils with orthography, grammar, and vocabulary (word families, definitions, synonyms, homonyms, antonyms) of the French language. Why can we date this period so precisely? In 1860, dictation was introduced in literacy teaching, in the 1960s, the *cahier* was gradually replaced by new teaching materials and curricula. During these hundred years, the exercise book organized a set of writing practices that used to be, as Hébrard (p. 175) puts it, "the framework for the school literacy which enabled rural France to enter 'modern' writing culture." Fundamental for this modern writing culture is that students learn a writing practice *and* acquire a consciousness of language which has been, from the very beginning, fused with this writing practice.

Modern language education is in several respects a case in point. Arguably, formal schooling in all modern alphabetic cultures has a twofold goal, one is to teach reading and writing skills, the other to teach a particular metalinguistic conception of language (Astington & Pelletier, 1996) – that is, of *written* language. Children are instructed to apply this conception not only to their own writing, but also to all linguistic practices in which they become involved. That is to say, they learn to read and write, and in addition, although in practice intimately intertwined, they learn to understand language in the light of written language. This usually implies that they learn to endorse the dominant "literate view" of their educational system regarding the moral and social superiority of writing over speech, a view which is characteristic of our entire culture of literacy. In other words, children come to take what Harris (1999, p. 48) describes as a "thoroughly unSaussurean view" and believe "that the written form of language is somehow superior to spoken forms, or at least provides a standard by reference of which 'correctness' is to be measured."

To make this point about the relationship between consciousness of language and literacy education, we can draw not only on historical evidence and linguistic and philosophical arguments, but also on recent psychological investigations which have shed new light on the development of children's understanding of metalinguistic concepts. For example, as several authors have shown, children's ideas about a "word" and their awareness about the difference between common nouns and proper names are closely connected to the metalinguistic (that is, more precisely, metadiscursive) practices in which they become involved when they begin to write (Ferreiro, 1997; Ferreiro & Vernon, 1992; Homer & Olson, 1999; Homer et al., in press).

It is, I believe, precisely for this reason – the fusion of the metalinguistics of writing with our consciousness of language – that literacy has become what Olson (1994) called a model for language in general, not only for the educated, but for the entire societal culture of literacy. The place of this fusion is not in the mind of the individual language learner, nor is it in the textbooks of linguistics; it is in the symbolic space of literacy. This symbolic space of our culture, I have suggested, has historically developed into the *a priori* of our consciousness of language. It is this space of a societal synthesis which comprises a continuum between linguistic and metalinguistic discourse, oral and literate practices, verbal and nonverbal forms of discourse, and material and symbolic practices. Notwithstanding, to live in a culture of literacy is to use and to understand all language as if it were an application of the metalinguistics of writing.

Note

1   A similarly pluricentric picture emerges from the studies in Heath (1983, 1990); John-Steiner, Panofsky, and Smith (1994); and Verhoeven (1994). Some of these studies also examine literacy practices and literacy events in different language cultures, and in communities who use non-oral language (such as the North American deaf community who uses *American Sign Language*).

References

Andresen, H. (1995). Spielentwicklung und Spracherwerb [Development of play and language acquisition]. *Flensburger Papiere zur Mehrsprachigkeit und Kulturenvielfalt im Unterricht, 10/11*. Flensburg: Bildungswissenschaftliche Hochschule Universität Flensburg.

Astington, J. W., & Pelletier, J. (1996). The language of mind: Its role in teaching and learning. In D. R. Olson & N. Torrance (Eds.), *The handbook of education and human development* (pp. 593–619). Oxford, UK: Blackwell.

Bazerman, C. (1988). *Shaping written knowledge: The genre and activity of the experimental article in science*. Madison, WI: University of Madison Press.

Bialystok, E. (1988). Levels of bilingualism and levels of linguistic awareness. *Developmental Psychology, 24*, 560–7.

Brockmeier, J. (1994). L'esperienza dello scrivere e gli inizi della coscienza metalinguistica.

[The experience of writing and the beginnings of metalinguistic consciousness]. *Rassegna di Psicologia, 21,* 99–123.

Brockmeier, J. (1996). Raccontare "ciò che è veramente accaduto": tecniche di persuasione e di giustificazione nel conflitto tra bambini [Telling "how it really was": Techniques of persuasion and justification in children's conflicts] *Scienze dell'Interazione. Rivista di Psicologia, Psicosociologia e Psicoterapia [The Science of Interaction: Journal of Psychology, Psycho-Sociology, and Psychotherapy], 3,* 31–41.

Brockmeier, J. (1998). *Literales Bewusstsein. Schriftlichkeit und das Verhältnis von Sprache und Kultur* [The literate mind: Literacy and the relation between language and culture]. Munich, Germany: Fink.

Brockmeier, J. (1999, April). *The literacy episteme: The rise and fall of a cultural discourse.* Paper presented at the Conference on Literacy and Conceptions of Language. OISE/ University of Toronto.

Bruner, J. S. (1999, April). *Narrative as distancing: Prerequisites to literacy.* Paper presented at the Conference on Literacy and Conceptions of Language. OISE/University of Toronto.

Carruthers, M. (1990). *The book of memory: A study of memory in medieval culture.* Cambridge, UK: Cambridge University Press.

Clark, H. H. (1992). *Arenas of language use.* Chicago, IL: University of Chicago Press.

Derrida, J. (1974). *Of grammatology.* Baltimore, MD: Johns Hopkins University Press.

Feldman, C. (1991). Oral metalanguage. In D. R. Olson & N. Torrance (Eds.), *Literacy and orality* (pp. 47–65). Cambridge, UK: Cambridge University Press.

Ferreiro, E. (1997). The word out of (conceptual) context. In C. Pontecorvo (Ed.), *Writing development: An interdisciplinary view* (pp. 47–59). Amsterdam: Benjamins.

Ferreiro, E., Pontecorvo, E., Ribeiro Moreira, N., & Garcia Hidalgo, I. (1996). *Caperucita Roja Aprende a Escribir* [Little Red Riding Hood learns to write] Barcelona: Gedisa, ColecciÛn L.E.A. (also in Italian and Portuguese).

Ferreiro, E., & Teberosky, A. (1982). *Literacy before schooling* (Siglo Veintiuno, Trans.). Exeter, NH & London: Heinemann. (Original work published in 1979)

Ferreiro, E., & Vernon, S. (1992). La distinction de palabra/nombre en ninos de 4 y 5 anos [The difference between word and name in 4- and 5-year-olds]. *Infancia y Aprendizaje, 58,* 15–28.

Finnegan, R. (1988). *Literacy and orality: Studies in the technology of communication.* Oxford, UK: Blackwell.

Foucault, M. (1973). *The order of things.* New York: Vintage.

Geisler, C. (1994). *Academic literacy and the nature of expertise: Reading, writing, and knowing in academic philosophy.* Hillsdale, NJ: Lawrence Erlbaum.

Gombert, J. E. (1992). *Metalinguistic development.* Chicago, IL: University of Chicago Press.

Goody, J. (1987). *The interface between the written and the oral.* Cambridge, UK: Cambridge University Press.

Goody, J., & Watt, I. (1968). The consequences of literacy. In J. Goody (Ed.), *Literacy in traditional societies.* Cambridge, UK: Cambridge University Press.

Haas, C. (1996). *Writing technology: Studies on the materiality of literacy.* Mahwah, NJ: Erlbaum.

Hamilton, M., Barton, D., & Ivanic, R. (Eds.) (1994). *Worlds of literacy.* Toronto, Canada: Ontario Institute for Studies in Education/Clevedon, Philadelphia & Adelaide: Multilingual Matters.

Harré, R., Brockmeier, J., and Mühlhäusler, P. (1999). *Greenspeak: A study of environmental discourse*. Thousand Oaks, London, & New Delhi: Sage.

Harris, R. (1986). *The origin of writing*. London: Duckworth.

Harris, R. (1989). How does writing restructure thought? *Language and Communication, 9*, 99–106.

Harris, R. (1996). *The language connection: Philosophy and linguistics*. Bristol, UK: Thoemmes Press.

Harris, R. (1999). Integrational linguistics and the structuralist legacy. *Language and Communication, 19*, 45–68.

Havelock, E. A. (1963). *Preface to Plato*. Cambridge, MA: Harvard University Press.

Havelock, E. A. (1982). *The literate revolution in Greece and its cultural consequences*. Princeton, NJ: Princeton University Press.

Heath, S. B. (1983). *Ways with words: Language, life and work in communities and classrooms*. Cambridge, UK: Cambridge University Press.

Heath, S. B. (1990). The children of Trackton's children: Spoken and written language in social change. In J. W. Stigler, R. A. Shweder, & G. Herdt (Eds.), *Cultural psychology: Essays on comparative human development* (pp. 496–519). Cambridge, UK: Cambridge University Press.

Hébrard, J. (1997). The graphic space of the school exercise book in France in the 19th–20th century. In C. Pontecorvo (Ed.), *Writing development: An interdisciplinary view* (pp. 173–89). Amsterdam: Benjamins.

Herriman, M. (1986). Metalinguistic awareness and the growth of literacy. In S. de Castell, A. Luke, & K. Egan (Eds.), *Literacy, society, and schooling: A reader* (pp. 159–74). Cambridge, UK: Cambridge University Press.

Homer, B. D., Brockmeier, J., Kamawar, D., & Olson, D. R. (in press). Children's metalinguistic understanding of words and names. *Genetic Epistemology*.

Homer, B. D., & Olson, D. R. (1999). Literacy and children's conception of language. *Language and Literacy, 2*, 113–40.

Ivanic, R. (1997). *Writing and identity: The discoursal construction of identity in academic writing*. Amsterdam: Benjamins.

Kirtley, C., Bryant, P., McLean, M., & Bradley, L. (1989). Rhyme, rime, and the onset of reading. *Journal of Experimental Child Psychology, 48*, 224–45.

Lévi-Strauss, C. (1962). *La pensée sauvage*. Paris: Plon.

Lotman, UI. M. (1990). *Universe of the mind: A semiotic theory of culture*. Bloomington, IN: Indiana University Press.

Lüdi, G. (1997). Towards a better understanding of biliteracy. In C. Pontecorvo (Ed.), *Writing development: An interdisciplinary view* (pp. 206–218). Amsterdam: Benjamins.

Luria, A. R. (1976). *Cognitive development: Its cultural and social foundations*. Cambridge, MA: Harvard University Press.

McLane, J., & McNamee, G. (1990): *Early literacy*. Cambridge, MA: Harvard University Press.

McLuhan, M. (1962). *The Gutenberg galaxy. The making of typographic man*. Toronto, Canada: University of Toronto Press.

Nagy, W. E., & Anderson, R. C. (1999). Metalinguistic awareness and literacy acquisition in different languages (pp. 155–60). In D. A. Wagner, R. L. Venezky, & B. V. Street (Eds.), *Literacy: An international handbook*. Boulder, CO: Westview Press.

Olson, D. R. (1977). From utterance to text: The bias of language in speech and writing. *Harvard Educational Review, 47*, 257–81.

Olson, D. R. (1991). Literacy as metalinguistic activity. In D. R. Olson & N. Torrance

(Eds.), *Literacy and orality* (pp. 251–70). Cambridge, UK: Cambridge University Press.

Olson, D. (1993). The development of representations: The origins of mental life. *Canadian Psychology, 34,* 293–306.

Olson, D. R. (1994). *The world on paper: The conceptual and cognitive implications of writing and reading.* Cambridge, UK: Cambridge University Press.

Olson, D. R. (1995). Writing and the mind. In J. V. Wertsch, P. del Rio, & A. Alvarez (Eds.), *Sociocultural studies of mind* (pp. 95–123). New York: Cambridge University Press.

Olson, D. R. (1999). The written word. Inaugural lecture as University Professor, University of Toronto. In *Redefining Literacy: Newsletter of the Language, Literacy, and Mind Research Group,* Spring issue. Ontario Institute for Studies in Education/University of Toronto.

Olson, D. R. (in press). The cognitive consequences of literacy. In P. Bryant & T. Nunes (Eds.), *Handbook of literacy.* Dordrecht, The Netherlands: Kluwer.

Olson, D. R., & Astington, J. W. (1990). Talking about text: How literacy contributes to thought. *Journal of Pragmatics, 14,* 557–73.

Olson, D. R., & Torrance, N. (2000). *On the making of literate societies.* Unpublished Manuscript, OISE/University of Toronto.

Ong, W. J. (1982). *Orality and literacy: The technologizing of the word.* London: Methuen.

Pellegrini, A. D. (1993). Ten years after: A reexamination of symbolic play and literacy research. *Reading Research Quarterly, 28,* 163–75.

Pellegrini, A. D. (1997). Bridges between home and school literacy: Social bases for early school literacy. *Early Child Development and Care, 127–8,* 99–109.

Piaget, J. (1951). *Play, dreams and imitation in childhood.* New York: Norton.

Pontecorvo, C., Orsolini, M., Burge, B., & Resnick, L. (Eds.) (1996). *Children's early text construction.* Mahwah, NJ: Erlbaum.

Russell, D. R. (1997). Writing and genre in higher education and workplaces. *Mind, Culture, and Activity (Special issue) The activity of writing/The writing of activity), 4,* 224–37.

Scholes, R. J. (1993). *Literacy and language analysis.* Hillsdale, NJ: Erlbaum.

Scholes, R. J., & Willis, B. J. (1991). Linguists, literacy, and the intensionality of Marshall McLuhan's western man. In D. R. Olson & N. Torrance (Eds.), *Literacy and orality* (pp. 215–35). Cambridge, UK: Cambridge University Press.

Stevenson, H. W., Lee, S., & Schweingruber, H. (1999). Home influences on early literacy. In D. A. Wagner, R. L. Venezky, & B. V. Street (Eds.), *Literacy: An international handbook* (pp. 251–7). Boulder, CO: Westview Press.

Sulzby, E., & Teale, W. (1991). Emergent literacy. In R. Barr, P. D. Pearson, M. L. Kamil, P. Mosenthal (Eds.), *Handbook of reading research, vol 2.* New York: Longman.

Venezky, R. L. (1999). Reading, writing, and salvation: The impact of Christian missionaries on literacy. In D. A. Wagner, R. L. Venetzky, & B. V. Street (Eds.), *Literacy: An international handbook* (pp. 119–24). Boulder, CO: Westview.

Verhoeven, L. (1997). Acquisition of literacy by immigrant children. In C. Pontecorvo (Ed.), *Writing development: An interdisciplinary view* (pp. 219–40). Amsterdam: Benjamins.

Vygotsky, L. S. (1976). Play and its role in the mental development of the child. In J. Bruner, A. Jolly, K. Sylva (Eds.), *Play – Its role in development and evolution* (pp. 537–54). Harmondsworth, UK: Penguin.

Vygotsky, L. S. (1978). *Mind in society: The development of higher psychological processes* (M. Cole, V. John-Steiner, S. Scribner, & E. Sauberman, Eds.). Cambridge, MA: Harvard University Press.

Vygotsky, L. S. (1987). *Thinking and speech* (N. Minick, Ed. and Trans.). New York: Plenum.

Wells, G. (1985). *Language development in the preschool years.* Cambridge, UK: Cambridge University Press.

Wells, G. (1990). Talk about text: Where literacy is learned and taught. *Curriculum Inquiry, 20*, 369–405.

5

Cognition and the Lexicon in the Environment of Texts

Rita Watson

"The conceptual boundary between words and their meanings ... has been re-drawn under the impact of a literate tradition."

Olson (1994, p. 32)

Olson's work has ranged across many important issues in language, mind, and culture. His influence has been arguably most profound on the subject of literacy and mind. He has long argued (Olson, 1977, 1994) that the emergence of literacy engendered a new form of thought, distinguished by a conscious, reflective attitude to the processes and products of cognition, and by new conceptions of world, self, and language. Literacy, he claims, has played a central role in the rise of scientific thinking, the development of rationality, and specifically, metacognition.

This chapter explores an aspect of this claim on which we worked together (Watson & Olson, 1987): the influence of a literate tradition on the idea of "word" as a meaning-bearing constituent of language, and attempts to articulate the meaning of words by definition. In the following, the role of literacy and orthographies in the emergence of conceptions of language is re-examined, and evidence from pre-classical texts is presented to support an orthography-neutral account. Pragmatic theory is used to suggest how the process of text interpretation (Olson, 1994) could influence reflection on language and the resulting conception of words as meaningful and definable.

The Development of the Concept "Word" in the Classical and Post-classical Periods

We argued (Watson & Olson, 1987) that it was the preservation of the word in written form that led to its identification as a meaning-bearing constituent in language. The argument about word meaning that we developed was based primarily on two phenomena. The first was that the formal word definition achieved importance during the period of classical Greek thought. We claimed that this was a consequence of the rise of alphabetic literacy in the classical period. The second line of reasoning was the relation between the authority of dictionary definitions and the rise of print-based literacy. These two lines of argument are outlined below.

Word definition and the classical period

A preliterate or common-sense understanding of "word" is that it constitutes an utterance (cf. Ong, 1976). Expressions such as "I must have a word with him" or "a word to the wise is sufficient" both imply complete utterances rather than what we usually think of as a single word. The notion of the word as an isolated, meaningful element of a linguistic code is evident from the classical period. The earliest recorded attempts at definitions of words *qua* words emerged in ancient Greece.

The Greeks were masters of definition. For Aristotle, to have a true definition was to have the most important possible knowledge (Robinson, 1950), although he acknowledged the difficulty of arriving at an essential defining expression for the words of natural language. According to Havelock (1963, 1976) Hesiod made the first known attempts at defining words, analyzing the various uses of words throughout the written versions of the Homeric epics. Plato believed that the words of natural language had abstract, formal features that could be expressed in a definition. This ideal is, however, only realized in stipulative definition, central to the formal languages of mathematics and philosophy, in which the meaning of a term is fully circumscribed by a given expression. Statements of the stipulative form "Let X be Y," in which "X" is a word and "Y" is a formal expression that defines its meaning, allow formal logical inquiry to proceed by circumventing the ambiguities of natural language.

Seeing a word written down gave rise to the idea of the word as a linguistic element possessed of an identity across contexts of use, and a sense that its meaning must likewise be constant. On what could be called the standard account of literacy and the classical period (Goody, 1987; Havelock, 1963; McLuhan, 1962; Olson; 1977; Ong, 1976), the representational adequacy of the phonetic alphabetic adopted in ancient Greece was the basis of this development. On this account, the advent of a phonetic alphabet that represented speech unambiguously enabled meaning to be more easily ascribed to, and deduced from, texts. It became easier to analyze the form and content of propositions contained within the text and "word" came to be thought of as an element of the linguistic code, the meaning of which could be defined.

Word definition and the rise of print literacy

The widespread popular notion that words have definitions emerged in the age of print literacy. The precursors to the English dictionary were simple vocabularies, interlinear glosses of English equivalents of Latin or Greek words that were used to help in translation, that included no definitions. The first English dictionary that consisted of words and their associated definitions appeared only after the invention of the printing press (Starnes & Noyes, 1946). These early works were characterized by nonstandard lexis as well as nonstandard definitions. "Floure" and "flower," for example, were interchangeable forms, "floure" being defined as the bloom of a plant and "flower" as the main ingredient in bread in an early dictionary.

The underlying purpose of these early works could be revealed by an inspection of their title pages. A primary objective of the dictionary was to aid the new literati, "Ladies, gentlewomen and other unskillful persons . . ." with the meanings of hard words as they appeared in texts, an undertaking "very useful to all such as desire to understand what they read."[1] The definitions often consisted only of synonyms or brief paraphrases of such "hard words."

While the new printers of books were trying to decide which lexical forms to adopt in the absence of any agreed upon standard, writers of early dictionaries had to decide not only on lexical forms but also on how to establish and express conventions of meaning. By the 18th century, in what has been called the age of the dictionary, many scholars tried their hand at dictionaries as a growing reading public created an active and competitive market for such volumes. Dr. Johnson, a practical man by all accounts, had a more far-reaching aim than his predecessors: the compilation of a systematic reference book of the meanings of all the words in the language. He set a standard for the definition that was universally adopted. Just how formidable a task faced him is expressed by this excerpt from the preface of the 1806 edition of his famous dictionary.

> When I took the first survey of my undertaking, I found our speech copious without order, and energetic without rules. Wherever I turned my view there was perplexity to be disentangled, and confusion to be regulated; choice was to be made out of boundless variety, without any established principle of selection, adulterations were to be detected without a settled test of purity; and modes of expression to be rejected or received, without the suffrages of any writers of classical reputation or acknowledged authority . . .

Johnson adopted Hesiod's strategy. The "authorities" to whom he ultimately turned were the best writers of his day. This tradition of taking words as they are used in texts as the basis of dictionary definitions persists to the present day, as is evident on the examination of works such as the *Oxford English Dictionary*. His concern with authority presages the role that dictionaries would come to assume. Beyond simply recording conventions of use, dictionaries have assumed an authority as the ultimate arbiters of word meaning. We turn to the dictionary when we want to know the "true" meaning of a word. Dictionaries essentially legislate what words mean in today's western literate culture (Robinson, 1950). But the actual nature of a dictionary definition is, and has been since Johnson's time, simply a record of how a word is used. Any authority it may possess is an attribution of the users of dictionaries, modern-day literates.

Literacy and the concept of "word"

The chaos that Johnson observed in the above quote about language was not unique. Aristotle bemoaned the difficulty of defining the words in natural language and many great historical thinkers have complained about the difficulties presented by the meanings of words. Olson (1994, p. 166) makes a number of references to this in his discussion of the distinction between signs (words) and ideas that became focal in the early modern period. He cites Locke (1690/1961) referring to words as a "perfect cheat"; Descartes (1637–44/1968) as claiming that the certainty of his own ideas could only be achieved by divesting his thought of words; and Bacon's (1857) exhortation to "imitate the wisdom of the mathematicians" and define words, "so that others may know how we . . . understand them . . . for (in) want of this, we are sure to end . . . in questions and differences about words." These observations reflect an awareness of the non-uniqueness of word-sense relations in natural language, and the enormous difficulty of pinning down meaning at all.

The ordinary use of language is, as expressed by these philosophers, replete with ambiguity. The idea of fixed definable meanings for words, the absence of which so troubled these thinkers, is clearly an idea that has been imposed on natural language. The words of ordinary discourse become worrisome troublemakers only in the process of reflecting upon signs and their meanings such as in the pursuit of the philosophy of ideas.

Olson (1994) points out that this development constituted a move from metonymic understanding, in which word and thing are directly related, to representational understanding. When meaning is conceptualized as a property of the relation between signs and ideas, rather than by direct reference to things, the notion of words *qua* words and what they represent becomes opaque, the object of reflection and interpretation. The above quotes seem to suggest a sense of the irresolute ambiguity of the code. Aristotle and Johnson express the desirability of fixed defined meanings, of identifying one meaning with one word, but together with Locke and Descartes, express an awareness of the difficulty of attaining such a goal. Indeed, the problem remains central to present-day philosophy of language.

The question is, whether the issue of words and their meanings would have risen to consciousness at all in the absence of a written language. Did literacy cause this awareness, and if so, by what mechanism was it achieved? In the next section, an account of the emergence of the concept "word" is offered that draws on evidence from pre-classical texts. It suggests that this development may be orthography-neutral rather than a unique consequence of phonetic alphabets.

Orthography and the Word: Pre-classical Evidence

Figure 5.1 shows a document written in cuneiform orthography. It is a bilingual stone vocabulary dating from between 1200–800 BCE, that lists the Akkadian equivalents of 48 Kassite, or middle Babylonian, words.

Figure 5.1 Stone vocabulary showing the Akkadian equivalents of 48 Kassite (middle Babylonian) words. 1200–800 BCE, British Museum Western Asiatic collection, reference # 93005. © The British Museum.

The author of this artifact must have had a conceptual category for the linguistic element "word." Such a tablet could not have been constructed without at the very least a concept of "word" as a translatable element of a language. This artifact is not an isolated example. Hurrian texts found at Ugarit dating from 1500 BCE include a Sumero-Hurrian vocabulary. Hittite documents from around the same period found in modern-day Turkey show that scribes frequently interchanged lexical items in Hittite, Sumerian, and Babylonian (Walker, 1990).

These vocabularies are very similar in form to those that appeared in the English language in medieval times prior to the development of print, as noted above. They probably resulted from a similar need: to translate between languages. Even as medieval English scholars needed help in translation between English and Latin or Greek, ancient scribes would have needed artifacts such as the vocabulary in Figure 5.1 to translate between the working languages of their day. The need for Kassite-using scribes to refer to Akkadian documents, and vice versa, would engender a need for bilingual vocabularies of this type. Most literate individuals in this era were necessarily conversant with more than one script and more than one language. The residents of coastal cities in the eastern Mediterranean, such as Ugarit or Byblos, the center of Phoenician commerce, had to be conversant with as many as five different scripts and innumerable languages in order to carry on their daily business transactions (Robinson, 1995). The need for translation between languages thus may have been one influence on the development of the concept "word."

Another influence could have been the frequent adaptations of scripts to languages for which they were not invented. This was a common phenomenon in the pre-classical world (Robinson, 1995). Figure 5.1 shows an adaptation of cuneiform script to write Kassite, a middle-Babylonian language. Cuneiform was also adapted to numerous other languages, including Persian and Elamite. Adapting a script in this way would have necessitated some reflection on the properties of the language it was being used to represent, and hence could have led to a heightened awareness of linguistic elements such as "word."

A third possibility is the presence of a pre-classical, syllabic alphabet. While the above artifact is not in alphabetic orthography, alphabets had emerged by this period and could have been known by the writer(s). Cuneiform itself was used in the construction of an alphabet in ancient Ugarit, on the coast of what is now Lebanon, in the 14th century BCE. This cuneiform alphabet was inspired, according to Walker's (1990) account, by existing linear alphabets of Phoenician and Old Hebrew, since the order of signs in all three is almost identical. Shorter versions of the cuneiform alphabet were also used in Cyprus, Syria, Lebanon, and Palestine. In the second and early first millennium BCE, the eastern Mediterranean was the site of extensive commercial activity, cultural interaction, and population exchange. A recent indicator of this is found in an inscription on an arrowhead in which a citizen of Crete is found to be fighting in the army of a Canaanite chieftain (Deutsch & Heltzer, 1994, 1997). As Robinson (1995) points out, a vital, heterogeneous, and multilingual cultural and commercial context would necessitate the invention of a simple and unambiguous script, such as an alphabet. And it was in this context that the Phoenician alphabet evolved. The following offer similar accounts of its origin:

> For some time after Flinders Petrie's discovery of Proto-Sinaitic script at Serabit el-Khadim in Sinai, the inscriptions were taken to be the missing link between Egyptian hieroglyphics and Phoenician alphabetic scripts. But why should lowly miners in out-of-the-way Sinai have created an alphabet? Prima facie, they seem to be unlikely inventors. Subsequent discoveries in Lebanon and Israel (of fragmentary proto-canaanite inscriptions from the 17th and 16th centuries BCE). . . . suggest that the Canaanites were the inventors of the alphabet, which would be reasonable. They were cosmopolitan traders, at the crossroads of the Egyptian, Hittite, Babylonian and Cretan empires; they were not wedded to an existing writing system; they needed a script that was easy to learn, quick to write and unambiguous. Although unproven, it is probable that the Canaanites created the first alphabet. (Robinson, 1995, p. 161)

> The modern consensus on the origin of the alphabet favors the North Semitic alphabet as the earliest known form, dating from the first half of the second millennium BCE. (Diringer, 1968, cited in Harris, 1986)

On Robinson's (1995) account, it becomes clearer why the Greeks may have decided to adopt the Phoenician alphabet, when for them, the Mycenean writing system was a more likely candidate. The latter had been used to write Greek for centuries before they adopted the Phoenician system, and the two cultures had much more in common than the Greeks and the Phoenicians, including a shared pantheon (Ventris, in Robinson, 1995). The fact that the Phoenician version was chosen for adaptation by the Greeks could reflect the recognition that it was a clear and efficient method of writing, already widely disseminated and probably already widely recognizable.

The Greek adaptation of this script may have influenced the emergence of the concept "word," but the above suggests that it was probably not the sole cause. Alternative explanations are first, a need for translation; second, the frequent adaptations of scripts to new languages; and third, the long-standing presence and wide dissemination of the Phoenician alphabet.

But what of orthography itself? Could basic literacy, in any orthography, cause a reconceptualization of language, a new awareness of the elements of language? An older artifact, also cuneiform, that predates the emergence of the alphabet, suggests that this is the case.

Further Evidence for the Influence of Pre-classical Orthographies on Conceptions of Language

Figure 5.2 shows an Akkadian school text from Girsu, dated 2250 BCE. It lists personal names, sorted not by any property of their referents such as nationality, social status, gender, wealth, or height. Rather, they are sorted on the basis of the

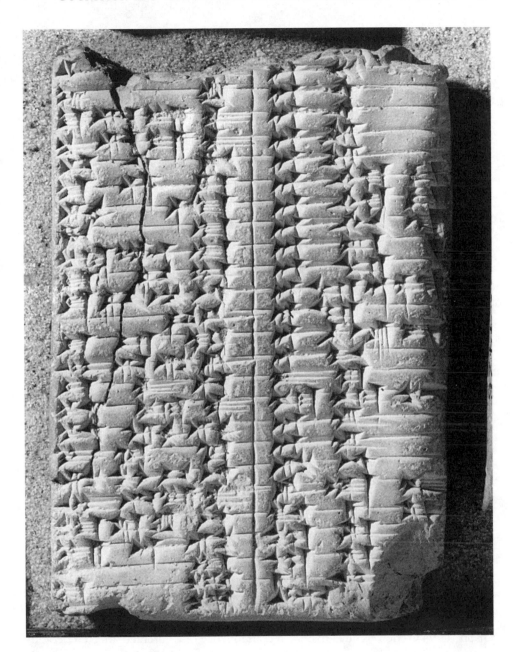

Figure 5.2 An Akkadian school text from Girsu, dated 2250 B.C. British Museum Western Asiatic Collection reference # 86271. A list of names beginning with the same cuneiform sign. © The British Museum.
Note: The orientation of the figure reflects the common view that texts from this period are read from left to right, but it should be noted that a minority holds that they be read from top to bottom. Thanks to Wayne Horowitz of the Assyriology Department, The Hebrew University of Jerusalem, for his helpful comments.

way in which they are written. It is a list of names whose written form begins with the same cuneiform sign. That is, all names beginning with a particular sign are listed in sequence. Thus we see in this text the referential or metonymic properties of words (names) being superseded by the orthographic properties of their written form. The writer of this Akkadian text organized it according to an isolated orthographic element, the first sign of the word. Thus, an orthographic element defines the conceptual category on the basis of which the writer organized the text.

Literacy and orthographic segmentation

The cognitive aspects of orthographic segmentation have been extensively investigated and constitute one of the strongest kinds of evidence for cognitive consequences of literacy. The phonemic segmentation performance of alphabetic literates (Goswami, 1991; Goswami & Bryant, 1990; Liberman, Shankweiler, Fisher, & Carter, 1974; see Walton, 1992 for an extensive review) is characterized by the phonemic categories associated with alphabetic orthographic units, or letters. For example, they will identify three separable phonemes in words like bat (b-a-t) and cat (c-a-t).

Preliterates and nonalphabetic literates don't usually segment words in this way. Instead, they will tend to segment words into nonalphabetic phonemic units, such as onsets and rimes (cat : c = onset -at = rime, c + at = onset + rime), which are more syllabic in nature (Goswami, 1986; Treiman, 1985, 1991). This segmentation into onsets and rimes is much easier for preliterates than separation into alphabetically represented phonemic units (Treiman, 1985). After acquiring an alphabetic orthography, children will segment words phonemically according to alphabetic phonemic constituents. That is, they separate out the phonemic elements that correspond to the orthography that they have acquired. The conceptual categories with which the phonemic segmentation task is accomplished, it seems clear, are influenced by the properties of the orthography acquired in learning to read.

As in the standard account of the cognitive consequences of literacy, in which the phonetic alphabet is held to be representationally more adequate, this change has been viewed as a development from inadequate phonemic segmentation abilities to adequate abilities. However it no longer seems tenable to view alphabetic literacy as the endpoint of a historical progression toward better orthographies (Harris, 1986; Olson, 1994). The very idea may be a consequence of a "literacy-infected" cognitive state, in much the same way as Dennett (1994) has claimed that human cognition is language-infected. Harris argues something along this line.

> Describing a syllabary in alphabetic terms makes it seem defective, when in fact alphabets do not represent a perfect or unambiguous correspondence of symbols to linguistic units. Neither alphabets nor syllabaries succeed in perfectly representing speech. The bias toward the alphabet may derive from the conceptual categories of alphabetic-literate scholars. (Harris, 1986, p. 38)

The clear presence of syllabic orthographic segmentation as an organizing principle in the artifact pictured in Figure 5.2 overwhelmingly supports this idea. The concept "orthographic segment," then, like the concept "word," seems to be a consequence of literacy irrespective of the orthography that is used.

The emergence of phonemic categories is a more difficult issue. While as cited above, there is ample empirical evidence that alphabetic literacy influences the phonemic conceptual categories of alphabetic literates, there is no such evidence for the consequences of other orthographies, except for some negative evidence that logographic script literates do not segment phonemes in the same way as alphabetic literates (cf. Olson, 1994). While we have no way of investigating post hoc the phonemic segmentation performance of cuneiform literates, it seems that acquiring a syllabic cuneiform script at least allows its users to conceptualize their language in terms of the properties of the orthography used to write it.

We see in the artifact in Figure 5.2 the emergence of a conceptual category, "same first sign," or "the sign X." We see linguistic entities, names, sorted according to this orthographically derived category. It is interesting to note, as Olson (1994) suggests, that the onset-and-rime segmentation preferences of preliterate children corresponds quite closely to syllables, and that syllabic scripts were historically antecedent to alphabetic writing. It may be that syllabic phonemic categories are conceptually basic, and that syllabic scripts were constructed according to their corresponding conceptually basic phonemic units. However, even if this were the case, an orthography could still have a causal effect in bringing such conceptual categories to conscious awareness. The use of a basic conceptual category in creating an orthography could be quite transparent, but once the orthography is constructed and learned by a linguistic community and regularly used, these formerly transparent categories would necessarily be rendered opaque.

The above discussion of orthographic segmentation and literacy can be expressed in the form of two competing claims:

Claim 1: Orthography-Specific:
Alphabetic literacy provides us with the conceptual categories for thinking about language because it provides a representationally adequate working model of the language.
This is the implicit assumption under much current work on phonemic segmentation and literacy. There is convincing evidence that acquiring alphabetic orthographies influences the conceptual categories used for thinking about language. Acquiring alphabetic orthography influences the phonemic segmentation performance of alphabetic literates away from onsets and rimes (syllables) toward units corresponding to letters.

Claim 2: Orthography-Neutral:
Orthographies influence the conceptual categories that are used to think about language. Acquiring and using any orthography to write a language will influence the phonemic segmentation preferences of the users of that orthography.

On this second claim, the explanation for why logographic literates or preliterates don't segment texts according to alphabetic phonemes seems clear. They don't do it because they have no reason to. No conceptual category is constructed or maintained unless it has a functional role. Alphabetic phonemic conceptual categories are constructed by the users of alphabetic scripts because they are needed to read and write. Users of logographic or syllabic scripts could be expected to form conceptual categories corresponding to the orthographic elements that they need to use.

Orthographies, Literacy, and Conceptions of Language

This analysis suggests that the user of an orthography creates the conceptual categories needed to relate the orthography to the language that it is being used to represent. Hence orthographies necessarily create conceptual categories for thinking about the language. Orthographies, in fact, could be conceptualized as theories of the language they are created or adapted to represent. Deciding what features of the stream of speech need to be represented in order to successfully reconstruct a message is a theory-like decision. So at some level, then, all orthographies can be expected to have in common that they cause or at least influence the conscious or working conceptions of language of the people who use them. This explains how the concept "word" could have arisen.

Writing, however, is a product of the human mind. It thus becomes difficult to conceptualize how orthographies could have effects on the mind, such as enhancing metacognition or creating new conceptions of language and world, as Olson (1994) has claimed. It may be useful to consider a contagion metaphor that has been used to describe both the influence of language on cognition and the influence of cultural or "public" representations on cognition. Dennett (1994) has argued that human beings have "language-infected" cognitive states; that is, while language enables the cognitive flexibility and reflective thought that set human beings apart from other species, the products of such higher level cognitive processes are necessarily influenced by the properties of language. Orthographies and texts are cultural or "public" representations of language. The pattern of distribution of cultural or "public" representations in a population has been likened to the pattern of distribution seen in the epidemiology of disease (Sperber, 1996), and their influence on cognition could be conceptualized in a manner similar to the way in which Denett has characterized the general effects of language.

This contagion metaphor suggests that orthographies and texts may have both tacit and overt consequences in cognition, and also suggests that these consequences are grounded in the biological nature of human cognition. Orthographies are cultural phenomena but they are also inescapably products of the human mind, and their influence on cognition could only be a result of their representation and interpretation in human minds in the process of text understanding.

The cognitive consequences of literacy, then, would have to be a consequence of the use of orthographies in the cumulative episodes of text understanding in a literate cultural tradition. The resulting orthography-based theories of language could be expected to vary according to differences in the communicative functions and interpretive requirements of the texts they are used to construct. That is, some interpretive requirements could be expected to be more sophisticated than others. We saw above, for example, how literate scholars and philosophers bemoaned the ambiguity of words in natural language. They complained that whatever rules operate in natural language to allow the use of words, they seemed inadequate for the exactness required in their intellectual pursuits.

If the use of written language had some influence in raising this awareness of ambiguity, what was the cognitive mechanism by which it was achieved? Simple orthography influences the concept "word" as a translatable element of language but there is no evidence that it raised awareness of words as meaningful, or of the idea of definition. Olson (1994) claims that interpretation, specifically an opaque theory of interpretation, is the causal mechanism underlying the influence of literacy. We now turn to an examination of how interpretation may have influenced the development of the conception of words as meaningful and definable.

Literacy and Communication

The idea of representational adequacy discussed above was based on a conception of writing as the representation of speech. On this view, the phonetic alphabet provides a better representation of speech than a syllabic script because it enables an easier recovery of the words of an utterance and hence an easier recovery of meaning. The "writing as transcription" idea has been quite pervasive (Gelb, 1963), and has led to conceptualizing the effects of literacy on cognition as a code-based phenomenon.

Recent theories of writing suggest that this is a mistaken idea. Historically, writing systems were not invented to transcribe speech, but rather to convey information (Gaur, 1987; Harris, 1986). On this account, texts are primarily communicative. The "goodness" of an orthography, then, lies not in its representational adequacy with respect to a spoken language, but rather with its communicative adequacy with respect to the messages that it is designed to convey. No script, it is claimed, accurately represents speech. This suggests that the effects of literacy on cognition may be better conceptualized not as code-based, but as event-based.

In post-Gricean pragmatics, specifically relevance theory (Blakemore, 1987; Sperber & Wilson, 1995), all comprehension is seen as inferential. Propositional forms and explicatures of an utterance are not given, but derived on the basis of assumption schemas. The idea of code-based literal meaning is itself problematic. It is far from obvious that a hearer first computes a literal interpretation of the words of a sentence in the process of understanding, and only then considers contextual factors. In relevance theory, the hearer selects a context within which the utterance has maximal contextual effects. This is accomplished by appeal to a set of assump-

tions about the hearer's and the speaker's communicative and informative intentions. The process of inferential understanding, potentially lengthy and complex, is
constrained by the principle of relevance. The hearer does not process all the
explicatures and implicatures of an utterance, only enough to derive a relevant enough
interpretation, that is, relevant to him or her. The most relevant interpretation is
the one in which the minimum amount of effort yields the maximum contextual
(cognitive) effects.

Relevance theory is event-based. It presents a theory of how communicative events
are understood. The linguistic code is one source of information processed by a
hearer in arriving at a relevant interpretation of an utterance. Communicative events
are understood by means of assumption schemas in the cognitive environment of
the hearer/reader. The difference between text understanding and utterance understanding, on this account, lies in a change in the sources of inference available to
the reader, and not, as is often claimed, in the decontextualization of written expressions. Any text-understanding event has a "con-text," features that define the
environment in which the interpretive process takes place.

If writing is indeed communicative in nature, its effects on cognition may be best
understood by examining how it differs from communicative events in ordinary oral
language. If interpretation is the mechanism by which writing, or literacy, has its
effect, it should be clear how the interpretation of communicative events involving
orthographies and texts differs from the inferential and interpretive processes underlying ordinary verbal communicative events. What is unique to the interpretation of texts?

Reflection

Does a reader necessarily reflect? On a pragmatic account there is no reason to
expect that a reader's goal would necessarily be any different than a hearer's. Both
want to recover an interpretation that is relevant enough to warrant the effort invested. Reflection is possible but is neither necessary to, nor unique in, processing
written forms. It involves extra processing and would only be expected to occur
when a relevant interpretation is not arrived at on a first attempt at understanding.
This would be true of both oral and written language, and indeed, reflection does
occur with oral forms as well (Feldman, 1991).

However, the change in the sources of inference available to the reader, in contrast
to the hearer, could be expected to make reflection on the code more frequent in text
understanding. The hearer of an utterance can appeal to a number of sources to
enrich his or her cognitive environment, including the interlocutor and their shared
situation. The reader of a text, in contrast, has fewer options. In the case of failure to
arrive at a relevant interpretation, for example, when a sentence is ambiguous, the
reader must return to the written representation of the code if interpretation fails.
Under these conditions, then, the role of the code can be seen to be more prominent
and more opaque as a source of information than in ordinary oral discourse.

The role of the code in resolving ambiguity could thus be expected to be greater in written communicative events, because of the limited sources of inference available to the reader. Reflection, on this account, is a consequence of ambiguity, of interpretive requirements, rather than a direct consequence of the representation of the code in written form.

Interpretation

On a pragmatic account, an opaque notion of interpretation is not unique to text understanding. Strategies for the interpretation of oral language can range from the naive to the sophisticated, depending on the complexity of the oral form. Irony and deception in oral language, for example, require sophisticated understanding and several orders of metarepresentation (Sperber, 1994).

However, sophisticated or opaque notions of interpretation could be expected to arise in text understanding under cases of high representational demand, such as scientific or philosophical uses of written language. These go beyond the understanding of single utterances or sentences to the representation of extended arguments and discourse. These forms do have unique interpretation requirements and unique representational demands.

Whether interpretation is simple or sophisticated, then, is a consequence of the use to which an orthography is put, the kinds of texts that it is used to create and their interpretive requirements, rather than a direct consequence of the presence of a written representation of the code.

Interpretation as a causal mechanism

Sophisticated or opaque interpretation, then, whether in oral or written language understanding, requires metarepresentation. The sophisticated interpretation of a text requires that the text be explicitly represented, not simply processed transparently as a means to a communicative end. In order to define a word, or even to recognize that a word is in need of definition, requires that "word" become an opaque metalinguistic category for the interpreter. The question raised by Olson (1994) is whether sophisticated interpretation simply takes advantage of existing metarepresentational capacities or whether it causes the development of metarepresentational capacity itself.

Interpretation is unlikely to have played a causal role in the evolutionary or developmental emergence of metarepresentation itself. Literacy is a relatively recent development in cognitive evolutionary terms (cf. Cosmides & Tooby, 1994), too recent to have caused the basic metarepresentational capacity in the human brain. Metarepresentation in children, as has become increasingly clear in recent research on children's theory of mind (Astington, 1993; Astington, Harris & Olson, 1988; Gopnik & Meltzoff, 1997; Leslie, 1994), clearly predates their acquisition of literacy, and happens long before they are capable of sophisticated interpretation.

It seems more likely that the consequences of sophisticated interpretation are in the nature of an amplification of existing metacognitive abilities. Since, on current views, there may be more than one kind of metacognition (Sperber, in press), it is not unreasonable to suggest that the interpretive requirements of certain kinds of texts, the frequent need for, and use of, a sophisticated interpretation strategy, could enhance the development of existing metarepresentational capacity in particular ways. Sophisticated interpretation strategies could conceivably, then, lead to the development of a specific kind of metacognition that would underwrite the specific representational demands of text understanding.

Interpretation, word meaning, and definition

The concept "word," it was argued above, came into consciousness with early uses of orthography. The concept of words as meaningful, and the problematic nature of identifying meanings, was a consequence of certain uses of orthography and the kinds of interpretation those uses required. The emergence of the definitional form was in response to the interpretive requirements of philosophy and mathematics. The importance of definition in the classical period is a consequence, it is suggested by the evidence and discussion above, of the use to which texts were put.

The emergence of the dictionary definition, and the popular notion of its authority, was a response to the interpretive requirements of a dispersed and populous community of readers. This development had a profound effect on conceptions, or theories, of language. Putnam (1975) suggested that the phenomenon of writing and needing dictionaries gave rise to the whole idea of semantic theory. The idea of words as meaningful and definable may itself be a consequence of "literacy-infected" cognitive states (cf. Dennett, 1994).

Both the definitional form and the common dictionary definition, then, arose in response to the interpretive demands of sophisticated uses of texts. Definitions can be conceptualized as axioms in an explicit, sophisticated theory of language. An opaque, sophisticated theory of interpretation requires explicit formulations of meaning, such as definitions.

Conclusions

Several claims have been made in this chapter. An orthography-neutral account of the effects of literacy on conceptions of language was presented. Any orthography that is used to represent a language will cause its user to articulate and develop new conceptions of that language.

Orthographies are likened to theories of the language they are used to represent. Deciding which aspects of the language it is necessary to represent and how the orthography can be used to do so are theory-like decisions. The sophistication of the theory depends on the use to which the orthography is put.

The conception of "word" emerged with other conceptions of language as a consequence of the use of orthographies. The role of words in theories of language developed as orthographies were used in more sophisticated ways. The conception of words as meaningful was evident with the emergence of the word definition. Both the definitional form and the common dictionary definition arose in response to the interpretive demands of sophisticated uses of texts. Definitions can be conceptualized as axioms in an explicit, sophisticated theory of language. An opaque, sophisticated theory of interpretation requires explicit formulations of meaning, such as definitions.

The effects of the code are due to its role in the inferential processes underlying text understanding. The code is important to recovering meaning in text understanding because the reader turns to it in cases of inferential or interpretive failure. Other sources of enrichment in the cognitive environment of the reader are sparse. The written version of the code, then, has its effect when ordinary interpretation fails. Conceptualizing this inferential prominence of the code as "decontextualization" leads to the faulty conclusion that no extratextual inference is taking place. This would contradict most existing theories of communicative event understanding.

The interpretive requirements of certain kinds of texts, the frequent need for, and use of, a sophisticated interpretation strategy, could be expected to influence the development of a kind of metarepresentational capacity. Literacy is too recent in our evolutionary history to have caused the basic metarepresentational capacity in the human brain, but sophisticated interpretation could influence the development of metarepresentational capacity in ways that would underwrite such interpretive activity.

Note

1   R. Cawdrey, an English schoolmaster, is credited with having written the first English–English dictionary in 1604, by Starnes and Noyes (1946). The quotes listed are from the title pages of Cawdrey's "A Table Alphabetical" and Blount's "Glossographia" as they appear reproduced in Starnes and Noyes.

References

Astington, J. W. (1993). *The child's discovery of the mind*. Cambridge, MA: Harvard University Press.

Astington, J. W., Harris, P. L., & Olson, D. R. (Eds.). (1988). *Developing theories of mind*. New York: Cambridge University Press.

Bacon, F. (1857). The advancement of learning. In J. Spedding, R. Ellis, & D. Heath, (Eds.), *The works of Francis Bacon (Vols. 1–14)*. London: Longmans.

Blakemore, D. (1987). *Semantic constraints on relevance*. Oxford, UK: Blackwell.

Cosmides, L., & Tooby, J. (1994). Origins of domain specificity: The evolution of functional organization. In L. A. Hirschfeld & S. A. Gelman (Eds.) *Mapping the mind: Domain specificity in cognition and culture* (pp. 85–116). New York: Cambridge University Press.

Dennett, D. (1994). Language and intelligence. In Khalfa, J. (Ed.) *What is intelligence?* Cambridge, UK: Cambridge University Press.

Descartes, R. (1968). *The philosophical works of Descartes.* (E. S. Haldane & G. R. T. Ross, trans.) Cambridge, UK: Cambridge University Press. (Original work published 1637–44)

Deutsch, R., & Heltzer, M. (1994). *Forty new ancient west Semitic inscriptions.* Tel Aviv, Israel: Archeological Center Publication.

Deutsch, R., & Heltzer, M. (1997). *Windows to the past.* Tel Aviv, Israel: Archeological Center Publication.

Diringer, D. (1968). *The alphabet: A key to the history of mankind (3rd edn).* New York: Funk & Wagnalls.

Feldman, C. F. (1991). Oral metalanguage. In D. R. Olson & N. Torrance (Eds.), *Literacy and orality* (pp. 47–65). New York: Cambridge University Press.

Gaur, A. (1987). *A history of writing.* London: The British Library.

Gelb, I. J. (1963). *A study of writing (2nd edn).* Chicago: University of Chicago Press.

Goody, J. (1987). *The interface between the oral and the written.* Cambridge, UK: Cambridge University Press.

Gopnik, A., & Meltzoff, A. (1997). *Words, thoughts, and theories.* Cambridge, MA: MIT Press/Bradford.

Goswami, U. (1986). Children's use of analogy in learning to read: A developmental study. *Journal of Experimental Child Psychology, 42,* 73–83.

Goswami, U. (1991). Learning about spelling sequences: The role of onsets and rimes in analogies in reading. *Child Development, 62,* 1110–23.

Goswami, U., & Bryant, P. (1990). Rhyme, analogy, and children's reading. In P. B. Gough, L. C. Ehri, & R. Treiman (Eds.), *Reading acquisition* (pp. 49–64). Hillsdale, NJ: Erlbaum.

Grice, P. (1989). *Studies in the way of words.* Cambridge, MA: Harvard University Press.

Harris, R. (1986). *The origin of writing.* London: Duckworth.

Havelock, E. (1963). *Preface to Plato.* Cambridge, UK: Cambridge University Press.

Havelock, E. (1976). *Origins of western literacy.* Toronto, Canada: OISE Press.

Leslie, A. (1994). Pretending and believing: Issues in the theory of ToMM. *Cognition, 50,* 211–38.

Liberman, I. Y., Shankweiler, D., Fisher, F. W., & Carter, B. (1974). Explicit syllable and phoneme segmentation in the young child. *Journal of Experimental Child Psychology, 18,* 201–12.

Locke, J. (1961). *An essay concerning human understanding.* London: Dent. (Original work published 1690)

McLuhan, M. (1962). *The Gutenberg galaxy.* Toronto, Canada: University of Toronto Press.

Olson, D. R. (1977). From utterance to text: The bias of language in speech and writing. *Harvard Educational Review, 47,* 257–81.

Olson, D. R. (1994). *The world on paper.* Cambridge, UK: Cambridge University Press.

Ong, W. (1976). *The presence of the word.* New Haven, CT: Yale University Press.

Ong, W. (1982). *Orality and literacy: The technologizing of the word.* London: Methuen.

Putnam, H. (1975). *Mind, language and reality: Philosophical papers. Vol. 2.* Cambridge, UK: Cambridge University Press.

Robinson, R. (1950). *Definition.* Oxford, UK: Clarendon Press.

Robinson, A. (1995). *The story of writing.* London: Thames & Hudson.

Sperber, D. (1994). Understanding verbal understanding. In J. Khalfa (Ed.), *What is intelligence?* Cambridge, UK: Cambridge University Press.

Sperber, D. (1996). *Explaining culture: A naturalistic approach.* Oxford, UK: Blackwell.

Sperber, D. (in press). Metarepresentation in an evolutionary perspective. In D. Sperber (Ed.), *Metarepresentation*. Oxford, UK: Oxford University Press.

Sperber, D., & Wilson, D. (1995). *Relevance: Communication and cognition*. (2nd edn). Oxford, UK: Blackwell.

Starnes, D. T., & Noyes, E. (1946). *The history of the English dictionary from Cawdrey to Johnson*. Chapel Hill, NC: University of North Carolina Press.

Treiman, R. (1985). Onsets and rimes as units of spoken syllables: Evidence from children. *Journal of Experimental Child Psychology, 39*, 161–81.

Treiman, R. (1991). Phonological awareness and its role in learning to read and spell. In D. J. Sawyer & B. J. Fox (Eds.), *Phonological awareness in reading: The evolution of current perspectives* (pp. 159–89). New York: Springer-Verlag.

Treiman, R. (1992). The role of intrasyllabic units in learning to read and spell. In P. B. Gough, L. Ehri, & R. Treiman (Eds.), *Reading acquisition* (pp.65–106). Hillsdale, NJ: Erlbaum.

Walker, C. B. F. (1990). Cuneiform. In J. T. Hooker (Ed.), *Reading the past: Ancient writing from cuneiform to the alphabet* (pp. 15–72). London: The British Museum Press.

Walton, P. (1992). *Effects of training on the orthographic segmentation abilities in young children*. Unpublished doctoral dissertation, University of British Columbia.

Watson, R., & Olson, D. R. (1987). From meaning to definition: A literate bias on the structure of word meaning. In R. Horowitz & J. Samuels, (Eds.), *Comprehending oral and written language* (pp. 329–53). San Diego, CA: Academic Press.

6

Rhetorical and Aesthetic Form: Poetry as Textual Art

Joan Peskin

As I sat in an undergraduate class on thought and language in Johannesburg, South Africa, listening to the arguments of Vygotsky, Luria, Piaget, Bruner, and Olson, I felt the first thrill in discovering what was to be my life's work. This was my initial encounter with the work of David Olson. I could not have wildly imagined then, that after emigrating to Toronto I would be having fascinating discussions with David about my 3-year-old son's mind in the making. I would bring anecdotes from home, and David would seamlessly weave them together, his elegant analyses matched by his eloquent language. Recently I had cause to remember one of these discussions, where David, pulling together my half-formed thoughts into cogent arguments, articulately reeled off predictions regarding behaviors of children who do not yet represent beliefs. Ten years later I reviewed someone's manuscript examining one of these predictions. The editor's praise of the manuscript as most "timely and interesting research" underscored for me how David is a thinker ahead of his time.

Those exciting discussions on children's first representations of their own and other people's thinking, framed my PhD thesis and early work on young children's misrepresentations of text. But my choice of David as supervisor was based on my admiration for his heart as well as his mind. In his research groups I noticed his curiosity, modesty, interest in, and attempt to make sense of what everyone was trying to say; how he brought out the best in his students, and showed no interest in taking kudos for himself. And I quietly observed his kindness when I shared an office with one of his overseas students, whose English was poor and who desperately was trying to finish her PhD to return home to her young daughter whom she had last seen at birth. I observed, week after week, draft after draft, line by line, David's painstaking help on her thesis. He went beyond any call of duty.

After my research on young children (Peskin, 1992, 1996), I changed direction, or thought that I did. I revisited a pilot study from my earlier course work with another professor and began an expert-novice study on how university students make sense of difficult period poetry. Seemingly far from David's domain, however, I still kept encountering his insights and his lucid writings. As this chapter will demonstrate, in areas as diverse as literary theory; the representation of the poet's intentions; metaphor as what is meant, not said; and the relationship between literature and the appreciation of the visual arts, my mind continues to be shaped by Olson's thinking.

Rhetorical Form

Rhetorical form is that aspect of the text which concerns itself with how the text is taken by the reader. In *The World on Paper* (1994) David Olson writes that Maimonides, in the 12th century, demonstrated an awareness of this relationship between the writer and the intended audience: Maimonides explained that Biblical writers used expressions such as the "hand of God" because simple folk would understand the term. This concern with rhetorical form involves increasingly recursive questions such as: Who is the author? Who is the author addressing? What does the author want the reader to think? When do readers think about what the author believes? And when do readers consider what the author intends the reader to believe? These questions form part of the very foundation of critical thinking about the written word.

The rhetorical (or semiotic) level of interpretation is to be distinguished from what Umberto Eco (1990) refers to as a semantic level of interpretation. A semantic reading is directed to understanding the semantic content of the text. In a purely semantic reading, what the text says is expected to be understood without any knowledge of who was writing the text and for which purpose. The text content is treated as "autonomous" (Olson, 1977).

Consciousness of these two levels of interpretation – rhetorical form and autonomous content – separates the critical reader from the naive reader. The naive reader attends to what the text is saying, accepting the written statements as objective facts. The sophisticated reader focuses not only on what the text is saying, but also on what the author wants the reader to believe. In text interpretation in disciplines as diverse as history and science, this critical reader is concerned with interpreting apparent facts as authorial beliefs, and distinguishing between the two. Wineburg (1991) compared historians and high school students reading historical texts. The historians pay early attention to the source of the document. The author and date and place of writing provide the historian with predictions as to the content, and consideration of the intentions or goals of the writer enable judgments about authorial bias and reliability. While advanced readers pay close attention to rhetorical form, questioning, "Why does the author think this?" "What is the motive?" and "What was going on at the time of writing?" less advanced readers are limited to considerations of semantic content. They focus their attention on what the text means, that is, its referential meaning, as if viewing the text merely as a conveyer of objective information. The format of textbook writing with its "unremitting flow of assertions, that is, statements offered as true" does not make this discrimination easier (Olson, 1994, p. 192). The author is irrelevant in the students' task of recovering the "autonomous" content. History appears to speak for itself.

In the sciences and social sciences there is a similar distinction between rhetorical form and semantic content. The novice reader focuses only on content while the expert readers attend to both levels of interpretation. The advanced reader reconstructs the context of the textual statements in order to decide just how to interpret them (Geisler, 1994; Olson & Astington, 1993). Olson and Astington refer to "ways of taking utterances," that is, deciding on the illocutionary force of the statement (1993, p. 11). Metadiscourse becomes the source of clues enabling the reader to decide on the level of certainty to grant the claims. Does the author say that X hydrolyzes Y, or appears to hydrolyze Y, or may hydrolyze Y? Did the original speaker intend the expression to be taken as confident claim or as hesitant conjecture? The knowledgeable reader also tries to reconstruct the contextual factors to evaluate the author's claims and attribute possible error. The scientist understands that the text is attributable to an author and is therefore, subjective and interpretive. On the other hand the novice reader does not talk of the scientific text as having authors, referring rather to what "the book said" (Geisler, 1994, p. 173.)

The rhetorical stance to a text therefore facilitates critical interpretation. For the expert reader, the author is opaque; for the novice, the writer is transparent and the reader looks through the rhetorical form to the referential content. Advanced readers evaluate and judge knowledge while novices merely absorb it.

Reading Poetic Texts: Early Awareness of Rhetorical Form

In most domains the ability to take factual statements as expressing audience-directed intention is a skill which becomes evident only in the graduate years. Even Honors students read the semantic content of historical texts as objective facts rather than as authorial beliefs (Wineburg, 1991). However, in recent studies that I have carried out, there is evidence of precocious awareness of authorial intention – even in the high school years – when students are reading poetic texts (Peskin, 1998). These studies have taken the form of expert-novice comparisons, a procedure currently proving fruitful in cognitive research.

Studies on expertise look at what experts know and what strategies they use that novices do not know and do not use. In this way, any systematic changes in the patterns of interpretation and the operations underlying the reading of poetic texts can be examined. An expert refers to a person with special skills and knowledge acquired through experience, rather than inherent talent (Ericsson & Charness, 1994). "Expert" and "novice" are relative terms in that the novice may indeed be fairly experienced in reading poetic texts, but is less experienced than the expert.

The 8 "experts" in my study were Ph.D. candidates in the English department at the University of Toronto, and the 8 "novices" were either undergraduates in their first two years of English studies who had taken one course on poetry, or high school students in their last two years of an advanced private school with intensive poetry instruction. The students were tested individually. They were given a short poem for practice in thinking aloud, with the following instructions: "I'd like you to think aloud as you try and make sense of each of the poems. Say everything that you are thinking. It's just as if you are 'turning up the volume' on your associations, inferences or any minor thoughts as they flit through your mind. Don't censor anything." They were then provided with the target poems with no author's name visible, presented individually. One was a metaphysical poem, "On a drop of dew" by Andrew Marvell. The other was an Elizabethan love sonnet, "Lyke as a hunts-man" by Edmund Spenser. As advocated by Ericsson and Simon (1991), probes were nonspecific prods such as "What does this poem suggest to you?" and, at moments of silence, reminders to think aloud. Their verbalizations were tape re-corded and transcribed.

One of the questions explored was whether the novices would show awareness of rhetorical form in poetic discourse. The literary theorist, Jonathan Culler, has pro-posed a structuralist model, distinguishing between meaning or semantic interpre-tation on the one hand, and semiotic conventions (rhetorical form) on the other hand. Culler (1976) states that reading poetry is not a natural activity but is charged with artifice, that is, animated by a special set of expectations or conventions which the reader has assimilated and which are also part of the implicit knowledge of the author. The study of one poem facilitates the reading of the next, and readers must have considerable experience in these conventions. For Culler (1976, p. 115), the primary expectations are first, the "rule of significance: read the poem as expressing a significant attitude to some problem concerning man and/or his relation to the universe," secondly, the "convention of thematic unity" whereby all the parts of the poem are related to create a unified, coherent whole, and thirdly, the "conventions of metaphorical coherence" which was operationally defined as an expectation that "the basis of poetic expression is the metaphor" (Frye, 1978, p. 91).

The protocols were examined for evidence of the above three conventions as an indication of the novice reader's awareness of the goals and intentions of the poet. The experts' awareness of these basic conventions was not examined as pilot studies demonstrated that their knowledge was too automatic for conscious articulation (Peskin, 1998). Expert performance will be discussed later in this chapter. In the interests of simplicity, throughout this chapter illustrative examples will be restricted to the metaphysical poem, "On a drop of dew" (presented in Appendix A). And as the poem may be difficult to grasp on a first reading, an interpretation of the sus-tained metaphor will be provided (an interpretation common to all the experts, but to only two of the novices in the study). In the poem, Marvell compares a drop of dew in a flower to the soul in the human body. In the first part of the poem he describes the mournful drop of dew, restless on the flower as it waits to be evapo-rated and can thereby return to the skies. The second half introduces the soul which, in the same way, is unhappy in the body and longs to return to heaven. It must be noted here that text reading generates both consensual and personal meanings, and although no two responses will be identical, in a period poem which is highly con-strained by the textual pressure of a conceit, a specialized group of readers may share a response (Purves, 1989).

Analysis of the protocols made it clear that all three theoretical conventions or expectations hypothesized by Culler (1976) guided most novice readings of both the poems in this study. To begin with the *rule of significance*, on each poem there were at least seven verbalizations from the group of novices, demonstrating an awareness that the reader must "attempt to read any brief descriptive lyric as a moment of epiphany," a process of finding ways to grant a poem "significance and importance" (Culler, 1976, p. 175). For instance, Novice Four thinks aloud:

> I'm not sure if the poet is writing this to point out to the reader or perhaps to her or himself the importance of dew but, to make us realize the importance of everything in our lives, and how the smallest little thing that we take for granted should be considered, and we should take some time to, excuse the expression, stop and smell the roses.

There is an anticipation that the poet is intending to make a point, even if the point hypothesized is ultimately unsatisfying to the novice.

A second expectation hypothesized by Culler (1976) is that of *thematic unity*, an awareness that this point will function as a central unifying element to which all the puzzle pieces should fit. One "should prefer those (explanations) which best succeed in relating items to one another rather than offer separate and unrelated explanations" (p. 170). Novice Seven thinks aloud:

> I can get many streams of ideas but I don't know how to tie them together. What is he telling me?

And later when Novice Seven begins to make the poem coherent:

> It seems to be funneling, like pinning each thing on to the previous thing, feeling a little more secure about what I have established. Each new thing I am taking and fitting in. I have some core, some parts fitting, I can tack on.

And Novice Two comments,

> I don't know, some of the phrases don't, I'm sure they, like, fit together, but I can't see how they fit together . . . I got a little confused at the end because I want to understand the poet's meaning but I don't understand some of the words in the last two lines so I'm not sure what the message is totally. . . . I still don't know why, if the poet is trying to associate the dew with a human experience or emotion. . . . but then . . . at the end . . . I can't quite grasp what the entire meaning is.

The novices clearly verbalize their expectation that the poet has intended that the propositions relate to each other in order to create a coherent and unified whole.

The third expectation is that of *metaphorical significance*. As the extended metaphors in this study were difficult for the novices, they were not always able to make them coherent, but most of the novices recognized the importance of metaphor in poetry, and searched for, observed, and attempted to make sense of the symbolic content of the poems. Novice Three comments:

> It seems to me to equate dew with goodness and innocence and purity and part of the skies and part of the heavens.

She is attempting to unravel the terms of comparison, but she does not perceive the role of the soul as one of the terms and she later expresses dissatisfaction with her reading.

And Novice Seven, for instance, thinks aloud:

> The poem seems to be not really filled with metaphors and similes but pretty straight-forward, when you first look at it.

While Novice Seven missed the extended simile, her comment clearly demonstrates the expectation that metaphor is a vehicle of poetic expression.

Recognition of a metaphor "will depend upon a consciousness of language, of the discrepancies between possible ways of relating what is said and what is meant" (Olson, 1988, p. 221). Even when the novices didn't mention metaphor directly, there was the awareness that what the poet was saying and meaning were not the same. Novice Six comments,

> It's not just about a drop of dew, so I was trying to look at . . . um . . . trying to look for the other meanings under the words, what the author's trying to say.

This early awareness of the textual (or rhetorical form) on the part of the novices is probably scaffolded by the idiosyncratic language of poetry. In prose, ideas are connected by putting words in an established order. It tends to be written in an expansive way conforming to the combinative rules. The language is usually transparent, in that it is processed automatically with the aim of comprehending the meaning or message. Poetry, on the other hand, tends to compress, and in doing so, it inclines toward the comparisons and the condensation of figurative language. By emphasizing image formation it often disregards syntax, the connectives and the linear order of language. Jakobson (1987) wrote of poetry as a system not belonging to ordinary communication because the language of poetry calls attention to itself.

To sum up to this point, it seems that when reading poetry, undergraduates and even advanced high school students do not just interpret the content of the poem but have a concept of interpretation. They ruminate over the poet's intentions, the unifying theme and the difference between what the poet said and what is meant. With regard to poetic discourse there appears to be a precocious awareness of the rhetorical form.

Aesthetic Form

The two interacting levels, form and content, are evident not only in textual analysis but also in artistic interpretation in the visual arts. To view aesthetically is to see the form and how it expresses its meaning rather than simply to see through the form to the meaning (Olson, personal communication, 1998). The ability to see both the intended object – as well as the features which give rise to that perception – is an important aesthetic achievement. However, in the attempts of theorists to demystify cognition in the visual arts, the concern with form appears to be directed less toward the intentions, perspective, and persuasions of the artist, (rhetorical form in textual analysis) and more toward *how*, aesthetically the form expresses and amplifies its meaning.

In his writings on "visual thinking," Rudolf Arnheim refers to intuitive and intellectual cognition (1968, 1969). Intuitive cognition is the perception of the "effect" of the painting, such as perceiving a sad face. In observing a painting, the components (shapes, colors, and relations between them) interact in such a way so that the total image is perceived with very little of the highly complex perceptual process reaching consciousness. This intuitive cognition of effect appears to be similar to the cognition of semantic content in textual reading. Intellectual cognition, on the other hand is when "an observer, instead of absorbing the total image of the painting intuitively, wishes to identify the various components and relations of which the work consists. He describes each shape, ascertains each color. . .and proceeds to examine the relations between the individual elements, for example, the effects of contrast or assimilation. . ." (Arnheim, 1969, p. 234). The viewer may note, for instance, that the downward lines of the mouth and eyes contribute to the perception of sadness and are echoed in the droopiness of the tree in the background.

In artistic interpretation in the visual arts, the awareness of form concerns "interaction between parts and wholes, between color and shape, between the representation and the represented" (Jakobson, 1987, p. 4), and how these interacting components effect meaning. In textual interpretation, on the other hand, the concern with form has been directed more toward reader awareness of the beliefs and persuasions of the author, what Geisler (1994) calls the rhetorical aspects of the texts. But poetry occupies a place somewhere between text and art. To a far greater extent than other kinds of literature, the reader of poetic discourse needs to be aware not only of textual or rhetorical form but of aesthetic or artistic form. A poem can be viewed as textual art.

Reading Poetic Texts: Later Appreciation of Aesthetic Form

In aesthetic interpretation of poetry, consciousness of how the interacting components effect meaning becomes center stage. The reader's focus on artistic form not only facilitates the construction of meaning but also gives readers an understanding of just how the poem amplifies that meaning. A second research area in the studies on reading poetry (Peskin, 1998) involved a comparison of experts and novices in their awareness of these interacting components.

Protocols were examined for those interpretive strategies which appeared to be useful in appreciating the way in which the text says what it says. In a domain as abstruse, idiosyncratic and unexplored as poetry, some of the more interesting data cannot be accounted for in terms of current theories of text processing. As Bereiter and Bird (1985), Flower and Hayes (1985), and Johnston and Afflerbach (1995) have all noted in their studies of skilled readers or writers, it may be less productive to systematically classify verbal reports, than to intuitively examine, catalogue, and illustrate elements that facilitate success. The list of elements was pared down according to the criteria that the operation differentiated the experts from the novices, and appeared in at least three expert or three novice protocols on *both* of the poems. While an operation may have been valuable in making sense of one of the two texts, the aim was to attempt to delineate more general operations.

From the elements in the initial coding list, the following interpretive operations appeared to demonstrate an appreciation of aesthetic form. First, the experts showed greater evidence of observing the *structure* of the poems. Expert Two, for instance, ponders aloud:

> The *Sun* ends the first part, *Till the warm Sun pitty it's Pain*, and ends the poem itself, *Into the glories of th' Almighty Sun*. Not that this tells me anything at the moment yet. I'm just looking for patterns.

A few of the novices also consciously focused on the endings of each of the poems, for instance, Novice Six:

> I can't quite grasp what the entire meaning is. I'm looking at the last four lines because I know that in most poetry they're usually pretty important.

However, the experts, but none of the novices, also showed evidence of integrating structural elements with the poem's meaning in more subtle ways, focusing on, for instance, the relationship between the last line of each section (as in the example from the expert above); the break-up into grammatical units; how the arrangement by stanza corresponds to the sense; the division into lines and stanzas, and the resonance between structure and content as in a grouping of very short lines or a particularly long or circular sentence as in the following example from the protocol of Expert Two:

> . . . and then at the end of the sentence the skies *exhale it back again* . . . So the whole sentence isn't closed. It's circular. It starts at the sky and goes back to the sky. So the whole structure of the sentence and those thoughts are circular, like the dewdrop.

Secondly, there was the recognition by the experts that poets often use *binary oppositions* as important thematic devices. The experts displayed an effective strategy of looking for the meaning of the poem at the locus of the contradictions, juxtapositions, or dialectic. Expert Seven comments:

> One of the things that comes right away is the definite sense of polarity, of inside, outside, where elements are first established as something distinct and then at some point dissolve into each other.

Novice Eight, on the other hand, reading the same lines, observes the binary oppositions but rejects them as too confusing:

> So you've got sort of an equation, or you've got a scale there, but it doesn't give me any sense of clarity. The one word seems to negate the other somehow, and it just jumbles everything for me. I don't like lines like these. They just jumble things.

Not aware of the significance of the binary oppositions in constructing meaning in literary texts, this novice then ignores these lines.

Thirdly, most of the experts (but only one of the novices) commented on the *word play and language*. For instance, after reading the last line, *Into the Glories of th' Almighty Sun*, Expert Five comments:

> The word, *Sun*, is probably a play on son, like Jesus, and it gets Christian overtones.

Compare this to Novice Five who does not recognize the pun:

> *Into the Glories of th' Almighty Sun.* So it evaporates into the air when the sun comes out. (She rereads the line) So I don't know. That seems to have a happy connotation rather than the dew just going away, but I don't really know. I guess at the beginning it was just talking about when it's morning and then it gets into the day and the dew goes into the sun.

She misses the religious overtones and the extended comparison of the dew to the human soul.

And finally, on each poem the group of experts verbalized at least seven observations of *rhythm and rhyme* as amplifiers of meaning. As Expert Three thinks aloud:

> . . . gg . . . hh . . . . ii . . . So we see that, okay, wherever he's actually closing an argument he gives us a rhyming couplet to sort of slam the door shut so that we get the idea . . . The circle imagery is reflecting the rhyme-scheme which reflects the name of the poem which is about the round perfection of God. It's all so beautifully interconnected it makes me shiver.

Only two of the novices even looked at the rhyme scheme, and that was only on one of the poems.

Poetic language is unique in the emphasis on its semiotic aspect, that is, on the signifier rather than the signified. For Umberto Eco (1990) literary texts (poetry, in particular) "aim at producing two Model readers, a first level, or a naive one, supposed to understand semantically what the text says, and a second level, or critical one, supposed to appreciate the way in which the text says so" (p. 55). But there is an intimate relationship between these two types of reading for it is clear from the above examples that the experts' critical reading of *how* the text "says so" provides cues to facilitate a semantic understanding of what the text is saying. The novices, on the other hand, while showing proficient consideration of the rhetorical form (the significant attitude of the poet and how the parts of the poem relate to this unifying theme, and that what the poet is saying may not be what he is meaning), showed little awareness – and consequent appreciation – of aesthetic form, that is, how the components of the poem effect and amplify the meaning.

When Meaning Breaks Down

Alexander Pope asserted alliteratively: "The sound must seem an echo to the sense" (1965, p. 155), and the question arises as to whether there needs to be some understanding of what the text says semantically (Eco's naive reading, 1990) before there can be a "second level" critical appreciative reading. Hence, a third area I have investigated, concerns the attempts by novices and experts to construct meaning when they cannot make semantic sense of the lines.

To begin with the novices, they more frequently stated *that* they didn't understand, as well as specifically *what* they didn't understand. Novice Six ponders:

> I don't understand the difference between the sun, the eternal day and the dew. Somehow I'm not understanding what these represent, and . . . how the dew is being compared to those things.

Novice One comments:

> *Into the blowing roses* . . . Blowing? Blowing? Why are roses blowing? Blowing wind maybe.

The novices also more frequently backtracked, rereading from the beginning of a confusing segment. For example, Novice Six thinks aloud:

> I'm going to go back again. (She rereads the same lines.) I'm just keeping reading it till something sticks out.

Or the novices set text aside and pressed on in the hope of later resolution. Novice Three reads:

> *Till the warm Sun pitty it's Pain,/And to the Skies exhale it back again.* It goes back. I get a little bit lost. (She reads the next three lines) I'm going to carry on reading down.

So when meaning broke down, novices expressed their lack of understanding and either reread the confusing segment or did the opposite, that is, set the lines aside and read on in the hope that the confusion would be resolved in later lines. These techniques or strategies are similar to those observed in studies of general reading comprehension (Bereiter & Bird, 1985; Johnston & Afflerbach, 1985).

While the experts did not frequently verbalize a lack of clarity, there were 10 very cryptic lines (lines 27–36) in "On a Drop of Dew" which even these experts did not find easy. The first four of these lines seem quite incomprehensible, and none of the experts (or two English professors) felt that they had made the lines intelligible. One may have expected, therefore, that when reading these particular lines, the experts would behave as the novices did. On the contrary, it seemed that at precisely these moments of difficulty, the experts do not use general strategies from the discipline of reading comprehension to attempt construction of semantic meaning, but rather focus on the aesthetic form.

Although two of the experts acknowledged that the lines were difficult, they all turned away from trying to construct sense, to rather focusing on the tempo and movement, dialectic and images, language and word play, and on shape, structure, and rhythm as cues. Expert Four comments on the effect of line length and the tempo:

> . . . shorter lines. They look kind of punchy, an epigrammatic effect. The tempo of the poem is sped up in a kind of interesting fashion as if the poet is trying to carry forward very quickly the ideas he's trying to express.

Expert Five focuses on the juxtapositions or dialectic:

> *How loose and easie hence to go:/ How girt and ready to ascend.* I get the idea of the tightness, "girt and ready to ascend", but then it would dissolve, "loose and easy".

And she comments on the imagery in these two lines:

> It's a kind of neat image because you get this idea of a very tenuous hold on bodily life.

She reads the next two lines:

> *Moving but on a point below,/ it all about does upwards bend.* Once again a very lovely image. You get the idea of all the lines tending upwards.

Expert Three examines the poet's word play:

> It's hard . . . It's hard . . . I can't. I'm thinking and I don't know what I'm thinking. The first thing that occurs to me is that it's full of puns and what that suggests to me since this is the type of poem in which the language mirrors the theme, that a pun is a paradox, just as man is a paradox being half human, that is half fallen and subject to time and mutability. Just as the fallen world is full of paradoxes, that is, we have day and night.

Expert Two focuses on form, movement, and the dialectic:

> *Dark beneath, but bright above:/Here disdaining, there in Love.* This section seems to be structured in that there's here and there's there, there's the definite idea of above and below . . . I get the feeling of this back and forth movement.

But most interesting was Expert Six, who was quite unfazed by her difficulty in making the lines intelligible.

> It's becoming more and more obscure. It's becoming mysterious, I guess, in the religious sense of mystery. Okay, what was the subject? (She rereads these lines) This sounds like a riddle. It sounds like a nursery rhyme. It's a passage which is more pleased with language and with creating a mystery than it is with making itself clearly understood.

She interprets the obscurity as deliberate on the part of the poet, contributing to an atmosphere of strangeness, incoherence, and mystery in the religious sense.

Compare these examples to Novice Five reading the same lines, who backtracks and then laboriously tries to build a representation of the literal meaning of each broken-up line. She rereads line 27:

> *In how coy. . . .* (She pauses there and paraphrases in prose) In how shy. (She continues reading) *a Figure wound/Every way it turns away:/So the World excluding round*, I don't know what the "world excluding round" means. *Yet receiving in the Day*. It means that the day is coming. *Dark beneath, but bright above*: Dark on the earth and bright in the sky. I don't know. *Here disdaining, there in Love*, I have no idea what love has to do with it. Maybe that's the whole point of it. I don't know. *How loose and easie hence to go*: Okay so maybe they're saying that maybe love is easy to go. It comes and goes. I don't know. (She continues in frustration).

As distinct from the novices, it seems that when the experts cannot make clear sense of a passage, they move from trying to construct a representation of what the poem is saying to how the poet is saying it. As Expert Five comments as he reads these lines:

> I'm swerving away from what the poem means and onto how the poem is meaning it.

One could say that the experts' expertise lay not only in what they know, but also in what they know to do when they do not know. And what they know to do seems to exemplify Eco's model critical reader (1990) who focuses on appreciating the way in which the text says what it says.

Furthermore, it appears that the experts derived greater enjoyment from these critical readings. Most of the experts, but only one of the novices, expressed pleasure, whereas most of the novices, but none of the experts, expressed interpretive dissatisfaction understanding the poems. Expert One, for instance, thinks aloud:

> I like this poem. It's saying the same thing basically over and over again, but always making it more intriguing. It's just a wonderful exercise in using language.

And Expert Three comments:

What is absolutely magnificent is that the poem pulls itself apart, so that part of it pulls down and parts of it pulls up. It's unbelievable. . . . When you understand the structure, and a couple of the pieces of the puzzle you're solving lock in, that's when the magic of the poetry happens.

The novices, on the other hand, very frequently expressed frustration. Novice Two says:

I don't get it. I don't know, like I feel that I'm missing some hidden things and if I knew them then I'd be able to, you know.

And Novice Five comments:

If I understood it I could go on and on 'cos I always do that but I really don't get it.

Knowledge of Aesthetic Form as the Discipline Expertise when Reading Poetic Texts

The argument above is that understanding poetry is a particular category of reading comprehension in that constructing meaning involves not only a focus on rhetorical or textual form but also an advanced appreciation of aesthetic or artistic form. And while the novices demonstrated a precocious understanding of rhetorical form, their frustrated search for meaning in the difficult period poetry used in these studies, appeared to preclude a concern with the poetic art. On the other hand, the experts not only showed an appreciation of both the textual and artistic forms, but when "sense" failed them, they redirected their attention to aesthetic form, for instance, ruminating on just how it is that these lines give one a feeling of the strange and the mystical.

This tendency to utilize discipline expertise (Rouet, Favart, Britt, & Perfetti, 1997), that is, one's expert knowledge of the methods of the discipline when the semantic content of the problem is not easily accessible, has been found in studies on mathematics as well as history. Wineburg (1998) quotes from a study on mathematics where an expert in number theory was presented with a problem in geometry, an area that he hadn't worked on for years, "Rather than the quick mobilization of knowledge, he scratched his head and said, 'Hmmm. I don't exactly know where to start'" (p. 320). He then slowly worked through the puzzle applying and adapting his knowledge of the general forms of the discipline so that it addressed this new situation in which ready knowledge was lacking. A group of college students, with more specific knowledge of geometry than the mathematics expert, were, however, unsuccessful in solving the problem. Similarly, Wineburg recently gave a set of documents concerning Abraham Lincoln's stance on slavery, to an historian who knew little about American history. This non-Americanist, after much cognitive flailing, used his structure of knowledge from his experience in the general discipline of historical thought, to work through the confusion and to build an adequate interpretative structure (Wineburg, 1998, 1999).

Minds in the Making: Educational Implications

In the interpretation of texts, Olson highlights the importance of "an understanding of audience-directed intentions – what the author wants the putative audience to do or think" (1994, p. 156). In the present study it was clear that the novices reading poetic texts grasped the importance of understanding the poet's audience-directed intention; however, they lacked the historical and cultural knowledge necessary to create a coherent sense of what the author was meaning. These novice readers lacked Olson's shared system of interpretation (Feldman, this volume, Chapter 2). The concept of an interpretive community is particularly relevant in understanding period poetry where there are vast disjunctions in time between the writing and reading. Writers make use of conventions in their writings, and if the modern reader is not able to use them to understand the text, the resulting error may be "presentism," a default psychological propensity to select a context from one's current experience (Peskin, 1998). This was obvious in the novice readings of the poem, "Lyke as a Huntsman," where Spenser compares the pursuit of a lover to a huntsman pursuing a deer in the forest. Five of the novices, missing the terms of the comparison, tried to assimilate the sense of the poem to their current life themes, such as "cruelty to animals," or "judging a person not by looks but what they're really like," or trying to be "laid-back." In reading comprehension, words and phrases trigger spreading activation, and it is the structure of knowledge as well as higher interpretive processes which must constrain this automatic processing.

As Culler notes, both the poet and the reader bring to the text expectations about the cultural forms of poetry. "To write a poem . . . is immediately to engage with a literary tradition . . . made possible by the existence of the genre, which the author can write against, certainly, whose conventions he may attempt to subvert, but which is none the less the context within which his activity takes place (Culler, 1976, p. 116–117). It is the knowledge of the patterns of the genre which allow the reader, centuries later, to categorize and contextualize the poem and anticipate what is to come. As one expert in the present study noted, "I now have a portable context. I'm seeing an imaginary transparency which has Donne's name at the bottom with notes in the margin." While the poem was actually by Donne's contemporary, Marvell, she had a frame of reference, a structured and integrated representation that systematically cued her knowledge.

The expectations about poetry remind one of the schemata, of which Gombrich (1961) writes, in the production and appreciation in the visual arts. Gombrich, in demystifying the creative process of artists, writes of the "canon," the mass of schemata in the form of geometric relationships which the painter must know in order to draw a plausible figure. It appears that the tool kit of the poet is also stocked with canonical forms and themes, and like the artist, the poet often works according to Gombrich's "rhythm of schema and correction." The artist knows and constructs a schema before he can modify and mold it to the needs of the particular portrayal. The poet is writing by creating a distinctive instantiation of some core schema, and the reader's understanding may depend on having and retrieving this schema so that what the poet did with it can be appreciated.

Ironically, however, (and possibly because of the aesthetic, as well as the intensely personal nature, of poems) knowledge of poetry is frequently seen as implicit knowledge to be acquired tacitly through naive perception. While in the early high school years poetry appreciation may be fostered best by choosing straightforward poems rich in rhythm, rhyme, relevance, and humor, in the later high school years, when more abstruse poems begin to be introduced, bottom-up information seems to be inadequate in the search for meaning. A lack of knowledge of the structure, the methods, and the culturally attuned standards of the discipline may contribute to an antipathy toward poetry.

The present research has demonstrated that literary education can be based on empirical research. Studies on the cognitive operations of expert readers make salient the important conventions, expectations, and aesthetic components relevant to poetry as discourse. This may help teachers elaborate the structural properties of poetic texts which may, in turn, enable students to appreciate the new shape of the poem that is being read.

There is a difference between liking, for instance, a dog picture or poem because one likes dogs, and on the other hand, enjoying how the painter or poet used form – words, rhythm, movement, contrasts, light, color, and so on – to achieve the meaning or effect. Education appears to have neglected this side of knowledge. There has been little emphasis on directing students' attention to the forms by means of which meaning is expressed. Yet the appreciation made possible by seeing how form gives rise to meaning, is the very beginning of aesthetics.

In David Olson's early work on young children learning to construct the diagonal (1970), he argued for a more active teaching approach whereby a knowledgeable other uses language to direct the listener to the "critical features of an event which permit the choice between (the) alternatives" (p. 199). This may apply no less to the making of the minds of young adults as they construct meaning when reading a poetic text.

Acknowledgments

I am grateful to the Spencer Foundation for its support of my research through a National Academy of Education Postdoctoral Fellowship, and later, an award under the Small Grants Program.

References

Arnheim, R. (1968). From perceiving to performing: An aspect of cognitive growth. [Special Issue: Comments and discussion] *Ontario Journal of Educational Research, 10,* 213–10.

Arnheim, R. (1969). *Visual thinking.* Berkeley, CA: University of California Press.

Bereiter, C., & Bird, M. (1985). Use of thinking aloud in identification and teaching of reading comprehension strategies. *Cognition and Instruction, 2*, 131–56.

Culler, J. (1976). *Structuralist poetics: structuralism, linguistics and the study of literature.* New York: Cornell University Press.

Eco, U. (1990). *The limits of interpretion.* Indianapolis: Indiana University Press.

Ericsson, K. A., & Charness, N. (1994). Expert performance: Its structure and acquisition. *American Psychologist, 49*, 725–47.

Ericsson, K. A., & Simon, H. (1991). *Protocol analysis: Verbal reports as data.* Cambridge, MA: MIT Press.

Flower, L. S., & Hayes, J. R. (1985). The cognition of discovery: Defining a rhetorical problem. *College Composition and Communication, 31*, 21–32.

Frye, N. (1978). *Anatomy of criticism.* Princeton, NJ: Princeton University Press.

Geisler, C. (1994). *Academic literacy and the nature of expertise: Reading, writing, and knowing in academic philosophy.* Hillsdale, NJ: Lawrence Erlbaum.

Gombrich, E. H. (1961). *Art and illusion: A study in the psychology of pictorial representation.* Kingsport, TN: Kingsport Press.

Jakobson, R. (1987). *Language in literature.* Cambridge, MA: Harvard University Press.

Johnston, P., & Afflerbach, P. (1985). The process of constructing main ideas from text. *Cognition and Instruction, 2*, 207–32.

Olson, D. R. (1970). *Cognitive development: The child's acquisition of diagonality.* New York: Academic Press.

Olson, D. R. (1977). From utterance to text: The bias of language in speech and writing. *Harvard Educational Review, 47*, 257–81.

Olson, D. R. (1988). "Or what's a metaphor for?" *Metaphor and Symbolic Activity, 3*, 215–22.

Olson, D. R. (1994). *The world on paper: The conceptual and cognitive implications of writing and reading.* Cambridge, UK: Cambridge University Press.

Olson, D. R. , & Astington, J. W. (1993). Thinking about thinking: Learning how to take statements and hold beliefs. *Educational Psychologist, 28*, 7–23.

Peskin, J. (1992). Ruse and representations: On children's ability to conceal information. *Developmental Psychology, 28*, 84–9.

Peskin, J. (1996). Guise and guile: Children's understanding of narratives in which the purpose of pretense is deception. *Child Development, 67*, 1735–51.

Peskin, J. (1998). Constructing meaning when reading poetry: An expert-novice study. *Cognition and Instruction, 16*, 235–63.

Pope, A. (1965). Poems: 1700–1717: An essay on criticism. In J. Butt (Ed.), *The Poems of Alexander Pope* (pp. 143–168). London: Methuen & Co. Ltd.

Purves, A. C. (1989). That sunny dome: Those caves of ice. In C. R. Cooper (Ed.), *Researching response to literature and the teaching of literature* (pp. 54–69). New Jersey: Ablex Publishers.

Rouet, J., Favart, M., Britt, M. A., & Perfetti, C. A. (1997). Studying and using multiple documents in history: Effects of discipline expertise. *Cognition and Instruction, 15*, 85–106.

Wineburg, S. (1991). Historical problem solving: A study of the cognitive processes used in the evaluation of documentary and pictorial evidence. *Journal of Educational Psychology, 83*, 73–87.

Wineburg, S. (1998). Reading Abraham Lincoln: An expert/expert study in the interpretation of historical texts. *Cognitive Science, 22*, 319–46.

Wineburg (1999) Historical thinking and other unnatural acts. *Phi Delta Kappa, 80*, 488–99.

Appendix A

"On a Drop of Dew" by Andrew Marvell

See how the Orient Dew,   1
Shed from the Bosom of the Morn
  Into the blowing Roses,
Yet careless of its Mansion new,
For the clear Region where 'twas born,   5
  Round in its self incloses,
  And in its little Globes Extent,
Frames as it can its native Element,
How it the purple flow'r does slight,
  Scarce touching where it lyes,   10
But gazing back upon the Skies,
  Shines with a mournful Light;
    Like its own Tear,
Because so long divided from the Sphear.
  Restless it roules and unsecure,   15
    Trembling lest it grow impure:
  Till the warm Sun pitty it's Pain,
And to the Skies exhale it back again.
    So the Soul, that Drop, that Ray
Of the clear Fountain of Eternal Day,   20
Could it within the humane flow'r be seen,
  Remembring still its former height,
  Shuns the sweet leaves and blossoms green;
  And, recollecting its own Light,
Does, in its pure and circling thoughts, express   25
The greater Heaven in an Heaven less.
  In how coy a Figure wound,
  Every way it turns away:
  So the World excluding round,
  Yet receiving in the Day.   30

Dark beneath, but bright above:
Here disdaining, there in Love,
How loose and easie hence to go:
How girt and ready to ascend.
Moving but on a point below,   35
It all about does upwards bend.
Such did the Manna's sacred Dew destil;
White, and intire, though congeal'd and chill.
Congeal'd on Earth: but does, dissolving, run
Into the Glories of th' Almighty Sun.   40

7

Building on the Oral Tradition: How Story Composition and Comprehension Develop

Anne McKeough

My first contact with David Olson was when I was a student at OISE in the early 1980s. David's class was the first I attended upon returning to graduate work after a decade of working as a teacher, counselor, and psychoeducational consultant. I had only one year of sabbatical leave from my school district and wanted desperately to learn all the latest techniques for diagnosing and remediating children's intellectual and social/emotional difficulties. I was unprepared for what I was about to encounter.

When I first began to read the articles and books listed in the course syllabus, I feared that I had enrolled in the wrong program. The theoretical positions laid out in the papers we read seemed far removed from the children I had recently worked with and planned to return to. But I knew an outstanding teacher when I met one – I was struck by the breadth of David's knowledge and I was well aware of what I stood to gain from contact with such a teacher. So I labored on, reading and rereading the texts and struggling to see some link to the flesh and blood children who were so familiar to me. I came to class each week armed with many questions and I marveled as David "romanced" us with his descriptions of cleverly designed studies that offered a glimpse into the minds of children. Until this point in my career, behavioral and psychometric theory had largely informed my thinking about children's social and cognitive development and I thought, "So this is what's in the black box!" I began to read with a different goal; instead of trying to find the children I had known in the literature I was reading, I began using it to discover things about them I had previously been blind to. That small shift made a huge difference for me. As I recalled individuals I had taught, assessed and counseled, I saw them in a new light. Under David's teaching that first semester, I began to change the way I thought about children. I began to consider their behaviors in light of their thoughts and intentions, instead of considering only the environmental factors and psychometric factors that shaped their performance. With this view of children came not only a different and richer understanding of children, but also a desire to be a practicing member of the new interpretive community David had introduced me to. My one year of full-time study at OISE grew to three and other scholars of great distinction, most importantly Robbie Case, also influenced my development. And when I returned to work with children, it was as one who seeks to understand how they "make up their minds" (Olson, 1989).

My contact with David has, fortunately for me, extended beyond my time as a student at OISE. I have met him at conferences where his love of ideas and enthusiasm for knowing enlivens every conversation he is a part of. During his stay as a visiting scholar at The University of Calgary, David attended my research group, and it was a pleasure to see him engage with my students in that same playful yet purposeful way I had experienced two decades earlier. His presence also brought members of our faculty together in the Olson Colloquium – meetings that occasioned many stimulating discussions. His writings have been an important part of the courses I teach and his thinking has continued to impact on my research. In the discussion that follows, I will elaborate on this latter point, highlighting how David's insights into the development of the literate tradition and the changes in individuals' thinking as they develop as members of a literate society have affected my work on the development of story composition and comprehension. I will also tap into David's discussion of how and why the process of meaning construction changed with the advent of widespread writing – his proposal that hermeneutics, the science of interpretation, essentially replaced folk wisdom as an interpretive framework, and how children gradually become enculturated into this interpretive community as they take up literacy practices.

Olson on Oral and Literate Traditions

Olson proposed that, within the oral tradition, events were understood in light of a set of beliefs about how the world works – a folk psychology, which was shared by speakers and listeners within a given community. This folk psychology enabled speakers and listeners to share meanings and understand even unusual occurrences. Within this view, folk psychology brought the unexpected into canonical form, by contextualizing it in one of life's truths, and thus making it less unusual and more plausible. For example, actions that were highly atypical of people in general might be rendered meaningful through the adage, "Like father, like son." It also bound those who shared the beliefs into an *interpretive community* – one where the meaning a speaker intends and the meaning a listener takes can be counted on to be similar (Feldman, this volume, Chapter 2).

Olson (1988) further suggested that certain narrative forms that are rooted in oral tradition, such as folk tales and oral histories, also deal with the "givens" or truths of life. These narratives offer a clear message, often explicitly stated at the end of the story in a moral or piece of folk wisdom, and so no further interpretation is necessary or even possible. Contextualized in folk psychology, these stories serve to validate the group's shared understandings and beliefs, again supporting the exist-

ence of an interpretive community where the gap between what is known through
personal experience and what the community takes as given is a small one (Olson &
Bruner, 1996).

With the advent of widespread literacy, however, there was no guarantee that
writers and readers shared the same meaning-making frameworks and belief systems. As Carol Fleisher Feldman (this volume, Chapter 2) highlights, readers could
not necessarily draw on their personal experience to understand what a writer
intended, and writers could not count on their readers to be members of the same
interpretive community. Olson proposed that this required individuals "to see
what was thought and said in a new way" (Olson, 1994, p. xv). He argued that
writing occasioned the creation of a set of concepts for thinking about speech,
concepts such as words, the very words, literal meaning, and saying as distinct
from meaning (Olson, 1996). Hence, for Olson, literacy is primarily a metalinguistic
activity (Olson, 1994). This allows us, as readers of written text, to revisit them, to
determine if they said what we took them to mean; as writers, we can examine our
texts, asking ourselves, "Does this text say what I mean?" Literate individuals
reach what is meant by examining what was said, thus making a distinction between what is *given* and what is *interpretation*. As a function of literacy, then, we
tend to view the text as an entity, separate from its interpretation. Feldman (this
volume, Chapter 2) argues that, to help the reader glean intended meaning from
what is given in the text, conventions such as genre signals and markers for tropes
were developed. As interpretive communities formalized these conventions, they
were institutionalized in the roles of, for example, editors and teachers (Olson,
personal communication, June 29, 1999). With this institutional knowledge came
a code of fairly clear standards – standards that it is essential for novices to reach
before they can be considered a member of a particular community. In this new
type of interpretive community, the gap between what was taken as given by the
interpretive community and individuals' personal knowledge was considerably wider
than in the oral tradition where personal and social knowledge were so closely
related.

Low-literate and Literate Individuals' Interpretive Stances in the Narrative Domain

My colleagues and I utilized Olson's distinction between the interpretive stances
taken within the oral and literate traditions to examine the literacy efforts of individuals who had not achieved a functional literacy level and compare them to the
practices of literate individuals (see McKeough, Templeton, & Marini, 1995). Our
low-literacy group comprised 10 volunteers who attended publicly funded literacy
programs and who achieved an independent reading level score of grade 3 or less
on the Silvaroli Classroom Reading Inventory, Form D (Silvaroli, 1986). The literacy group of 10 volunteers was recruited from post-secondary colleges and all
subjects were assessed as having reached ceiling on the same reading inventory, that

is, above a grade 8 level. Criteria for inclusion in the study was average to high average ability as assessed by the Wechsler Adult Intelligence Scale-Revised (Wechsler, 1981). We asked the participants to compose an original story and to listen to another story, then retell it, and describe the main character.

Story composition

For the narrative composition component, participants were asked to compose a story "about somebody who had a problem he or she wanted to solve." The story was to be geared to an adult audience and was to include a surprise or unexpected ending. The goal was to elicit optimal performance and to encourage subjects to include what Bruner (1986) has referred to as narrative's dual landscapes – the landscapes of action and of consciousness.

We used a developmental model developed in earlier work (McKeough, 1992; 1997a; 1997b; McKeough et al., 1995; see Figure 7.1) to analyze the compositions. This model is base on Case's (1985, 1992) theory which asserts that, while cognitive development follows a general pattern that can be accounted for, in part, by stage-related increases in processing capacity, it also requires domain-specific conceptual knowledge that is constructed through experience and reflection. Our model comprised three categories of narrative compositions – *action, intentional*, and *interpretive* and was constructed by analyzing the original story compositions of individuals aged 4 to 18 years of age. Briefly, the least structurally complex stories are action stories. They relate a sequence of events wherein actions are ordered in the following form: within some specified setting, the protagonist does "A" and then "B" and then " C." These stories are stereotypic social scripts (Nelson, 1981) and do not differentiate action from the mental states that motivate them or occur in association with them. Intentional stories, in contrast, consist of a plot wherein action is motivated by characters' intentions (i.e., what they want, feel, or think). They typically have the structure of folk tales and comprise a problem and its resolution. In their more complex form, complications, sub-plots, and failed attempts at problem resolution also appear. To construct this type of story, authors need to reflect on the actions and states that occur in the physical world and to account for, or respond to them by describing story characters' internal mental worlds. Consequently, intentional stories begin to differentiate between Bruner's (1986) two landscapes. The third and most complex type of story has been termed interpretive, to indicate that authors reflect on, interpret, and account for why characters hold particular mental states. That is, relations among the protagonist's actions and mental states are established, for example, on the basis of personal history and long-standing psychological traits. Interpretive stories follow the general pattern of the western short story, with its psychological focus – where, as Bruner has stated, the "engine of action moves from the plot to the character" (Bruner, 1986, p. 37). As shown in Table 7.1, a scoring scheme based on this model has been developed (McKeough, 1992; McKeough et al., 1995). Stories that are entirely action-based are assigned a score of 1; intention-based stories are assigned a score of 2, 3, or 4 depending on

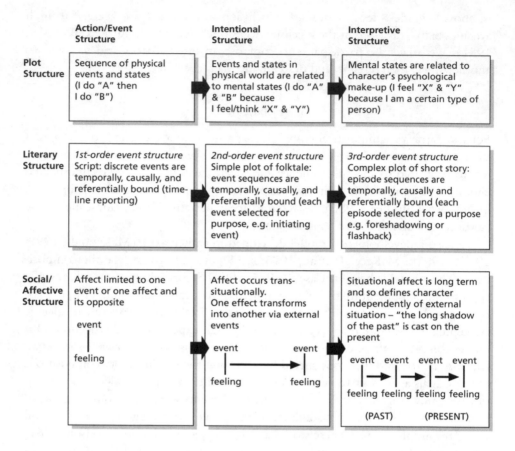

Figure 7.1   Model of narrative development.

the level of complexity; interpretive stories are assigned scores of 5, 6, or 7, again, depending on their level of complexity. (For a more complete discussion of the scoring scheme, see McKeough, 1992; 1997a; 1997b.)

In general terms, statistical analyses of the data determined that, as predicted, two distinct interpretive frameworks existed – one that reflected the folk psychology similar to that which is found in folk tales and that formed the backbone of the oral tradition (the intentional category) and another that drew on the literate tradition typical of the western novel or short story (the interpretive category). Low-literate participants typically utilized a folk tale structure that centered on a hero whose actions are driven by both external circumstance and internal motivation. In these stories, unusual actions and events were frequently made plausible by reference to folk psychology, as the following orally generated story illustrates:

Bill and Bob were having problems with chest pains and Bill decided to go to the doctor's and get it checked out because it was always hurting and he had a big mark on

Table 7.1 Developmental Scoring Scheme

Action	Does the story have a sequence of events that are temporally, causally, or referentially related and that occur exclusively in the physical world of action and events? (Note: "happily ever after" not scored as a mental state)	⟶ NO – Level 0

| YES
↓

Intentional	Does the story include explicit or implicit reference to the mental states that motivate action in the physical world and is there a problem that is immediately resolved in the end?	⟶ NO – Level 1

| YES
↓

	Does the story have a problem, a series of failed attempts or complications followed by a resolution (not necessarily solving the problem), such that additional mental states are mentioned or implied in the context of the story?	⟶ NO – Level 2

| YES
↓

	Does one impediment or a well-developed sub-plot have more significance than the others, thereby also broadening the characters' intentions/mental states? Is the impediment dealt with in the outcome, with the result that the resolution has a well-planned feeling?	⟶ NO – Level 3

| YES
↓

Interpretive	Does the focus of the story shift from the characters' mental states to *why* particular mental states are held? Does a constellation of mental states or constellation of social circumstances create a psychological profile or character trait that is represented across time and situations?	⟶ NO – Level 4

| YES
↓

	Are additional traits represented, such that a dialectic is created wherein the interaction of two states or traits lead to further psychologically oriented complications?	⟶ NO – Level 5

| YES
↓

	Does the dialectical relation between states or traits act as an integrating device lending a greater sense of coherence to the story?	⟶ NO – Level 6

| YES
↓

Level 7

his chest like a hard ball. It kept going in and out. So he went to the doctor's one day
and the doctor turned around and he said, "You got cancer." So Bill went home and
told Bob because he had the same problem. So Bill said he was going for the operation. So Bill went in, had the operation done. And the doctor told Bob he should have
it done. Bill died on the table, soon as they cut him open. And Bob turned around and
he said he'd stay alive because he didn't want it to be done. The doctor turned around
and said, "Six months at the most." So Bob turned around and he said, "I'll take my
chances with the six months." He's been going, oh, about 16 years now or more. And
he's still got his family and kids and he's happy and he says he's not going to pay the
doctor until he dies.

The action in this story is clearly driven by both circumstances that exist in the
world – Bill's experiences, and the main characters' thoughts, beliefs, and intentions. Moreover, the author uses folk psychology to create and account for his main
character's unusual actions, his refusal of the recommended surgery. There is nothing within the story to explain why someone might choose this course of action,
beyond referring to the mental state that motivated it ("he didn't want it to be
done"). When Bob's decision is considered in light of folk wisdom – if a cancerous
growth is exposed to air when the body is cut open, like fire, it often rages out of
control – his refusal of surgery is reasonable, however. As Olson has noted, folk
psychology makes the unusual more understandable (Olson & Bruner, 1996). Although the author does not state this explicitly, within a certain folk psychology it is
taken as given – there is an assumption of a shared belief. And according to Feldman
(this volume, Chapter 2), in oral practice, speakers (and storytellers in the oral
tradition) orient to the interpretive system they expect their listeners to hold.

In contrast, literate participants did not rely on folk psychology, but instead,
accounted for their characters' unusual actions by creating a context within the
story world that made them plausible. They use a different set of conventions –
conventions that allow them to explore the psychology of their characters through
the use of figurative language, symbolism, and flashbacks or potent memories, for
example. The following written story illustrates this point:

The busses roared by the stops like great dinosaurs. Paul watched them with blank
eyes, waiting for the right number to trigger a response. At last his bus arrived and he
slowly milled with the rest of the people to it. He found his seat overlooking the right
picture ad. It was important to find an appealing ad so he could quickly avert his eyes
to it when caught staring. It wasn't that people were unusual, it was just that they all
had that look. You know, the one that says, "Help, I don't know what it's all about."
Maybe he stared because he always felt as though he was staring at a mirror.

   Soon he started recognizing landmarks and buildings. This signaled the end of his
ride, and after ringing for his stop, he labored his way off. The office. The place where
most of his time was spent. The sight of it made him remember how he'd felt the first
day. Excitement for his first job, nervousness because of the fear. More than anything
he wanted to succeed.

   Three years later and all that was left was the desire to succeed. But not at the job, at
life. What did it mean to him? Well, nothing really grand. He wasn't unreasonable, he

just wanted to be happy with his work. He stopped at the door to pick up the mail. Always the first here, he thought. Not because he was excited to start, just in a hurry to get it over with.

He heard a noise from around the alley and peered around the corner. There was a bagman, one of the homeless, quickly filling his shopping bag with discarded paper. Paul didn't want to scare him, but he felt a sudden urge to talk with this man.

"Good morning," he said. "Are you finding what you need?"

The bagman looked up, he wasn't old, just weathered and worn.

"I don't need anything except the air I breathe my friend," he said.

Paul felt a sudden wave of sorrow. For himself, but also for many like him.

"How can you be so free?" he cried.

"Freedom is an everyday effort, not a commodity. It comes when you enjoy the journey and forget about the destination," said the man.

Paul turned from him and went back to the front door. Slowly he turned the key in the lock, feeling the tumblers fall. Just as the lock clicked open, he knew his final tumbler had fallen and his lock was open. He pushed open the door, knowing that today would be the last day he saw this office. As he stepped in, a bus roared by on the street, and he turned and saw the faces in the windows. Each one unique and individual, not without fear, but it was their fear, not his.

The author of this story created a fairly coherent, albeit stereotypic picture of the character's psychological make-up within the story by, for example, across-situation contrasts (i.e., earlier in his working career Paul was emotionally and intellectually alive but now he is numb) and comparisons with other "lost souls" similarly afflicted (e.g., "Maybe he stared because he always felt as though he was staring at a mirror."). The psychological profile he presents allows readers to understand the character's unusual actions throughout the story; appeal to folk wisdom is not necessary. This capacity to create a text that can stand on it own, decontexualized from what the reader knows of the specific writer's beliefs, is part of the legacy of written text (Olson, 1996). The type of characterization evident in this story reflects two features of the Western novel: Bruner's second landscape, the landscape of consciousness, occupies center stage and the engine of action lies in the character, not in the plot, as is the case with folk tales (Bruner, 1986).

In summary, the low-literacy participants composed stories that were qualitatively different from those composed by the literate group. The latter were more similar to the short story or modern western novel. In spite of the differences, however, it is clear that the low-literate participants' stories clearly met Bruner's (1990) four narrative criteria, namely, events occurred in a sequence, they focused on something in particular, dealt with intentionality, and highlighted both canonicality and breach.

Story recall and interpretation

For the narrative recall task participants were asked to listen to a taped story, approximately 4,700 words in length, and to retell it as though they were telling it to

someone who had not heard the story before. The goal was to elicit the most complete retelling possible, without suggesting exact recall. The story we used was a
slightly edited short story (Duczek, 1988) that appeared in an anthology of short
stories composed by adolescents. Very briefly, it is about a woman who runs out of
gasoline while driving along an isolated road. A man offers her a drive and she
reluctantly accepts it. Her reluctance is based, we are told, on long-standing feelings of distrust of men stemming from a lifetime of insensitive and sometimes cruel
treatment at their hands. Her worst fears are realized when the man kidnaps and
imprisons her. But she is determined to escape and end her victimization. Eventually she overpowers him, beating him into unconsciousness, and in so doing, feels
she is taking revenge for the wrongdoings of all men. While looking for his car keys
so that she can escape, she discovers that he is wealthy. Reflecting on her situation,
she decides not to inform the authorities (who are, of course, largely male) and
instead imprisons her captor and lives off his investments. We selected this particular story for two reasons: First, it met general standards for interestingness for an
adult sample in that the characters were adult, the story took place in a familiar
setting, and the goal was both important and difficult to attain (Hedberg & Stoel-
Gammon, 1986; Jose & Brewer, 1983; Mandler, 1982). Second, the story contained action, intentional, and interpretive elements and so allowed for retelling at
all three levels.

The gist paradigm was used to score the narrative recall protocols (Tindal &
Marston, 1990). This form of recall involves memory of story content rather than
verbatim recall (Kintsch, 1977). The unit of analysis used was the T-unit. T-units
are the shortest grammatically complete sentences that a passage can be cut into
without creating fragments. T-units, or terminable units, are defined as "a single
clause plus whatever subordinate or non-clauses are attached to, or embedded within,
that main clause. A clause is defined as a subject (or coordinated subjects) with a
finite verb or coordinated finite verb" (Hunt, 1977, pp. 92–93).

The initial step in our analysis was to conduct a T-unit analysis of the target story
as follows:

First, T-units were identified. A total of 95 T-units were identified in the target
recall text. Next, T-units were classified into the following three types, corresponding to the three levels of narrative described in Figure 7.1:

1   Action/Descriptive T-units: Action T-units describe physical movement (e.g.,
    "She ran across the gravel."), and descriptive T-units give information concern-
    ing settings or physical states and events transcribed by a copula verb (e.g.,
    "The sky was gray, dull, and heavy" and "She is on a deserted road."). Seventy
    action/descriptive T-units were identified and these comprised 73.68% of the
    target text.
2   Intentional T-units refer to first-order mental states, such as thoughts, needs,
    wishes, and plans, that motivate action (e.g., "She decided to escape") or social
    judgments (e.g., "The plan worked quite well"). Nineteen intentional T-units
    were identified and these comprised 20% of the target text.

3 Interpretive T-units refer to second-order mental states that underlie first-order mental states. Six interpretive T-units were identified and these comprised 6.32% of the text. They utilize a subordinate clause construction that can take one of three forms:

(a) A justification of an intention (e.g., "She was uneasy about getting in the van (first-order mental state) because she didn't trust men" (second-order mental state)). The initial clause, "She was uneasy about getting in the van" would have been considered an intentional T-unit if it had stood alone. With the addition of the underlying motivation, "because she didn't trust men," however, the entire statement is categorized as an interpretive T-unit.

(b) A justification of a character traits (e.g., "She never complained about bad service in restaurants because she was a shy person"). The initial clause, "She never complained about bad service in restaurants," would have been considered an intentional T-unit if it had stood alone. With the addition of the second clause that specified a personality trait, "she was a shy person," however, the entire statement is categorized as an interpretive T-unit.

(c) A consequence of an action or intention that extends to other times or situations (e.g., "She takes revenge not only against Ferdinand but against all the other males she hated"). The initial clause, "She takes revenge . . . against Ferdinand" would have been considered an intentional T-unit if it had stood alone. However, with the addition of the second clause that specified an extension of the vengeful feelings to "all the other males she hated," the entire statement is categorized as an interpretive T-unit.

The second step in the analysis was to use the above criteria to score the subjects' recall protocols for the type of T-units recalled (i.e., action/descriptive, intentional, and interpretive). By way of illustration, consider the following two recall segments dealing with the protagonist's escape from her kidnapper, Ferdinand, and her revenge. The first protocol segment, generated by a literate subject, contains the three types of T-units. (Action/description T-units are left unmarked, intentional t-units are italicized, and interpretive T-units are bolded).

She hunted around the room for some loose object to disable Ferdinand with so she could escape. It took her some time and she managed to get the bookshelves out. *(She) planned to clobber Ferdinand when he was locking up or unlocking the door, one or the other. The plan worked quite well, except her motivation took over from what was necessary* and **she took revenge on Ferdinand for every guy that had ever done anything to her in her life, by the look of it**. *Anyway he was beaten quite badly. She felt quite victorious about the whole situation, locking Ferdinand in the room and going upstairs* . . . While she was looking for the keys to get out of the place in his truck, she found a whole pile of papers *and it seemed like Ferdinand was quite well off*. **She decided, well, in this male dominated society where she would have to explain to a whole pile of males what may seem to be an incredulous story, and elevate herself**

again, and again, and again, she felt that, well, why bother? *She could have it all.* She had Ferdinand locked up downstairs, the fact that he had all this money here, *and took it upon herself to look after herself for the rest of her life.*

The following protocol segment, generated by a low-literate subject differs from the above sample in that it contains only action/descriptive and intentional T-units:

> After nine days, I finally got the shelf off. *I hardly slept that night at all because I was trying to think and that.* Then when he rang to come in he rang as usual. Ten minutes. I got up and went to the sink and told him to come in. He came in and he put the padlock on the top and when he bent down to put the other one, I rushed over from the sink and when he looked up I hit him over the head with the board quite a few times. He was bleeding pretty good. I dragged him away from the door, unlocked the door and ran up to the house. . . . *I knew I should have called the cops right away but there was no phone.* I started looking through a lot of papers *and I found out the guy was a very rich man. I figured, if I'm going to get revenge, I might as well go all the way* and *I decided to go downstairs, unlock the door.* I got a chain and I locked his leg against a steel pipe. Then I drove to town and did my tests that I had to do for my school. I invested some of his money and it paid out pretty good.

As can be seen in the above excerpts, the low-literacy subject described the main character's actions as occurring in response to her feelings and thoughts about Ferdinand, whereas the literate subject also made reference to the character's distilled and long-standing feelings toward males, in general. The low-literate subject's recall of descriptive/action and intentional T-units suggests that he focused more on the "given" of the text (i.e., what is assumed or taken for granted about people's actions, in the light of certain mental states), rather than on the interpretation of the text (i.e., why the characters feel or think as they do).

We also asked participants to describe the main character in a story they had just listened to, and found the two groups differed in a fashion similar to that Olson identified as characterizing the oral and literate traditions. Although both groups gave accurate accounts of the character, capturing her complexity and uniqueness, literate individuals engaged in metalinguistic activities and low-literate individuals assumed the folk psychology stance typical of the oral tradition. The following response is typical of the literate group. The participant reflects on the text, takes it as an object, and analyses it. That is, he differentiates between portions of the text that deal with the character's self-description and those that are part of the flow of events, identifies some descriptive elements as "the most obvious" and others as "the critical stuff," and disassociates himself from the character's appraisal of what might be considered "well being." (These portions of the text are italicized.) In other words, both the text and the contents of the text are discussed.

> She seemed to be a very repressed person . . . *in her early description of herself.* And even though it hurts inside, she won't let them know it hurts because that's the way she was told to be. *Looking at the evidence of her self-description,* she must have been a

very lonely person. . . . She (also) seemed a bit of a plotting person, a conniving person. *Not from her self-description but from the evidence that she plotted against Ferdinand. That's the most obvious, of course.* But also . . . to hold a lot of things back until the appropriate times, that requires a bit of forethought. . . *The critical stuff was that she . . . used Ferdinand, as* – well, he tried to use her – but she used Ferdinand as a channel for all of that – not just against Ferdinand but against all men, period – and put herself in a position of power and – *according to her* – well being.

Unlike the preceding character description, in the following sample produced by a low-literate subject no mention is made of the text as separate from its contents. Whereas the literate subject made distinctions between the various parts of the text, the low-literacy subject referred solely to its contents. Nevertheless, this description captures the main character's traits very adequately and highlights her transformation (from being fearful, isolated, and nervous to being happy and heedless). This participant also gave a good account of the factors in the world that occasioned the main character's various mental states and traits (e.g., ". . . everybody wanted to taunt her") and, albeit to a more limited extent, justification of one mental state with another (e.g., "She just couldn't control (her fear) after awhile" because "fear was building up in her more than she realized"). This is accomplished, however, mainly by the additive effect of problematic relations, which culminated in the unexpected and the unexpected is made canonical through reference to the folk adage – "Like they say, when you corner them, that's it."

> (She was) very scared and lived a sheltered life. Very hidden, kept to herself. Very hidden away from people. A very nervous type person. Very scared. It seemed like everybody wanted to taunt her and she didn't know how to deal with it. . . . So she seemed to get more scared every time and fear was building up in her more than she realized. She just couldn't control it after awhile. . . And she figured she might as well go all the way. If she got nailed, she didn't care. She was to the point of no return of caring. Like they say, when you corner them, that's it.

Based on these analyses, we concluded that the interpretive stance of individuals who lacked literacy skills was qualitatively different from their literate counterparts. Within Olson's view, the former stems from literate practices while the latter reflects practices largely derived from the oral tradition. Our literate participants used a set of conventions different from those used by the low-literate participants – conventions that reflected decontextualized thought and that were typical of the western novel rather than the folk tale. Moreover, they did not rely on shared meaning between reader and writer (Feldman, this volume, Chapter 2), referred to the text as an entity separate from its contents (Olson, 1986), and composed texts that were internally coherent (McKeough et al., 1995).

Adolescents' Use of Flashback as a Literary Convention

Although the study summarized above highlights some conventions typical of western literary practice, there are certainly other conventions that writers come to utilize as they become part of this interpretive community. In studies of young adolescents developing competence, we found that adolescents can use flashbacks in order to create the inner worlds of characters and to lend poignancy to events and depth to characterization (Genereux & McKeough, in preparation). They construct two or more time lines by manipulating the flow of the plot and juxtapose them in such a way as to contextualize one within the other. In order to achieve this effect, they must create text segments that deal with the story characters' presents and pasts and mark the event sequences as such in the text. In the following sample story, we see two instances of temporal manipulations of this sort – one that takes the narrator back in time and one that lays out past events in the life of the troubled young girl who the narrator meets.

Guilty!

The sun glared at the deep blue ocean and the ocean glittered back the touch of its warmth. . . . Everybody was happy. Children played on the beach . . . and couples walked along the shore, hand in hand.

On one side of the beach, the cliffs looked dangerous with its jagged edges sprouting out from its sides. There hung a sign covered with red warning tape that read, "Danger. Do not enter". . .

(The protagonist walks to the top of the cliff and sees a depressed adolescent sitting near the cliff's edge, staring out over the ocean. Seeing the girl occasions a flashback.)

I thought back to the last time I had come up to the cliffs. There was a teenager . . . I went to wake him up but at the sound of my footsteps, he got up with a look of fear. At his feet, I observed a gun . . . and when he saw that I noticed the gun, he became terrified. Suddenly, out of the blue, he jumped off. I was in shock and couldn't move a muscle. For the last year, I've been blaming myself for not stopping him and so I have a regular psychiatrist.

It was exactly a year today (since) . . . the incident had happened. I was scared. I could remember last night, how the psychiatrist had told me to return here and try to put the past behind me. Now, I can feel the mistake of her judgment.

(The protagonist starts a conversation with the girl who reveals that it was her boy friend who committed suicide and describes past events that make her feel responsible for his death because she had broken off the relationship.)

"We were in love. Well that's what we thought. A few weeks before he jumped, I told him it was over . . . He went 'berserk!' . . . Then, while I was in school, he jumped from this cliff . . . I shouldn't have broke up with him."

"You know that you're wrong in thinking his death was your fault," I explained. I tried to think back to my appointments with my psychiatrist and what she had told me. "You don't really know why he jumped. . . . I'll bet he had problems at home that probably made him depressed . . . No one knows why a person commits suicide but you must think of it as an accident.

"Thank you. I feel better talking about it. . . ." She walked away. I sat by the tree and stared out at the ocean. . . . The water below looked calm. The sun slowly slid away and left an aurora of lights in the sky.

In this story, the young author manipulated the time line by presenting a central event, the youth's suicide, out of chronological order as a recollection. In so doing, she uses it to explore the psychology of guilt, rather than telling about the act itself. The recalled event unites the two strangers, placing them on a similar mission – to expunge the inappropriate and counter-productive guilt they feel because of the part they played in the event. The recollections of the suicide by both the narrator and the young girl contextualize their actions and psychological states. By having both characters tell the story of the youth's suicide, the author makes their unusual behavior plausible. That is, the recollections explain both the narrator's trek away from the idyllic beach, up the forbidden trail and the young girl's sad presence on the cliff's edge. Thus, by using the two flashbacks, the author managed to do much more that provide background information; she created characters with greater psychological depth than might exist otherwise and created a context within the story world that helped the readers to understand the characters' psychology. Although creating flashbacks is not the only literary convention this young writer used (for example, she has tried her hand at using a version of the *sympathy of nature* device), it is a device that has been found to occur in a significantly greater proportion of stories at this age range (Genereux & McKeough, in preparation).

What is lacking in this account, however, is an explanation of how these different conventions come to be taken up by young writers. Olson proposed that the conventions are "canons" and are institutionalized in the person of editors and teachers who insist that they be used by all of those who claim membership in certain interpretive communities (Olson, pers. comm. June 29, 1999). A preliminary analysis of young adolescents writing journals suggests that they are aware of these "canons" and strive to integrate them into their writing practices (McKeough, 1998). Very briefly, we conducted a T-unit analysis of grade 7 students' journals, written while they were being taught to compose *interpretive* stories and, following the procedure outlined in the low-literate/literate comparison study, we categorized the T-units as action/descriptive, intentional, or interpretive. Although anecdotal in nature, our data suggest that students are aware of, and recognize, the importance of certain of these conventions including developing psychological depth in characters, making substantive revisions, and using writing to explore the perspective of others. The following statements illustrate this awareness:

(a) "I learned a lot from this whole thing (the instruction sessions) like how to dig deeper into a character's mind which I think is very important because you really have to know the character or else the whole point is lost. (b) Most of all I learned to let go of a first draft." (c) "I thought it would be a neat thing or a sad thing to try to put myself in their shoes or situation."

The mental practices illustrated in the comments of these novice writers are the hallmarks of a literate interpretive community. Within the literate community, writers practice a set of conventions which are different from those practiced within the oral tradition and which are, according to Olson, supported by the type of decontextualized practices found in institutions such as schools. These practices require writers to take a metaposition to the texts they create – to take them as the object of their cognition, treating them as entities that are distinct from their contents. Thus, as Olson proposed, literacy is largely a metalinguistic activity (Olson, 1994).

Conclusion

A good deal of work remains to be done, however, before we understand how novices come to use the conventions of a literate community. One promising approach is to investigate the various developmental pathways young writers take in striving to compose what we have called *interpretive* narratives. Literary devices that published authors use and that adolescents manage fairly effectively clearly are not limited to those discussed in this chapter. Besides creating characters in increasing psychological depth via flashbacks, adolescent authors use devices such as creating a story within a story (Genereux & McKeough, in preparation) and surprise endings (Case et al., 1996). These literary techniques require them to construct a double meaning – one that is immediately apparent as the text is read and another that becomes evident when the story's end is reached. To accomplish this feat, authors need to understand that "the very words" they write can carry two meanings, depending on the reader's position in the text. This awareness of readers' capacity to interpret, according to Olson, is part of our literate legacy and stems from the set of categories that writing has allowed us to develop (Olson, 1994).

In closing as I reflect back upon the process of writing this chapter, two thoughts stand out from all the others. The first is that David Olson continues to teach me. In attempting to do as Janet Astington requested – to discuss how David's work has influenced mine – I have had to view my developmental analyses from a different perspective. It has made me more aware of the need to focus on the cultural conventions and literary practices that surround and inform young writers and that provide a context for their developing competence.

The second thought that surfaces is not new to me. At the outset of this chapter, I commented that during my first few contacts with David, I recognized him as a superb teacher. His love of ideas and his willingness to share his knowledge, his intellectual curiosity and commitment to understanding and knowing make him a model of all that is best in our academic community. I count myself among the very fortunate because I know him.

References

Bruner, J. (1986). *Actual minds, possible worlds.* Cambridge, MA: Harvard University Press.

Bruner, J. (1990). *Acts of meaning.* Cambridge, MA: Harvard University Press.

Case, R. (1985). *Intellectual development: Birth to adulthood.* New York: Academic Press.

Case, R. (Ed.) (1992). *The mind's staircase: Exploring the conceptual underpinnings of children's thought and knowledge.* Hillsdale, NJ: Erlbaum.

Case, R., Okamoto, Y., Griffin, S., McKeough, A., Bleiker, C., Henderson, B., & Stephenson, M. K. (1996). The role of central conceptual structures in the development of children's thought. *Monographs of the Society for Research in Child Development, 61* (1–2, Serial No. 246).

Duczek, J. (1988). Reversal. In T. Bowen (Ed.), *Anthology 88: Significant perceptions* (pp. 142–50). Calgary, AB: Calgary Catholic Schools.

Genereux, R., & McKeough, A. (in preparation). *The development of narrative composition and interpretation in adolescence.* Unpublished manuscript, University of Calgary.

Hedberg, N., & Stoel-Gammon, C. (1986). Narrative analysis: Clinical procedures. *Topics in Language Disorders, 71,* 58–69.

Hunt, K. (1977). Early blooming and late blooming syntactical structures. In C. Cooper and L. Odell (Eds.), *Evaluating writing* (pp. 90–104). Urbana, IL: National Council of Teachers of English.

Jose, P., & Brewer, W. (1983). *The development of story liking: Character identification, suspense, and outcome resolution* (Report No. 291). Urbana, MI: University of Urbana Study of Reading. (Eric Document Reproduction Service No. ED 236 547).

Kintsch, W. (1977). On comprehending stories. In M. A. Just and P. A. Carpenter (Eds.), *Cognitive processes in comprehension* (pp. 33–62). Hillsdale, NJ: Erlbaum.

Mandler, J. M. (1982). Recent research on story grammars. In J. F. Le Ny and W. Kintsch (Eds.), *Language and comprehension* (pp. 207–18). Amsterdam: North Holland.

McKeough A. (1992). The structural foundations of children's narrative and its development. In R. Case (Ed.), *The mind's staircase: Exploring the conceptual underpinnings of children's thought and knowledge* (pp. 171–88). Hillsdale, NJ: Erlbaum.

McKeough, A. (1997a). Changes in narrative knowledge across the school years: Evidence from typical and atypical populations. In A. Smorti (Ed.), *The self as text: Construction of stories and construction of the self* (pp. 277–307). Florence, Italy: Giunti.

McKeough, A. (1997b). Narrative knowledge and its development: Toward an integrative framework. *Issues in Education: Contributions for Educational Psychology, 2,*146–55.

McKeough, A. (July, 1998). *Examining narrative thought in story compositions and learning journals: A developmental approach to teaching adolescents.* Paper presented at the Biennial Meeting of the International Society for the Study of Behavioral Development, Berne, Switzerland.

McKeough, A., Templeton, L. N., & Marini, A. (1995). Conceptual change in narrative knowledge: Psychological understandings of low-literate and literate adults. *Journal of Narrative and Life History, 5,* 21–49.

Nelson, K. (1981). Social cognition in a script framework. In J. H. Flavell & L. Ross (Eds.), *Social cognitive development: Frontiers and possible futures* (pp. 97–118). Cambridge, UK: Cambridge University Press.

Olson, D. (1986). The cognitive consequences of literacy. *Canadian Psychology, 27,* 109–21.

Olson, D. (1988). Mind and media: The epistemic functions of literacy. *Journal of Commu-*

nication, 38, 27–36.

Olson, D. (1989). Making up your mind. *Canadian Psychology, 30*, 617–27.

Olson, D. (1994). *The world on paper*. Cambridge, UK: Cambridge University Press.

Olson, D. (1996). Toward a psychology of literacy: On the relations between speech and writing. *Cognition, 60*, 83–194.

Olson, D., & Bruner, J. (1996) Folk psychology and folk pedogogy. In D. Olson and N. Torrance (Eds.), *The handbook of education and human development* (pp. 9–27). Cambridge, MA: Blackwell.

Silvaroli, N. (1986). *Classroom Reading Inventory*. Dubuque, IO: Wm. C. Brown.

Tindal, G., & Marston, D. (1990). *Classroom-based assessment*. Columbus, OH: Merrill.

Weschler, D. (1981). *Weschler Adult Intelligence Scale-Revised*. New York: The Psychological Corporation, Harcout Brace Jovanovich.

8

From Action to Writing: Modes of Representing and Knowing

Gordon Wells

In his book, *Before Writing*, Gunter Kress (1997) discusses the many modes in which children represent meaning before they master the system of writing. His illustrations include: drawings, some of them colored in, or cut out and adorned with further material; three-dimensional figures; and – my favorite – a photograph of a "pillow car," made from two wire-mesh drawers, a pillow, a red toolbox and other objects, all carefully arranged so that the two girls who made it could sit in the car with their doll passengers. Surprisingly, it might seem, the car has neither gear-shift nor steering wheel. However, as Kress comments, this is "not because this car's makers do not know about them, but because they are not relevant for the purposes of this car's users and makers" (p. 32). The point of the illustrations is to support his central argument: in making meaning with and through signs of various kinds, people – old as well as young – act out of their current *interest* and put to use in sign-making *whatever is to hand*. Furthermore, since the sign is almost always a means to an end in some larger activity, usually involving others as well as the signmaker, he claims that "all signs show rationality, logic, human desire and affect" (p. 19).

It is these claims that I want to explore in this chapter. My ultimate purpose is to consider the modes of representation that are available for exploitation in developing understanding in educational settings and, in so doing, I will argue for a broadening of the current limited – and limiting – focus on written text that is typical of most classrooms. This is perhaps ironic in a book honoring David Olson, who has done so much to clarify the potential of writing for knowing and understanding. Since I moved to OISE in 1984, David and I have spent many hours discussing writing and related issues and I have benefited enormously from his provocative observations, even when I don't agree with them. Indeed, there is nothing so stimulating for one's own thinking as the attempt to construct arguments to counter the opposition. Thus, I do not wish to decry the value and versatility of written text and its role in the classroom. However, like Kress, I believe that children make meaning in many ways before mastering writing and educators need to value and build on these other modes. Before broaching this topic, however, I first wish to consider the perspectives on representation offered by writers from a number of other disciplines.

It is generally agreed that human mental activity has to do with representations but, beyond that, there is considerable difference of opinion on such questions as: Do other species also make representations? If so, for what purpose? What is the nature of representations? Are they stored in the mind and retrieved in a relatively fixed form, or are they created on the fly in response to the demands of the situation? How are representations related to propositions realized in linguistic form? Following Vygotsky's (1981) precept, I shall adopt a genetic approach in my attempt to answer these questions, starting with a phylogenetic perspective from contemporary work in brain science.

A Phylogenetic View from Neuroscience

While studying the brain activity of rabbits in response to sensory stimulation, Walter Freeman made an interesting discovery. Contrary to the generally accepted view, he found that "the traces of [sensory] stimuli seemed to be replaced by constructions of neural activity, which lacked invariance with respect to the stimuli that triggered them. The conclusion seemed compelling. The only knowledge the rabbit could have of the world outside itself was what it had made in its own brain" (Freeman, 1995, p. 2).

This finding and the conclusion drawn from it may seem to be very far removed from the study of human meaning making; but Freeman argues otherwise. There are important continuities in the evolution of brain structure, organization, and function, he claims, that link humans to much simpler organisms even than rabbits and, in developing his thesis, he draws not only on studies of mammalian brains but also on recent work made possible by the development of non-invasive techniques for scanning the activity of human brains (cf. Deacon, 1997; Edelman, 1992).

On this basis, Freeman proposes that, in origin, meaning arises from an organism's activity in fulfilling its needs to find and ingest food, to mate and reproduce its kind, and to avoid predators and other threats to its survival. For species that are mobile, this activity requires a "cognitive map" that enables the organism to orient itself in space and time and this, in turn, is constructed on the basis of the information derived from the organism's actions into the world. As in the case of the rabbit, Freeman argues, information from the sensory systems is incorporated into the cognitive map, constantly updating it. It is also incorporated into the brain's continuing unity of intentionality (i.e., purposefulness) and so contributes to the changing focus of attention and of action.

What an organism "knows," therefore, it knows as a result of its own actions, which are uniquely situated in space and time. Over its lifetime, it constructs its own trajectory and cognitive map from the genetically determined groundwork by grasping for available sensory input from within and outside its own body. Thus, although to a considerable degree each member of a species shares a common genetic inheritance and a common ecological niche, its intentional structure is unique, as is the "knowledge" that it constructs.

However, although solipsistic, brains do not exist in isolation. If only for the reproduction of the species, they need to interact with other brains. Furthermore, in the case of humans, in particular, brains and minds develop in a social as well as a material world. Brains are members of societies, Freeman argues, and this requires them to coordinate their intentionality with the intentionality of others. In part, this is made possible by the fact that the world into which humans act is a cultural world that has been shaped by prior generations of human artifact-mediated activity. And in part it occurs through the attempt to establish mutual understanding while acting into the social world of joint activity, in the course of which human brains create the shared channels, codes, and protocols that make possible the give and take of information in sign-mediated dialogue.

> Thinking is a process by which some pattern [of neuroactivity] is actualized from the intentional structure into meaning and deployed into the world. Thoughts . . . enact the emergence of meaning as a set of relations in a place in an intentional structure, in accordance with which representations are shaped by actions into the world. A representation formed and sent by one brain evokes thought that leads to the construction of meaning in a brain receiving the representation. (Freeman, 1995, p. 107)[1]

However, there is no suggestion that the representations themselves persist or become the material on which further operations are performed. On the contrary, representations are constructed for the occasion on the basis of the constantly emerging and developing self-organization of neuroactivity. For Freeman, representations are "actions into the world," not the contents of an embodied mind.

Nevertheless, although it is undoubtedly the case that all representations, in whatever mode, are created in and through action, some human representations leave a record of their creation that gives rise to representational objects that can have a life of their own. With training, bards and orators were able to remember and reproduce spoken utterances and, with the advent of drawing, writing and other visuographic modes of semiosis, the demands on memory were offloaded on to representations that had a permanent existence, independent of the action that produced them. The question that must now be considered, then, is: Can such representational objects be considered to contain meaning? And if so, can one, by memorizing the representations created by others, acquire a store of knowledge that can be applied when the occasion arises? On both these questions, Freeman is quite unequivocal: although representations are intended to elicit thought in others, in themselves they have no meaning.

At one level, Freeman is undoubtedly correct. The text, as physical object, has no meaning other than as a collection of ink marks on a surface or, in the case of a computer file, as images on a screen; and even when treated as a text in a recognizable language, the meaning is not in the text itself but in readers' transactions with the text (Rosenblatt, 1978). And as others besides Rosenblatt have argued, different readers create different meanings in the course of these transactions and even the same reader will create different meanings on the first and subsequent readings of the same text. As a result, the idea that any text has a single unique meaning has had to be abandoned, even by its strongest supporters (cf. Olson, 1995).

However, there is another level at which representations have been considered to have meaning. To Popper (1972), for example, there is a distinction to be made between representational objects, seen as texts in the sense above, and the "content" that is represented in such texts. Once created, the latter is taken to have a continuing, immaterial existence in what he calls World 3.

> If we speak of Platonism, or of quantum theory, then we speak of some objective import, of some *objective logical content*; that is, we speak of the third-world significance of the information or the message conveyed in what has been said, or written. (1972, p. 157)

Even though they might not be comfortable with Popper's World 3 of immaterial objects, many people would accept the idea of the continuing existence of ideas, theories and supporting evidence, irrespective of whether they themselves were familiar with the "objects" in question. It is in this sense that we normally interpret references to "what is known" about a subject or to the cumulative nature of scientific knowledge. Indeed, the very idea of a culture, when considered as an entity independent of the beliefs and values enacted by its particular members, past or present, seems to be based on such an assumption.

Nevertheless, as I have argued elsewhere (Wells, 1999, in press a), such assumptions have no basis in reality. "Scientific knowledge" and "what is known" are no more than reifying abstractions, created by the nominalizing process that is characteristic of the synoptic registers of western theoretical discourse; they are convenient ways of talking that, when unpacked, are seen to refer to the situated activities of particular individuals using representational objects as mediators of their other-oriented acts of knowing in specific situations. As Freeman (1995) argues, "all knowledge originates in the brains of individuals" (p. 2) and representation is the "product of behavior that is used to cross the solipsistic gulf" (p. 6).

A Cultural Historical Perspective

If rabbits make representations through acts into the world of other conspecifics, what more human beings? In *Origins of the Modern Mind*, Merlin Donald (1991) sets out to trace the development of representation from apes to modern humans. The gist of his argument is that, over the course of this evolutionary trajectory, there have been a number of major modifications of "cognitive architecture," each associated with a new representational system. As he puts it, "Humans did not simply evolve a larger brain, an expanded memory, a lexicon, or a special speech apparatus; we evolved new systems for representing reality." What is more, "each successive new representational system has remained intact within our current mental architecture, so that the modern mind is a mosaic structure of cognitive vestiges from earlier stages of human emergence" (pp. 2–3).

Episodic culture

The starting point for Donald's proposed trajectory is the culture of the australopithecines, approximately 4 million years ago, which can be plausibly reconstructed from the cognitive achievements of contemporary great apes. This he describes as an "episodic" culture. Higher primates, as we know them today, are extremely adept in the realms of event perception and episodic memory. Chimpanzees, our nearest relatives, also have social structures that depend upon remembering large numbers of individually learned dyadic relationships; they also have a nuclear family structure, with division of labor and sharing of food. The same would equally have been true of the earliest hominids, he argues and, as with chimpanzees, these characteristics would have required the ability to perceive and remember complex events and to use this situationally based knowledge to guide their actions.

However, episodic culture has serious limitations. Despite their skill in the analysis and recall of situational information, higher primates cannot *deliberately* construct representations in order to elicit thinking in others. They have no "semantic" memory and, as a result, they cannot re-present a situation to reflect on it, either individually or collectively. It was thus the emergence of the ability to produce conscious, self-initiated, representational acts that marked the first major transition on the trajectory from ape to modern human.

Mimetic culture

This transition occurred sometime between two and one and a half million years ago with the changes that can be seen in the culture of *Homo erectus*. Not only did these protohumans have a much larger brain, but they made more elaborate tools, used fire, and built shelters in seasonal base camps. They were also able to pass on these procedural forms of knowing from one generation to the next and to transport them as, over many generations, they migrated from Africa into Eurasia. Such achievements obviously required a means of recalling and sharing information in the absence of environmental cues. From fossil evidence, however, it seems clear that *Homo erectus* had not yet developed language. On this basis, Donald proposes that their governing mode of representation was "mimetic", using a combination of gesture, mime, facial expression, and modulated phonation. Mimesis would have constituted an important advance in that it enabled coordination of joint activity and pedagogic interaction in acculturation of the young.

Mythic culture

The next transition occurred only half a million years ago, or less, with the advent of *Homo sapiens*. The major development here was associated with the development of language in the modality of rapid, grammatical speech. However, language did not develop simply because of a further enlargement of the brain or a lengthening of the vocal tract. As Deacon (1997) argues, the development of language and the brain show a pattern of co-evolution, in which the emergence of language was part of a more general pattern of adaptation that, building upon the cognitive achievements of mimetic mind, strove to integrate the unconnected bits of information in a more comprehensive and coherent account of being-in-the-world.[2]

The invention and refinement of spoken language must have brought about a radical change from the cultures preceding that of *Homo sapiens*. Speech added a new and more powerful mode of interpersonal interaction, utilizing a representational system with greater precision and comprehensiveness of reference to objects and actions and their location in space and time. It also provided means for reflectively connecting events through relationships of purpose, reason, and causality, and so for the development of narrative meaning making.

However, according to Donald, the most significant achievement made possible by the use of language was "mythic invention". Exploiting the fundamental narrative organization of oral language (Bruner, 1986), language-using cultures began to construct overarching myths in order to explain human existence and its relation to the nonhuman world. As Donald argues: "Myth is the prototypical, fundamental, integrative mind tool. It tries to integrate a variety of events in a temporal and causal framework. It is inherently a modeling device, whose *primary* level of representation is thematic." And on this basis he concludes that, "modern humans developed language in response to pressure to improve their conceptual apparatus, not vice versa" (1991, p. 215).

Writing and theoretic culture

Mythic culture emerged some 50,000 years ago. Underpinning it were the physical, cognitive, and interpersonal skills that we still deploy in everyday life, together with the "dynamic" everyday uses of oral language (Halliday, 1993a), with their bent toward narrative construal of experience. For most people in all cultures, this way of life continued, relatively unchanged, until very recently. This may be somewhat difficult to appreciate, given the changes, particularly of a technological kind, that have taken place in the last two or three hundred years, but these only began to impinge on the lives of most of the earth's inhabitants during the course of this century. However, as with all the transitions that preceded, the emergence of theoretical culture (or "knowledge society," as it is currently named) did not occur overnight. In fact, the first recorded steps were taken some 4,000 years ago, with the first use of written marks to represent articles traded.[3]

In *The World on Paper*, David Olson (1994) has given us a convincing account of the way in which writing developed, first as a means of giving visual representation to the meanings communicated in speech, and only later, in the alphabetic script developed by the Greeks when they adopted another culture's writing system, as a representation of the sounds of speech itself. As he points out, it is the representation of meaning, not of sound, that is the crucial feature of writing, and not all orthographies have arrived at the same solution. In contrast to alphabetic scripts, writing systems based on Chinese characters, for example, are logographic (Taylor & Olson, 1995), while others are syllable-based, such as the script invented relatively recently by the Vai (Scribner & Cole, 1981). Whatever the orthography, however, the crucial cognitive consequence of writing was that, because by design it produced relatively permanent artifacts, it also created a medium in which memory could be externalized. As Donald observes: "Visuosymbolic invention . . . [created] the *exact* external analog of internal, or biological memory, namely, a storage and retrieval system that allows humans to accumulate experience and knowledge" (1991, p. 309).

This is not the place to trace the history of writing which, from its origins in accounting, has come to permeate almost all aspects of contemporary life.[4] Suffice it to say that, in addition to its early uses in recording information for administrative purposes – a function that has proliferated and diversified over the centuries – writing has, over time, come to serve two major groups of functions. On the one hand, it provides an external representation of "mythic" or "aesthetic" meanings, as in narrative, poetry, drama, and history; and on the other, it serves to archive information of a substantive, practical kind, based on observation and investigation, and in this way to provide the basis for "theory building." Although this distinction was slow to become marked, and is still blurred in many contexts, the development of the latter function in the form of "prose" genres (Olson, 1977, 1994) has played a critical role in the development of meta-activity of all kinds, and represents probably the chief contribution of written representation to the development of theoretical activity. As Olson observes: "What literacy contributes to thought is that it turns the thoughts themselves into worthy objects of contemplation" (1994, p. 277).

Of course, writing is not the only semiotic modality in which meaning can be given a fixed representation. However, even among the other visuographic modalities there is a similar division of functions. Drawing, together with painting and sculpture – all of which, in their first appearance, antedated writing and numerical notation by many millennia – tend to be used to create evocative, aesthetic representations that still maintain their mythic origins; musical and choreographic notations, although functioning more like writing, also have an aesthetic purpose in allowing compositions in these media to be performed even when their composers are not present to direct them. Mathematical formulae, maps, graphs, diagrams, and three-dimensional models, by contrast, are typically used to represent information for practical and analytic purposes. For this reason, these modes of representation, together with prose writing, have played an important role in the development of theoretical understanding.

From this brief review, it seems clear that while the transition to theoretical thinking would not have occurred without the externalization of memory made possible by relatively enduring visual representations, the invention of writing and other visuographic means of representation was not, in itself, sufficient to cause the shift.

What was also required was a new reason for exploiting the external memory system, which was provided, in large part, by the emerging interest in scientific investigation, together with the ideological changes that accompanied it, at the time of the European Renaissance (Hacking, 1990). Particularly important among these was the tendency toward the reification of knowledge artifacts (Ueno, 1995), which was itself associated with the creation of a new register of written language with which to represent and communicate the outcomes of scientific activity (Halliday & Martin, 1993).

In sum, although exploitation of the new modes of visuographic representation as external memory devices has clearly been instrumental in the development of our contemporary theoretical culture, equal weight in explaining the transition needs to be given to the changing cultural values and purposes that have led to the increasing valorization of the knowledge that can be constructed by these means. However, it is probably correct that, as Donald argues, "once the devices of external memory were in place and once the new cognitive architecture included an infinitely expandable, refinable external memory loop, the die was cast for the emergence of theoretic structures" (1991, p. 356).

However, an equally important aspect of Donald's (1991) argument is that although, over the course of the cultural-cognitive transitions that he proposes, the semiotic systems of mimesis, speech, and external symbolic storage (ESS) each powered a new mode of cognitive activity, they did not replace those that preceded, but were additive in their effects. The result is that "our modern minds are thus hybridizations"(p. 356), with a variety of modes of functioning at their disposal; furthermore, most activities call for more than one mode of thinking and require the complementary and interdependent use of more than one mode of representation.

It is to further explore the relationship between representations and knowing that I turn next to the views of Marx Wartofsky, a philosopher of science.

Representing as Primary

Like Donald, Wartofsky was interested in the historical development of knowing. As he put it, "what we take knowledge to be is itself the subject of an historical evolution" (Wartofsky, 1979, p. xiii) which has resulted from the progressively more highly developed modes in which humans have acquired the ability to make representations. However, there is no ambiguity about Wartofsky's conception of what it is to make a representation.

1 *Anything* can be a representation of anything else.
2 It is *we* who constitute something as a representation of something else. It is essential to something's being a representation, therefore, that it is *taken* to be one.
3 From (1) and (2) it follows that a representation is whatever is taken to be a representation; that representing is something *we do*, and that nothing is a representation except insofar as we construct or construe it as one; and in this, it is precisely the representation we make it, or take it to be.

Thus, although representations are clearly important for Wartofsky, what is primary is the actual *activity of representing*. Representing, he argues, is a fundamental human activity; it is something we do as an essential means of perceiving and of knowing, and is central to all forms of action. Whether internal or external, then, representations have their origin in the primary act of representing. "They come to be what they are, are sustained or maintained as such, and are exhaustively describable in terms of our own intentions" (1979, p. xxi). Representing is also the distinctively human way of constructing knowledge; it is through the intentional making and using of artifacts of different kinds that we become conscious of our own activity and at the same time come to understand that which the artifact is used to represent.

Wartofsky distinguishes three kinds of artifacts that can function as representations. First are material tools and the social practices in which they are employed; these are *primary* artifacts in that they are directly involved in the transformation of the environment for the production and reproduction of the means of existence. The first such artifacts were simple tools (knives, spears, and pots); today, they include aircraft, computers, and automatic banking machines. Such artifacts are not created for the purpose of representing, but they can be so used, particularly to represent the activities in which they are typically involved. The second category consists of those that are created for the purpose of preserving the tools and practices by means of which primary activities are organized, and their motives, goals, and knowledgeable skills passed on to new participants. These *secondary* artifacts are symbolic representations of the primary activities which they are used to plan, manage, and evaluate. Face-to-face mimetic acts would have been the earliest form of secondary artifacts; nowadays they may be in one of a variety of semiotic modes or even in a combination. Finally, *tertiary* artifacts: these are the imaginative, integrative representational structures (myths, works of art, as well as theories and models) in terms of which humans attempt to understand the world and their existence in it.

Like Donald's, Wartofsky's central thesis is that human cognition has developed historically as a function of the different types of artifact that have been used to represent activity and its constitutive objects and actions and at the same time to allow reflection on the various types of relationships involved. As these artifacts have become capable of representing more complex relationships as well as of remaining fixed in form over time and space, they have made possible more complex modes of perception, action, and cognition, and the development of more integrative modes of knowing and understanding. As he puts it:

> . . . our own perceptual and cognitive understanding of the world is in large part shaped and changed by the representational artifacts we ourselves create. We are, in effect, the products of our own activity, in this way; we transform our own perceptual and cognitive modes, our ways of seeing and of understanding, by means of the representations we make. (1979, pp. xx–xxiii)

Like Freeman, Wartofsky also emphasizes the active, social nature of representing – of making representational artifacts to mediate activity with others. Furthermore, as he points out, it is through the attempt to make such representations with and for others that we make meaning for ourselves and, in the process, develop an understanding of our experience of being-in-the-world construed in terms of the theories made available by, and appropriated from, other members of our culture. As Vygotsky so aptly suggested, "the individual develops into what he/she is through what he/she produces for others" (Vygotsky, 1981, p. 162).

Representing and Knowing

In the previous sections, following Freeman, Donald, and Wartofsy, I argued that it is the activity of representing that plays the defining role in characterizing human cognition. We represent those aspects of the world that are *currently of interest to us*. And because with each advance in representing, the previous modes were not lost, we have a repertoire of modes *to hand* for representing what is of current interest. In some cases, this involves pressing into service cultural artifacts that are already available, as when we refer to or quote from others' work or, as in the case of Kress's daughter, by arranging items of furniture to represent a car. On other occasions, we may create novel artifacts in any of the semiotic modalities that we have mastered, for example by composing a written text or by taking a photograph. Often, we make use of a variety of artifacts in a complex interdependency, as when we consult a work of reference, exploit a metaphorical connection in speech to explore the significance of what we have read, simultaneously gesturing to clarify our meaning, and then go on to create a visuographic representation of the relationship thus grasped.

I want now to propose that the same arguments apply to the activity of knowing, since this is mediated by representational acts of various kinds. Just as Wartofsky observes that "there is no human knowledge without representation" (1979, p. xviii), I argue that the same is true of knowing. Furthermore, knowing, like representing, is always situated in a particular moment in relation to the activity that it furthers. In fact, knowing is best understood as a central mode of participating in any ongoing activity. Sometimes it is conscious and deliberate, as when solving a problem, and sometimes it is an operation, routinized and below the level of conscious attention (Lave & Wenger, 1991; Leont'ev, 1978). Viewed in this light, knowing is the use of one or more representations to mediate the achievement of the end in view which, in the theoretical mode, may well be to create a further representation. This being so, we can distinguish modes of knowing in the same way as Donald and Wartofsky distinguish modes of representing (see Table 8.1).

Table 8.1 proposes two modes of knowing for which there is no direct warrant in the work on which I have been drawing. The first of these concerns what I call "substantive knowing." In each domain of everyday experience, we construct piecemeal representations, often in language, of objects, persons and events, organized in terms of the activities in which they are involved. These are the "facts" that are shared by co-participants in an activity system, along with the relevant procedural

Table 8.1 Modes of Knowing: Phylogenetic and Cultural Development

Time BP	Mode of knowing	Participants	Donald (1991)	Wartofsky (1979)
2 million years	Instrumental	Individual in action	Episodic	Primary artifacts: material tools
1–1.5 million years	Procedural	Between individuals while engaged in action	Mimetic	Secondary artifacts: tools and practices; mimetic interaction
50,000 years	Substantive	Among members of a cultural group, reflecting on action and as a basis for planning further action	(Linguistic)	Secondary artifacts: representations of tools and practices; spoken interaction
50,000 years	Aesthetic	Among members of a cultural group, making sense of the human predicament	Mythic	Tertiary artifacts: artistic representations in myth, narrative, graphic, and musical modes
2,500 years	Theoretical	Among members of a specialist community seeking to explain the natural and human world	Theoretic	Tertiary artifacts: decontextualized representations, such as taxonomies, theories, models, etc.
?	Meta	Among members of a cultural group, also individuals, seeking to understand and control their own mental activity		Tertiary artifacts: representations of mental and semiotic processes

knowing. In their discursive organization such linguistic representations are "dynamic" rather than "synoptic" (Halliday, 1993b), or "narrative" as opposed to "paradigmatic" (Bruner, 1986), and they make up a large part of what Halliday (1993a) calls our everyday, or common-sense, knowledge, which is derived from our own and other people's experience. These everyday linguistic representations are, in my view, quite different from the genres of myths or overarching narratives that Donald (1991) sees to be the major achievement of the narrative use of speech. For this reason, I distinguish a substantive mode of knowing, which in all probability preceded and provided much of the material on which the more aesthetic, mythic mode of knowing built.

The second addition is that of "metaknowing." The family of "meta" terms ("metalanguage," "metacognition," etc.) is of fairly recent origin, but the activity of metaknowing itself is probably almost as old as language itself. All languages include terms for referring to linguistic events – nouns such as "story," or "argument," and verbs such as "tell," or "persuade." Reflecting on our actions, including our linguistic and mental actions, is a necessary precursor for constructing explanatory representations of them, whether in a narrative or a paradigmatic genre. For this reason, metaknowing cannot be located as one stage in the sequence of phylogenetic development that is summarized in Table 8.1. It might perhaps be best thought of as orthogonal to the others (Astington, pers. comm. 9 December, 1998), functioning as a facilitator of each transition from one stage to the next in Donald's developmental model.[5]

Three final points need to be made about the modes of knowing set out in Table 8.1. First, as with the priority ascribed to representing in relation to representations, it is the activity of knowing that is primary. Knowledge is constructed in the process, but this knowledge does not thereby become a mental object that can be recalled and applied, ready-made, on subsequent occasions; rather it has to be constructed anew on each occasion in order to fit the intentions of the participants and the specifics of the situation in which they act. To be sure, one outcome of knowing is often the production of a representational artifact, or "knowledge object." However, as argued by Freeman (1995), such objects do not contain knowledge, although they have the potential to mediate the knowing of others, provided those others can bring the necessary resources to their transactions with them. Even Popper, who clearly thought of knowledge as "autonomous and immaterial," insisted that to make it one's own requires an active transaction with the knowledge object, "by trying to reinvent it or to reconstruct it, and by trying out, with the help of our imagination, all the consequences of the [object] which seem to us to be interesting and important" (Popper & Eccles, 1977, p. 461).

Second, although the different modes of knowing emerged over time in the course of the developmental trajectory of human cultures, the earlier were not supplanted by those that emerged later. All remain available, once mastered, and all are interdependently involved in contemporary activity systems of any scope and complexity, although they may be distributed over different participants and different phases in the activity.

This brings me to the final point. Knowing certainly requires the active participation of individual knowers on each and every occasion but, because of the social nature of activity, it is never an individual achievement, even when carried out in solitary seclusion. Each of us makes use of (some part of) the accumulated knowing of others and of the representational tools and knowledge objects that they have created. In "acting into the world" (Freeman, 1995) we also contribute to an ongoing dialogue, often with others who are engaged in the same activity as ourselves. In knowing, each of us acts out of our own interests, while at the same time seeking to establish some intersubjectivity of interest with co-participants in the activity. As Kress (1997) argues, too, we also make use of what is to hand, both those resources of the culture that we have mastered and are able to deploy, and also whatever meanings we have personally made or are currently making of our unique individual experience.

Ontogeny Recapitulates Cultural History

The sequential development of different modes of knowing over the course of human history that I have just traced might at first sight seem to be of little educational significance. However, it begins to take on considerable importance when the parallels are recognized between this sequence and the sequence of intellectual development in ontogeny. Of course, this is not a simple recapitulation; children growing up in a contemporary literate culture are surrounded from birth by artifacts and practices that result from and embody all the available modes of knowing (Cole, 1996). Appropriating existing cultural tools is thus very different from inventing them *de novo*, as Scribner (1985) points out. Nevertheless, as Nelson (1996) has argued, children during the preschool years traverse similar stages in progressively making sense of more and more complex aspects of their experience, as they appropriate the semiotic tools for representing that correspond to Donald's "episodic," "mimetic," "mythic," and "theoretic" minds.

Nevertheless, although Donald's stages are repeated in Nelson's ontogenetic account, her main focus is on the role played by the semiotic system of linguistic representation. In this, she has considerable affinity with Halliday, who also ascribes a preeminent role to language: "When children learn language, they are not simply engaging in one type of learning among many; rather, they are learning the foundations of learning itself. . . . Hence the ontogenesis of language is at the same time the ontogenesis of learning" (1993a, p. 93).

However, in the light of the work reviewed above, I would argue that such a logo-centric emphasis misrepresents the multimodal and "hybrid" nature of knowing characteristic of contemporary humans. Humans do not "act into the world" solely in the linguistic mode; nor is language the only mode in which the inner "cognitive map" is represented (Freeman, 1995).[6] Language may be the most pervasive mode for making and representing meaning and, with the mathematical and other notational systems derived from it, it is essential for theoretical knowing. But it is important not to discount the roles played by action, gesture, and drawing, as well as the aesthetic modes of music and dance, as modes of representation in which humans establish intersubjectivity of purpose and reference and develop mutual understanding in the full range of activities in which they participate (Lemke, in press; Wells, in press b). So, while I agree with the general thrust of Nelson's argument, I would want to place greater emphasis on the different kinds of artifacts that mediate knowing across activity systems (Engeström, 1990; Wartofsky, 1979) and emphasize their complementarity rather than focusing on one alone. Further, Nelson's (1996) account of ontogenetic development focuses primarily on the preschool years. In what follows, I wish to consider the implications of the recapitulationist view for later development during the years of schooling.[7]

Building on a Solid Experiential Foundation

One of the most important consequences of adopting a historical perspective is the recognition that, in the development of human cultures, each advance in construing and representing experience was built on the modes of knowing that preceded. And on a very different time-scale, the same developmental sequence applies in ontogenesis. As each new mode of representation is appropriated from interactions with others and constructed as a resource for intramental functioning, it expands the range of modes of knowing by means of which the individual can make sense of his or her experience.

As we have seen, historically, speech and narrative emerged as more powerful means of representing and communicating the understandings developed by the mimetic mind; similarly writing and other visuographic semiotic modes provided more powerful, externally accessible, means of working on the knowledge developed by the narrative mind. It seems likely, too, that in each case the transition was facilitated by "going meta" on the knowledge base already established (Olson & Bruner, 1996). However, the slow time-scale on which these developments took place can easily lead to the cumulative nature of this process being ignored and, ironically, this seems to be most true with respect to the most recent development, that of theoretical knowing. Certainly, once established, the development of theoretical knowing in any field tends to become an independent activity, carried on largely by extending and improving existing knowledge artifacts in the form of theories and models. However, in almost every case, the initial impetus for theorizing had a practical orientation and required a broad base of accumulated observations and experience of the phenomena in question, encountered in the practical activities of everyday life. Furthermore, as Wartofsky pointed out, theoretical models, although temporarily detached from primary activities, do not exist in and for themselves. They are "representations to ourselves of what we do, of what we want, and of what we hope for. The model is not, therefore, simply a reflection or copy of some state of affairs, but beyond this, a putative mode of action, a representation of prospective practice, or of acquired modes of action" (1979, p. xv).

I emphasize this point because, in planning how to induct young people into the culture's valued knowledge, particularly its theoretical knowledge, the approach adopted often ignores the historical nature of knowledge building. Curricula are designed in terms of the internal structure of the knowledge domain as currently understood by experts, rather than by building on the first-hand experience of learners in the sort of everyday practical activities from which that structure was initially derived (Nelson, 1996). Not surprisingly, many learners have difficulty in understanding the experts' decontextualized theoretical formulations and, as has been amply documented, a high proportion lose interest and abandon the attempt to understand.

Thus, the significance of recognizing the parallels between ontogenetic development and the cumulative development of the modes of knowing over the course of human history is that it reminds us of the solid basis for each advance that was constructed in the modes that preceded; it also reminds us of the continuing inter-dependence of the modes that make up the intellectual toolkit at any moment in development. As I have argued elsewhere (Wells, 1999), what is required to put this understanding into practice in education is for teachers to find ways of organiz-ing classroom activities so that theoretical knowing builds more organically on the modes of knowing that students already deploy and grows out of their attempts both to solve the problems arising from the specifics of the "primary" activities in which they engage and to create representations of the understandings that they achieve in the process. Clearly, not every new topic needs to be rooted in proce-dural, substantive, and narrative construals of first-hand practical experience; how-ever, I am suggesting that such an organic, developmental approach should be adopted with respect to each new domain of theoretical knowing that is encoun-tered in school and that, whenever possible, theoretical knowing be put to use in further practical situations. For it is in the attempt to apply knowledge taken over from others that it is most fully understood and made part of one's own resources for future problem solving.

Inquiry, Talk, and Text

In education, we are concerned with the development of meaning making, that is to say, with enabling people to increase their ability to construe their environment and act effectively in it. In undertaking this endeavor, three principles must be treated as paramount. First, meaning is a process of "acting into the world" that transforms both the world and the actors. Second, although this process of mean-ing making is carried out by individuals, it is dependent on, and takes its signifi-cance from its role in, collective activity. As Leont'ev observed, the individual's action only has meaning "in the system of social relations" (Leont'ev, 1981, p. 47). This is related to the third principle, namely that the modes of representation through which meanings are constructed are neither given innately nor invented anew by each individual; rather, they are cultural resources that each individual appropriates from others through participation in joint activity. Individual development thus involves the active appropriation of the practices used to mediate meaning making between people and the personal reconstruction of these practices in relation to one's own unique experience and "continuing unity of intentionality" (Freeman, 1995).

There is a further principle that follows from the interaction of the first three: while what individuals can mean depends on both their personal experiences and the opportunities they have had to appropriate the mediational means that are uti-lized within the culture, the continuation and renewal of the culture itself depends, in turn, on the unique meanings that its individual members contribute to the local activities in which they participate. Each occasion of activity therefore both repro-duces cultural practices and modes of knowing and also to some degree transforms

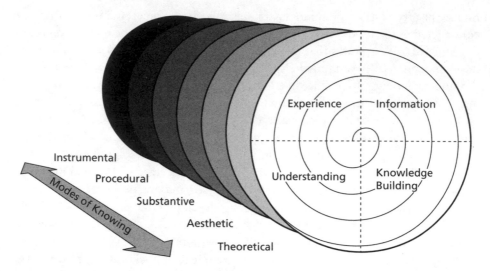

Figure 8.1　The spiral of knowing.

them. There is thus an inevitable but creative tension between homogeneity and diversity, and between convention and invention.

Combining these four rather abstract principles with the arguments developed in the previous section has led us to conceptualize the ideal classroom as a community of inquiry, in which individual development is seen as both occurring through, and contributing to, jointly undertaken activities that start from the collective's individual experiences and have as their continuing goal the construction of enhanced understanding (Wells, 1999). This can be represented as in Figure 8.1.

This figure is to be read as a spiral, with each cycle starting from personal experience, to which information is added from the environment in the form of feedback from action or symbolically through representations produced by others. The goal of each cycle is to arrive at an enhanced understanding through integrating the new information into the individual's existing "cognitive map," which is achieved through knowledge building. As the term implies, this latter is an active process of making connections and testing interpretations and conjectures, through action and/or the making of further symbolic representations. As already mentioned, this phase is essentially interpersonal and collaborative. As Bereiter puts it, "the important thing is that the [knowledge building] be progressive in the sense that understandings are being generated that are new to the local participants and that the participants recognize as superior to their previous understandings" (Bereiter, 1994, p. 9). If this goal is achieved, each cycle results in an improved and more coherent base of understanding in terms of which to construe further experiences and interpret new information. However, the process is never complete, for with each increase in understanding comes a recognition of how much more there still is to understand (Nickerson, 1985).

The figure should also be read as a spiral in a second sense. Most activities require more than one of the modes of knowing and, as suggested above, when embarking on a new domain, it is desirable to start with experience of everyday practical activities and with the modes of knowing in which they are most readily construed. Moving from shared procedural and substantive knowing to the theoretical mode of knowing, and back and forth between them as necessary, involves another kind of spiral and an interpenetration of each of the modes, as Vygotsky (1987) explained in his account of the relationship between everyday and scientific concepts.

Inevitably, in the classroom, it is linguistic representations that figure most prominently in the interpersonally oriented phases of the cycle, that is to say, in the uptake of information and in knowledge building. However, as both Lemke (in press) and Smagorinsky (1995) emphasize – as does Kress (1997) and Roth and McGinn (1998) – we need to give much more scope in educational settings for the exploitation of other modes of representation and for their use in combination with language.

Nevertheless, it is still in the written mode that knowledge building can most effectively be conducted. As Olson (1977, 1994) and many other writers have pointed out, the great advantage of a written text in this context is that it demands that writers make their meanings explicit, both for themselves and for others – that they make clear how their utterances are to be taken and provide warrant for the propositions that they assert. The other major advantage of a written text is that it is an "improvable object" (Scardamalia, Bereiter, & Lamon, 1994), a representation of meaning that can be reviewed and revised in an understanding-enhancing dialogue with oneself as well as in collaboration with others. To be most beneficial in its contribution to the development of understanding, then, writing needs to be seen as just one arc in the spiral of knowing, complementing practical activity and exploratory talk and consolidating the basis for another cycle.

The following example, taken from research carried out in the "Developing Inquiring Communities in Education Project" (DICEP),[8] illustrates one way in which the principles I have outlined can be realized in practice.

Studying Energy Through Constructing Elastic-Powered Vehicles

In a private school in North Toronto, Mary Ann Van Tassell and Barbara Galbraith had, for several years, arranged their timetables so that they could team teach science with their grade two students. Together, they had developed a number of curricular units that allowed their students to explore various aspects of the natural environment through practical investigations that they found interesting and challenging. However, as they reviewed their program in July in preparation for the coming year, the two teachers were not entirely satisfied. When starting each new topic, they had made a point of encouraging the children to think about the questions they would like to try to answer and these were then written on chart paper and displayed on the classroom wall. What they now realized, however, was that

that was as far as these questions went. The activities that followed were almost entirely selected by the teachers, and they were chosen with reference to the questions that they, the teachers, thought ought to be answered rather than to those that the children had actually asked (Galbraith, pers. comm. March 1995).

In planning the first science unit for the new year, therefore, they decided to try to allow it to evolve more organically in response to the children's questions; they also intended to become more involved themselves in the resulting problem solving. The theme selected for this new approach was "energy," to be explored through the making and testing of "rollers" powered by elastic bands. The children brought from home a variety of cylindrical containers and, following the design found in a children's guide to technology (Richards, 1990), they each began to make their own roller and to conduct tests to see how far it would travel for a given number of turns of the elastic band. Immediately, however, there were problems. Apart from the difficulties of construction encountered by these 7-year-olds, there were unexpected variations in the manner in which the rollers functioned. In some cases, it took a very large number of turns to get the roller to move at all; others unwound very fast but hardly moved; and some veered to one side or the other. As can be imagined, these problems generated a number of very real questions of an initially instrumental nature. In general, attempts were made to solve these problems as they arose, but they were also addressed more reflectively in the whole class discussions that either started or ended each lesson.

The problem of the rollers that did not go straight gave rise to a particularly interesting discussion. In some cases, the difficulty had arisen because a child had used a container such as a film canister that, with its lid on, had a greater diameter at one end than at the other. In other cases, the problem had been created by adding rubber bands round the circumference of the container in order to give the roller better grip. Part way into the discussion, one of the teachers took one of the rollers that had an elastic band around one end (thus making it slightly conical) and asked the children to predict whether it would travel in a straight line or veer to one side. Most predicted that it would veer, but they were divided as to which way it would circle – to the right or to the left. After it had been observed to circle to the right, I wondered aloud what would happen if the elastic band was moved to the other end. When the adjustments had been made, the children were asked to predict again and then invited to explain their predictions. Most who tried were unable to be at all specific, but Alexandra made an interesting connection:

> I think it will [turn] because on a car if you turn the wheel this way (motioning to the left) the wheels go this way (motioning to the left) if you turn it this way (right) it goes this way (right)

Then the roller was released but, contrary to predictions, it traveled in an almost straight line. Finally, after the rubber band had been moved even further toward the end of the container, another trial was conducted and the roller circled – somewhat erratically – around the end with the smaller diameter.

The teachers had intended to end the unit after experimenting with the rollers. But, because of the children's enthusiastic interest and the indeterminate results of the tests, they decided to extend it further. Following Alexandra's connecting the roller with the wheels of a car, a decision was made to explore the making and testing of similarly powered "cars." Again, each child brought from home a small cardboard carton and, with dowel and wooden wheels obtained by the teachers, they constructed vehicles that were powered by an elastic band that was attached to the front of the box and the center of the rear axle. After a period of general experimentation (and modification of malfunctioning vehicles), it was decided in a general class discussion that the questions to which they wished to find answers were: how far the vehicle would travel for a given number of turns, and whether the addition of rubber bands or Scotch tape as "tires" would affect the vehicle's performance on the wooden floor as compared to on the carpet.

Since no one, teachers or children, had attempted such an experiment before, it took some time to develop a satisfactory procedure. One very important invention, proposed by one of the children, was to make a mark on the circumference of one of the rear wheels so that the number of turns could be counted accurately. Conventions also had to be established concerning the use of a tape measure to calculate the distance traveled. Once these procedures were in place, (relatively) systematic trials were carried out by children working in pairs and the results recorded in a chart form that had been collaboratively constructed for the purpose.

At the end of one session, Whitney approached me excitedly. From looking at her chart of results, she had noticed that, for each additional turn of the rear wheels when the car was pushed backwards, it traveled forwards a further 19 cm – approximately – when released. I asked her if she could think about these interesting results and come up with an explanation by the following week's lesson. When the time came, Whitney did not, in fact, have an explanation (or was perhaps too timid to attempt one in public). However, the problem was taken up in a class discussion and, with the chart of results written up on the blackboard, a collaborative attempt was made to solve it.

Initially, although the children were able to see the pattern, they could not make a connection between an additional turn and the additional 19 cm traveled. In an attempt to help them, I asked one of the children to stand on a tape measure. Her foot was exactly 20 cm long and, as she stepped along the tape, each additional foot-length added a further 20 cm. "So now, what connection can we make?" I asked. At this point there was a rush of suggestions, all of them inaudible because spoken at once, and Matthew, sitting unseen on the floor beside the teacher, made a circular gesture with his hand. Eventually, Lindsay can be heard.

| 135 | *Lindsay:* | The first foot was on- . the first foot was twenty-one . and then her next foot was forty-one, so that's twenty in between . and that's exactly like that (Whitney's results) with nineteen in between. |
| 136 | *Teacher 2:* | So how does that connect to the pattern? |

137   *Peter*:   How much- how long is the box?
138   *Teacher 2*:   How long is this box? (checking) OK, let's measure the box
                      and see how long the box is (taking tape measure and
                      measuring). It's twenty-three centimeters

When it has been generally agreed that it is not the length of the box that is relevant, the teacher prompts them again by asking what else on the car they could
measure, but nobody has a suggestion. At this point, I take one of the children's
cars and put a drop of ink on the elastic band that had been added to the marked
rear wheel as a tire and push the car across a large sheet of chart paper. With each
turn of the wheel, it leaves an ink-spot on the paper. Several children immediately
fetch tape measures and the teacher measures the distance between the marks. What
follows is worth quoting in full.

157   *Teacher 2*:   Kind of between nineteen and twenty actually
158   *Teacher 1*:   Lindsay?
160   *Lindsay*:   When she <moves> her box . when she's doing that . when
                      she moves all the centimeters, the reason why it's doing .
                      Nineteen maybe more is because- . . . (Other children are
                      indicating that they want to speak)
161   *Teacher 2*:   Yes . the distance-
162   *Lindsay*:   – the distance of her turning around her wheel
163   *Teacher 1*:   – is-
164   *Lindsay*:   – is . twenty
165   *Matthew*:   Each time . she winds it back it's twenty centimeters
166   *Teacher 1*:   So how can we find out for sure?
167   *Carrie*:   <Count> it?
168   *Teacher 1*:   Of- of what? You've *just said the distance* of the -
169   *Lindsay*:   *Measuring the distance* . . . back wheel
170   *Children*:   – of the wheel
171   *Teacher 1*:   Measure what?
172   *Matthew*:   Measure um <the distance between the wheels>
173   *Sam*:   Maybe . you can take a tape measure round and round it
174   *Teacher 1*:   Around the wheel?
175   *Matthew*:   Yeah, *meas-*
176   *Teacher 2*:   *Measure* around the wheel?
177   *Children*:   Yes
178   *Matthew*:   – and see if it's twenty
179   *Teacher 2*:   Like this? (measuring round the circumference of one
                      wheel)
180   *Julia*:   I don't think it's twenty (she is sitting next to Teacher 2
                      and can see the measurement)
181   *Teacher 2*:   No, you're right. D'you know what it is?
182   *Children*:   *What?*

183	*Julia*:	*Nineteen*
184	*Teacher 2*:	Nineteen
		(Many speak at once)
185	*Teacher 2*:	It's kind of between nineteen and twenty
186	*Teacher 1*:	Which is why you get the difference, right? (referring to Whitney's less than consistent results)
187	*Charlie*:	That's why- that's why she's getting nineteen in between
188	*Children*:	Yeah
189	*Charlie*:	That's *why she's -*
190	*Matthew*:	*That's nineteen* . . . adding nineteen every- every minute
191	*GW*:	(to Whitney) You go and tell everybody because you made this discovery
192	*Whitney*:	(gives her explanation with much hand gesture to indicate the wheel's circumference, but her speech is too soft to hear)
193	*Teacher 2*:	So what would happen if everybody measured . their wheel the way I just *measured this?*
194	*C?*:	*They would see-*
195	*Matthew*:	They could see how much it would keep on going . like *** (*Several children speak at once*)
197	*Teacher 2*:	*You should be able* to PREDICT . how far it will go (Observation, 15 February, 1995)

As is always the case when classroom activity is systematically observed, there are multiple perspectives from which a curricular unit can be viewed. Here, however, I shall focus mainly on the evidence that the observations provide for the thesis of this chapter. Most striking in this respect, perhaps, is the central role performed by the rollers and cars, first as the outcome of the instrumental and procedural knowing involved in their construction, and subsequently as tools in the shift toward the more theoretical knowing involved in explaining the results of testing them. These "vehicles" thus functioned both as working mechanical artifacts and as embodied representations of mathematical relationships, which latter role they performed for precisely the reason offered by Wartofsky, namely that that they "carried" information about the mode of their own production and functioning.

Initially, the children's concern was to have the artifacts work properly and this involved them first in instrumental knowing as they each attempted to construct one, and then in procedural knowing as they assisted each other with those aspects that were proving problematic. Later, this same concern led to a search for ways of getting the cars not to skid on the smooth surface of the floor, in the course of which they generated substantive knowledge about the properties of different surfaces and the function of tires in enabling the wheels to get a better grip. However, from early on, the children were also interested in the relationship between the number of turns of the rubber band as it wound up on the rear axle and the distance the vehicle would travel. This started, as one might expect, in a context of competition, as children sought to outdo each other with respect to the prowess of their respective cars. But it did not take much persuasion on the part of the teachers to turn this into a more general problem, to be tackled experimentally through sys- tematic trials. And it was the pattern that Whitney noticed in her results that led to the discussion quoted above which, from the point of view of the move toward theoretical knowing, must count as one of the most successful episodes in the whole unit. Throughout the unit, then, in their dual role as artifacts and tools, the elastic-powered vehicles not only mediated different modes of knowing, but they also mediated between the different modes, integrating them in a larger activity structure of doing and knowing.

So far I have said very little about the role of discourse in the collaborative knowledge building that occurred at many points throughout this unit. However, it is very evident in the extracts already quoted, as is the role of the teachers in helping the children to extend and clarify their contributions so that, as a community, they advance toward a shared understanding of the issues that are addressed. It is this goal of achieving a common understanding, I suggest, that, orchestrated by the teachers, enabled individual children to construct their own representations and to respond to, and build on, those of others. One further point, that is not apparent from the transcribed speech, is the multimodal nature of this discourse. As already mentioned, the chart of Whitney's results, written on the blackboard, played a significant part in the discussion; from time to time reference was also made to other written texts on display – the questions that the children had posed in previous discussions and the interim conclusions that they had reached. But most striking was the mimetic meanings expressed through gesture and posture, as the children used their whole bodies to communicate. Indeed, I would argue that it was Matthew, in his silent circular gesture, who first 'saw' the direction in which the solution might be found. Certainly his contribution at 165, "Each time . she winds it back it's twenty centimeters," suggests that he had by then figured it out, and it is probable that it was partly his desire to share his growing understanding that earlier prompted him to make his unnoticed gesture.

However, in arguing for the quality of the knowing together demonstrated in this episode, I am not claiming that all the children had achieved the same understanding by the end of the unit. From a constructivist perspective on knowing and learning, such an outcome would be most unlikely, since the development of each individual's understanding builds on his or her prior understanding, which itself depends on the range and nature of previous relevant experience. As classes of children are rarely, if ever, homogeneous with respect to prior understanding, identity of outcome is not to be expected. On the other hand, it is reasonable to expect that each individual will extend or deepen his or her own understanding through the interplay of solo, group, and whole class activity and interaction. And this, in the teachers' view, could be observed, over the course of the unit, in the changes in the children's manner of participation and in the quality of their contributions to the discourse.

As a final step in each activity, the children were asked to write in their science journals, reflecting on what they had observed and attempting to provide an explanation. Here is what Alexandra wrote as they were still perfecting their cars:

> Today our group made sure we got acurat answers on how far our cars move. First we looked at Jansens car. After 2 minutes me and katie realizised that Jansons cars wheels were rubbing against the box thats called friction. Then the car wouldent go very far because there was to much friction.

The teachers also made a practice of recording ideas that emerged in whole class discussion on large sheets of chart paper, the exact formulation being negotiated in collaboration with the children. Here, the process of composing the written text helped the children to focus on what was happening, and why; the resulting text also provided a collective record of the group's emerging understanding, to which individual children could refer as they made their own entries in their science journals.

Engaging in writing as well as in talking certainly helped the children to extend and consolidate their understanding of the concepts involved in this investigation of energy. They themselves were aware of its importance as an integral part of "doing science" and approached it enthusiastically. This was apparent from their comments in the interviews that were conducted at the end of the unit, which included a question asking if writing in science had helped their learning. Alexandra replied:

> When you write stuff .. You can always remember it and then, when you share in groups you can write more stuff so . so whatever you share you learn more.

In conclusion, two things stand out from the preceding example. First is the way in which the unit as a whole developed from instrumental and procedural knowing, as the children built and tested their vehicles, to a community effort to construct more theoretical explanations of the substantive knowledge gained in the process. And second is the evidence for the crucial role of collaborative knowledge building in each cycle of activity as the means whereby the individual students' experience and the information that each contributed to the discussion were developed into a common understanding.

However, it is by recalling the perspective on meaning making and representing proposed by Kress and reiterated by Freeman that I wish to conclude. As they both emphasize, meanings are actions into the world made out of *current interest*; furthermore, since a complete understanding of any topic or phenomenon is never fully achieved, they are also made with whatever resources are available *to hand* – and, it should be added, *to mind* – however incomplete or inadequate these may be for the purpose. Nevertheless, when interest drives action in an activity undertaken with others there is real motivation to appropriate the resources needed to understand and act more effectively. These are important reminders for those trying to create ideal classrooms.

Notes

1   In this context, it is interesting to see how Halliday (1993a) describes the ontogenesis of language: "Children are predisposed, from birth, (a) to address others, and be addressed by them (that is, to interact communicatively); and (b) to construe their experiences (that is, to interpret experience by organizing it into meanings). Signs are created at the intersection of these two modes of activity. Signs evolve (a) in mediating – or, better, in enacting – interaction with others, and (b) in construing experience into meaning" (pp. 94–5).

2   Like Donald, Deacon convincingly argues that language could not have emerged without a co-evolving change in the organization of brain function that predisposed human infants to value symbolic referential relationships over purely indexical ones. Tellingly, he also argues that, although linguistic structure, as described by Chomskyan linguists, may appear to be so complex as to be unlearnable, it has the particular forms found in particular languages because these forms are well adapted to the learning abilities of infant brains: "The key to understanding language learnability . . . [lies] in language change. Although the rate of social evolutionary change in language structure appears unchanging compared to the time to develop language abilities, this process is crucial to understanding how the child can learn a language that on the surface appears impossibly complex and poorly taught. The mechanisms driving language change at the sociocultural level are also responsible for everyday language learning" (Deacon, 1997, p. 115).

3   While writing this chapter, I have been reading a summary of evidence that suggests that a theoretical culture may have arisen as long ago as 12,000 years and, although it disappeared in some catastrophe, it was the know-how that it developed that made possible the building of the pyramids in Egypt and also in South and Central America.

4   But see Olson (1994b) as well as Goody (1986), Harris (1989), Havelock (1976), and Ong (1982).

5   Another perspective on metaknowing is suggested by Egan (1997), who also adopts a genetic approach to human intellectual development. He proposes a developmental sequence of four kinds of understanding that are mediated by language use: mythic, romantic, philosophic, and ironic (there is also a prelinguistic kind that he calls somatic). In this scheme, ironic understanding can be seen as a form of metaknowing in that it results from self-conscious reflection about the language one uses and about the different, and sometimes mutually incompatible, ways of understanding experience that are generated by different modes of language use. However, although ironic understanding has been potentially available as long as language itself, Egan sees its current flowering as in some ways a postmodern response to our 20th-century recognition of the ultimately uncertain and relative nature of all kinds of understanding.

6   The same hybridity also characterizes what Vygotsky (1987) refers to as "inner speech."

7   A somewhat similar case is developed by Egan (1997).

8   The "Developing Inquiring Communities in Education Project" (DICEP) was initiated with assistance from the Spencer Foundation. The group includes teachers from grades 1 through 8 and university-based educators. More information about the group, together with details of publications (some available on-line) can be found at the project's webpage: http://www.oise.utoronto.ca/~ctd/DICEP.

References

Bereiter, C. (1994). Implications of postmodernism for science, or, science as progressive discourse. *Educational Psychologist, 29*, 3–12.

Bruner, J. S. (1986). *Actual minds, possible worlds.* Cambridge, MA: Harvard University Press.

Cole, M. (1996). *Cultural psychology: A once and future discipline.* Cambridge, MA: The Bellknap Press of Harvard University Press.

Deacon, T. W. (1997). *The symbolic species: The co-evolution of language and the brain.* New York: Norton.

Donald, M. (1991). *Origins of the modern mind: Three stages in the evolution of culture and cognition.* Cambridge, MA: Harvard University Press.

Edelman, G. (1992). *Bright air, brilliant fire.* New York: Basic Books.

Egan, K. (1997). *The educated mind.* Chicago: University of Chicago Press.

Engeström, Y. (1990). *Learning, working and imagining: Twelve studies in activity theory.* Helsinki: Orienta-Konsultit.

Freeman, W. J. (1995). *Societies of brains: A study in the neuroscience of love and hate.* Hillsdale, NJ: Erlbaum.

Goody, J. (1986). *The logic of writing and the organization of society.* Cambridge, UK: Cambridge University Press.

Hacking, I. (1990). *The taming of chance.* Cambridge, UK: Cambridge University Press.

Halliday, M. A. K. (1993a). *Language in a changing world.* Sydney, Australia: Applied Linguistics Association of Australia, Occasional Paper 13.

Halliday, M. A. K. (1993b). Towards a language-based theory of learning. *Linguistics and Education, 5*, 93–116.

Halliday, M. A. K., & Martin, J. R. (1993). *Writing science: Literacy and discursive power.* London: Falmer Press.

Harris, R. (1989). *The origin of writing.* Cambridge, UK: Cambridge University Press.

Havelock, E. (1976). *Origins of western literacy.* Toronto, Canada: OISE Press.

Kress, G. (1997). *Before writing: Rethinking the paths to literacy.* London: Routledge.

Lave, J., & Wenger, E. (1991). *Situated learning: Legitimate peripheral participation.* New York: Cambridge University Press.

Lemke, J. L. (forthcoming). *Teaching all the languages of science: Words, symbols, images, and actions.*

Leont'ev, A. N. (1978). *Activity, consciousness, and personality.* Englewood Cliffs, NJ: Prentice Hall.

Leont'ev, A. N. (1981). The problem of activity in psychology. In J. V. Wertsch (Ed.), *The concept of activity in Soviet psychology* (pp. 37–71). Armonk, NY: Sharpe.

Nelson, K. (1996). *Language in cognitive development: The emergence of the mediated mind.* New York: Cambridge University Press.

Nickerson, R. S. (1985). Understanding understanding. *American Journal of Education, 93*, 201–239.

Olson, D. R. (1977). From utterance to text: The bias of language in speech and writing. *Harvard Educational Review, 47*, 257–81.

Olson, D. R. (1994). *The world on paper.* Cambridge, UK: Cambridge University Press.

Olson, D. R. (1995). Conceptualizing the written word: An intellectual autobiography. *Written Communication, 12*, 277–97.

Olson, D. R., & Bruner, J. S. (1996). Folk psychology and folk pedagogy. In D. R. Olson & N. Torrance (Eds.), *The handbook of education and human development* (pp. 9–27). Cambridge, MA: Blackwell.

Ong, W. (1982). *Orality and literacy*. New York: Methuen.

Popper, K. R. (1972). *Objective knowledge: An evolutionary approach*. Oxford, UK: Clarendon Press.

Popper, K. R., & Eccles, J. C. (1977). *The self and its brain*. Berlin: Springer-Verlag.

Richards, R. (1990). *An early start to technology*. London: Simon & Schuster.

Rosenblatt, L. (1978). *The reader, the text, the poem: The transactional theory of the literary work*. Carbondale, IL: Southern Illinois University Press.

Roth, W.-M., & McGinn, M. (1998). Inscriptions: Toward a theory of representing as social practice. *Review of Educational Research, 68*, 35–59.

Scardamalia, M., Bereiter, C., & Lamon, M. (1994). The CSILE project: Trying to bring the classroom into World 3. In K. McGilley (Ed.), *Classroom lessons: Integrating cognitive theory and classroom practice* (pp. 201–28). Cambridge, MA: MIT Press.

Scribner, S. (1985). Vygotsky's uses of history. In J. V. Wertsch (Ed.), *Culture, communication and cognition: Vygotskian perspectives* (pp. 119–45). Cambridge, UK: Cambridge University Press.

Scribner, S., & Cole, M. (1981). *The psychology of literacy*. Cambridge, MA: Harvard University Press.

Smagorinsky, P. (1995). Constructing meaning in the disciplines: Reconceptualizing writing across the curriculum as composing across the curriculum. *American Journal of Education, 103*, 160–84.

Taylor, I., & Olson, D. R. (1995). An introduction to reading the world's scripts. In I. Taylor & D. R. Olson (Eds.), *Scripts and literacy* (pp. 1–15). Boston: Kluwer Academic Publishers.

Ueno, N. (1995). The reification of artifacts in ideological practice. *Mind, Culture, and Activity, 2*, 230–9.

Vygotsky, L. S. (1981). The genesis of higher mental functions. In J. V. Wertsch (Ed.), *The concept of activity in Soviet psychology* (pp. 144–88). Armonk, NY: Sharpe.

Vygotsky, L. S. (1987). Thinking and speech. In R. W. Rieber & A. S. Carton (Eds.), *The collected works of L. S. Vygotsky, Volume 1: Problems of general psychology* (pp. 39–285). New York: Plenum.

Wartofsky, M. (1979). *Models, representation, and scientific understanding*. Boston: Reidel.

Wells, G. (1999). *Dialogic inquiry: Towards a sociocultural practice and theory of education*. Cambridge, UK: Cambridge University Press.

Wells, G. (in press a). Dialogue about knowledge building. In B. Smith (Ed.), *Liberal education in a knowledge society*. La Salle, IL: Open Court.

Wells, G. (in press b). Modes of meaning in a science activity. *Linguistics and Education*.

Part II
Representation, Language, and Theory of Mind

9

Minds in the (re)making: Imitation and the Dialectic of Representation

Philip David Zelazo

"Mimesis is an action about action."

Paul Ricoeur (1981/1991, p. 150)

I've known David Olson for about seven years, which is a small fraction of his professional career but nearly the full extent of mine. Indeed, I met him for the first time following my job talk at Toronto, in the spring of 1992. Although I was well aware who he was, I had no idea how much our interests overlapped; and of course, I could hardly anticipate the extent to which he would eventually influence my work. This influence, which has been both direct and indirect, and almost always difficult to gauge, will perhaps be apparent in this chapter, but if the ideas put forward owe much to Olson, I hope they might serve as a partial requital, too.

In this chapter, I describe a theory of representational understanding and use that draws heavily on the hermeneutics of Paul Ricoeur and the genetic epistemology of James Mark Baldwin. This theory, which construes representation to be intrinsically mimetic, speaks to a number of issues that Olson has identified in his work. Accordingly, I first summarize a few key aspects of Olson's approach to representation in an attempt to establish the background against which this theory is proposed. These aspects, which by no means exhaust the import of Olson's oeuvre, include the following: (a) a characterization of qualitative age-related changes in children's representational abilities; (b) the explicit rejection of the Vygotskian (e.g., 1934/1962) notion of internalization (especially, of language); and (c) the notion that literacy transforms the epistemology of the reader.

Background: Olson

Qualitative changes in representational ability

In a series of articles and book chapters, Olson and his colleagues (Olson, 1988, 1989, 1993; Olson & Campbell, 1993) develop the suggestion that in the course of child development, there are several qualitative transformations of children's representational abilities. Although many authors have imagined similar changes – for example, they can be found in the work of Baldwin (e.g., 1892), Piaget (e.g., 1936/ 1952), and Bruner (e.g., 1973) – Olson's approach is unique insofar as it is concerned particularly with the emergence of intentional states such as beliefs and desires, and with the ability to represent these states (i.e., "theory of mind").

According to Olson, infants do not actually have intentional states, and hence, their behavior is not properly explained in mentalistic terms. Instead, their behavior is mediated by "perceptual" schemata, which Olson characterizes as "simply causal functions" (Olson, 1993, p. 292). Nonmentalistic, behaviorist accounts therefore suffice to explain infant behavior, according to Olson. Eventually, however, children acquire the ability to form propositions that relate an idea to something perceived; that is, they acquire the ability to *predicate* something (i.e., a schema held in mind) about something else (i.e., a perceptual schema). For Olson, predication is the first step toward the formulation of beliefs. The second, constitutive step occurs when children are able to consider this predicative relation between two schemata relative to a third schema. It is only at this third stage, which occurs at about 4 years of age, that mind emerges on Olson's account:

> Beliefs, we recall, are the mental structures identified with Mind. No beliefs, no mind. So how do beliefs arise? Beliefs arise when the child becomes capable of relating the propositions constructed at stage 2 with the perceptual schemata constructed at stage 1. (Olson, 1989, pp. 623–624)

Olson suggests that these saltatory increases in representational ability are made possible by corresponding increases in children's "resources for holding in mind" (Olson, 1993, p. 302). Here, Olson follows the neo-Piagetian proposals of Pascual-Leone (1970) and Case (1985). As Olson (1993, p. 303) puts it, ". . . [T]his resource grows from essentially zero at birth, to one at about one-and-a-half years of age (at which time naming, pretense, and the like become possible) to about two at age four (at which time ascriptions of mental states become possible)." He further notes that this "growing ability to hold in mind is not to be viewed as simply a growth in memory, but rather a growth in capacity of a secondary memory, perhaps a form of episodic memory, separate from on-line processes" (Olson, 1993, p. 303). This identification of holding in mind with episodic memory (see Tulving, 1985; Wheeler, in press) presumably underlies Olson's (1989) suggestion that it is not until 4 years of age that "children come to specify the Self – the self-conscious self" (p. 624).

Rejection of the notion of internalization

Language plays a curious role in Olson's account of representational development. In several places, Olson highlights the correlation between language acquisition and the development of internal representation. Indeed, he goes so far as to claim that "children actually acquire the cognitive machinery that makes intentional state ascription literally true of them" when they acquire the ability to use language for "making statements, requests, and promises" (Olson, 1988, p. 420), although as noted, he elsewhere (e.g., in Olson & Campbell, 1993) makes it clear that it is not first-order statements that correspond to mental states but statements about propositions. (See Olson & Kamawar, 1999, and Kamawar & Olson, in press, for further parallels between metacognition and metalinguistic understanding.) Despite this emphasis, however, Olson rejects the suggestion that children's internal representations are somehow formed, or at least informed, by the external representations that they use.

More specifically, Olson rejects the Vygostkyian (e.g., 1934/1962) suggestion that developmental correspondences between internal and external representations are due to internalization, a process whereby the formal structure inherent in a cultural practice, such as language use, is first acquired in overt behavior and then reflected in one's private thinking. Olson and Campbell (1993, p. 13) note: "The view we shall adopt here is that the appearance of thought mediated by external representations (public symbols) runs exactly parallel with the development of thought mediated by internal representations. This concurrence is not due to internalization, a concept of doubtful application, but rather is a direct consequence of the fact that the same cognitive structures are required for both." Later, they emphasize the logical independence of language and internal representation: "[T]here seems to be no necessary relation between knowing a language and keeping an object in mind or even keeping a proposition in mind" (Olson & Campbell, 1993, p. 23). Thus, instead of adopting a Vygotskian view according to which the growth of internal representation depends causally on the use of language, they seem to favor the more Piagetian position that language and other forms of external representation are logically contingent expressions of children's developing representational ability.

Writing as a model of speech: the cognitive consequences of literacy

Although Olson argues that the early development of representation does not depend on the acquisition of language, he has written at length about the cognitive consequences of literacy (Olson, 1977, 1986, 1994). The point of departure here is Olson's (1977) observation that development involves a transition from "language as utterance" to "language as text," which Olson glosses in terms of Grice's (1957) distinction between "speaker meaning" and "sentence meaning." That is, children become less dependent on paralinguistic context to constrain their interpretations of language, and hence, their interpretive strategies become more like those that are normally brought to bear on text, which is typically decontextualized – abstracted away from the circumstances of its creation.

According to Olson (1994), literacy plays an instrumental role in bringing about this decontextualization of language, primarily because it effects an appreciation of the difference between text, on the one hand, and its meaning, on the other. This appreciation engenders a hermeneutic stance that makes text an isolable object of consideration. Further, because writing provides a relatively explicit model of speech (Olson, 1994), this hermeneutic stance can be applied not only to text, but also to speech. In fact, as Olson suggests, it can be generalized even further, giving rise to a scientific epistemology where observations can be treated as data and considered in relation to hypothetical models of reality. Thus, by transforming language as utterance into language as text, literacy imparts to speech the degree of reflection that is required for formal operational thought (Inhelder & Piaget, 1955/1972). Recast in cultural/dialectic terms, the influence of literacy may be summarized as follows: learning to speak (which is at least in part a consequence of enculturation) prepares children for learning to read (which is perhaps wholly a consequence of enculturation) and permits the self-reflective use of text as a model of speech. This use of text in turn transforms one's notion of speech, and thereby creates further opportunities for self-reflection and metalinguistic understanding.

Summary

Although there are, naturally, numerous differences between Olson's proposals and my own positions on these often controversial issues, there are also several important points of contact. First, I share Olson's belief that there are age-related increases in the complexity of children's representations that can ultimately be attributed to more general aspects of cognitive development (although we disagree about which aspects; for discussion see Zelazo & Frye, 1997). Second, I, too, am inclined to emphasize that in the course of development, children's thinking becomes (potentially) more reflective and decontextualized. These are crucial characteristics of cognitive development, and they have profound consequences for behavior. Third, I am impressed by his comprehensive account of literacy, which I believe provides a paradigmatic illustration of a more general cultural/dialectic process.

   In contrast to these points of contact, I have three primary disagreements with Olson's approach. First, I believe that the empirical evidence indicates convincingly that mental representation is a fundamental function of human cognition, present at birth and probably before (for review, see Zelazo & Zelazo, 1998; for related arguments, see Meltzoff & Moore, 1998). Second, in addition to the cognitive changes that Olson identifies, I believe that there is also good evidence for changes in representational structure at the end of the first year of life (Zelazo & Zelazo, 1998) and at the end of the third year (Zelazo & Jacques, 1996). Third, I believe that internalization, including the internalization of language, plays an important role in the development of representation, and I am optimistic that it can be explicated adequately. In fact, in this chapter I sketch a mimetic theory of representational understanding and use (see also Zelazo, 1999a), based on the writings of Ricoeur and Baldwin, that relies heavily on the notion of internalization as a characterization of developmental change (though not as an explanation). Although this sketch hardly provides an adequate explication of internalization, it will perhaps persuade the reader that such an explication is possible.

Representation as Imitation: Ricoeur and Baldwin

The traditional copy theory of representation, which is a generalization of Aristotle's (1927) brief remarks on tragedy (in *Poetics*), is widely disparaged. According to this theory, representation (Aristotle uses the term *mimesis*) imitates the structure of reality. This feature of representation is perhaps most clearly seen in the case of visual representation. As Gombrich (1960) notes, (mimetic) visual representations will vary in verisimilitude, with some representations being realistic likenesses of reality and others being relatively abstract. In any event, however, there is a reproduction of some aspect of reality and the reality-representation relation becomes paramount in any consideration of the nature or quality of the representation.

The importance of this relation may have appeared self-evident in the case of visual representation as painters in Europe and North America perfected a long tradition of representational painting. However, this importance was directly challenged at the beginning of the 20th century by artists such as Kasimir Malevich (1878–1935), Pablo Picasso (1881–1973), and Marcel Duchamp (1887–1968).[1] By painting, for example, a black square on a white background (*Black Square*, 1913), Malevich questioned the necessity, and perhaps even the possibility, of evaluating representations in terms of their relation to (real) referents. In what sense is *Black Square* an imitation? To what does it refer? What, if anything, is imitated? Similar questions were also raised, but with a bit more humor, by Picasso's collages (e.g., *Still Life with Chair Caning*, 1912, which incorporated "real-world" elements, including an oilcloth and a rope frame) and Duchamp's readymades (e.g., *Bicycle Wheel*, 1913, which consisted of a bicycle wheel mounted on a stool; see Figure 9.1). *Bicycle Wheel* was not a representation of a wheel, in the traditional sense; rather, it *was* a wheel.

If the traditional copy theory fails to respond readily to questions regarding the nature of the representation-reality relation, it is downright stumped by questions concerning the status of reality itself. The copy theory seems to presuppose the a priori existence of an un-represented, but none the less known, reality. This assumption is clearly problematic – even in those cases where the explicit aim of representation is reproduction. As Gombrich (1960, p. 14) and Goodman (1968, p. 7) note, there is no "innocent eye," and consequently, the copy theory seems "stopped at the start by an inability to specify what is to be copied" (Goodman, 1968, p. 9).

Notice, however, that because these post-positivist considerations apply to cases in which the explicit aim of representation is imitation, they may reveal the inadequacy of the traditional theory, but they should not be taken to indicate that imitation is not involved in representation. Most likely, as Ricoeur (1981/1991) suggests, the limitations of the traditional copy theory consist in an overly simple characterization of the mimetic process. According to Ricoeur, the simple notion of re-presenting a present reality is an artifactual formulation that follows from an ill-advised abstraction of two moments from a continuous coordination (cf. Dewey,

Figure 9.1 Bicycle wheel, by Marcel Duchamp (1913). Readymade: bicycle wheel, diameter 64.8 cm, mounted on a stool, 60.2 cm high. Original lost; this version in the collection of Arturo Schwarz, Milan. © Succession Marcel Duchamp/ADAGP Paris & DACS London 2000.

1896). Instead, Ricoeur recommends that mimesis be understood as a dialectic process, which he traces through three moments or phases. Following Aristotle, he focuses on literary representation and discusses mimesis mainly as a narrative imitation of action: the creation of a story.

For Ricoeur (1981/1991), mimesis depends first on the presence of actions – significant behavior – to be represented. Actions are significant, or meaningful, because they refer to something beyond themselves – they are *about* something (inter alia, they are about their goals). Given the availability of actions to be represented, the first moment of mimesis (mimesis$_1$) prefigures these actions, providing a partial, and perhaps implicit, understanding of their significance. Indeed, Ricoeur suggests that actions are, to some extent, *interpretants* (in Peirce's, 1932, terminology) offering rules for their own reading or interpretation (at least to those who are literate in the language of action). This point is important because it underscores the subjectivity of the mimetic process even in this first phase, where mimesis is anchored to external events.

The second phase of mimesis (mimesis$_2$) corresponds to the active configuration of the actions that are prefiguratively understood in mimesis$_1$. Ricoeur (1981/1991) refers to this process of configuration as *emplotment* – the arrangement of events into a coherent story in order to "augment their readability" (p. 141). The actions are not only understood, as in mimesis$_1$, they are *interpreted*, and their interpretation is achieved in the context of a variety of constraints (e.g., narrative constraints) particular to that phase of mimesis. The resulting interpretation, or story, is then "actualized" (p. 151), by reading, in the third and final phase of mimesis. That is, through reading, the actions that were prefigured in the first phase and configured in the second now become transfigured – understood differently in light of the story. Ricoeur borrows the term *iconic augmentation* from Dagognet (1973) to emphasize that mimesis is productive, rather than reproductive. Instead of re-presenting a present reality, mimesis transforms that reality.

This transformation undermines the distinctions between internal vs. external and representation vs. reality, and it further underscores the subjectivity of the entire mimetic process. As Goodman (1968, p. 33) puts it, "Nature is a product of art and discourse."

Ricoeur's (1981/1991) account of mimesis provides an alternative to the traditional copy theory of representation that none the less preserves the insight that representation captures the structure of something. Although Ricoeur was concerned with external representation, aspects of his account arguably apply to internal representation, too. Indeed, there are striking parallels between this account and the earlier developmental theory of James Mark Baldwin, according to which the roots of internal representation (particularly of self and other) can be seen in imitation in infancy. Generalizing from Ricoeur and Baldwin, I suggest that all representations (external and internal) are intrinsically imitative, although at every phase, they are also interpretative. Thus, internal representations, like external representations, are mimetic in Ricoeur's sense: they accommodate the structure of something and transfigure one's subjective experience of reality as part of an ongoing, circular process.

I begin the following section with a brief summary of Baldwin's (e.g., 1892, 1894, 1894/1968, 1897) theory of mental development, which I then discuss in terms of Ricoeur's hermeneutics, Olson's ideas as outlined earlier, and my own theoretical formulations regarding representation and the development of self-reflection.

"My sense of myself grows by imitation of you, and my sense of yourself grows in terms of my sense of myself." Baldwin (1894, p. 42)

Baldwin's theory of mental development

Baldwin (1894) defines imitation functionally as a reaction that "normally repeats its own stimulus" (p. 48). For Baldwin, babies are imitative from birth, although the character of their imitation develops considerably over the course of infancy. Initially, imitation is automatically elicited ("suggested") by the infant's experience of his or her own behavior or by the perception of stimuli in the environment (Baldwin refers to what is imitated as "the copy"). The former case corresponds to what Baldwin calls a *circular reaction* – the self-imitative repetition of a pleasurable response. The latter case, instinctive mimicry, includes "those reactions which re-produce subconscious, vaguely present stimulations: for example, the acquisition of facial expression, the contagion of emotion . . . " (Baldwin, 1894, p. 48). In both cases, there is responding that reinstates (to some degree) the circumstances that triggered it (the copy), but there are also opportunities for learning. First, because instinctive mimicry is fairly indiscriminate, the infant imitates painful as well as pleasurable responses, and only the latter will be selected for repetition. Second, efforts at repetition are subject to accidental variation, which allows fortuitous, useful variations to be retained in a manner that Baldwin considered an application of Darwin's notion of natural selection (Baldwin, 1892).

Eventually, imitation becomes less automatic and more deliberate. In fact, Baldwin suggests that the very origin of volition can be seen in changes in imitation that occur at the end of the first year of life. At this time, according to Baldwin, the maturation of a coordinating center makes possible the conscious comparison of (i.e., deliberation between) a target action to be imitated and a response in the infant's behavioral repertoire (see Figure 9.2). Now, instead of simple imitation, the infant exhibits persistent or try-try-again imitation because, as Baldwin (1892) puts it, there is a "stimulus to repeated effort [that] arises from a lack of co-ordination or identity in the different stimulations which reach the centre of co-ordination simultaneously" (p. 287). When one of these stimuli is selected for repetition (transforming a state of poly-ideism to one of mono-ideism), the infant feels the sense of effort that is a hallmark of will.

The dialectic of personal growth. For Baldwin, imitation, whether simple or persistent, is the primary way in which human beings learn about the world, including most particularly, the personal world of self and other (by *personal*, Baldwin refers

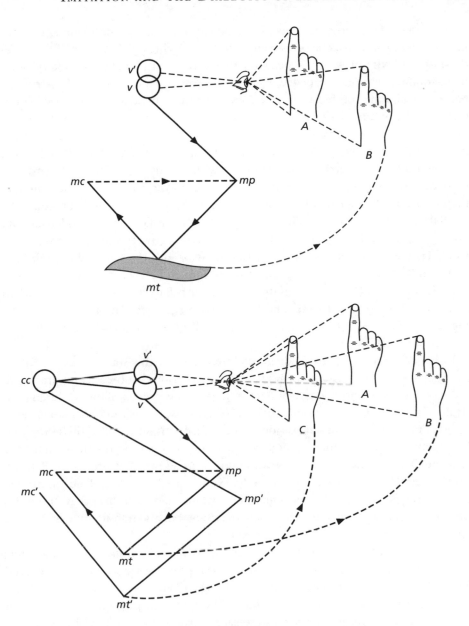

Figure 9.2 (a) Baldwin's depiction of simple imitation. *v, v′* = visual seat; *mp* = motor seat; *mt* = muscle moved; *mc* = muscle-sense seat; *A* = "copy" imitated; *B* = imitation made. The two processes *v* and *v′* flow together in the old channel *v, mp*, fixed by association, and the reaction is repeated without change or effort. (b) Baldwin's depiction of persistent imitation with effort. *C* = successful imitation; *cc* = co-ordinating centre, either local or purely functional. Other letters same as in Figure 2(a), with the added circuit *cc, mp′, mt′, mc′*. The processes at *v* and *v′* do not flow together in the old channel *v, mp*, but are co-ordinated at *cc* in a new reaction *mp′, mt′*, which includes all the elements of the "copy" (*A*) and more. The useless elements then fall away because they are useless and the successful effort is established. (Reproduced from Baldwin, 1894/1968).

both to oneself and to other persons). Baldwin describes the development of this understanding as a dialectic process of identification through imitation. The dialectic starts with the presence of behavior that is (at least partially) outside of one's behavioral repertoire, and hence, viewed in terms of its outward or *projective* aspects. By imitating this behavior, one comes to comprehend the *subjective* side of it; for example, one comes to appreciate the affect that accompanies it, or the effort involved. Once this happens, one tends automatically to *eject* this subjectivity back into the original behavior. So, for example, when a father pricks himself with a pin, his daughter may observe this behavior but without any appreciation of its painful consequence. When she imitates the behavior, however, she will feel the pain, and then immediately infer that her father felt it too. Subsequently, and consequently, she will view the behavior of pin pricking in a different fashion; her understanding of the behavior will have been transformed from projective to subjective to ejective. In effect, the child will have brought the behavior into the scope of her self- and social understanding, expanding the range of human behavior with which she can identify. Baldwin (1897) captures the ever-crescent character of identification when he writes, "It is not I, but I am to become it" (p. 36), a formulation that anticipated Freud's (1933/1940) famous dictum, "Where It was, there I shall be (Wo Es war, soll Ich werden)" (p. 86).

In general, according to Baldwin, children learn in this way, by appropriating new behaviors from suitable projects (e.g., parents) and subsequently practicing these behaviors on *ejects* (e.g., younger siblings). This process allows children (and adults, for that matter) to modify their *ego* (their sense of self) and *alter* (their sense of other), which Baldwin sees as (ideal) ends of a continuum, called the *socius*, that inevitably develop together through the dialectic of personal growth. To illustrate that the dialectic operates at every age and in a broad range of situations, Baldwin (1897) recalls being amazed by a friend's proficient typing. After Baldwin himself learned to type, he incorporated a first-person appreciation of this behavior into his own socius, adding to his own behavioral repertoire, but also transfiguring his friend's prestidigitation into a more mundane skill.

It should, perhaps, be emphasized that the socius is essentially, fundamentally, subjective. Projects are defined from one's own point of view and so is the alter. Thus, Baldwin (1897) reminds us that when the child imitates his or her father, it is a representation of the father, the "father-thought" (p. 23), and not the father himself, that is being imitated. This inescapable subjectivity follows from the fact that experience – including one's own experience of the copy to be imitated – is always phenomenal, never *noumenal* (to use the Kantian, 1781/1927, term). For Baldwin, the development of self-consciousness was understood to be the way in which phenomenal experience, and indeed history itself, unfolds in time – a point made more explicitly by James (1904).

Another point worth emphasizing is that actions to be imitated are prefigured in Baldwin's account just as they are in Ricoeur's. To see this, consider the question, "What does one imitate, and why?" Although Baldwin (1897, p. 17) writes that the child "imitates everything, being a veritable copying machine," the statement is manifestly hyperbolic. Some behavior is *already* understood by the child and corresponds to the accomplishments that he or she practices on ejects. What does get imitated is behavior that is moderately discrepant from what the child already understands, from what the child has already incorporated into his or her socius. Baldwin does not develop this suggestion, but he does make it (albeit somewhat obliquely) in his book, *Social and Ethical Interpretations of Mental Development*:

> . . . [I]f [the child] only acts strictly on the revived elements of content which come up in his own consciousness from within, then he is acting strictly as he has acted before, and that teaches him nothing. On the other hand, he cannot act in ways absolutely new, for they come into his consciousness with no tendency to stir up any appropriate kinds of action. He cannot act suitably upon them at all. Hence it is only new presentations which are assimilable to old ones that can get the benefit of habits already attached to the old ones and so lead to action more or less suited to the new. (Baldwin, 1897, p. 101)

Early in development, then, what gets imitated are new elements that are not entirely novel but instead bear some relation to what the child already knows. It is within the range of these dimly understood, prefigured behaviors that imitation is indiscriminate.

Development of conceptual understanding. In addition to appropriating partly new behaviors through imitation, children also learn about themselves and others by reflecting on the moments in the dialectic of personal growth and abstracting these moments from the continuous circular process. Initially, infants exist in a state of *adualism*, which Baldwin envisions as a kind of prelapserian innocence akin to that conveyed by Wordsworth (1904) in his famous line, "Heaven lies about us in our infancy!" (from *Ode: Intimations of Immortality from Recollections of Early Childhood*, first published in 1807). Although they are conscious in some minimal sense, infants are unaware of any distinctions that might be implicit in the structure of experience (e.g., inner vs. outer, subject vs. object, ego vs. alter; Baldwin, 1906). During the course of development, however, children proceed through a series of "progressive differentiations between the knower and the known" (Cahan, 1984, p. 131) that culminates, ironically perhaps, in transcending these dualisms and recognizing their origin in the dialectic.

Although the dialectic of imitation operates throughout the life span, there are cognitive developmental changes that affect the kinds of abstractions one might make from the dialectic. Thus, for example, the growth of the coordinating center at the end of the first year makes possible persistent imitation with effort, which Baldwin (1894, p. 42) claims is "the first volition, and the first germinating nucleus of self-hood over against object-hood. Situations before accepted simply, are now set forward, aimed at, wrought; and in the fact of aiming, working, the fact of agency, is the sense of subject." The acquisition of additional distinctions is similarly subject to developmental constraints, resulting in a fairly reliable developmental sequence that continues well into adulthood (Baldwin, 1906).

Synthesis: Representation and its Development

The parallels between Baldwin's theory of mental development and Ricoeur's account of representation are particularly striking when one considers that Baldwin was writing nearly 90 years before Ricoeur and for a very different purpose. Ricoeur recommends that representation be understood as a dialectic of mimesis; Baldwin's theory, based on developmental data, suggests that a similar dialectic has its roots in infant imitation.

The conceptualization of representation as a kind of productive or generative imitation provides a rich alternative to the traditional copy theory. In all cases of representation, an agent captures some aspect of the perceived structure of something (a "copy"), interprets this aspect in light of various constraints (epistemic, artistic, etc.), and consequently changes one's construal of whatever was imitated (changes one's copy). As shown in Figure 9.3, a prefiguration (prefiguration$_n$) is the basis of a configuration (configuration$_n$), which then leads to a transfiguration (transfiguration$_n$) of the initial prefiguration. The transfiguration can then reenter the circle as a new prefiguration (prefiguration$_{n+1}$), as can the configuration itself when it becomes an object of consideration. This basic process will be familiar to anyone who has ever written descriptively about something – say, about someone else's theory (to use a reflexive example). First, one's writing is obviously constrained by (what one perceives to be) the structure of the theory – that is, by the prefigured theory. Second, there are discursive (and other) constraints introduced by the writing process (i.e., in the process of configuration). Third, the entire exercise, including an appreciation of the resulting description, transfigures one's understanding of the theory described. The transfigured theory can then serve as the basis for another iteration of the mimetic process. Moreover, just as text can serve as a model of speech (Olson, 1994), the description of the theory itself (the configuration) can serve as a relatively concrete model of one's thinking about the theory. This model provides feedback that can scaffold the representational process and facilitate critical self-reflection.

Although the above-mentioned example may feel familiar to the reader, it is important to recognize that this same process is inherent in *every* instance of representation, including those that operate outside of focal attention. Indeed, consideration of different kinds of representation is instructive. For one thing, it helps clarify the relation between internal and external representations, which in turn permits one to chart the course of internalization. To see this, consider the case of behavioral imitation. This is a form of external or public representation insofar as it is the imitator's overt, publicly observable behavior that most conspicuously captures (some aspect of) the structure of the action that is imitated; the imitator's overt behavior is a kind of configuration. However, to the extent that the imitation is genuine imitation (and not, say, the elicitation of a fixed action pattern; Jacobson & Kagan, 1979), it is also undoubtedly mediated by internal or private representation, as Meltzoff and Moore (1998) and others have argued. That is, no matter how reflexive (in the full sense of the term) the imitation may be, the translation from the

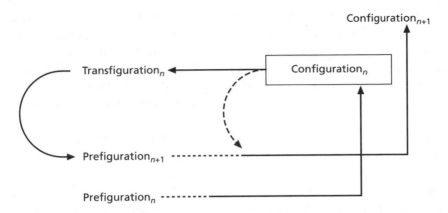

Figure 9.3 A schematic depiction of representation as a circular process. Prefiguration$_n$ provides the raw material for configuration$_n$, which then effects a transfiguration$_n$ when it is "read." Transfiguration$_n$ can serve recursively as prefiguration$_{n+1}$, as can configuration$_n$.

perception of another person's behavior to one's own imitative expression requires some form of intermediate (perceptual-cognitive) representation that preserves (some aspect of) the structure of the observed behavior at some level of abstraction. This is as true of yawning as it is of, say, my concerted efforts to improve my French pronunciation. We may identify moments in the imitative process that deserve to be called internal or external, but every instance of behavioral imitation involves both. More generally, all instances of external representation also involve internal representation.

One thing to notice about behavioral imitation is that one's own imitative behavior, being a relatively concrete expression of one's internal representation, scaffolds the whole process of representation by providing an interim model of one's thinking. This feedback allows one to reflect on the representation and potentially to modify it. Gradually, one may come to rely less on this feedback, much in the same way that we learn to do long division without the aid of paper and pencil.

Perhaps the most important thing to notice about behavioral imitation, though, is that the presence of the model's behavior provides a relatively rich set of constraints on the representation that is achieved and expressed. Indeed, we might say that the model's behavior serves as a fairly explicit suggestion or prop for the imitator's representational effort. Serving as a prop is one of the key characteristics of external representations (Walton, 1990). A painting, for example, invites one to imagine a certain configuration of events. In the case of a "realistic" painting, the suggestion is often fairly explicit, and our conceptual image will be relatively constrained. In other cases (e.g., impressionist painting), the suggestion may be more subtle (see Gombrich, 1963, p. 10). (Incidentally, so-called nonrepresentational painting often provides explicit props, it is just that the suggested conceptual image may be primarily formal, as in Malevich's *Black Square*.)

This characterization of external representations in terms of the degree to which they provide explicit suggestions regarding what is to be represented, and of behavioral imitation as representation that is constrained by a relatively explicit suggestion, suggests a metric by which we might measure the course of internalization. Consider the case of pretend play, which typically develops during the second year of life. In pretend play, one treats something (a pretense object) as something else (a real object). Over the course of the second year, children become more likely to perform pretend actions (e.g., talking on the telephone) with pretense objects (e.g., a spoon) that bear little physical resemblance to the real objects, and they also become more likely to perform pretend actions without objects altogether (e.g., Ungerer, Zelazo, Kearsley, & O'Leary, 1981). Moreover, there are proportional (complementary) age differences in children's ability to resist responding on the basis of the actions suggested by the real objects (Elder & Pederson, 1978; Pederson, Rook-Green, & Elder, 1981). Thus, in this context, one sees increasing independence from the literal context, and an increasing reliance on imagination (see also Overton & Jackson, 1973; O'Reilly, 1995, for work with preschoolers). As Vygotsky (1978, p. 103) puts it: "It is remarkable that the child starts with an imaginary situation that initially is so very close to the real one. A reproduction of the real situation takes place." He describes the child at this point in terms of a ratio where object properties dominate meaning (a relation he depicts as "object/meaning"). Initially, we might say that representation is relatively stimulus-bound, or context dependent, and, correlatively, that representational structure is determined primarily by something external. Eventually, however, children become capable of creating representations on the basis of more subtle suggestions, and we might say that their representations are less dependent on external context and more internally determined. (Note that representation is productive in all cases; this distinguishes internally determined representation from mere assimilation, which is internally driven but in a different, nonproductive way.) Thus, in pretend play, the locus of control shifts from external to internal during the course of the second year.

Conceptualized in this way, it becomes clear that internalization is not an explanatory mechanism, but an explanandum. In the course of internalization, structure in the environment is transferred into a representing organism. An explanation of this pervasive developmental process can perhaps be sought in an account of representation as productive imitation.

Conceptual understanding of representation

In addition to being a byproduct of mimetic representation, the internalization (and consequent decontextualization) of representations will undoubtedly also be affected by children's growing conceptual understanding of representation. Gombrich (1963, p. 9), for example, describes the cultural insight that representations might correspond to a particular visual experience rather than to reality, and he suggests that this had dramatic consequences for the history of painting (permitting Giotto, e.g., to depict a person as seen from behind). Several other authors (e.g., DeLoache,

Pierroutsakos, & Troseth, 1996; Liben, 1999) have described similar insights from an ontogenetic perspective, and they uniformly agree that the consequences for behavior are profound.

Like the decontextualization seen in children's use of objects, the development of children's conceptual understanding of representation can be considered in the context of pretend play. Olson and Campbell (1993, pp. 16–17) articulate one position on this issue: "Pretend play is one of the first clear indications of the understanding of symbols." They then go on to suggest that pretense objects (e.g., a bench used as a horse) are "not true symbols in that they do not yet represent any *particular* thing" (my emphasis). A similar point has been made by DeLoache and Burns (1993, p. 108), who suggest that toddlers generally fail to appreciate the "representational specificity" of symbols that they employ when pretending. I would suggest, however, that the limitations on children's conceptual understanding of pretense objects as symbols are more severe – even though their pretend play is certainly representational, as described above.

The severity of this conceptual limitation is suggested by DeLoache et al.'s (1996, p. 30) remark that babies "see through" pictures. Indeed, as Vygotsky (1978, p. 108) notes, it is the reality behind the picture that matters to infants and young children: "What is most important is the utilization of the plaything and the possibility of executing a representational gesture with it . . . A pile of clothes or a piece of wood become a baby in a game *because* the same gestures that depict holding a baby in one's hands can apply to them" (my emphasis). Similarly, Gombrich (1963, p. 4), who generally addresses the question of the history of representation, rather than its ontogeny, suggests, "The baby sucks its thumb as if it were the breast . . . But here too 'representation' does not depend on formal similarities, beyond the minimal requirements of function." This analysis, which suggests that pretend play initially corresponds to substitution rather than explicit symbolization, fits well with the gradual decontextualization that can be seen in this context. Although pretend play always involves representation, and (initially at least) involves the use of external representation, it does not strictly require an understanding of external representation.

Mechanisms underlying the acquisition of conceptual understanding of representation: use and reflection

Using representations involves both interpreting them and producing them, and as with the distinction between internal and external representations, they invariably occur together, so it is somewhat artificial to consider them separately. By using representations, one comes to understand more aspects of the representing relation. Vygotsky (1934/1962, p. 90) viewed this as one instance of a more general developmental law: ". . . [C]onsciousness and control appear only at a late stage in the development of a function, after it has been used and practiced unconsciously and spontaneously." The basic aspects of this law have been preserved in more recent accounts. For example, Bruner (e.g., 1973, p. 329) notes that the movement from an enactive representation to an iconic one is dependent on "a certain amount of motoric skill and practice." Similarly, Karmiloff-Smith (1992) suggests that the use of procedural representations drives their redescription into a more explicit (and conscious) format.

Both Liben (1999) and DeLoache (e.g., DeLoache et al., 1996) emphasize the transformative effect of using representations. For example, when DeLoache et al. (1996, p. 37) discuss the difference between 2- and 2.5-year-olds' use of pictures to guide search for a hidden object, they suggest that the older children understand the "intention regarding how pictures are to be used in this situation," and they further note that children at this age "have also begun to *produce* pictures" (their italics). Drawing may provide insight into the artist's intention to represent a particular referent. Without a first-person appreciation of this intention, it is no wonder that the purpose of pictures is obscure.

At the very least, using representations provides an opportunity for the discovery of certain of their properties. For example, sophisticated symbol users eventually identify various aspects of the representational process. This understanding develops gradually, and several authors have described its development in detail (e.g., DeLoache et al., 1996; Liben, 1999). As Liben notes, children first come to distinguish the representation from its meaning; then they come to appreciate the relation between them; and so on. These discoveries, however, will be constrained by age-related, domain-general limitations on the complexity of the relations children can formulate.

As noted, Olson (e.g., 1993) suggests that changes in the complexity of children's representations (and their understanding of representations) can be attributed to changes in memory or holding in mind. For reasons outlined elsewhere, I believe that this suggestion is too simple, on its own, to account for the extant data. An alternative, which is broadly consistent with the dialectic accounts offered by Ricoeur and Baldwin, is to attribute increases in complexity to a functional process of recursion whereby the contents of consciousness are fed back into consciousness so that they can become available to consciousness at a higher level. This suggestion follows from the Levels of Consciousness model (LOC model; e.g., Zelazo, 1999b), an information processing model of the role of reflection in the control of thought and action. According to the LOC model, there are four major age-related increases in the highest level of consciousness that children are able to muster in response to situational demands. These increases, which are brought about by recursion, have important consequences for the quality of subjective experience, the potential for recall, the complexity of knowledge structures, and the possibility of action control. First, recursion adds depth to subjective experience because more details can be integrated into the experience before the contents of consciousness are replaced by new environmental stimulation. Second, each degree of recursion causes information to be processed at a deeper, less superficial level (Craik & Lockhart, 1972), which increases the likelihood of retrieval (Craik & Tulving, 1975). Third, higher levels of consciousness allow for the formulation and use of more complex knowledge structures. The complexity of these knowledge structures, which is measured in terms of the number of degrees of embedding in the structures (e.g., an "if X then if Y then Z" rule is more complex than an "if Y then Z" rule), determines the scope of one's cognitive control. In general, recursion moves consciousness further away from the exigencies of environmental stimulation in what might be called *psychological distance* (cf. DeLoache, 1993; Dewey, 1931/1985; Sigel, 1993), and this allows for the formulation of increasingly complex, and more decontextualized discursive reasoning. It is this representational complexity that more directly constrains the development of children's conceptual understanding of representation (e.g., Frye, Zelazo, & Palfai, 1995; Zelazo & Frye, 1997).

Figure 9.4 illustrates several aspects of the LOC model, which is explained more fully elsewhere (e.g., Zelazo, 1999b). Briefly, the basic psychological processes that are depicted in the figure include: minimal consciousness (abbreviated as minC), semantic and procedural long-term memory (LTM), and working memory (WM). MinC, which is perhaps the most important theoretical primitive in the model, is meant to be the simplest, but still conceptually coherent, kind of consciousness that we can imagine. When an object in the environment (objA) triggers an intentional representation of that object (IobjA) from semantic long-term memory (LTM), the IobjA can become the content of minC, by way of which it can trigger an associated action program stored in procedural LTM. When the entire contents of minC are fed back into minC via a recursive loop, a higher level of consciousness is achieved, namely recursive consciousness (recC). The contents of this level of consciousness can be related to a corresponding description descA or label, which can then be deposited into working memory where it can serve as a goal (G1) to trigger an action program (stored in procedural LTM). Self-consciousness involves another degree of recursion, and makes possible the use of conditionally specified self-directed speech (i.e., rules). Additional degrees of recursion (not depicted in Figure 9.4) yield additional levels of consciousness, and each new level of consciousness affords a new degree of self-regulation by allowing the formulation and use of rules of greater complexity.

Conclusion

At this point, we might ask how this approach addresses the questions that proved so problematic for the copy theory. As we saw, certain kinds of visual art, for example, challenge the viewer to answer the question, What is represented? In light of our account, we can now say that all art is representational in some sense – just not in the sense supposed by the copy theory. The Canadian (abstract) painter Kazuo Nakamura recently pointed out that "most of what people call abstract art is, in fact, just decoration derived from the natural world" (Dault, 1999). While I am inclined to agree, I would add that we should liberate ourselves from the inclination to think that art represents a present and objective reality (the "natural world"). Instead, consistent with the (inescapable) subjectivity noted in the above account, it represents something subjective. This may be a particular perception of something or it

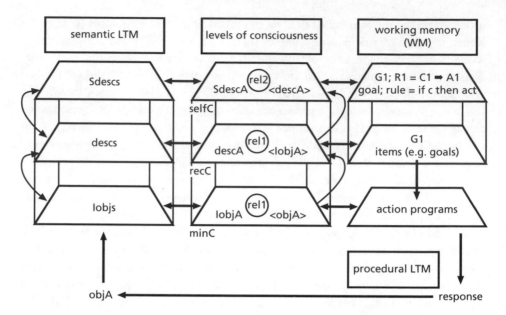

Figure 9.4 A process model of self-consciousness (adapted from "Children's rule use: Representation, reflection, and cognitive control" by P. D. Zelazo and S. Jacques, 1996, in R. Vasta (Ed.), *Annals of Child Development, Vol. 12*, p. 163). See text for an explanation.

may be an idea or even a feeling. An external representation is a prop that serves to elicit this subjective state in another person, and as such, it "repeats its own stimulus" (Baldwin, 1894, p. 48).

We might also, at this point, summarize the way in which our account speaks to the issues that Olson raised in his work. First, unlike Olson, the account maintains that representation is present throughout the life span. However, it is consistent with Olson's suggestion that there are qualitative changes in conceptual understanding that allow for the construction of increasingly complex representations. Whereas Olson attributed these to increases in holding in mind, the current approach attributes them to increases in self-reflection. These explanations are not necessarily contradictory: increases in self-reflection may depend on increased resources – in memory, as Olson suggests, or perhaps in speed of processing (Zelazo & Zelazo, 1998).

Second, far from being "a concept of doubtful application" (Olson & Campbell, 1993, p. 13), internalization proves to be a central feature of the development of representation. Just as children become less dependent on paralinguistic context to constrain the interpretation of speech (Olson, 1977), and presumably learn to supply the constraints themselves, we can see how the external support for representation may be gradually diminished, with the agent requiring fewer external constraints in order to achieve the appropriate conceptual image.

Third, literacy proves to be a paradigmatic case of a more general dialectic phenomenon. One must "read" representations whether they be literary, visual, or even behavioral, and in all cases, external representation serves as a model of the (pre- and configurational) internal representations that generated them. The use of this model facilitates representation in several ways, but it does so primarily by creating opportunities for critical self-reflection.

Finally, the current account contrasts with many contemporary models of cognition, including Olson's, in its rejection of certain rationalist assumptions. Olson (1994), for one, insists on the rationality of human cognition when he writes: "Although no one, these days, believes in the possibility of a non-rational mind . . . " (p. 15); and again, "Of course all people are rational; it is part of the definition of a human being . . ." (p. 22). Indeed, the rationalism of his approach is apparent not only in its position regarding the primacy of symbolic thought in development (and its independence from cultural conditioning), but also in its elegance and its scope. In contrast, however, the current account emphasizes interactions and collapses across familiar, and seemingly self-evident, distinctions. In addition, the cognitive developmental model that underlies this account of representation (the LOC model; Zelazo, 1999b) suggests that apparently irrational dissociations between knowledge and action are the norm not only during child development, but also across the life span. This alternative approach may be messy, but if so, then I hope that this is at least partly because it captures something of the dynamic structure of the phenomena themselves.

Acknowledgments

Preparation of this paper was supported in part by a grant from NSERC of Canada to P. D. Zelazo. I would like to thank Janet Astington, Laurel Bidwell, Stephen Cain, Sophie Jacques, Ulrich Mueller, David Olson, and Dean Sharpe for their helpful comments on an earlier draft of this chapter.

Note

1   A similar story could be told for other art forms, such as literature and music, but as Calvin Tomkins (1966) tells us, "The avant-garde painters and sculptors were ahead of their literary and musical colleagues. . . in their decisive break with the past" (p. 8).

References

Aristotle (1927). *Selections* (W. D. Ross, Trans.). New York: Charles Scribner's Sons.

Baldwin, J. M. (1892). Origin of volition in childhood. *Science, 20*, 286–88.

Baldwin, J. M. (1894). Imitation: A chapter in the natural history of consciousness. *Mind, 3*, 26–55.

Baldwin, J. M. (1897). *Social and ethical interpretations in mental development: A study in social psychology.* New York: Macmillan.

Baldwin, J. M. (1906). *Thought and things: A study in the development and meaning of thought, or, genetic logic; Vol. 1. Functional logic, or, genetic theory of knowledge.* New York: Macmillan.

Baldwin, J. M. (1968). *Mental development in the child and the race* (3rd edition). New York: Augustus M. Kelley. (Original work published in 1894).

Bruner, J. (1973). *Beyond the information given* (J. Anglin, Ed.). New York: Norton.

Cahan, E. (1984). The genetic psychologies of James Mark Baldwin and Jean Piaget. *Developmental Psychology, 20,* 128–35.

Case, R. (1985). *Intellectual development: Birth to adulthood.* New York: Academic Press.

Craik, F. I. M., & Lockhart, R. S. (1972). Levels of processing: A framework for memory research. *Journal of Verbal Learning and Verbal Behavior, 11,* 671–684.

Craik, F. I. M., & Tulving, E. (1975). Depth of processing and the retention of words in episodic memory. *Journal of Experimental Psychology: General, 104,* 268–294.

Dagognet, F. (1973). *Ecriture et iconographie* [Writing and iconography]. Paris: J. Vrin.

Dault, G. M. (1999, May 15). Kazuo Nakamura's lucky numbers. *The Globe and Mail,* p. E2.

DeLoache, J. (1993). Distancing and dual representation. In R. R. Cocking & K. A. Renninger (Eds.), *The development and meaning of psychological distance* (pp. 91–107). Hillsdale, NJ: Erlbaum.

DeLoache, J. S., & Burns, N. M. (1993). Symbolic development in young children: Understanding models and pictures. In C. Pratt and A. F. Garton (Eds.), *Systems of representation in children: Development and use* (pp. 91–112). Chichester, England: Wiley.

DeLoache, J. S., Pierroutsakos, S. L., & Troseth, G. L. (1996). The three 'R's of pictorial competence. In R. Vasta (Ed.), *Annals of child development, Vol. 12* (pp. 1–48). London: Jessica Kingsley Press.

Dewey, J. (1896). The reflex arc concept in psychology. *Psychological Review, 3,* 357–70.

Dewey, J. (1985). Context and thought. In J. A. Boydston (Ed.) & A. Sharpe (Textual Ed.), *John Dewey: The later works, 1925–1953* (Vol. 6, 1931–1932) (pp. 3–21). Carbondale, IL: Southern Illinois University Press. (Original work published in 1931).

Elder, J. L., & Pederson, D. R. (1978). Preschool children's use of objects in symbolic play. *Child Development, 49,* 500–4.

Freud, S. (1940). Neue folge der Vorlesungen zur Einführung in die Psychoanalyse [New introductory lectures on psychoanalysis]. In A. Freud, E. Bibring, & E. Kris (Eds.), *Gesammelte Werke: XV* (Whole volume). London: Imago Publishing Co. (Original work published 1933).

Frye, D., Zelazo, P. D., & Palfai, T. (1995). Theory of mind and rule-based reasoning. *Cognitive Development, 10,* 483–527.

Gombrich, E. H. (1960). *Art and illusion: A study in the psychology of pictorial representation.* New York: Pantheon Books.

Gombrich, E. H. (1963). *Meditations on a hobby horse: And other essays on the theory of art.* London: Phaidon Press.

Goodman, N. (1968). *Languages of art: An approach to a theory of symbols.* Oxford, UK: Oxford University Press.

Grice, P. (1957). Meaning. *The Philosophical Review, 66,* 377–88.

Inhelder, B., & Piaget, J. (1972). *The growth of logical thinking from childhood to adolescence: An essay on the construction of formal operational structures* (A. Parsons & S. Milgrim, Trans.). London: Routledge & Kegan Paul. (Original work published 1955).

Jacobson, S. W., & Kagan, J. (1979, July 13). Interpreting "imitative" responses in early infancy. *Science, 205,* 215–17.

James, W. (1904). Does 'consciousness' exist? *The Journal of Philosophy, Psychology and Scientific Methods, 1,* 477–91.

Kamawar, D., & Olson, D. R. (in press). Children's representational theory of language: The problem of opaque contexts. *Cognitive Development.*

Kant, I. (1927). *Critique of pure reason* (F. M. Muller, Trans.). New York: Macmillan. (Original work published in 1781).

Karmiloff-Smith, A. (1992). *Beyond modularity.* Cambridge, MA: MIT Press.

Liben, L. S. (1999). Developing an understanding of external spatial representations. In I. E. Sigel (Ed.), *The development of mental representations: Theories and applications* (pp. 297–321). Mahwah, NJ: Erlbaum.

Meltzoff, A. N., & Moore, M. K. (1998). Object representation, identity, and the paradox of early permanence: Steps toward a new framework. *Infant Behavior and Development, 21,* 201–35.

Olson, D. R. (1977). From utterance to text: The bias of language in speech and writing. *Harvard Educational Review, 47,* 257–81.

Olson, D. R. (1986). The cognitive consequences of literacy. *Canadian Psychology, 27,* 109–21.

Olson, D. R. (1988). On the origins of beliefs and other intentional states in children. In J. W. Astington, P. L. Harris, & D. R. Olson (Eds.), *Developing theories of mind* (pp. 414–26). New York: Cambridge University Press.

Olson, D. R. (1989). Making up your mind. *Canadian Psychology, 30,* 617–27.

Olson, D. R. (1993). The development of representations: The origins of mental life. *Canadian Psychology, 34,* 293–306.

Olson, D. R. (1994). *The world on paper.* Cambridge, UK: Cambridge University Press.

Olson, D. R., & Campbell, R. (1993). Constructing representations. In C. Pratt & A. F. Garton (Eds.), *Systems of representation in children: Development and use* (pp. 11–26). Chichester, UK: Wiley.

Olson, D. R., & Kamawar, D. (1999). The theory of ascriptions. In P. D. Zelazo, J. W. Astington, & D. R. Olson (Eds.), *Developing theories of intention: Social understanding and self-control* (pp. 153–66). Mahwah, NJ: Erlbaum.

O'Reilly, A. W. (1995). Using representations: Comprehension and production of actions with imagined objects. *Child Development, 66,* 999–1010.

Overton, W. F., & Jackson, J. P. (1973). The representation of imagined objects in action sequences: A developmental study. *Child Development, 44,* 309–14.

Pascual-Leone, J. (1970). A mathematical model for the transition rule in Piaget's developmental stages. *Acta Psychologica, 32,* 301–45.

Pederson, D. R., Rook-Green, A., & Elder, J. L. (1981). The role of action in the development of pretend play in young children. *Developmental Psychology, 17,* 756–59.

Peirce, C. S. (1932). *Collected papers: Vol. 2: Elements of logic.* Cambridge, MA: Harvard University Press.

Piaget, J. (1952). *The origins of intelligence in children* (M. Cook, Trans.). New York: Vintage. (Original work published in 1936).

Ricoeur, P. (1991). Mimesis and representation (D. Pellaeur, Trans.). In M. J. Valdes (Ed.), *A Ricoeur reader: Reflection and imagination.* Toronto, Canada: University of Toronto Press. (Original work published in 1981).

Sigel, I. (1993). The centrality of a distancing model for the development of representational competence. In R. R. Cocking & K. A. Renninger (Eds.), *The development and meaning of psychological distance* (pp. 91–107). Hillsdale, NJ: Erlbaum.

Tomkins, C. (1966). *The world of Marcel Duchamp*. New York: Time Inc.

Tulving, E. (1985). Memory and consciousness. *Canadian Journal of Psychology, 25*, 1–12.

Ungerer, J. A., Zelazo, P. R., Kearsley, R. B., & O'Leary, K. (1981). Developmental changes in the representation of objects in symbolic play from 18 to 34 months of age. *Child Development, 52*, 186–95.

Vygotsky, L. S. (1962). *Thought and language* (E. Hanfmann & G. Vakar, Trans.). Cambridge, MA: MIT Press. (Original work published 1934).

Vygotsky, L. S. (1978). *Mind in society: The development of higher psychological processes*. Cambridge, MA: Harvard University Press.

Walton, K. L. (1990). *Mimesis as make-believe: On the foundations of the representational arts*. Cambridge, MA: Harvard University Press.

Wheeler, M. (in press). Varieties of consciousness and memory in the developing child. In E. Tulving (Ed.), *Memory, consciousness, and the brain: The Tallinn Conference*. Philadelphia: Psychology Press.

Wordsworth, W. (1904). *The poetical works of Wordsworth* (T. Hutchinson, Ed.). Oxford, UK: Oxford University Press.

Zelazo, P. D. (1999a). *Imitation and the dialectic of representation*. Unpublished manuscript, University of Toronto.

Zelazo, P. D. (1999b). Language, levels of consciousness, and the development of intentional action. In Zelazo, P. D., Astington, J. W., & Olson, D. R. (Eds.), *Developing theories of intention: social understanding and self-control* (pp. 95–117). Mahwah, NJ: Erlbaum.

Zelazo, P. D., & Frye, D. (1997). Cognitive complexity and control: A theory of the development of deliberate reasoning and intentional action. In M. Stamenov (Ed.), *Language structure, discourse, and the access to consciousness* (pp. 113–53). Amsterdam & Philadelphia: John Benjamins.

Zelazo, P. D., & Jacques, S. (1996). Children's rule use: Representation, reflection, and cognitive control. In R. Vasta (Ed.), *Annals of child development, Vol. 12* (pp. 119–76). London: Jessica Kingsley Press.

Zelazo, P. R., & Zelazo, P. D. (1998). The emergence of consciousness. In H. H. Jasper, L. Descarries, V. F., Castellucci, & S. Rossignol (Eds.), *Consciousness: At the frontiers of neuroscience: Advances in Neurology, Vol. 77* (pp. 149–65). New York: Lippincott-Raven Press.

10

Content and the Representation of Belief and Desire

Robin N. Campbell

I first met David Olson when we spent the session of 1978–79 together at the Netherlands Institute for Advanced Studies in Wassenaar. We were part of a group put together by Jerry Bruner which included Melissa Bowerman, Paul van Geert, Bea de Gelder, Margriet van Ierland, Herman Parret, Maire Logan Ryan, and Manny Schegloff. I had just finished a difficult and direly neglected paper which masqueraded as a review of work on the relationship between cognitive development and language acquisition but which was actually about the need to distinguish between what would now be called explicit and implicit knowledge.[1] I badgered David throughout the year about this topic, since it became evident that he was interested in it too and not afraid to try to make sense of what consciousness had to do with cognition. In the following years David's interest in left field psychology developed strongly, doubtless exacerbated by his involvement with the McLuhan Program at the University of Toronto, and, of course, the memory people in Toronto, notably Endel Tulving, had begun to grapple in their empirically orthodox ways with the distinction between implicit and explicit memory. So David must have thought of mc and my weird ideas and was kind enough to arrange a visit for me to the University of Toronto in the session 1986–7. We spent many happy hours that year discussing a different aspect of the content of cognition, namely whether cognitive development could be characterized as a process involving changes in what sorts of ontological categories children could think about, and whether some of Piaget's ideas about cognitive development could be reconstrued in this way. This collaboration resulted in three joint papers – Campbell and Olson (1990) and Olson and Campbell (1993, 1994) – and David presented most of the decent ideas in his Presidential Address to the CPA Conference in 1989 (see Olson, 1989). The ideas explored in this chapter – a further application of the principle that content matters – were also first put forward at that 1989 conference. What merit they have is thus due to our discussions in Toronto a few years before. I should also like to acknowledge the encouragement and influence of Ellen Bialystok, Gordon Wells, and especially Janet Astington, and the postgraduate group at OISE during that period. The arguments offered against John Searle's analysis of desire were developed later, but the impetus to examine Searle's analysis came from these OISE discussions of the development of understanding of belief and desire.

In this paper I attempt to apply some ideas about the importance of *content* to issues concerning children's ability to represent the beliefs and desires of others – or, in plainer language, to think about their thoughts. I will start by expressing some general reservations about the theory-of-mind enterprise as a whole. One of the insights to come out of Europe in the 1920s and early 1930s was the idea that cognitive development involved increase in powers of representation; this was not only a feature of the well-known works of Piaget and Vygotsky but was also strongly implied by the comparative psychological writings of Wolfgang Köhler. I incline strongly to the Piagetian position that children are initially devoid of representational powers. In short, that there is literally nothing that an infant can think about. According to Piaget, the first signs of such representational powers appear around the end of the second year with object permanence, deferred imitation, insightful solutions to detour problems, and so forth.

For Piaget, of course, perception did not imply representation: it was only when the infant could react to an object which was not present, or reproduce an action not recently performed, that it made sense to him to speak of *representation*. But the representational powers implied by these achievements of late infancy may be quite limited – perhaps only that children can now think about absent objects and anticipate the outcome of certain kinds of action, etc. The central theory-of-mind claim, on the other hand, is that by age 4, children can represent and therefore (to my way of thinking) – *think about* or *hold in mind* – the thoughts (beliefs, intentions, desires) of another actor. If one takes the Piagetian position, then, this sets a very demanding agenda for the 2-year period from around 2 to around 4 years of age: hard work for the child and even harder work for those who would explain the child.

If one is uncomfortable about such a rapid advance in representational powers, then there are two moves that might be made. On the one hand, there is the idea that the powers of the infant might have been underestimated. On the other, there is the idea that the powers of the 4-year-old may have been overestimated. Although my own mind remains more or less closed to the first possibility, it remains open to the second. After all, the key demonstrations of the new powers – the various Wimmer and Perner false belief tasks (see e.g., Astington & Gopnik, 1991a) – demonstrate only successful prediction of the actions of others in situations where the judging subject would act differently. We are accustomed to the idea, following Vygotsky, that young children may use language in a quite transparent way to control the behavior of others, without explicit knowledge of the linguistic means by which this control is achieved. It may be that 4-year-olds develop practical means for efficient prediction without having any explicit knowledge of these means. In that case we might prefer not to say that the false belief tasks show that 4-year-olds can think about the *thoughts* of others, but only that they can think about the possible actions of others, and evaluate their likelihood efficiently.

However, this is a bleak and skeptical view. Moreover, it fails to do justice to the care taken by Wimmer and Perner in seeking to exclude alternative explanations to the one that they prefer. Perner, too, (e.g., 1991a) has strongly resisted the tendency – now lamentably commonplace – to assume that everything of substance in cognitive development is innate and so has accepted the difficult agenda of strong development of representational powers in the period between 2 and 4 years of age.

The Content of Beliefs

If we are uneasy with this agenda of strong development of representational powers, but wish to save the general hypothesis that 18-month-olds can't think about anything much and that 4-year-olds can think about the thoughts of others, then what can we do to quell the uneasiness? In Campbell and Olson (1990) we explored the notion that development may be staggered for different representational content. Possibly thoughts of rather circumscribed content may be entertained by 2-year-olds, allowing us to maintain the view that there is not very much that they can think about while conceding that they may occasionally think about states of affairs other than the one that currently confronts them. Again, it may be that 4-year-olds can represent the thoughts of others only if these thoughts have a similarly circumscribed content.

Oddly enough, there is already some immediate encouragement for this idea. Surely, if we were to allow that 2-year-olds could represent a certain class of thoughts, a likely candidate class would be thoughts about the *location* of hidden or absent objects, because of the strong development of object permanence and other searching skills. It may then be no coincidence that the false belief task employed by Wimmer and Perner involves attribution by the subject of beliefs about the location of a hidden object.

There is another version of the false belief task in common use which does not require attribution of a false belief about the location of a hidden object. This is the unexpected contents task (in which, say, an eggbox is found to contain marbles) and children succeed with it at roughly the same age[2] (Hogrefe, Wimmer, & Perner, 1986, Experiments 1 & 2; Perner, Leekam, & Wimmer, 1987, Experiment 2; Wimmer & Hartl, 1991). However, the relative difficulty of constructing the target belief here – a belief about what *kind* of thing is in the box – and in the standard location task may be obscured by other differences in procedure. In the location task the subject (or informed puppet) knows that the chocolate is at B and her knowledge of this is carefully checked. When the owner of the chocolate returns, knowledge of its original hiding place, A, is checked and the subject is carefully informed that Maxi decides to get his chocolate. If Maxi wants his chocolate and thinks that it is hidden at A and is a rational being, he should therefore look at A. In the unexpected contents task the child is merely asked,

"If I show this box to Y [a second child or puppet], all closed up like this, what will she say/think is in it?'

Presumably the 4-year-old is supposed to say "Eggs" because:

(a) eggboxes usually contain eggs
(b) this is an eggbox with contents concealed
(c) Y is presumed to be rational

But in fact no attempt is made to verify that the subject knows that Y would assent to (a) and (b). Perhaps if the subject were given the following instruction instead, the task would be somewhat easier:

> "Look, here comes Snoopy. I'm going to show him the box all closed up like this. Snoopy sees that it's an eggbox and he knows eggboxes usually have eggs in them. What will he say is in the box?"

A second point of difference between the unexpected contents task and the location task concerns the degree of commitment to the judgment made. When shown a closed eggbox and asked "What do you think is in the box?" I am certainly disposed to say "Eggs" but whether it is right to say that I *believe* that there are eggs in the box is another matter. I am, we might say, making an educated guess, but I would not agree that I knew that there were eggs in the box or commit myself to other claims implying a firm representation of hidden eggs. So the task is very unbalanced: the subject has grounds – as good as they come – for her belief that there are marbles in the box (she just saw them), but Snoopy has rather poorer grounds for the target belief that it contains eggs. It follows that the subject has a correspondingly weak basis for belief ascription. So I am not dismayed by the coincidence that the two tasks are mastered at roughly the same age and in particular, I do not think that it shows that one type of false belief is as easily represented as another.

Once we are alerted to the idea that different sorts of belief might be differently representable, other relevant distinctions between kinds of belief come to mind. The tasks just described both involve updatable, revisable beliefs or guesses. Presumably, it is just this sort of belief which we might first learn was empirically vulnerable. Accordingly, such false beliefs might be the first to be ascribed to other actors. But many of our beliefs, although still *contingent* beliefs, are not readily revisable, for example, beliefs about the origins or causes of natural phenomena. Sticking with eggs, our subject might believe that eggs come from chickens. Suppose we established that our subject held this belief, and then introduced little John, whose mischievous father had misinformed him that eggs were laid by pigs. Little John goes on holiday to a farm and the farmer sends him out to collect some eggs. Where would he be predicted to look for eggs? In the chickenhouse or in the pigpen?[3] Obviously, more examples could be produced but the point may already be clear enough. The sorts of thoughts that a 2-year-old can have may be quite restricted in content and, equally, it may be that the sorts of thoughts that a 4-year-old can represent or think about may be similarly quite restricted.

As a bridge to my next topic, we may note that all the beliefs so far discussed are readily construed in a referential manner, or *de re* as some would put it. They are beliefs about a certain bar of chocolate, or about eggboxes, or about one particular box, or about eggs. However, notoriously, some beliefs are not about any definite thing – in the sense that we don't have anything in mind that the belief is about. So if I am nearly run over by a speeding car I might form the belief that the driver of the car – whoever he or she is – is a criminal lunatic. With such beliefs, truth-value changes when a co-designative expression is substituted. So, supposing the driver was in fact my mother, it does not follow that I believe that my mother is a criminal lunatic. Beliefs construed in this fashion as being about who or whatever satisfies the description of the subject of the target proposition are sometimes described as *de dicto* beliefs.

Desires and Beliefs

There are many possible ways in which desires and beliefs might be distinguished, and discussions by Perner (1991b) and by Astington and Gopnik (1991b) have helped clarify some of these ways. For example, it may be that beliefs are typically shared – thus making the ascription of a different belief hard – but that desires are typically not shared, making the ascription of a different desire somewhat easier. There are some problems here arising from uncertainty about what constitutes the same belief or the same desire. George and Henry each believe that they see a turnip, but George's belief is about George and Henry's is about Henry, so from a third-person logical point of view their beliefs are different, but ordinary usage and commonsense encourage us to say that George and Henry share the belief that they see a turnip. George believes that Henry sees a turnip (Henry is in the garden, while George is indoors); Henry also believes he sees a turnip. Here third-person logic says they have the same belief (that Henry sees a turnip) but ordinary usage and commonsense dictate the conclusion that George and Henry do not share a belief here. If we set aside the peculiar view of logic regarding the individuation of beliefs – according to which two people cannot have the same belief or desire about them-selves – then it seems quite plausible that members of the same community, viewing the same world, might share very many beliefs, but not quite so many desires.

Although beliefs and desires might well differ in the way just described, what I will attempt in this section is to discuss some possible ways of distinguishing beliefs from desires in terms of their typical contents, since I think that these have been ignored or underestimated.

In the first place the content of a belief seems undeniably propositional and our usage reflects this. The verb *believe* takes a full clause as its complement specifying a subject – what the belief is about – and a predicate – whatever is thought to be true of that subject. Desires may have this form, but very many desires seem to have much simpler content.

(i) X wants Y   (ii) X wants to [Verb] Y

are familiar formulae that fall short of the full propositional specification invariably found with *believe*. Of course, such formulae may be treated as elliptical and expanded as follows:

(i)′ X wants that X has Y   (ii)′ X wants that X [Verb]s Y

The notion that desires, like beliefs, have propositional objects is put forward by Searle (1983, p. 29), and his remarks on the question have not, so far as I know, been countered by other philosophers or linguists, so it is worth while to consider them here.

His argument is brief – barely a page – and is easily summarized. He begins by making clear that he is discussing a notion which is more general than that codified by individual English verbs like *wish, want, desire* and points out that whereas one can say of some previous act,

(1) I wish I hadn't done it,

it is "bad English" to say

(2) I want/desire I hadn't done it.

He considers that (1) expresses an intentional state of desire and that the absence of sentences like (2) is due to some arbitrary syntactic restriction associated with the verbs *want* and *desire*. Although this is presented as an argument for abstraction, Searle has also slipped in the claim that we may desire past events to have had a different outcome. He then discusses and rejects the *prima facie* evidence that desires may have simple (nonpropositional) objects as their contents, namely the existence of sentences like (3), by means of the following argument. The "surface structure" of

(3) I want your house

is said to be misleading. Searle considers the sentence:

(4) I want your house next summer

and argues that *next summer* cannot modify *want* since the sentence does not mean

(5) I – next summer – want your house,

since it is perfectly consistent to say

(6) I now want your house next summer though by next summer I won't want your house.

What the sentence (4) must mean, says Searle, is

(7) I want (I have your house next summer).

It is therefore evident that the content is the proposition expressed by the embedded sentence. He concludes that since all occurrences of sentences *S desires/wants X* can take such modifiers, they must all be considered as expressing attitudes to propositions.

It seems to me that this argument is easily challenged. In the first place, surely we would normally say that what (1) expresses is not desire but regret. Wishes regarding the outcome of past events rarely come true! Nor is the possibility that such past events were wrongly reported a presupposition of such a wish. There is little point in coveting, lusting after, or seeking a different outcome. One might feel guilty, or sorrowful, or ashamed, etc., about the actual outcome, but could hardly plan to have acted otherwise. So there is a good case for rejecting the notion that the object of desire could be a past event. Could it be a present event? I think the answer is also no. While one might enjoy some experience currently in progress (perhaps as we tuck into our caviar, desire lines up with the edge of the spoon), enjoyable consumption is not desire. So it seems natural to represent desire as an intentional state which is aimed at some unfulfilled, but potentially fulfillable, object.

If this is accepted, then it follows that sentence (4) differs from (3) only in that the future time when the desire is to be fulfilled is specified in (4) but unspecified in (3). Since, by hypothesis, expressions of desire always imply a future time of fulfillment (which may or may not be specified) there is no need to invoke arguments about what constituent is modified as Searle does. In any case, the locus of adverbial modifiers is always hard to establish with any certainty: they may be said to modify the verb, the verb phrase, or the sentence as a whole, and deciding between these alternatives is never straightforward. In the case of (4), it may be that "next summer" cannot be taken as modifying the verb "want" but this is hardly a sufficient reason for abandoning the analysis $S+V+O+Adv$. Consider the following argument, which is analogous to Searle's. The sentence

(8) I go to Paris next week,

predicts a journey, perhaps due to some business obligation. This cannot mean, following Searle,

(9) I – next week – go to Paris,

since it is perfectly consistent to say

(10) I now go to Paris next week but next week I may not go to Paris.

Although this argument looks no worse than Searle's, few would be satisfied with it and none would want to propose an analysis for (8) other than *S+V+Loc+Adv*. Sentences like (3), (4), and (8), which express states to be terminated by consummation at some future time admit both aspectual/temporal modification of the verb denoting the state and specification of the time of consummation.

Looking at Searle's argument from the other end, he proposes the analysis in (7) for sentence (4). But if there is an embedded sentence in such simple statements of desire, that sentence must be rather limited in the form it can take. Although the underlying structure of

(11) I want a pound of caviar,

uttered at the delicatessen counter, might look as if it might be

(12) I want (I buy a pound of caviar),

this cannot be, since such an analysis would allow the sentence

(13) I want a pound of caviar with my Mastercard

to mean that you want to buy it with your Mastercard. Instrumental and manner adverbials, which the verb *have* does not permit, are also not permitted as modifiers of the mode of consumption in simple desire statements. So if there is an embedded sentence in simple desire statements, its subject is always *I* and the main verb is always *have*.

Finally, if we look instead at desire statements with undeniably propositional objects, then we still find strong restrictions on the form of the verb. It cannot be finite ("I want you leave today" – cf. "I believe you leave today") and hence will not accept any modifications of tense, etc. Although some similar verbs readily accept internal negation (e.g., "I promise not to leave") and this may mean something quite different from external negation ("I don't promise to leave"), *want* and *desire* with internal negation are clumsy at best ("I want not to leave"), and – if they mean anything – mean the same as external negation ("I don't want to leave").

So there is a perfectly good case for treating desire as an intentional state which can have as its aim either an object (simple desires), or an event or state (complex desires, with propositions as complements). On the other hand, if for this reason or that it is decided to analyse simple desires as containing an embedded proposition, then that proposition has a very restricted and redundant form – in particular, much more restricted than is the case for beliefs.

Returning to the expansions (i)′ and (ii)′, it is therefore by no means evident that expanding them in this way does any sort of justice to the content of X's desire. On the contrary, if I want an apple it seems simply absurd to say that I want some proposition to be made true. It is perfectly conceivable that (i) and (ii) correctly characterize the content of X's desire as respectively an object and an action rather than as a proposition. Even if we translate simple desires in this way as:

(iii) X + *wants* + *that* + $S(ubject)$ + $V(erb)$ + $O(bject)$

it is plain that in the formula (iii) the default value of S is X and the default value for V is *have*.

Accordingly, and against some common views, there seems to be no good case for symmetry between belief and desire as psychological states. A desire may have a simple object as when "X wants a new dress" whereas a belief must have a propositional object. The content of the desire may simply be a representation of the desired object. Further, although occasionally it may make sense to speak of a *de re* desire – as when X desires not just any new dress but one particular dress on display in a particular high fashion shop, for example – in general desires are for any object that meets a certain vague specification. So the content of a typical desire is a nonreferential specification and is therefore *de dicto*. If the contents of such desires represent anything then they represent only a possible object satisfying some vague conjunction of properties. In Quine's famous example (1960, Chapter 4; 1966, pp. 183–94), "the man who wants a sloop" may be said merely to crave "relief from slooplessness."

In this respect, desires are like pretend play in that the child who pretends that a banana is a telephone most likely does not have any particular telephone in mind and so represents no telephone by means of the banana. Again, although to make the point effectively would involve another lengthy excursion, I would argue – following the analysis in Goodman (1969) – that drawings do not represent in a straightforward manner either. If I draw a fish, there may be no fish that I have in mind. I draw a fish-picture, not a picture of some particular fish. So studies of children's drawings often beg the representational question. We may put a cup in front of a child, give her pencil and paper and ask her to draw the cup. But unless the child accepts the task as given, as one of producing a representation of that cup, there is little point in pondering the differences between her cup – the cup she has drawn – and the cup before her.

On the other hand, when we turn to desires in which S and V do not have the default values discussed above, the content may be just as referential and specific as that encountered in a typical belief, and that is because the desires are now about whatever fills the Subject slot in the formula.

Some Conclusions regarding Methodology

I will try now to relate some of the distinctions discussed above to some recent studies of knowledge of belief and desire. There are a number of studies now published, in which children's ability to represent beliefs and desires are compared, with mixed results (Astington & Gopnik, 1991b). Sometimes it seems as though 3-year-olds can represent (think about) the desires of another or their own previous desires; sometimes the desire seems as hard to represent as the usual false belief. My suggestion is that in the first place these studies have all employed rather untypical desires and that it would be premature to draw any firm conclusion from them. I will not comment on Astington's studies in any detail; however, it seems to me that the desires investigated in them are all of the referential variety – desires for some specific thing. As I have suggested, such desires are perhaps not the simplest sort of desires and, besides, involve a referential element. In Astington's studies, clear developmental separations between representation of belief and desire seem rather elusive. Possibly such separations would be clearer for attributive desires.

I will conclude the chapter by discussing two studies conducted by Josef Perner's students, Nicola Yuill (Yuill, 1984) and Julie Hadwin (Hadwin & Perner, 1991). In Yuill's study subjects are presented with the information that a child has a highly specific desire, namely that a specific child should catch a specified thrown ball – "This boy wants that boy to catch this ball". There is another possible catcher, a girl. The story is presented with pictures and the thrower's desire is illustrated by means of a "think-bubble" illustrating the desired outcome. Subjects have to judge whether the thrower will be pleased or sad, given this or that outcome. It turns out that 3-year-olds judge – as we would – that the thrower is more pleased if the intended catcher catches it.

This study has many weaknesses and it is hard to know why Perner (1991b) set such store by it. To begin with, there is no reason why the subject should not share the desire of the story character and so we can have no confidence that the judgments reflect the represented thoughts of the story character rather than the wishes of the subject herself. In the second place, the story character's desire is represented by a drawn "think-bubble" and – as I have argued above – there is some question about how a 3-year-old takes such drawings – even when they are not think-bubbles! Thirdly, that the girl should catch the ball instead of the intended boy hardly seems a dismaying outcome. This criticism works in the opposite direction from the previous two, since it makes it the more surprising that 3-year-olds should consider this outcome unsatisfactory and a source of sadness for the thrower.

In Hadwin and Perner's (1991) study the think-bubbles are presented as representing the thrower's beliefs about the outcome of his throw. In the picture story there is a wall between thrower and catcher so that until he looks over the wall the thrower does not know whether his belief is correct or not. Subjects have to judge whether the thrower would be surprised or not, given the actual outcome. Hadwin and Perner found that even 5-year-olds had difficulty in making appropriate judgments of surprise. Aside from the difficulties raised in discussion of Yuill's task, this study introduces a further difficulty, for the thrower is apparently represented as having a certain belief, but without any grounds for holding it. Why should he think that the other boy had caught the ball? Or is this merely *wishful thinking*, that is, equivalent to a desire?

Surely we would only predict that the thrower would be surprised if the thrower had some grounds for his wrong belief. Wimmer, Hogrefe and Sodian (1988) and Sodian and Wimmer (1988) have investigated the child's developing knowledge of the grounding of beliefs in perception, inference, and so forth. On the face of it, desires are often similarly grounded. My desire for a new dress may be a simple consequence of my perception of the shabby and unfashionable nature of the one that I am wearing now. Or it may arise because my best friend tells me that it's time for a change. Or I may infer from the expressions of contempt on the faces of my peers that something is amiss, etc. So desires may be grounded in just the same range of ways as beliefs. So far as I know, no one has investigated children's ability to represent desires grounded in these or other specific ways. Notice that in the example just given, the desire for a new dress is clearly to be taken as *attributive*. On the other hand, when the desire is *referential* – directed at a particular toy, or sweet-meat, or (as in Yuill's study) a goal that a particular person should catch a ball, then rather different grounds may have to be adduced. As Astington has argued in recent papers, the intrinsic desirability of certain objects may be a ground for a desire or (as in Yuill's study) the referential desire may be left quite ungrounded as a whimsical urge of the child.

Once again I have, I believe, identified good reasons for thinking harder about desires from the point of view of content.

Notes

1   Published as Campbell (1979). A revised version appeared as Campbell (1986).
2   The relative difficulty of these two tasks is hard to establish, because of variations in procedure, and since within-subject designs are generally avoided here on account of probable strong order effects. While Wimmer & Perner (1983) found no success with 3-year-olds on their location task, later investigations (e.g., Hogrefe et al., 1986, Experiment 4) show about 20% success. Equally, Perner et al. (1987) found 45% success with 3-year-olds on an unexpected contents task, but others (e.g., Wimmer & Hartl, 1991, Experiment 1) have reported only 25–30% success. I understand that an unpublished recent meta-analysis of such experiments by Henry Wellman shows no clear priority for either task. However, they are only very weakly associated (e.g., Daniel Connolly reported a correlation of .29 to the 1999 BPS Developmental Psychology Section Conference) so lack of priority should not be taken to mean that the tasks are closely related.
3   Although they did not include causation/origins tasks, Flavell, Mumme, Green, & Flavell (1992) compared ability to ascribe false beliefs of the usual sort with false beliefs about aspects of morality, social convention, and ownership. Unfortunately for my argument, they found little difference in difficulty between the standard and the novel tasks, except that ascription of false beliefs about ownership was somewhat easier.

References

Astington, J. W., & Gopnik, A. (1991a). Theoretical explanations of children's understanding of the mind. *British Journal of Developmental Psychology, 9*, 7–31.

Astington, J. W., & Gopnik, A. (1991b). Developing understanding of desire and intention. In A. Whiten (Ed.), *Natural theories of mind: Evolution, development and simulation of everyday mindreading* (pp. 39–50). Oxford, UK: Blackwell.

Campbell, R. N. (1979). Cognitive development and child language. In P. Fletcher & M.

Garman (Eds.), *Language Acquisition* (pp. 419–36). Cambridge, UK: Cambridge University Press.

Campbell, R. N. (1986). Language acquisition and cognition. In P. Fletcher & M. Garman (Eds.), *Language Acquisition*, 2nd Ed., (pp. 30–48). Cambridge, UK: Cambridge University Press.

Campbell, R. N., & Olson, D. R. (1990). Children's thinking. In R. Grieve & M. Hughes (Eds.), *Understanding children: Essays in honour of Margaret Donaldson* (pp. 189–209). Oxford, UK: Blackwell.

Flavell, J. H., Mumme, D. L., Green, F. L., & Flavell, E. R. (1992). Young children's understanding of different types of belief. *Child Development, 63*, 960–77.

Goodman, N. (1969). *Languages of art.* Oxford, UK: Oxford University Press.

Hadwin, J., & Perner, J. (1991). Pleased and surprised: Children's cognitive theory of emotion. *British Journal of Developmental Psychology, 9*, 215–34.

Hogrefe, J., Wimmer, H., & Perner, J. (1986). Ignorance versus false belief: A developmental lag in attribution of epistemic states. *Child Development, 57*, 567–82.

Olson, D. R. (1989). Making up your mind. *Canadian Psychology, 30*, 617–27.

Olson, D. R., & Campbell, R. N. (1993). Constructing representations. In C. Pratt & A. F. Garton (Eds.), *Systems of representation in children: Development and use* (pp. 11–26). Chichester, UK: John Wiley.

Olson, D. R., & Campbell, R. N. (1994). Representation and misrepresentation: On the beginnings of symbolization in young children. In D. Tirosh (Ed.), *Implicit and explicit knowledge: An educational approach* (pp. 83–95). Norwood, NJ: Ablex Publishing Corporation.

Perner, J. (1991a). *Understanding the representational mind.* Cambridge, MA: Bradford Books/MIT Press.

Perner, J. (1991b). On representing that: The asymmetry between belief and desire in children's theory of mind. In C. Moore & D. Frye (Eds.), *Children's theories of mind* (pp. 139–55). Hillsdale, NJ: Erlbaum.

Perner, J., Leekam, S. R., & Wimmer, H. (1987). Three-year-olds' difficulty with false belief: The case for a conceptual deficit. *British Journal of Developmental Psychology, 5*, 125–37.

Quine, W. v. O. (1960). *Word and object.* Cambridge, MA: MIT Press.

Quine, W. v. O. (1966). *The ways of paradox and other essays.* New York: Random House.

Searle, J. (1983). *Intentionality.* Cambridge, UK: Cambridge University Press.

Sodian, B., & Wimmer, H. (1988). Children's understanding of inference as a source of knowledge. *Child Development, 58*, 424–33.

Wimmer, H., & Hartl, M. (1991). Against the Cartesian view on mind: Young children's difficulty with own false beliefs. *British Journal of Developmental Psychology, 9*, 125–38.

Wimmer, H., Hogrefe, J., & Sodian, B. (1988). A second stage in children's conception of mental life: Understanding informational accesses as origins of knowledge and belief. In J. W. Astington, P. L. Harris & D. R. Olson (Eds.), *Developing theories of mind* (pp. 173–92). New York: Cambridge University Press.

Yuill, N. (1984). Young children's co-ordination of motive and outcome in judgements of satisfaction and morality. *British Journal of Developmental Psychology, 2*, 73–81.

11

Lying as Doing Deceptive Things with Words: A Speech Act Theoretical Perspective

Kang Lee

There are two kinds of teachers, one who merely imparts knowledge and one who enlightens. From my experience with David Olson as his postdoctoral fellow between 1994 and 1996, I firmly believe, and many of his students would concur, that David is a mentor who enlightens. David's pedagogy of enlightenment is a student-centered one. He always gives his students a free rein to pursue whatever attracts their intellectual curiosity, while generously sharing his ideas. I have also enjoyed many conversations with him, sometimes over a cup of coffee and other times over a pint of beer. It is from these conversations, caffeine or alcohol notwithstanding, that I learned to think theoretically, not to be content merely with the collection of good data, and instead to seek what the data really mean. It is also during these conversations that David introduced me to the speech act theory approach, which forms the theoretical framework of this paper.

Speech Act Theory

In this paper, I will use a speech act theory approach to provide an account of the development of children's knowledge about lying, specifically its meaning and moral values. The speech act theoretical approach posits that lying is a type of speech act that is characterized by features common to all forms of speech act or verbal communication. Among the major components of speech acts, two are most pertinent to the present discussion. First, a speech act is a socially motivated, rule-governed action that is performed to serve an interpersonal function in a social/cultural context (the conventionality component); second, a speech act is an intentional act that is mediated by the intentional states of the communicator (the intentionality component).

The notion that the intentionality and conventionality components of speech acts are central aspects of verbal communication is derived from theoretical advancement in the last half century in the area of philosophy of language (Tsohatzidis, 1994) as well as developmental research on verbal communication (e.g., Astington, 1988; Olson, 1994). In the field of philosophy of language, many philosophers, notably J. L. Austin (1962), have noted difficulties with traditional theories' assumptions regarding verbal communication, which hold that a verbal statement merely serves to describe some state of affairs, to state certain facts which must be either true or false, and which must be objectively verifiable. Austin's revelation of the shortcomings of the traditional theories led to a "revolution in philosophy" (Austin, 1962, p. 3), and subsequently in other fields, in the treatment of language and verbal communication.

Austin (1962) in his book *How to do Things with Words* observed that many utterances do not merely describe reality but also have an effect on reality; they are the performance of an act rather than a report of performance. Austin came to believe that all language is performative and that it is made up of speech acts to serve certain social functions. Austin's proposal was later expanded by other philosophers into so-called speech act theories. Prominent among such philosophers are Paul Grice (1980) and John Searle (1969). Grice and Searle each advocated two important lines of analyses on speech acts, one focusing on the intentional aspect (the intentionality component), and the other focusing on the conventional aspect (the conventionality component).

Intentionality component

Speech acts, according to Searle (1969), are rule-governed intentional behaviors. Due to this "intentionality component," a speaker may mean more than, or differently from what is said; the meaning and function of a speech act is mediated and determined not only by the literal meaning of a sentence and the actual state of affairs, but also by the intentional states of the communication partners (e.g., the intention or belief of a speaker).

Hence, to determine what a specific speech act is and what function it serves, one must consider at least five factors involved in verbal communication. The first factor is factuality (whether a statement reflects the true state of affairs). The second is the surface/literal meaning of a statement (what is actually said). The next three factors are all intentional/representational ones: the deeper meaning of a statement (what is meant, i.e., the true meaning that the speaker wishes his or her utterance to convey); the intention of the speaker (what is intended, i.e., what the speaker intends to state publicly); and the speaker's belief (what the speaker actually believes). Different combinations of these five factors result in different forms of speech acts (see Table 11.1). For example, when all the factors are the same, it is an accurate statement; when all the factors are the same except that a statement is not factually true, it is an honest mistake; when what is said is not what is meant but is what is intended, and what is meant is what is believed, it is a metaphor (e.g., to comment on the heavy rain outside, one states: "It's raining cats and dogs outside") or irony (e.g., A who does not think highly of B's driving skill quips: "B drives like a pro").

Table 11.1 Five Factors of a Speech Act

Forms of verbal communication	Literal meaning	Deeper meaning	Intention	Belief	Factuality
1) accurate, honest statement	x	x	x	x	x
2) honest mistake	y	y	y	y	x
3) verbal error	y	x	x	x	x
4) metaphor	y	x	y	x	x ~ y
5) irony, sarcasm	y	x	y	x	not x
6) lie	y	y	y	x	irrelevant

Notes
1. Factuality refers to whether a statement reflects the true state of affairs; Literal meaning refers to what is actually said by the speaker; Deeper meaning refers to the true meaning that the speaker wishes his or her utterance to convey; Intention refers to what the speaker intends to state publicly; Belief refers to what the speaker actually believes.
2. x and y are the content of an expression or representation; "~" means "is analogous with."

Conventionality component

The conventionality component refers to the socially and culturally defined rules of conversation that are intersubjectively shared (Grice, 1980; Sweetser, 1987). These rules are mostly implicit; members of a social-cultural group often use these rules with no awareness of their existence. According to Sweetser, these rules are hierarchically organized. At the top of the hierarchy is a so-called general cooperative rule. The general cooperative rule is a metamaxim and governs all communicative acts in all settings. This rule states that the goal of social communication is to "try to help, not to harm" (p. 47). The general cooperative rule condemns harmfully motivated communicative behaviors and condones helpfully motivated speech acts.

Below this metamaxim lie two sets of conversational rules that guide verbal communication in two different settings: the informational setting and the politeness setting. In informational settings, the primary goal of communication is to relay information. In this setting, we are expected to follow – and we assume others to follow – Grice's maxims of conversation (1980). The Maxim of Quality expects the speaker to be truthful and avoid falsehood; the Maxim of Quantity requires the speaker to provide as much information as necessary; the Maxim of Relation dictates that the speaker must convey relevant information; the Maxim of Manner asks the speaker to avoid ambiguity and obscurity. In contrast to informational settings, in politeness settings, maintaining and enhancing amicable social relations is of most importance. In this setting, interlocutors are expected to follow R. Lakoff's (1973) rules of politeness (e.g., do not impose, provide options, be amicable).

Lying as a Speech Act

Lying is a unique form of speech act. Lying, like other speech acts, has both the intentionality and conventionality components, but it differs dramatically from other forms of speech acts in terms of the specifics of the intentionality and conventionality components involved. With regard to the intentionality component, lying is a communicative act wherein there is a discrepancy between what is intended and what is believed by the speaker (the speaker intends to say what she or he does not believe). In philosophy, this discrepancy is referred to as the "intent to deceive" (Bok, 1978; Chisholm & Feehan, 1977). The factuality dimension is irrelevant to lying, as it is the speaker's deceptive intent, not whether the speaker's statement is factually true, that determines whether a statement is a lie (e.g., a speaker may tell a lie that is factually true). With regard to the conventionality component, lying, unlike many other forms of speech acts (e.g., an honest mistake or metaphor), often violates the most fundamental convention of communication, the General Cooperative Metamaxim, and the most critical Gricean maxim, the Maxim of Quality. Due to these violations, lying often evokes strong emotive reactions from communicational partners.

From a developmental perspective, lying poses both a challenge and an opportunity for the developing child. It is a challenge because lying requires the child to understand intentions and beliefs involved in communication, both of which are intangible and thus can only be inferred; to understand lying or to lie, children must also learn social conventions that govern all verbal communications. These conventions are often not explicitly taught to them by adults; indeed, adults are typically unaware of the existence of these conventions. Lying also presents an opportunity for children because by lying to others and detecting others' lies children learn the intentional nature of verbal communication and how words not only can change others' behavior but also their mental states. Because lying violates the fundamental conventions of communication, society in general and children's parents and teachers in particular tend to make explicit the rules against lying, which may in turn highlight to children the fundamental conventions governing all forms of verbal communication.

In the following sections, I will review recent developmental research on children's understanding of the concept of lying and its moral implications from a speech act theoretical perspective. Specifically, I will examine the current evidence regarding how children acquire the two integral aspects of lying as a speech act: the intentionality and conventionality components.

Children's Concept of Lying

The main purpose of the study of children's concept of lying is to determine the developmental course through which children acquire a "mature" understanding of the concept. What is the "mature" understanding of the concept of lying? From the perspective of speech act theories, it is the understanding that a lie is a statement by a speaker who believes the statement to be untrue and intends to deceive or to instill a false belief into the mind of a hearer (Chisholm & Feehan, 1977). A lie may or may not be inconsistent with the true state of affairs, although many lies do often deviate from or contradict reality.

According to speech act theories, the intentionality component is a necessary but not sufficient component of the concept of lying. Whether or not a verbal statement that meets the above definition is truly a lie depends on whether the statement violates a particular culture's conventions for the conversational context in which the statement is made (Sweetser, 1987). The culture's conversational rules not only determine the degree of severity of a lie (e.g., prosocial lies, asocial lies, and antisocial lies), but also whether an untruthful statement is a lie at all. Two crucial factors must be considered when determining whether a verbal statement is truly a lie (Sweetser, 1987). First, what is the general motive of the speaker when making such a statement? Is the speaker motivated by the desire to help or to harm the hearer? Second, what are the cultural/social conventions for the conversational context in which the statement is made? Is an untruthful statement required for the setting? Is informational accuracy or politeness more important for the setting? Hence, from the speech act perspective, the sufficient component for a verbal statement to be defined as a lie is the conventionality component of verbal communication.

Now, let us turn to the empirical evidence concerning children's acquisition of the intentionality and conventionality components of the concept of lying.

Intentionality component

The study of the acquisition of the concept of lying, pioneered by Piaget (1932/ 1965), has been the major topic of research on the development of lying. Most studies, with one recent exception (Lee & Ross, 1997), have focused on the acquisition of the intentionality component of lying. Evidence to date suggests that children begin to understand that lying is a form of verbal communication as early as the preschool years (Bussey, 1992). Young children apparently do not confuse lying with other forms of behavioral misconduct (e.g., stealing). However, they tend to confuse lying with other verbal behaviors that are not sanctioned by parents and teachers. For example, in his seminal work, Piaget (1932/1965) asked 6- to 11-year-old children to identify acts that were lies. Children around 6 years of age considered "naughty" words (e.g., swearing) to be lies. Similar findings were obtained more recently by Bussey (1992) and Peterson, Peterson, and Sato (1983). However, both Bussey (1992) and Peterson et al. (1983) disagreed with another of Piaget's major conclusions that young children are more inclined to consider a punished lie to be a lie than an unpunished one. Both found that children as young as 5 years of age considered an factually untruth statement to be a lie irrespective of whether a child lie-teller is punished and whether the child's statement is believed by an adult hearer.

Many researchers have focused specifically on the emergence of three elements of verbal communication in children's concept of "a lie:" belief, intent, and factuality. Results to date suggest that these three elements are taken into consideration at different ages. The first element that children come to grips with is factual falsity. By around 5 or 6 years of age, children begin to use whether a statement is consistent with the true state of affairs as the yardstick in determining whether a statement is a lie. This leads to overextension of the word "lie" to refer to a number of statements that most ordinary adults as well as philosophers and linguists would not classify as lies. For example, Peterson et al. (1983) studied the definitions of lying in children between 5 and 11 years of age, and adults. They found that guessing was considered to be a lie more by younger children than older children and adults, although a substantial proportion of older children and adults also labeled it as a lie. Exaggeration and practical jokes were thought of as lies by most children but not adults. Results of this study are in line with the earlier work of Piaget (1932/1965) and more recent work by Bussey (1992), Strichartz and Burton (1990), and Wimmer, Gruber, and Perner (1984). These results suggest that both the early emergence of the factual falsity element and the overextension of the word "lie" are robust phenomena.

With regard to the other two elements (intent and belief), Piaget (1932/1965) reported that children did not consider speakers' intentions in their determination of whether a false statement is a lie until later childhood. Young children considered a verbal statement that was factually false to be a lie even though the speaker did not have the intent to deceive (i.e., a honest mistake). This finding is consistent with those of Peterson et al. (1983) who also suggested that the element of the intent to deceive begins to be incorporated into children's definition of the concept of "lie" at around 11 years of age.

Similar findings were obtained in a more elaborate and controlled study by Wimmer et al. (1984), who examined both the use of the intent-to-deceive and false belief elements in children's definition of lying. In their study, children were presented with a series of puppet-show-type stories. Three protagonists, *A*, *B*, and *C*, were involved. *A* passed information to *B* and then *B* passed information to *C*. In one key condition (XYY), *A*, who possessed information X, intentionally passed information Y to *B*. *B*, not knowing the falsity of the information, passed it (Y) to *C*. Children were asked to determine whether *A* and *B* were lying. Results indicated that children as young as 4 years of age had no difficulty determining that *A* was lying. However, most young children 4 to 6 years of age failed to consider *B*'s belief state in their evaluation. They based their judgment mainly on whether *B* passed on false information that was originally intended to be false. Since *B* passed on the intentional falsehood, even unintentionally, she was judged as lying. Similar results were found among some 8- and 10-year-olds. In contrast, the older children appeared to appreciate the cause/source of *B*'s false belief and judged *B* not to be lying when *B*'s false statement was derived from *B*'s false belief about the true state of affairs. However, when B's false belief was induced by an intended false statement from *A*, *B* was judged to be lying. Wimmer et al. (1984) suggested that, for many children, "a message which was intended as a lie stays a lie even when it is passed on by an innocent believer" (p. 20). Overall, the results replicated Piaget's findings that children define a lie as any false statement rather than an intentional false statement until adolescence.

Recently, several studies have challenged the above findings on both theoretical and methodological grounds. The first challenge came from Strichartz and Burton (1990), who made three important improvements over earlier studies. They examined whether the intention and belief elements play different roles in children's definition of "lie" in addition to the factual falsity. Second, they asked participants to choose from three alternatives (a lie, the truth, or something else), instead of the two alternatives available (a lie or not a lie) in the earlier studies. Third, and most importantly, Strichartz and Burton (1990) adopted a new theoretical approach toward the development of the concept of lying. Based on Coleman and Kay's (1981) theoretical analysis of the concept of lying, they hypothesized that children's concepts of lies and lying is prototypical rather than propositional. That is, factors such as intention, belief, and factuality do not determine a verbal statement to be a lie in an all-or-none fashion; these factors are elements of the prototype of lying with different weights, and hence contribute to the conception of lying to different degrees.

Following Coleman and Kay's paradigm, Strichartz and Burton designed puppet plays that systematically varied the presence or absence of the three prototypical elements, intention (the intent of the speaker, not necessarily a lie-teller), factuality (whether the statement is true), and belief (whether the speaker believes the statement). They found that nursery school children did not use the labels of "lie" and "truth" in a systematic manner. Preschoolers and first graders used "lie" or "truth" based solely on factuality. Intent and belief were yet to be incorporated into their conception of lies and truth. Fifth graders appeared to be transitional between younger children and adults. Although they took the three elements into consideration when deciding whether a statement was a lie, they were reluctant to let the belief element override the factuality element and did so only when the intent of the speaker was to deceive. Adults, on the other hand, weighted the belief element as more important than either the factuality element or the intent element. When the speaker believed the statement to be false, adults weighted intent more heavily than factuality. Further, belief combined with either factuality or intent yielded greater consistency in judgment than the belief component alone. The three elements together yielded the highest consistency in judgment. This evidence indicates that the concept of lies and truth in adults is not an all-or-none phenomenon but a prototypical one; and that the three elements have different weights in adults' and children's definition of lying. Further, the acquisition of a "mature form" of the concept of lying may not progress in a linear fashion with the three elements sequentially incorporated into children's concept of "lie."

Methodological problems of some earlier studies were also discussed by two psychologists in Australia. Peterson (1995) challenged a common finding in earlier studies that young children are unable to use the speaker's intention to define lying.

She argued that the failure of previous studies to show young children's use of the lie-teller's deceptive intent as a defining cue was due to a flawed assumption. That is the assumption that child participants share with researchers the same understanding of the stated intention of the speaker in stories that are presented to them. In the earlier studies, children were often read a story involving a story character making a false statement. The story also explains explicitly a speaker's deceptive or nondeceptive intention. This intention is presumed to be understood by children. Peterson (1995) directly assessed children's understanding of the speaker's intention, and their judgment of whether the speaker's statement was a lie. She found that children's perceptions of the speaker's deceptive intent were not always consistent with those of the researcher, which led some children to give a seemingly "immature" definition of "lie" (i.e., not using the researcher-provided information regarding the speaker's deceptive intent). However, when children's subjective perceptions were matched with the researcher's, even 5- and 6-year-olds were significantly more likely to base their definition of "lie" on intention.

Further, Siegal and Peterson (1996) suggested that another reason for the failure of the earlier studies was a violation of conversational rules in the traditional questioning method, particularly the form of question used in those studies and the context in which questions were asked. Siegal and Peterson created lying scenarios involving food situations which were ecologically salient to children and with which they were familiar. More importantly, they asked questions in the form of "Was it a lie or a mistake?" rather than the commonly used form of question, "Did she/he lie or not lie?" or "Was it a lie or not a lie?" These two questions may lead to a "yes" bias or imply that the speaker is indeed lying. Also, by contrasting lies with mistakes, the intention of the speaker is highlighted. They found that many 4- and 5-year-olds and some 3-year-olds showed a rudimentary understanding of the differences between lies and mistakes as distinguished by the speaker's intentions. In other words, preschool children do use the speaker's intention to define "lie" in a familiar and ecologically important domain when an appropriate question is asked.

It should be noted that Peterson and Siegal's (1996) findings do not necessarily invalidate some of the earlier findings (e.g., Bussey, 1992; Peterson et al., 1983; Strichartz & Burton, 1990; Wimmer et al., 1984). This is because they only demonstrate children's rudimentary understanding of the intentionality component of the concept of lying in conditions under which critical information is highly simplified, or made very explicit. This understanding is also limited to situations with which young children are very familiar. For this reason, I would argue that the difference between Peterson and Siegal's findings and those of the earlier studies are not due to methodological differences. Rather, they may reflect different points of a gradual developmental course in children's understanding of the concept of lying. While Peterson and Siegal's findings reveal an early emergence of the understanding of a lie, other studies indicate how this understanding is consolidated and refined in later years. For example, while preschoolers are able to differentiate between a mistake and a lie in situations with which they are familiar (Siegal & Peterson, 1996), elementary school children generalize this understanding to a number of situations (e.g., Bussey, 1992). Also, elementary school children, unlike preschoolers, understand that the factuality of a statement (i.e., whether a statement really reflects the true state of affairs) is not critical to the concept of lying (e.g., Bussey, 1992; Peterson et al., 1983). Further, while preschoolers take into consideration a speaker's belief when deciding whether a statement is a lie, it is not until adolescence that children begin to appreciate the most critical "belief" element in the concept of lying (Strichartz & Burton, 1990; Wimmer et al., 1984).

Conventionality component

Most studies on children's concepts of lying in the current literature focus on the intentionality component of lying. This focus is likely due to a strong bias in philosophy and linguistics with regard to defining concepts. Philosophical and linguistic discussions of the concept of lying have been dominated by a propositional approach. The propositional approach to lying focuses only on the intentional aspect of the concept while viewing social and cultural factors to be irrelevant to the definition of lying itself. The approach adopts a "checklist" strategy for definition (Fillmore, 1975) and defines "lie" in an all-or-none fashion. It stipulates that only when all necessary and sufficient conditions (i.e., the false belief element and the intent-to-deceive element) are satisfied can a statement be called a lie. A statement is dichotomously classified as either a "lie" (if all the conditions are met) or not a lie (if any of the conditions are not met). Some of the studies cited above (Coleman & Kay, 1981; Strichartz & Burton, 1990) cast doubt on the propositional approach toward the concept of lying. These new findings suggest that the development of the concept of lying may be better studied with the prototypical approach.

It should be noted, however, that the intentionality aspect of the concept of lying is still the primary focus of the prototypical approach, although contextual factors are also given some consideration. The critical roles of social and cultural factors in people's concepts of lying as suggested by Sweetser (1987) have not been directly tested until recently. A recent study by Lee and Ross (1997) examined predictions based on Sweetser's folkloristic model of lying. Eight vignettes were presented to 12- and 16-year-old adolescents and 19-year-old young adults. Half were prototypical lie-telling situations (e.g., a speaker tells a white lie about her friend's new haircut to avoid hurting the friend's feelings), and the other half were prototypical truth-telling situations. Each vignette depicted a speaker making a statement in either an informational setting or a politeness setting under one of two conditions (the help and harm conditions). The speaker's statement was intended to either harm or help the hearer (i.e., violating or conforming to the general cooperative rule). For example, in one of the vignettes for the help/politeness condition, a story character has a bad new haircut and her friend thinks that this new style does not look good on her. However, to avoid hurting the story character's feelings, the friend states that she likes the haircut. Participants rated how strongly they agreed or disagreed that the statement was a lie.

In both lie- and truth-telling situations, the help–harm condition effect was significant (Figure 11.1). Both adolescents and young adults rated the statement as more of a lie in the harm condition than in the help condition. The setting effect was also significant. Participants rated lie-telling in an informational setting as more of a lie than in a politeness setting (e.g., white lies). These results support Sweetser's model and suggest that the concept of "lie" is a social-cognitive construct with social conventions regarding verbal communication and contexts being an integral part of the concept of "lie." It should be noted, however, that all the prototypical lie-telling scenarios including those depicting white lies were categorized by participants as lie-telling. This result suggests that social conventions may only determine the extent to which a specific type of lie-telling (e.g., white lie-telling) belongs to the category of lie-telling behaviors; they do not, however, change the membership of all types of lies. In other words, any false statements told with an intent to deceive the hearer are considered lies regardless of whether they are told to help or to harm and whether they are told in informational or politeness settings.

Results from a recent study by my colleagues (Cameron, Xu, & Fu, 1999) are consistent with those of Lee and Ross (1997). This study examined Canadian and Chinese children's concepts of, and moral judgments about, lying. In the first experiment, 7-, 9-, and 11-year-old Chinese and Canadian children were read stories involving children doing something good or bad, and making truthful or untruthful statements about their own deeds. They were asked to determine (1) whether an untruthful statement was a lie and (2) the extent to which the untruthful statement could be labeled as a lie (in addition, they were asked to give positive or negative ratings to the statements; see the next section). Most children of both cultures labeled an untruthful statement as a lie regardless of whether it was told to be modest (i.e., lying about one's own good deed) or to conceal a transgression (i.e., lying about one's bad deed). However, they responded that a

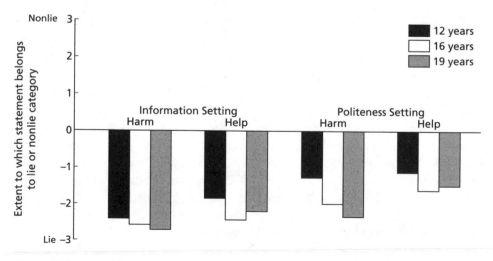

Figure 11.1 Canadian adolescents' and young adults' ratings of the extent to which various types of lie-telling belong to the category of "lie" (adapted from Lee & Ross, 1997).

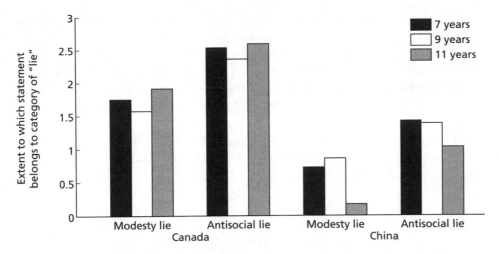

Figure 11.2   Canadian and Chinese children's ratings of the extent to which various types of lie-telling belong to the category of "lie" in Experiment 1 of Cameron et al. (1999).

modesty-motivated lie was a lie to a less extent than a lie told to conceal a transgression (Figure 11.2).

Experiment 2 of Cameron et al. (1999) examined Canadian and Chinese children's concepts of lying and their moral judgments about it when an untruthful statement was made to please or hurt another individual's feelings. Children were read four types of stories: Story 1 involves a child telling the truth to please another; Story 2, a child telling a lie to hurt another's feelings; Story 3, a child telling the

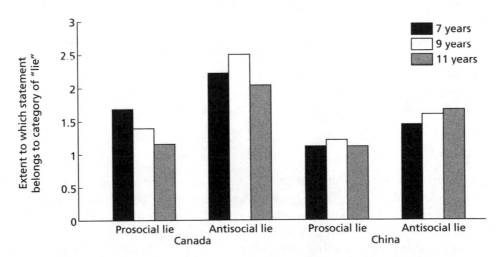

Figure 11.3   Canadian and Chinese children's ratings of the extent to which various types of lie-telling belong to the category of "lie" in Experiment 2 of Cameron et al. (1999).

truth to hurt; and Story 4, a child telling a lie to please. Again, no cultural difference was found with regard to whether a statement was a lie or the truth. Most children, regardless of age and the speaker's good or bad intention, considered an untruthful statement a lie. Nevertheless, when asked to determine the extent to which an untruthful statement is a lie, Canadian and Chinese children differentiated different types of lies. Like the adolescents and young adults in Lee and Ross (1997), they considered prosocial lies to be less of a lie than antisocial lies (Figure 11.3). These results suggest that social and cultural conventions of communication influence the extent to which an untruthful statement is considered by children to belong to the "lie" category, although they do not induce children to classify the statement out of the "lie" category.

Children's Moral Judgment of Lying

Lying is a morally charged and value-laden speech act. When children learn about lying, they must inevitably come to grips with its moral implications and must consider the question: Is lying right or wrong? To answer this question, one must first determine a speaker's intention. From the speech act theoretical perspective, the intentionality component concerning the moral implications of lying involves both the speaker's general communicative intention (i.e., to help or to harm) and the specific intention to deceive. Both intentions must be considered before a moral verdict is rendered. Following Sweetser's (1987) model, the two intentions have different levels of importance in determining a speech act's moral value, with the general communicative intention exerting greater influence than the specific intention to deceive.

To answer whether lying is right or wrong also involves the determination of whether and to what extent a specific act of lying violates certain social-cultural conventions (the conventionality component). From the speech act theoretical perspective, because lying is a form of verbal communication, it must adhere to such communicative conventions as Sweetser's metamaxim of cooperation (i.e., to help, not to harm), the Gricean maxims, and Lakoff's politeness rules. These conventions are value laden and morally charged. Hence, certain emotional and moral reactions may result when these conventions are violated or upheld.

Intentionality component

Research on the intentionality component in children's moral judgment of lying was again pioneered by Piaget (1932/1965) who focused mainly on how a speaker's specific deceptive intent is used in children's moral judgment of lying. He invented a testing paradigm that involved a pair of stories. Each story involved one story character who made a statement about their deed in various situations. Children were asked to judge which character was "worse" or "naughtier." When younger children were presented with stories in which one character lied and was punished and the other lied but was not punished, the latter was regarded as less "naughty" than the former. This reflects a typical reaction of children whom Piaget classified as preconventional. Later, children began to assess the severity of verbal statements by their deviations from the truth. The more a statement was different from the truth, the "naughtier" it was judged to be. For instance, guessing incorrectly a person's age by four years was judged "naughtier" than lying about a person's age by one year. Also, intention was found not to influence children's moral judgments. For example, in one story pair, one child intentionally gives the wrong directions, but the traveler finds his way none the less. In the other story, another child tries to help the traveler but the traveler gets lost. Children younger than 10 years of age thought the second child was naughtier. This illustrates the so-called "moral realism" in children's moral judgment. Only by approximately 10 years of age did Piaget find that children began to treat the intention of the speaker as an important factor in their moral judgment. Only at this stage did children judge the character with deceptive intentions as naughtier.

Piaget's findings were subsequently confirmed by many studies using similar procedures (e.g., Lickona, 1976). Recently, several researchers have questioned the methodology of the Piagetian paradigm (Bussey, 1992; Peterson et al., 1983; Wimmer et al. 1984). Peterson et al. (1983) suggested that the two-story format and the demand to weigh two protagonists' naughtiness might place too much of a cognitive load on younger children. When asked to evaluate only one protagonist's naughtiness, children between 5 and 11 years all used information regarding the protagonist's intention in their moral judgment. For example, they rated "white" and altruistic lies more positively than other types of lies. When a protagonist's deceptive or truthful intention is made explicit (Wimmer et al., 1984), children as young as 6 years of age gave significantly more rewards to the protagonist who had a truthful intention than the one who had a deceptive intention. Bussey (1992) further demonstrated that children as young as 4 years of age give more negative ratings to lying than to misdeeds. Children older than preschool age appreciated the value of truthfulness about misdeeds and gave a highly positive rating to truth-telling about one's misdeed. They even showed a strong sense of pride in making such a confession. Overall, these studies failed to confirm Piaget's major conclusions regarding children's moral judgment of lying. These recent results suggest that children as young as the late preschool years are able to give differential moral evaluations about lying versus misdeed and lying versus truth-telling. Children as young as 6 years of age also begin to use the protagonist's intention to make moral judgments, much earlier than Piaget concluded.

Conventionality component

The question of whether one's moral and emotional reaction to lying depends on a particular context or culture has been long debated in philosophy. Two opposing views exist. One view is the so-called deontological view that suggests that lying is intrinsically wrong and has a constant disvalue regardless of situations and cultural contexts (Bok, 1978; Kupfer, 1982). Many deontological theorists suggest that

although lying may sometimes be justified, all lies have negative values and therefore should be discouraged. The deontological view also suggests that there are
three main reasons that lying is intrinsically wrong: first, lying violates contractual
commitments between two interlocutors who assume by default that the other person always tells the truth; second, lying limits the lie-recipient's freedom of choice
and leads the person to make an uninformed decision; third, lying creates an internal conflict on the part of the lie-teller and cognitive dissonance in the lie-teller's
belief system, which can be hazardous to the lie-teller's mental health.

A social-conventional view of lying, in contrast, suggests that lying is not always
wrong, and lying in fact has inconstant values (Ochs, 1976). Whether a lie is right
or wrong is determined by social-cultural conventions. Some cultures may sanction
and even promote lying in certain contexts (Triandis, 1995). In these contexts,
lying has a positive value. In some other situations, lying is prohibited and discouraged. Only in these latter situations does lying have negative values. For example, in
some cultures (e.g., western cultures), the violation of the Gricean maxim of quality
may evoke a negative evaluation when a doctor lies to her patient about the patient's terminal illness, while in some other cultures (e.g., Asian cultures) it is a
common and morally sanctioned practice. Even within the same culture, lying in
certain contexts (e.g., malicious lies or lying to hurt others) may evoke more negative moral evaluations than lying in other situations (e.g., white lies, or lies to avoid
bringing embarrassment to others). Further, the social-cultural perspective suggests that the deontological perspective's view regarding the reasons for lying to be
wrong only represents the concerns of individualism which exist in many western
countries. In some other cultures (e.g., Asian cultures), the concerns for individual
rights to information, freedom of choice, and mental health are not necessarily
critical factors for deciding the moral implications of lying. Rather, the concerns for
group harmony, collectivity, and sometimes divine forces are the determinants of
whether lying is right or wrong (Shweder, 1991).

Limited empirical research has addressed whether cultural conventions have any
impact on children's moral judgment of lying. Most existing studies have been
conducted with children in western countries. As these children were raised in in-
dustrialized environments which emphasize individualism, self-assertion/promo-
tion, and competition, it is unclear whether findings with these children can be
generalized to children of other socio-cultural backgrounds. Although some anthropological studies and anecdotal reports seem to support the social-cultural perspective (Gilsenan, 1976; Ochs, 1976), little systematic developmental evidence
has been advanced (see Lee & Ross, 1997).

To bridge this gap in the literature, my colleagues and I conducted a series of
studies (Lee, Cameron, Xu, Fu, & Board, 1997; Cameron, Xu, & Fu, 1999) in
which we compared 7-, 9-, and 11-year-old Chinese and Canadian children's moral
evaluations of lie- and truth-telling in situations involving pro- and antisocial
behaviors. Children were presented with two stories involving a child who intentionally carries out a good deed and two other stories involving a child who intentionally carries out a bad deed. When story characters were questioned by a teacher

as to who had committed the deed, they either lied or told the truth. Children were asked to evaluate the story characters' deeds and their verbal statements. Both Chinese and Canadian children rated truth-telling positively and lie-telling negatively in antisocial situations, reflecting the emphasis in both cultures on the distinction between misdeed and truth-/lie-telling. A significant cultural effect was found in the prosocial condition: Chinese children rated truth-telling about one's prosocial deed less positively and lie-telling about it more positively than Canadian children; the cultural difference also increased with age (Figure 11.4). This effect appears to be due to the emphasis on self-effacement and modesty in Chinese culture and children's increasing exposure to it via schooling. Overall, these results fail to support the deontological view that lying has a universal disvalue.

Children's moral judgments of lying are also context-specific. One of the major issues that one must deal with when making moral judgments of lying is whether a lie-teller adheres to the general cooperative metamaxim (i.e., to help, not to harm). Based on Sweetser's (1987) analysis, when a speaker's general communicative goal is to help the hearer, the speaker's lie should have either a neutral or positive value. An example of such a situation is telling a white lie. Several studies (Bussey, 1992; Peterson et al., 1982) have shown that children as young as 6 years of age give less negative moral evaluations to white lies than to malicious lies. Some older children even give positive ratings to white lies when the hearer is an unfamiliar peer or adult (Walper & Valtin, 1992). However, as these studies were not designed to examine the role of the general communicative intention, it is unclear whether children's

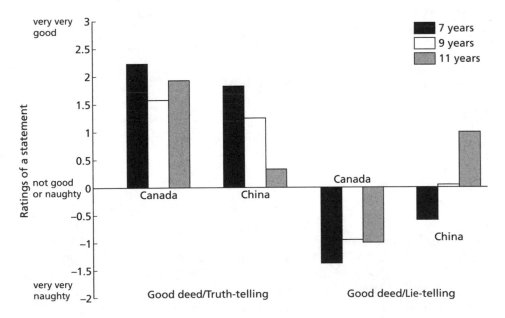

Figure 11.4 Canadian and Chinese children's moral evaluations of lie- and truth-telling in good deed situations (adapted from Lee et al., 1997).

differential moral evaluations on white and malicious lies were indeed due to children's understanding of the speaker's general communicative intention. It is possible that the children simply evaluated the *consequences* of both types of lies. They gave more negative evaluations to the malicious lies because they were presented in situations associated with explicitly stated, observable physical consequences. In contrast, the white lies' social consequences were often unobservable and not made explicit in those studies. This confound must be addressed before a firm conclusion can be reached regarding the role of the general communicative intention in children's moral judgment of lying.

A recent study by my colleagues addressed this issue (Cameron, Xu, & Fu, 1999). In this study, we presented both Canadian and Chinese children at 7, 9, and 11 years of age with stories depicting lie- or truth-telling in politeness situations (e.g., a child is given a sour apple by his friend and states that he dislikes the apple). To ensure that children understood the intention of the speaker, we made explicit why the child in the story tells a lie or the truth (i.e., to please the hearer or to hurt the hearer's feelings on purpose). Results show that both Canadian and Chinese children at all ages differentiated between lies told to help and lies told to harm as well as between lie-telling and truth-telling. Overall, they gave more positive ratings to lie-telling that is performed to please the hearer than lie-telling performed to hurt the hearer; they also gave more positive ratings to truth-telling with an intention to please than that with an intention to hurt the hearer. A cross-cultural effect was also obtained: As age increased, Canadian children's moral evaluations of white lie-telling shifted from negative to positive, while Chinese children's evaluations remained negative even though their negative ratings were significantly lower in the prosocial lie-telling situation than those in the antisocial lie-telling situation. This evidence further supports the social-cultural view of the moral values of lie-telling.

Conclusions and Future Research

In this review, I have examined current research on the development of the concept of lying and its moral implications from a speech act theoretical perspective. Specifically, I have reviewed studies that address how children acquire the intentionality and conventionality components of lying. Several major conclusions can be drawn from the review.

Development of the concept of lying

Overall, evidence to date suggests that children's understanding of the concept of lying emerges as early as 3 years of age. At this age, children already take a speaker's intention into consideration when deciding whether a statement is a lie, suggesting that the intentionality component of the concept of lying has already emerged. This early understanding, however, is rather limited. Young children only consider an untruthful statement (which is inconsistent with the speaker's belief) as a lie when the statement is also inconsistent with the true state of affairs. As age increases, children begin to understand more complex aspects of the intentionality component of lying. For example, they begin to realize that a factually true but untruthful statement is still a lie; they also realize that relaying of a lie by an unsuspecting speaker is not a lie, and understand that metaphor and irony are not lies even though they are not consistent with reality.

With regard to the conventionality component, no evidence exists regarding whether preschool children differentiate different types of lies according to whether they are told for pro- or antisocial purposes. Given that 7-year-olds in our study showed clear differentiation of prosocial and antisocial lies and that preschool children appear to understand white lies (Cavanagh, Lee, & Board, 1997) and they tell white lies (Talwar & Lee, 1999), we can infer that the conventionality component of the concept of lying also emerges during the preschool years. After this time, children gradually take into consideration the specific social conventions of their culture when deciding the extent to which an untruthful statement is a lie. By about early adolescence, children's understanding of lying has developed to a level that is similar to that of adults. Their concept of lying now reflects an integration of their understanding of social and cultural conventions of communication as well as the intentional states involved in communication. Now, the concept of a lie refers to an intentionally false statement motivated to achieve specific interpersonal impact in a specific social setting.

Development of moral judgments of lying

Evidence to date suggests that children begin to understand the moral values of lying during the preschool years. They take into consideration the intention of the speaker when making moral judgments about an untruthful statement. They not only use information regarding whether a speaker has a deceptive intent but also information about the general communicative intentions of the speaker (i.e., to help or to harm). In addition, as children become socialized to the conventions of their culture, they begin to understand that lying is not always wrong, and that the moral value of lying is context-specific. While lies told for antisocial purposes (e.g., to conceal a transgression or to hurt another person's feelings) are considered by children of preschool ages to be morally wrong, beyond this age, lies told for prosocial reasons (e.g., to be modest or to please another person) are increasingly viewed by children as not negative and sometimes even positive. In other words, social conventions regarding lying gradually become an important factor in children's moral judgments of lying.

Future research

A number of major questions need to be addressed in future research in order to develop a comprehensive theory about the development of the understanding of lying. The first question is how the intentionality and conventionality components interact in children's long journey toward a mature understanding of the concept of lying and its moral implications. Research to date has focused exclusively on either the acquisition of the intentionality component or that of the conventionality component. It is unclear whether and how children's understanding of the conventionality component of lying affects their understanding of the intentionality component and vice versa. The second question is how children's concept of lying is related to their moral judgments of lying. Most studies to date have not specifically examined this issue. One study by Wimmer et al. (1984) revealed that children who responded to a lexical question first (i.e., whether a statement is a lie) were more likely to mislabel a mistake as a lie and give harsher moral judgments than those who were asked a moral evaluation question first. This finding suggests that children's concept of lying and their moral judgments of it may indeed interact with each other.

The third question is whether and how children's conceptual knowledge about lying and its moral values is related to children's actual lie- and truth-telling behaviors in different social-cultural settings. Most studies in the literature tend to address exclusively either the development of the conceptual knowledge about lying or children's lying behaviors. It is unclear, for example, whether children who understand the prosocial value of white lies are more inclined to tell white lies than children who do not, and whether Chinese children who give positive ratings to lying for modesty are more likely to tell lies to conceal their own good deed than Canadian children who normally give negative ratings to this kind of lying. The fourth question is how children's understanding of the intentionality and conventionality components of lying interact with their acquisition of other forms of communication. Although there is some evidence suggesting that children demonstrate an earlier and better understanding of the intentional or conventional nature of verbal communication in deceptive situations, no research exists to ascertain whether children's experience and knowledge about lying facilitates their understanding of other forms of communication. Answers to these questions in the near future will undoubtedly provide a more comprehensive picture of the development of lying and bring us closer to the truth about children and lying.

Acknowledgments

This chapter was prepared with the support of grants from the Social Science and Humanities Research Council of Canada, the Premier's Research Excellence Award from the Ontario Government, and the Chancellor's Research Excellence Award from Queen's University. I would like to thank Janet Astington, Michelle Eskritt, Alejo Freire, and Victoria Talwar for their constructive comments and suggestions on earlier versions of this manuscript.

References

Astington, J. W. (1988). Children's understanding of the speech act of promising. *Journal of Child Language, 15,* 157–73.

Austin, J. L. (1962). *How to do things with words*. Cambridge, MA: Harvard University Press.

Bok, S. (1978). *Lying: Moral choice in public and private life*. New York: Pantheon Books.

Bussey, K. (1992). Lying and truthfulness: Children's definitions, standards, and evaluative reactions. *Child Development, 63*, 129–37.

Cameron, C. A., Xu, F., & Fu, G. (1999, April). *Chinese and Canadian children's concept of lying and their moral judgment: Similarities and differences*. Paper presented at the Biennial Meeting of the Society for Research in Child Development, Albuquerque, New Mexico.

Cavanagh, L., Lee. K., & Board, J. (1997, June). *Do actions speak louder than words? Children's use of the verbal-nonverbal consistency principle during incongruent social communications*. Poster presented at the Annual Meeting of the Canadian Psychological Association. Toronto, Ontario, Canada.

Chisholm, R. M., & Feehan, T. D. (1977). The intent to deceive. *The Journal of Philosophy, 75*, 143–59.

Coleman, L., & Kay, P. (1981). Prototype semantics: The English word lie. *Language, 57*, 26–44.

Fillmore, C. J. (1975). An alternative to checklist theories of meaning. In *Proceedings of the 1st Annual Meeting of Berkeley Linguistics Society* (pp. 123–131). Berkeley, CA: Berkeley Linguistics Society.

Gilsenan, M. (1976). Lying, honor, and contradiction. In B. Kapferer (Ed.), *Essays in social anthropology (Vol. 1): Transaction and meaning: Directions in the anthropology of exchange and symbolic behavior* (pp. 191–219). Philadelphia: Institute for the Study of Human Issues.

Grice, H. P. (1980). *Studies in the way of words*. Cambridge, MA: Harvard University Press.

Kupfer, J. (1982). The moral presumption against lying. *Review of Metaphysics, 36*, 103–26.

Lakoff, R. (1973). The logic of politeness: Or minding your P's and Q's. In *Papers presented at the Ninth Regional Meeting of the Chicago Linguistic Society* (pp. 292–305). Chicago: Chicago Linguistics Society .

Lee, K., Cameron, C. A., Xu, F., Fu, G, & Board, J. (1997). Chinese and Canadian children's evaluations of lying and truth-telling. *Child Development, 68*, 924–34.

Lee, K., & Ross, H. (1997). The concept of lying in adolescents and young adults: Testing Sweetser's folkloristic model. *Merrill-Palmer Quarterly, 43*, 255–70.

Lickona, T. (1976). Research on Piaget's theory of moral development. In T. Lickona (Ed.), *Moral development and behavior: Theory, research and social issues.* New York: Holt, Rinehart & Winston.

Ochs, K., E. (1976). On the universality of conversational implicatures. *Language in Society, 5*, 67–80.

Olson, D. R. (1994). *The world on paper*. Cambridge, UK: Cambridge University Press.

Peterson, C. C. (1995). The role of perceived intention to deceive in children's and adults' concepts of lying. *British Journal of Developmental Psychology, 13*, 237–60.

Peterson, C. C., Peterson, J. L., & Seeto, D. (1983). Developmental changes in ideas about lying. *Child Development, 54*, 1529–35.

Piaget, J. (1965). *The moral judgment of the child* (M. Gabain, Trans.). New York: The Free Press. (Original work published in 1932)

Searle, J. (1969). *Speech acts*. Cambridge, UK: Cambridge University Press.

Shweder, R. A. (1991). *Thinking through cultures*. Cambridge, MA: Harvard University Press.

Siegal, M., & Peterson, C. C. (1996). Breaking the mold: A fresh look at children's understanding of questions about lies and mistakes. *Developmental Psychology, 32*, 322–34.

Strichartz, A. F., & Burton, R. V. (1990). Lies and truth: A study of the development of the concept. *Child Development, 61*, 211–20.

Sweetser, E. E. (1987). The definition of lie: An examination of the folk models underlying a semantic prototype. In D. Holland (Ed.), *Cultural models in language and thought* (pp. 43–66). New York: Cambridge University Press.

Talwar, V., & Lee. K. (1999). *The development of white lie telling: Do children tell white lies and can adults detect them?* Manuscript in preparation, Queen's University.

Triandis, H. C. (1995). *Individualism and collectivism.* Boulder, CO: Westview Press.

Tsohatzidis, S. L. (Ed.). (1994). *Foundations of speech act theory: Philosophical and linguistic perspectives.* London: Routledge.

Walper, S., & Valtin, R. (1992). Children's understanding of white lies. In W. Winter (Series Ed.) & R. J. Watts, S. Ide, & K. Ehlich (Vol. Eds.), *Trends in Linguistics: Studies and Monographs, 59. Politeness in language: Studies in its history, theory and practice* (pp. 231–51). New York: Mouton

Wimmer, H., Gruber, S., & Perner, J. (1984). Young children's conception of lying: Lexical realism – moral subjectivism. *Journal of Experimental Child Psychology, 37*, 1–30.

12

Internal and External Notions of Metarepresentation: A Developmental Perspective

Deepthi Kamawar and Bruce D. Homer

For much of his academic career, David R. Olson has offered a graduate course in the Psychology of Language and Literacy at the Ontario Institute for Studies in Education (University of Toronto). Over the years, the course has covered David's far-reaching interests which include topics such as beginning literacy, philosophy of language, pragmatics, cognition and literacy, mental verbs, writing, history of reading, and semantic/syntactic development. For many, the issues that were raised in David's class began what would become a career, or at least an ongoing interest. In fact, the two of us took this course (together) and then went on to conduct our thesis research in the very topics we presented in that class. Others whose research careers have been influenced by Olson's class on Language and Literacy include Janet Astington, Rita Watson, Anne McKeough, Joan Peskin, Penny Vinden, Ted Ruffman, and Tom Keenan – all of whose work is represented in this volume. Without a doubt, Olson's course can be credited with influencing and inspiring research for many.

What follows is a discussion of our research, which was inspired by Olson's class on Language and Literacy and by his ongoing interest in the notions of representation and metarepresentation. We are two of his most recent doctoral students, having just completed dissertations in the two areas we discuss: internal and external metarepresentation.

Before moving on to the research, it is important first to clarify what the key terms "representation" and "metarepresentation" mean. The range of representations that we understand and employ is remarkably large. Not only are we able to deal with mental representations such as beliefs, we are also able to deal with pictorial and linguistic representations such as street signs, maps, musical notation, and script. Generally defined, a *representation* is something that "involves one thing's 'standing for', 'being about', 'referring to or denoting' something else" (Schwartz, 1995, p. 537). For many years, Olson has been interested and involved in research addressing the notion of representation and the recursive notion of *metarepresentation*; that is the ability to represent a representation. This ability has been found to be developmental in nature and the focus of this chapter is to examine the notions of representation and metarepresentation within a developmental framework.

The two broad categories of representational systems described in the above paragraph outline a major division between types of representations; there are those that exist without an external physical aspect (mental representations) and those that have an obligatory physical component, such as script. Both types of representation can be used recursively. Therefore, we can use the term metarepresentation to describe such things as: (1) the ability to have beliefs about beliefs; and (2) the ability to use written notations to represent language. We will refer to the first use of the term as "internal" metarepresentation and the second as "external" metarepresentation. This is not to say that there is nothing taking place internally (in the mind) in the second form; but rather, the term "external" is used to emphasize the necessity of the external aspect of the metarepresentation.

A great deal of research has been done examining children's developing ability to deal with internal metarepresentations (e.g., Astington & Gopnik, 1988; Perner, 1988, 1991) as well as with external metarepresentations (e.g., Ferreiro & Teberosky, 1979/1982; Olson, 1991; Pontecorvo, 1997; Snow, Hemphill & Barnes, 1991). In this chapter we will examine each type of metarepresentation in turn, and will then conclude with some general comments on the nature of metarepresentation and on the interplay between representation and metarepresentation. Some directions for future research in the area will be offered.

Internal Metarepresentation

In order to investigate children's ability to deal with internal metarepresentation, it is necessary to find situations in which different representations yield distinct responses on the part of the child. One such situation is false beliefs; an area in which a great deal of research has been conducted. In a typical false belief task (e.g., Wimmer & Perner, 1983), a child is told a story about a character who puts her toy in a concealed location (location A) and leaves the room. Her brother comes in, and unbeknownst to his sister, moves the toy to another concealed location (location B). The brother leaves, the sister returns and the child participant is asked where the sister will look for the toy. Children around the age of 3 years tend to say that the sister will look for the toy in location B (where it actually *is*). However, children around age 4 and up tend to correctly say that the sister will look in location A. Note that is the location where the sister believes/represents the object to be. Success on false belief tasks requires the understanding "that the protagonist's belief is a mental state that represents *something* (the real location) as *being a certain way* – as being different from what it really is" (Doherty & Perner, 1998, p. 280). Such an ability is said to be indicative of a representational theory of mind (Perner, 1991). Comparing representations is possible at this metarepresentational level.

In the case of false belief, an individual's representation is different from the state of the world. Therefore, it is possible to play these situations off one another by asking the child to predict another's actions (or beliefs). Such a request determines whether the child bases his or her predictions on reality (situation theorist; Perner, 1991), or on the other's representation of reality (representation theorist; Perner, 1991).

While much attention has been paid to how children deal with false beliefs, there exist other situations in which different representations yield distinct responses for the child with metarepresentational ability. One such situation is referentially opaque contexts; that is contexts in which a mental attitude is directed toward a proposition that contains a specific description (representation). It is to this type of context that we now turn.

An important distinction when discussing opaque contexts is that between the *sense* and the *reference* of a term. Frege (1892/1991) pointed out that there is more to meaning than just referring, and that something mediates between the word and the object. He called this mediating factor the sense of a word. The sense is considered to be objective, and is the word's meaning. It is a particular way of connecting a referent to its name or description. This can be made clearer using Frege's example. He noted that Venus is picked out differently when it is referred to as: (a) the "Evening Star," the first "star" visible in the evening (we now know it is not really a star); and (b) the "Morning Star", the last "star" visible in the morning. It is important to note that the referent is *represented* differently by each name or description.

In normal sentences (transparent contexts) one can freely substitute co-referential terms without changing the truth-value of the sentence as a whole. For example, since "Venus is the Morning Star" is true, replacing "the Evening Star" for "the Morning Star" produces "Venus is the Evening Star" and does not affect the truth-value of the sentence.

In referentially opaque contexts, however, this kind of substitution does not guarantee truth-value (Quine, 1955/1991). A context is considered opaque if replacing a term within it with another co-referential term can affect the truth-value of the sentence as a whole (Hookway, 1988). One familiar type of opaque context involves propositional attitudes such as believe, think, and desire; for example, "Jessie believes that Venus is the Morning Star." While this may be true, simply substituting co-referential terms can create a false sentence, so long as Jessie does not know that Venus is also called "the Evening Star." Here, Jessie has a mental attitude (that of "belief") toward the proposition "Venus is the Morning Star," not the referent. Therefore, one cannot make changes to the proposition without possibly affecting the truth of the whole sentence. Stated this way, one can see that dealing with referentially opaque contexts also requires some metarepresentational ability, since one must be sensitive to the fact that a mental attitude is directed toward a proposition (a linguistic entity) and not toward the referent (the object in the world). At a minimum, one must be aware that objects can be referred to in more than one way.

A crucial understanding in order to be sensitive to referentially opaque contexts is knowing how to deal with *partial knowledge*; specifically, knowing that having access to the referent under one description does not ensure access to it under all possible descriptions (Kamawar, 1996). Note that this is not the same requirement as false belief tasks, which require one to distinguish truth from falsity. Opaque contexts require the understanding that different descriptions may represent a referent in distinct ways, and that while someone may have a mental attitude toward an object under one description, he or she may not have that attitude toward it under a different one. These contexts require an understanding of the representational nature of language and beliefs; therefore, in order to be sensitive to opacity, one requires metarepresentational ability.

Given that both false belief and referential opacity tasks require the ability to metarepresent, it might be expected that performance on the two tasks would be related. De Villiers (1995) looked for just such a relation by giving 3- to 6-year-olds referential substitution (opacity) and false belief tasks. The opacity tasks involved an object that was referred to in three ways: based on its appearance (a silver box); based on its contents (candy); and based on its function (it is a birthday gift). Children were asked about story characters and whether those characters did something to, or thought about, objects under different descriptions. An example of a question with a transparent context is "Did the mom put the silver box/birthday present on the top shelf?" An example of a question with an opaque context is "Did the mom know the silver box/candy is on the table?" (p. 32). De Villiers reported that only the children who passed false belief tasks went on to appropriately constrain referential substitution, however, once age was partialled out, that relation disappeared. Though close, this study came just short of demonstrating a link between the two metarepresentational tasks.

Recently, Apperly and Robinson (1998, Study 1) had 4- to 6-year-olds perform a standard false belief task and an opacity task. Their opacity task involved a puppet who knew that A was in a box (where A is a dice) but didn't know that the A was a B (that the dice was an eraser). The participants' job was to decide whether the puppet (who saw the A in the box) knew that the A was a B (Q1), and whether it knew there was a B in the box (Q2). The authors found that those children who were successful on the false belief task were the same ones who were able to answer Q1, but their performance on Q2 (opaque context) was poor.

Apperly and Robinson took the opacity task to be a clear measure of metarepresentational ability, so that in finding that children could pass the false belief task but not the opacity one, they drew the conclusion that false belief tasks do not measure metarepresentational ability. However, they might have failed to find a relation between the two tasks for the simple reason that they used only one false belief task. With only a pass/fail score for false belief, they could say only whether the ability to deal with false belief is identical to the ability to deal with opaque contexts, thereby leaving out the possibility that the two are related but not equivalent. Their view is consistent with an all-or-nothing view of metarepresentational ability.

One of us (Kamawar & Olson, in press) designed a study to examine the relation between opacity and false belief more closely. Three- to seven-year-olds were given three opacity and three false belief tasks. The opacity tasks consisted of short stories about two characters: Mark and Anna. Each opacity story was about a referent that could be distinctly represented in many ways. One character had knowledge of the object under a specific representation (description), and it was made clear that he or she lacked knowledge about it under other representations (descriptions). For example, in one story, Anna and Mark were at a doctor's office. Mark stood next to the doctor (description A) while she (the doctor) put a bandage on Anna's knee. Unbeknownst to Mark, the doctor was in fact Anna's mom (description B). At the end of the story, comprehension questions ensured that the children understood the story and the key questions were asked: "Did Mark stand next to Anna's mom?" (transparent) and "Does Mark know that he stood next to Anna's mom?" (opaque). The correct answer to the first question was "yes," and to the second, "no." The first question (transparent) ensured that participants knew that it was permissible to substitute one description for another in some situations. The second question (opaque) tested whether participants were sensitive to the fact that substitution was not allowed because Mark's mental attitude of "knowing" was toward the proposition that represented the referent as "the doctor" and not as "Anna's mom."

Children earned a score of up to three points (one per story) for answering the opacity and transparent questions correctly. They also performed three false belief tasks for which they received a point for each correct answer. These points were summed to get each child's false belief score (out of three).

The general results are outlined here (see Kamawar & Olson, in press, for details). Consistent with other studies, children improved on false belief tasks with age, and there was a sharp increase in performance around age 4. Children at all ages performed quite well on the transparent questions showing little difference between the youngest and oldest age groups. Children's performance improved with age on the opaque questions, with the biggest jump in performance from age 4 to 5 (see Figure 12.1).

The question of whether performance on the two metarepresentational tasks is related was answered by examining the correlation between opacity and false belief scores. Even with age partialled out, there was a significant relation between opacity and false belief performance (pr (117) = .25, two-tailed, $p < .01$), supporting the view that the two are related, though not equivalent. Opacity proved to be more difficult, though both tasks are metarepresentational. This supports the view that development of metarepresentational ability is not all-or-nothing, but varies according to the specific nature of the tasks in question.

Comparison of false belief and opacity tasks

Like Apperly and Robinson (1998), we found that the ability to perform successfully on the false belief tasks was not equivalent to successful performance on the opacity tasks. However, unlike them, we do not interpret this to mean that false

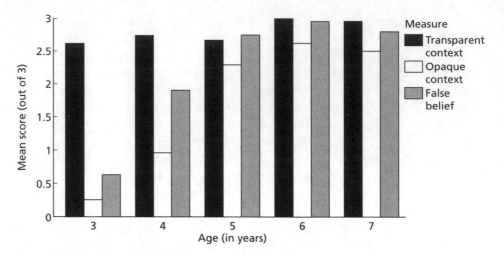

Figure 12.1   Children's performance on transparent context, opaque context, and false belief tasks, by age.

belief tasks are not metarepresentational. Instead, we argue that success on both false belief and referential opacity tasks are metarepresentational, but that opacity tasks require something extra, and that "something extra" is what makes them more difficult.

The difference in difficulty can be explained by appeal to the fact that while false belief tasks deal with *false*, or incorrect, information about a situation, opacity tasks deal with something more subtle. Opacity tasks demand that the child be able to deal appropriately with *partial knowledge*. This is a point that deserves more attention.

Earlier, we mentioned that success on false belief tasks requires the understanding "that the protagonist's belief is a mental state that represents *something* (the real location) *as being a certain way* . . . as being different from what it really is" (Doherty & Perner, 1998, p. 280). The important phrase here is " . . . different from what it really is . . ." (and therefore is a false belief). This needs to be contrasted with opacity tasks. In becoming able to deal with opacity, the skill that is required is not sensitivity to the fact that something is represented as being different from what it really is, but rather, that a representation might only represent one aspect of the referent. Therefore, just because someone knows an object under one description of it, she might not have access to it under another. It is possible that the younger children build composite mental representations of the referents. Instead of there being "the doctor" and "Anna's mom," the mental representation might be something like "the doctor mom." When asked if the character in the story knows that he stood next to "Anna's mom," younger children might not compare the way in which the two descriptions represent the referent (a more advanced skill), but rather, they may simply answer the question by appeal to the composite representation of the referent. To succeed on the opacity tasks, children need to be sensitive to the fact that an object can have more than one representation, and that these representations are distinct from one another.

Keeping representations distinct is easier with false beliefs than with opaque contexts. This is due to the fact that a composite representation is not an option when dealing with false beliefs. The situation sets up a "forced choice" for the child: "Where is the object? In Location A or in Location B?" The object cannot be represented as being in the composite location "AB." The situation requires that a choice be made between the two representations, one true and one false. Opaque contexts do not demand such choice because both options (e.g., "the doctor" and "Anna's mom") are permissible ways of representing the referent. In false belief tasks, successful children allow that beliefs can be different from, and false of, a situation. In opacity tasks, children have to allow that beliefs could be different because the way that a word conveys a sense or meaning goes beyond the way it refers to an object. What opacity tasks require that false belief tasks do not, is the ability to deal with partial knowledge. This is harder. This then helps to explain the difference in performance on the two tasks while allowing them both to be considered metarepresentational.

Our findings (Kamawar & Olson, in press) support the view that false belief and opacity are related, and that metarepresentational ability is not an all-or-nothing ability. Some metarepresentational tasks are harder than others because they require the ability to deal with more sophisticated concepts, such as partial knowledge. This raises the question of how other metarepresentational tasks are related to false belief and opacity, and what might make those tasks more or less difficult. This is the focus of future research which will attempt to map out factors that affect metarepresentational ability as a function of task demands. We will come back to the issue of future research, but let us now turn out attention to the concept of external metarepresentation.

External Metarepresentation

In the previous section we discussed developments in children's ability to coordinate internal metarepresentations which were recursions within the same representational system; that is, beliefs about beliefs. In this section, we turn our attention toward one form of external metarepresentations, namely writing, which is a representational system that is used to represent another representational system (i.e., language). Writing is therefore, by its very nature, a second-order representational system. This provides some unique challenges for learning to read and write and cognitive consequences thereof; two of which will be reviewed in this section. The first is that children seem to initially understand writing as a first-order representational system that represents the world directly, rather than a second-order system that represents language (Homer & Olson, 1999). The second phenomenon that we will discuss is that when children do begin to relate written text to spoken language, the metarepresentational system (i.e., writing) actually changes children's conception of the representational system (i.e., speech) (Olson, 1994; Homer & Olson, 1999).

In order to understand the cognitive challenges and implications of literacy, it is necessary to first have an idea of how children learn to read and write. One of the most fruitful approaches for research in this area has been to adopt a constructivist stance in which literacy is seen as a cultural object that children actively attempt to understand by forming, testing, and modifying "theories" (e.g., Ferreiro, 1996). Two implications of this approach are that children start the process of becoming literate well before they receive any formal instruction, and that the "errors" made by young children during their early attempts to read and write are actually indications of their current understanding or "theory" of writing.

Drawing on these insights, Emilia Ferreiro has developed a technique for identifying preliterate children's conceptions of writing. The basic approach is to ask children to read and write, telling them to "just try" or "pretend" if they are reluctant. (In procedures where children are asked to write, they are also asked to "read" what they have written.) This technique has allowed Ferreiro (1985; Ferreiro & Teberosky, 1979/1982) to identify several common "stages" or levels of understanding that children pass through in their acquisition of literacy.[1]

One interesting finding is that children at a certain level, usually around 5 years of age, will often differentiate between what is written and what can be read. For example, if shown a picture of three ducks and asked to write "three ducks," children will often make three marks. When asked to "read" each mark individually, the children will say "duck, duck, duck," however, when asked what they say all together, they will answer "three ducks" (Ferreiro & Teberosky, 1979/1982). Ferreiro (1986) has also found that children at this level have great difficulty "writing" counterfactual statements such as, "no birds fly." She has found that in general, children have trouble with the notion of representing no, not, and nothing. Young children claim that statements such as, "There aren't any birds" cannot be written because "We see birds." Ferreiro has argued that these children have difficulty reconciling the presence of letters with the absence of the thing referred to. However, it is unclear if the preliterate children object to writing "no birds fly" because it is false, or because they cannot think of any way to represent negation.

In a more recent study, one of us, in collaboration with David Olson (Homer & Olson, 1999), investigated young children's (3 to 6 years old) conception of the representational nature of writing by asking them to write a series of expressions which included a quantity (e.g., "two dogs") and a negation (e.g., "no dog"). We hypothesized that the written representation of negation would provide a particular problem for children who did not understand that writing is a representation of language (i.e., who did not conceive of writing as a metarepresentational system).

We (Homer & Olson, 1999) found that children's conception of writing could be classified according to one of three categories:

1   *Other/Non-representational.* Children in this category would typically make a single, undifferentiated mark for each phrase. When asked to "read" a segment of the mark, they would repeat the entire phrase. Although children at this level do seem to know that writing involves making marks on paper and do differentiate writing from drawing, they do not appear to have any idea of the representational nature of these marks.

2   *Token/First-order.* Children in this category would use a separate mark to represent each object described in the expression. For example, "two dogs" was represented by two marks, both of which the child identified as being "dog" (i.e., "two dogs" = "dog" "dog"). When asked to write, "no dogs," children in this category would say that "no dogs" could not be written or else they would make a mark and claim that it said something completely different (e.g., "cat"). We suggest that children at this level are attempting to use writing to represent the world directly (i.e., the children conceive of writing as being a first-order representational system).

3   *Word representation.* The final group of children used one mark to represent each word of an expression. These children understand that writing represents language, and have begun the process of identifying how language is represented. It is interesting to note that many of these children attempted to represent words before they could actually write words, and some, even before they could write letters.

Although we (Homer & Olson, 1999) do not make any strong claims about the categories representing a developmental sequence, more of the younger children are in the Other (non-representational) category and more of the older children are in the Word (metarepresentational) category (see Figure 12.2), and the categories do roughly correspond to levels identified by Ferreiro (1985; Ferreiro & Teberosky, 1979/1982). However, Ferreiro's work has primarily been done with Spanish-speaking children – it is possible that the levels would be different for children learning to write English. Also, Ferreiro suggests that children's understanding of writing is always metalinguistic (i.e., metarepresentational). In her own words:

> Writing is related, from the very beginning, to language but not to the adult-conceptual object called "language" . . . It is related, if you will, to some privileged "pieces of language": proper nouns and common nouns (nouns that, in turn, could be conceived of as properties of objects that are left aside in drawing them). (Ferreiro, 1994, p. 120)

That is to say, Ferreiro suggests that young children think of proper and common nouns as being properties of objects, a phenomenon known as *nominal realism* (Piaget, 1929). Interestingly, there is some evidence to suggest that literacy is involved in children's transition from *nominal realism* to *nominalism*, the understanding that proper and common nouns are arbitrary symbols (Homer, Brockmeier, Kamawar, & Olson, 1999).

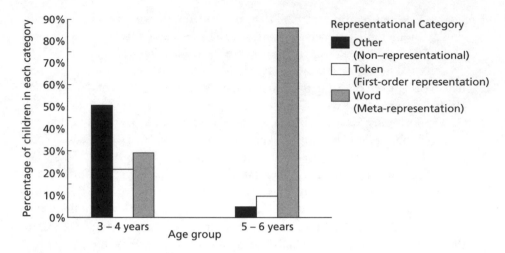

Figure 12.2   Children's assignment to representational category, by age (adapted from Homer & Olson, 1999).

More research is needed to obtain a clearer understanding of the beginning stages of literacy acquisition. Longitudinal research is required to determine if the different categories we identified (Homer & Olson, 1999) are indicative of a developmental sequence and if English-speaking children who are learning to read and write pass through the same levels identified by Ferreiro for Spanish-speaking children. Additional research will also be required to determine if children at the transitional level described above (i.e., Token/First-order) are attempting to use writing to represent objects directly or if they are attempting to represent nouns, which they consider to be properties of objects. However, the research on children's early conceptions of writing does clearly indicate that children have begun the process of learning to read and write well before they receive formal instruction. The question we shall now consider is how becoming literate affects children's understanding of language. We will argue that the process of learning to read and write is at least partially responsible for children being able to consciously reflect on language.

Most theories claim that the ability to consciously reflect on language, to understand language *as language* (i.e., *metalinguistic awareness*), is either part of more general cognitive developments (e.g., Hakes, 1980; Piaget, 1929; Sinclair, 1970) or an aspect of language acquisition (e.g., Karmiloff-Smith, Grant, Sims, Jones, & Cuckle, 1996; Smith & Tager-Flusberg, 1982). According to these theories, metalinguistic awareness involves only internal metarepresentation (i.e., language used to reflect on itself). In contrast, Olson's (1994) *model* theory of literacy argues that external metarepresentation (i.e., literacy) is responsible for certain aspects of metalinguistic awareness. More specifically, Olson argues that writing provides the set of categories that is used to reflect on language.

Olson's model theory reverses the traditional view of the relation between writing and speech. Researchers who contend that metalinguistic awareness develops independently of literacy suggest that children must be metalinguistically aware before they can learn to read and write. Most commonly, it has been argued that children must become aware of the phonological properties of language before they can become literate. Bradley and Bryant, for example, have conducted several studies which examine the relation between young children's phonological awareness and their later literacy skills (e.g., Bradley & Bryant, 1983; Bryant, MacLean, & Bradley, 1990; Kirtley, Bryant, MacLean, & Bradley, 1989). The authors have argued that children's awareness of "onset" (i.e., the first consonant or consonant cluster in a syllable) and "rime" (i.e., the remaining vowel sound and any subsequent consonants in the syllable) is essential in the process of learning to read. In a series of studies, Bradley and Bryant have demonstrated that prereading children's ability to segment words into onset and rime is related to their subsequent reading ability.

Other authors have claimed that children are aware of different aspects of language before they are literate. For example, Karmiloff-Smith (1992; Karmiloff-Smith et al., 1996) has recently argued that preliterate children have a concept of "word." Using a task that was more "on-line" than the usual metalinguistic judgment tasks, Karmiloff-Smith et al. investigated children's knowledge of what counts as a word. Children were read a story, during which the experimenter would stop occasionally and ask the children to "repeat the last word." With this task, even prereaders succeeded after only a brief training session, whereas with other methods, such as moving a token for each word (e.g., Bialystok, 1986), it is only around 6 or 7 years of age that children succeed. This finding led the authors to suggest that "metalinguistic awareness could turn out to be a part of language acquisition itself rather than the mere product of literacy" (Karmiloff-Smith et al., 1996, p. 215).

Although research has demonstrated that children are aware of certain aspects of language from a young age, it is still possible that literacy is playing a role. Typically, studies that argue for metalinguistic awareness before literacy have used a very formal definition of "literacy" (e.g., ability to recognize words in a word list). Considering the data reviewed above on children's acquisition of literacy, we know that the process of becoming literate begins well before children can read and write actual words. Measures such as "word recognition" do not capture children's early understandings of writing, and it may be – as implied by the model theory of literacy – that it is this early understanding which is essential for the development of metalinguistic awareness.

Olson (1994; Homer & Olson, 1999) has argued that literacy plays a crucial role in the development of metalinguistic awareness. He suggests that in learning linguistic concepts such as *word*, children are both learning something about their own speech practices and also learning something about the conventions of their particular literate, linguistic community for analyzing speech. That is to say, children are not only learning to reflect on speech, but they are also learning to think about their speech in terms of some historically evolved, conventional coding scheme, compatible with the structure of writing. For this, children must have available two types of representation or knowledge structures. First, they must have access to the structures of their own speech – this provides data for reflecting on language – and secondly, they must have a set of conventional categories (e.g., written words and letters) into which the data can be sorted – this provides a model for reflecting on language. Olson claims that familiarity with both written text and spoken language is necessary; the task for children is to bring the two together. In learning what a word is, children are learning to use this convention of writing as a model to introspect and categorize the properties of their own speech.

If the model theory is correct, then children who are able to identify words using the "on-line" task of Karmiloff-Smith et al. (1996) should have some understanding of the nature of writing, even if they are not functionally literate. This is exactly what we have found in our recent work (Homer & Olson, 1999). We investigated young children's understanding of word as a unit of written text and as a part of speech. Our results indicate that children's understanding of both increases with age. Even when controlling for age, children's understanding word as a unit of text correlates significantly with their ability to identify words in speech, both in a "pre-training" ($pr = .40$, $p < .001$) and a "post-training" ($pr = .30$, $p < .001$) version of Karmiloff-Smith et al.'s task.

Although this finding does not indicate a causal connection, we (Homer & Olson, 1999) argue that when it is considered along with the earlier observations of such anthropological writers as Scribner and Cole (1981) and Finnegan (1977) who reported that the traditional cultures they studied had no concept of word as a lexical entity, it seems fair to conclude that writing is a causal factor in acquiring a concept of word. This is not to say that literacy is the only way that metalinguistic concepts can be learned. We found, similar to Karmiloff-Smith and her colleagues (Karmiloff-Smith et al., 1996), that oral training tasks significantly improved children's ability to segment speech into words. Rather, the claim is that literacy is the usual way in which these concepts are learned.

The findings described above support Olson's *model* theory of literacy, however, more research is needed to further specify the precise relation between reading and oral metalinguistic knowledge. The correspondence between text and speech needs to be tested with linguistic concepts other than words. For example, children's phonological awareness should be predicted by their understanding of letters. Another implication of the model theory is that there should be significant differences in the development of metalinguistic awareness in cultures with qualitatively different scripts: children should develop an awareness of the components of speech which are actually captured by their culture's writing system. For example, children whose culture's script is logographic (e.g., Chinese) should develop a very different understanding from children whose culture's script is alphabetic (e.g., English – see Read, Zhang, Nie, & Ding, 1986). Currently, we are comparing literacy and metalinguistic awareness in Canadian and Chinese children (Homer, Xu, Lee, & Olson, 1999). Finally, it may be the case that there are some aspects of language that are more "natural" components of speech and are not, therefore, dependent on text (e.g., the syllable – see Bryant et al., 1990).

Comparison of Internal and External Metarepresentation

Both lines of research presented in this chapter reflect children's developing ability to deal with representations, and more specifically, with metarepresentation. While the specifics differ, many similarities can be seen in the development of internal and external metarepresentational ability. Young children treat descriptions of objects as referring to the world directly, in the same way that they treat writing as representing the world directly. It is only once they are able to metarepresent that they can see that people refer to objects in the world via their representations of them, and that script represents the world via representing language (which itself is representational).

As we have shown (Homer & Olson, 1999), developing metarepresentational ability in written form brings to mind an awareness of certain features of language and not others (e.g., words). The development that takes place in regard to opacity tasks is similar; once the child is able to metarepresent, he or she can become sensitive to the particular representations (descriptions) to which an individual has access, and become sensitive to the fact that representations of a referent can be distinct from one another (Kamawar & Olson, in press).

Given the similarities between the two types of metarepresentation, it is natural to ask how they are related to one another. An area for future research is to examine the developmental trajectories of the types of tasks discussed in this chapter in relation to each other. If they are found to be related, that would be support for the view that metarepresentation is an underlying ability that can be brought to bear across a wide range of situations; that is, it is an ability that is domain general and is required to deal with opacity, writing, and false belief. Alternatively, such a result may be indicative of a more specific metarepresentational ability that is based on the metalinguistic aspects of the tasks in question, and could therefore be the result of a literate culture and practices. Teasing apart these options will prove to be both challenging and interesting. Only more research can demonstrate which is the appropriate one.

On a final note, it must be said again that these two pieces of research are united in that they reflect the authors' interests which were inspired by David Olson. Olson's influence on current research is farther reaching than even he may realize, as many of the students who took his course have gone on to inspire their own students, who are now taking up the very same topics.

Note

1   Although the claim is that children pass through the levels in a specific sequence, it is important to point out that these are not "stages" in a strict sense. Ferreiro does not suggest that children's current levels will predict all of their reading and writing activities: at any one time, children may demonstrate behaviors that correspond with more than one level.

References

Apperly I. A., & Robinson, E. J. (1998). Children's mental representation of referential relations. *Cognition, 67*, 287–309.

Astington, J. W., & Gopnik, A. (1988). Knowing you've changed your mind: Children's understanding of representational change. In J. W. Astington, P. L. Harris, & D. R. Olson (Eds.), *Developing theories of mind* (pp. 141–72). New York: Cambridge University Press.

Bialystok, E. (1986). Children's concept of word. *Journal of Psycholinguistic Research, 15*, 13–32.

Bradley, L., & Bryant, P. E. (1983). Categorizing sounds and learning to read – A causal connection. *Nature (London), 301*, 419–21.

Bryant, P., MacLean, M., & Bradley, L. (1990). Rhyme, language, and children's reading. *Applied Psycholinguistics, 11*, 237–52.

de Villiers, J. (1995). Questioning minds and answering machines. In D. MacLaughlin & S. McEwan (Eds.), *Boston University conference on language development*, vol. 1 (pp. 20–36). Somerville, MA: Cascadilla Press.

Doherty, M., & Perner, J. (1998). Metalinguistic awareness and theory of mind: Just two words for the same thing? *Cognitive Development, 13*, 279–305.

Ferreiro, E. (1985). Literacy development: A psychogenetic perspective. In D. R. Olson, N. Torrance, & A. Hildyard (Eds.), *Literacy, language and learning* (pp. 217–28). New York: Cambridge University Press.

Ferreiro, E. (1986). *Proceso de alfabetizacion: La alfabetizacion en proceso* [The process of alphabetization: Alphabetization in process]. Buenos Aires, Argentina: Bibliotecas Universitarias.

Ferreiro, E. (1994). Two literacy histories: A possible dialogue between children and their ancestors. In D. Keller-Cohen (Ed.), *Literacy: Interdisciplinary conversations*. Cresskill, NJ: Hampton Press.

Ferreiro, E. (1996). The acquisition of cultural objects: The case of written language. *Prospects, XXVI*, 131–40.

Ferreiro, E., & Teberosky, A. (1982). *Literacy before schooling* (Siglo Veintiuno, Trans.). Exeter, NH: Heinemann. (Original work published 1979)

Finnegan, R. (1977). *Oral poetry*. Cambridge, UK: Cambridge University Press.

Frege, G. (1991) On sense and nominatum. In J. L. Garfield & M. Kiteley (Eds.), *Meaning and truth: The essential readings in modern semantics* (pp. 35–52). New York: Paragon House. (Original work published in 1892)

Hakes, D. H. (1980). *The development of metalinguistic abilities in children*. Berlin, Germany: Springer-Verlag.

Homer, B. D., Brockmeier, J., Kamawar, D., & Olson, D. R. (1999). *Between realism and nominalism: Learning to think about words and names*. Manuscript submitted for publication, University of Toronto.

Homer, B. D., & Olson, D. R. (1999). The role of literacy in children's concept of word. *Written language and literacy, 2*, 113–37.

Homer, B. D., Xu, F., Lee, K., & Olson, D. R. (1999). *The role of literacy in Chinese and Canadian children's conception of language*. Manuscript in preparation, University of Toronto.

Hookway, C. (1988). *Quine*. Stanford, CA: Stanford University Press.

Kamawar, D. (1996). *Children's development of a representational theory of language*. Master's thesis, Ontario Institute for Studies in Education of the University of Toronto.

Kamawar, D., & Olson, D. R. (in press). Children's representational theory of language: The problem of opaque contexts. *Cognitive Development.*

Karmiloff-Smith, A. (1992). *Beyond modularity: A developmental perspective on cognitive science.* Cambridge, MA: MIT Press.

Karmiloff-Smith, A., Grant, J., Sims, K., Jones, M., & Cuckle, P. (1996). Rethinking metalinguistic awareness: Representing and accessing knowledge about what counts as a 'word'. *Cognition, 58,* 197–219.

Kirtley, C., Bryant, P., MacLean, M., & Bradley, L. (1989). Rhyme, rime, and the onset of reading. *Journal of Experimental Child Psychology, 48,* 224–45.

Olson, D. R. (1991). Literacy as metalinguistic activity. In D. R. Olson (Ed.), *Literacy and orality* (pp. 251–270). Cambridge, UK: Cambridge University Press.

Olson, D. R. (1994). *The world on paper.* Cambridge, UK: Cambridge University Press.

Perner, J. (1988). Developing semantics for theories of mind: From propositional attitudes to mental representation. In J. W. Astington, P. L. Harris & D. R. Olson (Eds.), *Developing theories of mind* (pp. 141–72). New York: Cambridge University Press.

Perner, J. (1991). *Understanding the representational mind.* Cambridge, MA: Bradford Books/MIT Press.

Piaget, J. (1929). *The child's conception of the world.* London: Routledge and Kegan Paul.

Pontecorvo, C. (Ed.). (1997). *Writing development: An interdisciplinary view.* (Vol. 6). Philadelphia: Benjamins.

Quine, W. V. O. (1991). Quantifiers and propositional attitudes. In J. L. Garfield & M. Quietly (Eds.), *Meaning and truth: The essential readings in modern semantics* (pp. 323–33). New York: Paragon House. (Original work published in 1955)

Read, C. A., Zhang, Y., Nie, H., & Ding, B. (1986). The ability to manipulate speech sounds depends on knowing alphabetic reading. *Cognition, 24,* 31–44.

Schwartz, R. (1995). Representation. In S. Guttenplan (Ed.), *A companion to the philosophy of mind* (pp. 536–41). Cambridge, MA: Blackwell Publishers Ltd.

Scribner, S., & Cole, M. (1981). *The psychology of literacy.* Cambridge, MA: Harvard University Press.

Sinclair, H. (1970). The transition from sensory-motor behavior to symbolic activity. *Interchange, 1,* 119–26.

Smith, C. L., & Tager-Flusberg, H. (1982). Metalinguistic awareness and language development. *Journal of Experimental Child Psychology, 34,* 449–68.

Snow, C., Hemphill, L., & Barnes, W. S. (1991). *Unfulfilled expectations: Home and school influences on literacy.* Cambridge, MA: Harvard University Press.

Wimmer, H., & Perner, J. (1983). Beliefs about beliefs: Representation and constraining function of wrong beliefs in young children's understanding of deception. *Cognition, 13,* 103–28.

13

RUM, PUM, and the Perspectival Relativity of Sortals

Josef Perner

When I was a student in the Department of Psychology at the University of Toronto there was little cognitive development on offer for me besides Barney Gilmore's one-term Piaget course. So I sauntered over to OISE to attend the weekly colloquia of David Olson's research group and became a fairly regular attendant. At the time I was interested in logical reasoning, in particular, Piaget's class inclusion task on which Bill Ford was working under David's supervision. Their approach sensitized me to the pragmatic aspects of the language used with children and influenced by David's *Psychological Review* paper (Olson, 1970) I developed a long-lasting interest in pragmatics. This interest resurfaced with vigor later when trying to relate children's problems in Piagetian tests to their developing theory of mind. I not only had a theory like Margaret Donaldson's (1978) of why they failed Piaget and Inhelder's conservation test (because the questions asked are not genuine questions since the experimenter knows the answer). I also could explain why the older children passed (because they are able to understand second-order epistemic interest: the experimenter wants to know whether I know). Unfortunately my paper "The Insincerity of Conservation Questions" (Perner, Leekam, & Wimmer, 1984) made it only to two conferences because reality did not cooperate sufficiently for turning it into a proper publication. Our initial data indicated that children's problems with the conservation question were alleviated when the test question was turned into a genuine looking question asked by a seemingly ignorant newcomer. Unfortunately, this could not be replicated (Arthur, 1985).

David's paper with Elizabeth Robinson (Robinson, Goelman, & Olson, 1983) had another devastatingly strong influence on me. It led me into a spate of activity trying, with the help of Nicola Yuill, to find a link between children's understanding of knowledge formation and their appreciation of the ambiguity of referential expressions. My memories are vague, but I remember as many as 10 studies none of which yielded coherent, interpretable, publishable results. However, the experience was valuable in forcing me to think about the relation between children's metarepresentional and metalinguistic abilities.

Less directly I could also blame David for my efforts trying to prove that under certain conditions mutual knowledge was logically justified. Fortunately for David, this enterprise led to some success. Although we basically rediscovered the original solutions proposed by David Lewis (1969) and Steve Schiffer (1972) (but ignored by Herb Clark: Clark & Marshall, 1981) we were able to add to them and publish our findings (Garnham & Perner, 1990; Perner & Garnham, 1988).

Clearer success resulted from David roping me in to be the external supervisor of Deborrah Howe's MA thesis. Deborrah and David had some neat experimental ideas, which Deborrah and I worked into the still clearest evidence against "introspectionist" simulation theory (Perner & Howes, 1992). By the time of this collaboration David's influence on me had taken a quite different form – as a great and effective sponsor of "theory-of-mind" research. It began with an invitation to his theory-of-mind symposium at the Society for Philosophy and Psychology meeting in Toronto in 1985. Then the following year David, with the help of Janet Astington, Lynd Forguson, and Alison Gopnik, beat Paul Harris by one month to holding the first-ever theory-of-mind conference. The joint proceedings of both conferences appeared in the well-known opus edited by Astington, Harris, and Olson (1988) which gave a tremendous (some would claim, overly effective) boost to theory-of-mind research.

Legitimately blended with his self-interest in this area, David continued his moral and financial support of theory-of-mind research. Whenever I happened to be in North America there was a reason and some money for a stop-over in Toronto and stimulating explorations of meta-this-and-meta-that in David's office. The latest occasion was David's workshop "Literacy and Conceptions of Language" in April 1999. He invited me to this workshop because he had been very interested in our report (Doherty & Perner, 1998) of a close relationship between understanding false belief and metalinguistic abilities. David's excitement about this finding came just in time to rescue me from interpreting it the wrong way due to some recent incommensurable data. Here is the story and the correct interpretation (so I hope).

The Original Finding

Martin Doherty and I (Doherty, 1994; Doherty & Perner, 1998) discovered a surprisingly strong correlation between children's mastery of the traditional false belief test (Wimmer & Perner, 1983) and our "synonyms" task.

In the false belief task a story character, Maxi, puts his chocolate bar into one location (A) and leaves. In his absence the chocolate is unexpectedly transferred to another location (B). On his return hungry for his chocolate, children are asked where he will look. Typically young 3-year-olds answer incorrectly that he will look in location B where the chocolate bar is. After 4 years of age most children give the correct answer, at about the age that they are able to understand our "synonyms" task: children are first tested for their knowledge of word pairs that come close to being synonyms, for example bunny–rabbit, lady–woman, television–TV, etc. On different occasions children were shown the same object among three distractors and asked, "Which one is the *bunny*?" and later, "Which one is the *rabbit*?" Then they were given training on three training pairs. It was pointed out that the item could be called a bunny and a rabbit. So when a talking puppet (operated by the experimenter) says that it's a *bunny*, then the child's task is to call it a *rabbit* and the other way around. Then five test pairs followed. As one would expect, the younger children made more errors. They tended to repeat what the puppet had just said, while most older children correctly used the alternative expression. What was the pleasant surprise was that this ability did, indeed, as we had predicted, correlate strongly with mastery of the false belief task ($r = .71$ in Experiment 3 and $r = .65$ in Experiment 4) even when children's age and some measure of verbal intelligence (BPVS) were partialled out ($pr = .66$ and $pr = .60$, respectively). Because children had to produce a suitable alternative expression, we called this the *production* version of the synonyms task.

We also turned the paradigm around, in order to check to what degree the difficulty of the production version has to do with finding an alternative expression. In the new judgment version the child names the item first (e.g., "a rabbit") and the puppet then has to produce the alternative expression. The child's task was to judge whether the puppet had conformed to the instructions in each of three trials presented in a random sequence. The puppet either (1) correctly used the alternative description ("a bunny," correct judgment: "yes, puppet said the right thing"), or (2) repeated the child's label ("a rabbit," correct judgment: "no"), or (3) said something wrong ("an elephant," correct judgment: "no"). Again correctness of judgments was strongly correlated with passing the false belief task: $r = .83$ in Experiment 1 and $r = .82$ in Experiment 2, and stayed so even when the effects of a structurally similar control task and verbal intelligence in Experiment 2 were partialled out ($pr = .70$).

These correlations between the false belief task and the judgment version of the synonyms task have since been replicated by Martin Doherty (1998): $r = .71$ and $pr = .55$ after BPVS was partialled out. In a study by Wendy Clements children were taught four German color words and then had to use the German word if puppet had used the English word and the other way around. Again the correlation with the false belief task was high: $r = .75$ and $pr = .73$ after memory for the German color words was partialled out (Clements, Heider, Brooks, & Garnham, 1998). A mixed result was obtained in one study with German-speaking children in Austria by Waldhör (1996). In one experiment there was a clear correlation ($r = .55$ and $pr = .46$ with age and the K-ABC, a verbal intelligence test, partialled out), but in the second experiment the correlation was lower and not statistically significant: $r = .23$ and $pr = .10$ after age and verbal intelligence had been partialled out. This, however, appears to be one deviant sample, because Sandra Stummer (Perner & Stummer, 1998) found very strong correlations with Austrian children (see Table 13.1, bottom panel).

Our Original Explanation: Representational Understanding of Mind (RUM)

At face value the false belief task and the synonyms task have little in common. Their strong correlation is, therefore, highly surprising. The only explanation available was the one that led us to conceive of this study. This was the claim that mastery of the false belief task indexes the onset of a representational understanding of mind (or *RUM*, an acronym coined by Martin Doherty). I have argued for some time (Perner, 1988; 1991) that understanding false belief is tied to an understanding of representation. I will retrace this argument below. Martin and I then reasoned that the synonyms task also requires an understanding of words as representations. To understand words as representations one needs to be aware of them as a representational vehicle and to be aware of their representational content (meaning). The synonyms task requires both. The child has to monitor the meaning of the word used (it has to describe the item correctly; "elephant" won't do) and monitor the particular means (representational vehicle) used to express this meaning, that is to use a synonym. The data provided a better confirmation of this theory than we had originally hoped for. Too good to be true.

One nagging problem has always been that most linguists claim that there are no true synonyms. Certainly the word pairs that we have used are not synonymous, at best they are pseudosynonyms. Nevertheless, we argued that they were synonymous for such young children.

Troublesome Data

Using the production version only we started to use words other than "synonyms" (Perner & Stummer, 1998). All these tasks can be characterized as *say-something-different* tasks. In one condition we used basic and superordinate categories, for example dog–animal. Children had a natural tendency either always to use the basic term ("it's a dog") or to repeat the puppet's expression. To use "animal" when the puppet had said "dog" was as difficult as the synonyms task and the false belief task and it correlated highly with the false belief task. Essentially the same results came from another categories task using basic and subordinate categories, for example dog–poodle. Children again had a tendency to use the basic term (dog) or repeat the term used by puppet. The ability to use the subordinate term after the puppet had used the basic term was as difficult as and correlated highly with the false belief task. (See Experiments 1 and 2 in Table 13.1: The top panel shows the percentage of children passing each task for each experiment, for example the false belief task, synonyms task and categories task. The lower panel shows the correlations between the various tasks and the false belief task.)

These data are an embarrassment to the RUM theory because children can obey task instructions purely at the level of the meaning of words: say something true but different about the item. There is no need to look for differences at the level of the representational vehicle (different word form with identical meaning) and yet the task is mastered at the same time as the false belief task.

RUM received even greater embarrassment in the two-color condition. When the puppet named one of the colors of an item with two colors then the child was instructed to name the other color of the item. Again the young children tended to

Table 13.1 Results from Perner and Stummer (1998)

	Exp. 1	Exp. 2	Exp. 3	Exp. 4
Age range	3;0–6;1	3;4–4;9	2;9–5;7	3;1–5;0
Tasks	n = 36	n = 40	n = 30	n = 39
% Children correct on all items				
False belief	61	73	50	54
Say-something-different				
Synonyms	67	—	53	—
Categories	64	73[a]	—	62
Color/Color	—	—	50	64
Color/Name	94	95	83	90
Correlations [with age and verbal intelligence partialled out]				
FB (synonyms)	.64**[.45**]	—	.93**[.82**]	—
FB (categories)	.59**[.42*]	.77**[.65**]	—	.74**[.62**]
FB (color/color)	—	—	1.0**[1.0**]	.70**[.51**]
FB (color/name)	.38* [.32]	.37* [.20]	.39* [.09]	.36* [.11]

Note. [a] Average of number of children passing all superordinate/basic tasks and of number passing subordinate/basic tasks.
*$p < .05$, **$p < .01$

repeat the color named by the puppet and the ability to name the other color emerged with the false belief task (see Table 13.1).

To complete the story I should also mention the color–name condition with items of a single color. If the puppet gave the name of the object ("It's a bird" then the child had to name its color ("It's yellow") or the other way around. This task was much easier than any of the others (see Table 13.1). This fact suggests that the difficulty with the other tasks is not one of monitoring truth, that is that children who fail the false belief task find it difficult to follow task instructions in terms of "say something true but different about the item." If that were their problem then the color–name task should be as difficult.

A Near Miss Explanation: Executive Inhibition

There is an explanation from a totally different theoretical background that would fit these data quite neatly. As we have argued (Perner & Stummer, 1998), the correlation with our say-something-different tasks and the false belief task could be explained by the fact that the say-something-different tasks require executive inhibition of initial response tendencies and we know that such executive inhibition emerges with the mastery of the false belief task (for review see Perner & Lang, 2000; Perner, Stummer, & Lang, 1999). The say-something-different tasks require executive inhibition on the following grounds: When one is asked a question (or asks oneself a question due to prior instruction) then an automatic answering routine is triggered which produces the first suitable answer that comes to mind. If several answers are possible, of which a particular one should be chosen on the basis of further criteria, then executive control is needed to monitor the automatic answering routine, in particular to inhibit the first predominant answer that comes to mind automatically. This is exactly the case in all our say-something-different tasks except the color–name task.

For instance in the color–color task the child is instructed to name that color of the object that the puppet has not mentioned. Thus, the child has to answer the question, "What color is the object?" This triggers an automatic answer-finding routine for which there are two suitable answers (e.g., black and white, in the case of a black and white cat). Of these two colors the puppet's earlier answer (e.g., "black") will have made that color more prevalent in the child's mind than the other option. The automatic answering routine will, therefore, be more likely to encounter black before white and, thus, produce the wrong answer, "black." Executive control is needed to avoid this error and because executive control develops with the mastery of the false belief task these tasks correlate developmentally.

In contrast, in the color–name condition the child has been instructed to specify the color (of say a yellow bird) if the puppet said what the item is (e.g., "bird"). The color-finding routine triggered by the internally asked question will find "yellow" as the only suitable answer and that is correct. That the puppet said "bird" doesn't matter since that is not an acceptable answer to the routine triggered by, "What color is it?" There may be some tendency to simply repeat what the puppet had said, but such a tendency cannot be very prevalent since children this age do not routinely repeat what other people say.

Although this executive inhibition explanation fits our set of data with the production version of the say-something-different tasks very well, it does not generalize easily to the judgment data on the synonyms tasks. There is one way it could. If children judge what the puppet should have said by simulating the puppet's response and judging the puppet's performance by whether its response does or does not match the simulated response. Since the child's simulation would be subject to the same executive demands as the child's overt responses in the production paradigm, the same explanation can be applied to the judgment tasks. A clear error pattern would be predicted. For instance, if in the color–color task the child says, "it's black," then when the puppet is asked to say what color the item is the child will simulate the puppet's answer. In his or her simulation the answer-finding routine for color will hit first upon "black," because the child's own earlier answer has made it more prevalent than "white." If the puppet then correctly says, "it's white," the child will judge wrongly that the puppet should not have said this because it does not match the simulated answer. If the puppet incorrectly repeats the child's answer then the child will wrongly judge it as correct since it does match the simulated answer.

The problem with this attempt to extend the executive function explanation to the judgment data is that the predicted error pattern is extremely rare. In Doherty's (1994) original experiments this error did not occur consistently (over a repeat of the two relevant trials) and it did not occur in Waldhör's (1996) first experiment which showed good correlation with false belief.

At this point in the story I was at a real loss how to explain this interesting and without RUM inexplicable correlation between the false belief task and the relevant say-something-different tasks. Thanks to David's enthusiasm for the original finding and his prodding not to settle for the executive inhibition option I kept looking for a way out.

Retracing RUM

Let me start my analysis of the representational understanding of mind with simple propositions. Simple propositions are predications of a property (CAT, DOG, BLACK, . . .) to some individual (a, b, . . .): CAT(a), DOG(b), BLACK(a); or relations to several individuals: ON-TOP(a,b). The predicates (CAT, BLACK) *specify* what kind or sort of individual something is (cat) and what properties (black) it has. Timeless knowledge of the world (here and now), one could argue, can be given as an accumulation of such basic propositions. Such knowledge can be contained in a single mental space (Fauconnier, 1985) or mental model (Johnson-Laird, 1983; Perner, 1991). For instance, if I see something *a* which is a small cat on top of something else *b*, then I can represent this in a little model: [CAT(a), SMALL(a), ON-TOP(a,b)]. If I now learn that the something else is a dog then I can add information to my single model: [CAT(a), SMALL(a), ON-TOP(a,b), DOG(b)].

Now, however, if I observe that the cat and dog change places so that the cat is now underneath the dog, then I can't just add this new information, because my model would then contain incompatible information: From UNDER(a,b) it follows that NOT-ON-TOP(a,b) and my model would then have contradictory information in it [. . . ,ON-TOP(a,b), NOT-ON-TOP(a,b), . . .] which renders it informationally useless since any information can be inferred from a set of contradictions. I have two options. I can delete the outdated information and replace it with the new information, thereby updating my single model. Alternatively, if I want to retain the information about the earlier state then I need to partition my model into *submodels, subspaces* or *contexts*. In the present case it would be two temporal contexts or situations at two different times t_1 and t_2: [CAT(a), ON-TOP(a,b), DOG(b)]$_{t1}$ and [CAT(a), UNDER(a,b), DOG(b)]$_{t2}$. Each temporal model *specifies* the state of affairs at a particular time.

A similar need to create multiple models arises when considering possibilities. Instead of temporal contexts we need to represent a possible world in addition to the real world, for instance, when I consider the possibility that the black cat is white: [BLACK(a)]$_{RW}$ and [WHITE(a)]$_{PW}$ where "RW" indicates the *real world* and "PW" a *possible world*. The former model specifies how the real world is; the latter specifies a possible world.

Aboutness

Now notice, in so far as these models are vehicles of mental representation that specify something, they are *about* that which they specify. For instance [BLACK(a)]$_{RW}$ is about the real world and [WHITE(a)]$_{PW}$ is about a possible world, and both are about the individual *a*. Because they are both about individual *a*, we can say that they are about the same thing. However, and this is a critical feature, the things specified by each model are NOT *about* other things. That is, I cannot say that the possible world is about the real world, or that it is about individual *a*.

There are, however, occasions when we need to create different models in order to accommodate incompatible propositions, where the things specified by the models are *about* other things. For instance, if someone mistakenly thinks (believes) that the dog is a sheep, then we cannot just have a single model representing what the individual *b* really is and what that person thinks it is because the model [DOG(b), SHEEP(b), ...] has the contradictory implication that *b* is and is not a dog. A partition needs to be made, quarantining the misinformation [SHEEP(b)] from reality [DOG(b)]$_{RW}$, giving us two models. If we now ask what the former model specifies we would say that it specifies that person's belief (BEL). Now notice, a belief is not like a different possible world. Rather, it is something that is itself *about* something else. The belief that this dog (b) is really a sheep is *about* the real world. So we can say that the model [SHEEP(b)] specifies a belief which is about the real world:

[SHEEP(b)] – specifies → BEL – about → RW,

and thereby also (mis)specifies the real world. The model [DOG(b)] also specifies the real world (how it really is):

[DOG(b)] – specifies → RW.

Perspectives

It is not just belief which is about other things. Models that specify something that is about something else are required in many different cases, for example difference of visual perspective (point of view), difference in appearance, false beliefs, false representations, etc. In order to gain a suitably general expression for what models of this sort specify, I opt for *perspective*. There are other terms I could have chosen: point of view, mode of presentation, sense. Each of them has a specific history of use. Point of view has strong visual connotations, mode of presentation sounds unnatural in connection with misrepresentations and false beliefs, and Frege's "sense" is tied to definite descriptions that determine reference. So I opt for *perspective*.

Let me define *perspective* for my purposes as that which is specified by a mental model and which specifies something else in turn. In the simple case where a model specifies the world, perspectives (P) are redundant and can be ignored:

Model 1 – specifies → P – specifies → RW,

amounts to the same as:

Model 1 – specifies → RW.

Perspectives (P1, P2) become relevant whenever there are two alternative models that specify the same thing (the world) – see Figure 13.1.

Taking, switching, understanding perspectives

Although it may be difficult or impossible for an organism to understand a particular perspective, any sentient being capable of mental representation does *take* a perspective, since representations always present the world under a certain mode of presentation. But for taking a perspective one does not need to understand perspective. Some cognitive flexibility is required to *switch* perspectives. An understanding of perspectives may be useful for such a switch but not necessary. Understanding of perspective is necessary to represent the existence of two perspectives and that they are perspectives on the same entity (world).

Perspectival understanding of mind (PUM)

There is much developmental evidence that fairly young children can switch perspectives but are not able to understand perspective. An understanding of perspective develops around the age of 4 years and the ability to comprehend false belief is one reliable and major indicator of this ability. At this age children develop a perspectival understanding of mind (PUM).

Other examples are children's ability to represent the world from one per-

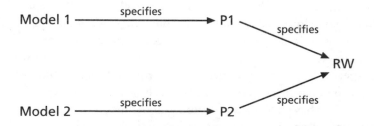

Figure 13.1 Two models specifying alternative perspectives on the same world.

spective and switch to the other perspective as illustrated by John Flavell's research on level 2 perspective taking and the appearance-reality distinction. For example, Flavell and his colleagues (Flavell, Everett, Croft, & Flavell, 1981; Masangkay et al., 1974) showed 3- to 5-year-old children a turtle drawn on a piece of paper lying on the table between child and experimenter who faced each other. When the children had the normal view (the turtle's feet closer to the child) they identified the turtle as *standing on its feet*. When the picture was turned around (so that the turtle's back was now closer to the child) they identified it as *lying on its back*. In other words, children were perfectly capable of switching between these two perspectives prompted by the change in visual input. What the younger ones could not do, however, was to understand the difference in perspective between themselves and the experimenter. This they mastered around the age of 4 years.

Similarly, Flavell, Flavell, and Green (1983) showed children a piece of sponge that looked deceptively like a rock. They identified it as a rock. But once they had been allowed to touch it and find out that it was spongy, they identified it as sponge. Again, they were capable of switching perspectives in one direction, from [ROCK(a)] to [SPONGE(a)] due to additional information. The younger children were incapable of understanding that two perspectives are involved, that is, that the object is a piece of sponge but looks like a rock. In this case children were also not able to switch back to their original perspective. This was, presumably, not possible because there was no change in the visual display. Similarly, these young children have difficulty seeing the second interpretation of an ambiguous drawing like Jastrow's (1900) duck-rabbit (Gopnik & Rosati, 1998; Rock, Gopnik, & Hall, 1994).

Importantly, the ability to acknowledge false appearances in the face of reality emerges at the same time as an understanding of false belief (e.g., Gopnik & Astington, 1988). A misleading appearance as well as false belief are cases of perspectives that (mis)specify reality and that conflict with the true specification. The same holds true for misleading, false representations. For instance, Parkin (1994; Parkin & Perner, 1996) told children a story about a princess who is in a castle and there is a direction sign on the road showing where the princess is. It points to the castle. Then the princess hops over to the woods to get some greenery. The direction sign still points to the castle. "Where does the sign show that the princess is?" The 3-year-old children answer wrongly "in the woods," the 4-year-olds correctly, "in the castle." Correct answers correlate strongly with correct answers on the false belief test. This is to be expected under the current analysis, because both the false belief (the prince has been told that his princess is still in the castle) and the direction sign have to be understood as specifying a false perspective on the story world.

In contrast, when the direction sign is replaced by a picture showing the princess in the castle (intended by us as showing where the princess is in the story world) even the youngest children answered the question, "Where does the picture show that the princess is?" correctly with "in the castle." This is possible because, unlike the direction sign, the picture can be read as specifying an independent situation that isn't about the story world. That is, in the case of the picture we can say that *in the picture the princess is in the castle while in the story she is in the woods.* Whereas we cannot do this for the direction sign. If we say that *in the sign the princess is in the castle while in the story she is in the woods,* this sounds awkward because there is no princess or castle in the sign. That means, the "false picture" can be understood by the younger child as specifying a different situation (the world in the picture) than the child's specification of the story world, while the "false sign" cannot be understood until the child can represent two different perspectives on the story world.

In sum, at the heart of the proposed development is an understanding of *perspective* and *aboutness.* Perspective and aboutness are intricately linked: A perspective is by necessity about something, and everything that is about something specifies a certain perspective.

Propositions and truth

Many other concepts also closely depend on aboutness and perspective, and thus might develop at the same time. A proposition is something with a truth value. To determine the truth of a proposition I need to evaluate it against the world. I do not need to represent that the proposition is about the world and that I am evaluating it against the world. However, in order to understand that someone (as in the false belief task) evaluates a false proposition as true I need to represent that the proposition is about the world against which it is evaluated and to represent its content which specifies a (false) perspective of the world. We have used this as one characterization of what is difficult for children in the false belief task (Perner, Leekam & Wimmer, 1987).

Representational understanding of mind (RUM)

Representations represent things as being a certain way as Goodman (1976) has made clear for photographs. The photo of a horse on the distant horizon depicts the horse *not as a* (recognizable) horse but *as* a tiny speck. A representation can, thus, represent a thing or fact as being one way while another representation represents the very same thing or fact as being another way. This corresponds to two different perspectives on the same entity. Hence, proper understanding of representations requires mastery of perspective and aboutness. However, in contrast to perspectives, which are abstract entities, representations are actual physical entities (representational vehicles) that carry perspectives as (part of) their representational content. As representational vehicles they are characterized by at least two important features: formal and etiological properties (causal efficacy). In the case of mental representations our folk psychology does not attempt to specify any formal properties, only etiological properties. A case can be made that when children solve the false belief task at 4 years of age, they also come to understand the causal efficacy of mental states (Leslie, 1988; Perner, 1991; Wimmer, Hogrefe, & Sodian, 1988).

In sum, a representational understanding of mind (RUM) implies a perspectival understanding of mind (PUM). Both seem to emerge at the same developmental juncture around 4 years of age. I have therefore characterized this development as a transition from the child being a situation theorist (who does not understand perspective) to being a representation theorist (who understands representations including their perspectival relativity).

The problem with RUM

Our problems in explaining the strong developmental relationship between understanding false belief and mastery of the say-something-different tasks shows the danger of focusing uniquely on understanding the mind as representational. Our explanation of children's mastery of the synonyms task was that it reflects the understanding of the formal properties of words as representations. However, as we have seen, the recent data make this untenable. A new explanation is required. A new theory is possible by keeping RUM and PUM conceptually separate. The difficulty that the say-something-different tasks share with the false belief task – as I am about to argue – is not an understanding of representation (RUM component in understanding belief) but an understanding of perspective (the PUM component in understanding belief).

Perspective and Sortals

Back to basic propositions again. If I have identified an individual b then I can specify it in various ways and as long as these specifications add up they can be accommodated in a single mental model, for example, b is a cat and it is brown and it is large and it is beautiful, etc. If incompatible propositions need to be represented, different models (partitions, contexts, spaces) have to be created, as for instance when change over time or alternatives to the real world are contemplated. However, even if we restrict ourselves to describing truthfully the real world here and now a problem requiring multiple models can occur. This problem attaches to the use of sortals.

Sortals specify what *sort of thing* an individual is. Importantly, though, they not only apply to the individual as other properties do, like color, size, beauty, etc. but they also (partly) determine the exact identity of the individual (Hirsch, 1982; Wiggins, 1980). In our example, the property of *being a cat* is a sortal. Let me introduce the relevant problems created by sortals with an example by Hirsch (1982). Assume I am pointing at an object in the woods and say "Look at this *tree*!" You point to more or less the same object but say "Look at that *trunk*!" We have identified two different objects. I have identified a tree [TREE(a)] you have identified a tree trunk [TRUNK(b)], which is part of the object that I have identified as a tree:

PART-OF(a,b). Now assume that the object we point at is a tree that has lost all its branches; reduced to its trunk. In this case the thing I identify as a tree and that you identify as a tree trunk is the same physical object: a = b. It now looks as if the information that this object is a tree and a trunk can be incorporated in a single model: [TREE(a), TRUNK(a)]. This, however, is deceptive, since different propositions are true about the object depending on whether it is identified as a tree or a trunk. As a trunk it may be beautiful (lovely bark and straight and fairly thick) but as a tree without branches it is exceedingly ugly and skinny: [UGLY(a), BEAUTIFUL(a), THICK(a), SKINNY(a)]. These are obviously contradictory implications which do not belong in a single model.

The same problems arise for CAT and ANIMAL. If I point to something and say "This is a cat," and you point to it and say, "This is an animal," we are identifying one and the same physical being, but these facts are not additive so that they can be incorporated in the same mental model. They support different inferences. For instance, if it is a fairly large cat then I may say with justification that *it is big* (as a cat), while you may say that *it is small* (as an animal).

So, we see that identifying an entity by different sortals requires different mental models. What do these models specify? Evidently they do not specify the world at different times or a different world but they specify the same world at the same time. Therefore they specify different *perspectives* on the world. Children who do not yet understand perspective are in an awkward position. They have come to accept that something can be a *cat* and that it can also be an *animal*. They can take one or the other perspective but they cannot entertain both descriptions simultaneously since that requires representing two distinct perspectives. But that is exactly what our say-something-different tasks require them to do. It forces them to keep in mind how the other person has identified the individual in order to then use another sortal, or in the judgment paradigm to remember what they themselves had used in order to be able to judge whether the puppet has appropriately used another descriptor.

John Flavell (1988) and Ellen Markman (1989) have made a connection between children's understanding of perspective and their reluctance to use different labels for a single object (mutual exclusivity). However, there are two reasons that made it difficult for me to see a connection with our "synonyms" and the other say-something-different tasks. One reason was that the mutual exclusivity principle is usually conceived of as a rule that governs word learning. If the child knows that the individual is a *rabbit*, then the child will try and attribute the information "This is a *bunny*" to another object or to a part of the rabbit. This, however, is not the issue in the say-something-different tasks because only terms were used that children already had in their vocabulary (they had surpassed the mutual exclusivity principle for these terms).

The other reason that made it difficult to see a connection was that the proposal was couched in John Flavell's (1988) theory of *cognitive connections*: "Children of this age also believe . . . that each object or event in the world has only one nature – one 'way that it is' – at any given point in time. It cannot be two or more very different, mutually contradictory, and incompatible things at the same time . . ." (p. 245). My problem with this characterization was that – contrary to Flavell's intentions – pretend play would also be made impossible by this restriction on what the young child can think. For, pretending that the banana is a telephone receiver requires thinking that the object identified as a banana has at this particular time a different nature, namely, being a telephone receiver. In contrast, characterizing children as failing to understand perspective does not preclude pretend play because the pretend model need not specify a different perspective on reality but specifies a different, possible world that shares some of the objects with the real world. So, we see that the distinction between alternative models that specify different worlds and alternative models that specify alternative perspectives on the same world is critical.

Switching perspectives–switching sortals

It is interesting to notice that the younger children, although they are able to switch sortals when the experimenter is using another sortal, have lingering doubts about the appropriateness of such a shift. Martin Doherty (1994, Experiments 6–8) had two puppets use different sortals (synonyms or superordinate categories) and asked the child to remember what each puppet had said, for example TV and television, and then asked whether the object really is a TV and a television. Many children tended to deny this. There was, however, only a weak relationship with children failing or passing false belief tasks. This is compatible with PUM theory, which does not imply specific constraints in this respect. Some children who fail to represent perspective (fail the false belief task) may tend to switch perspectives with each mention of a new sortal and, thus, agree that the item is a *TV* and then also agree that it is a *television*. Other members of this group, however, may get fixated on the use of one sortal and then deny the use of the other. Furthermore, children who start to understand that there can be alternative perspectives on the same reality (and pass the false belief task), may still remain unclear as to whether both perspectives have equal claim to reflecting reality. When directly confronted with the question whether something is really a *TV* and really a *television* they may feel compelled to prefer one as being really real.

Clements, Kvarv, and Garnham (1999) seem to be getting at a similar issue, that is, the younger children's tendency to deny that something can be, for example, a *rabbit* and a *bunny* at the same time, with a task more closely resembling the original synonyms task. For instance, one of four pictures showed a rabbit. Children were asked to point to the *rabbit*. The puppet was then asked to point to the *bunny*. Children had to judge whether that was where the puppet should have pointed. The younger children had problems and often answered "no." This indicates that these children might have thought that if it is a rabbit, then it can't be a bunny and the puppet shouldn't point to it. There was also a good correlation with the false belief task ($r = .55$, but perhaps not quite as strong as the correlations between the false belief task and the original synonyms task; see Tables 13.1 and 13.2).

One relevant difference to Doherty's assessment procedure might be the following. In the procedure used by Clements et al. (1999) the child defines the item with his or her pointing response as a rabbit. This definition is not explicitly reversed through any statement by the puppet. The child is thus likely to remain within the once defined perspective and judges the puppet's action within this perspective, that is, as wrong. In contrast, in Doherty's procedure the child and the puppet explicitly define different perspectives: "it is a rabbit," "it is a bunny," and children may therefore be more likely to switch between these perspectives and consequently agree that it is a *bunny*, and then agree that it is a *rabbit*.

The result by Clements et al. (1999) are, thus, compatible with the emergence of an understanding of perspective (PUM). However, a weaker correlation would have also been compatible, since there is no guarantee that children might not switch perspectives when the puppet is pointing to the rabbit under the description of "bunny." In any case, it is in important ways not the same as the original synonyms task.

False Belief and Say-Something-Different: A New Explanation

At this point we have gained a new account of why children who fail the false belief task have difficulty with the original "synonyms" task (Doherty & Perner, 1998). Both tasks require an understanding of perspective. This explanation has several advantages. One advantage is that it need not cling to the problematic claim that the pseudosynonyms of our studies constitute true synonyms for young children. Furthermore, it also explains why children's difficulty extends to other sortals like superordinate and subordinate categories (Perner & Stummer, 1998). Also the fact that the color–name task posed practically no difficulty for the young children fits this explanation nicely. What something *is* (name) and what *color it has* are additive facts that fit into a single mental model and need no juxtaposition of perspectives. In addition, the new explanation applies to *production and judgment* versions of the say-something-different tasks alike, which gives it the edge over the executive control explanation.

However, there is one finding in our more recent study (Perner & Stummer, 1998) that does not fit this explanation: the difficulty of the color–color condition and its good correlation with the false belief task. Color is not a sortal and the two facts of one part of the object being white and another part being black are additive facts combinable in a single mental model. So why is that condition so difficult? A suggestion by an anonymous reviewer of our paper provided the helpful hint. The reviewer suggested that the difficulty with the say-something-different tasks is not the sameness of meaning as suggested by RUM but the sameness of referent. The critical point then is that, although the instructions to name the other color could be construed as naming the color of another part, the actual question refers to *the* color of the object: one person says: "It is white," the other one: "It is black." Strictly speaking this would be a contradiction. Either it is white or black but it cannot be both. However, it is quite common, in fact, when characterizing the color of an object, that one abstracts away from the other colors it actually has in some parts and focuses exclusively on the predominantly occurring color. If one does that with an object of two roughly equally prevalent colors then the decision to call it red (rather than green) has a similar function for *the object's color* as using a particular sortal has for identifying *the object*. Although color is not a sortal apt to identify objects, a particular color is a sortal for an object's color: it identifies the color of an object. And it thereby creates a *color perspective*. If I identify the cat as white then I commit myself to it being light or it having my favorite color, whereas when I identify it as a black cat then I commit myself to calling it dark and not being of my favorite color. That means that the color–color condition also requires understanding of perspective which explains its developmental linkage with the false belief task.

In addition to being able to apply PUM theory to the color–color condition, there are also a series of obvious testable predictions. For instance, the color–color condition can be changed to animals whose head is a different color from their body, for example a cat with a white head and a black body and the child is instructed: "If puppet says the color of one part (e.g., 'white' because its head is white) then you tell me the color of another part (e.g., 'black' because its body is black)." This condition should be easy, as easy as the color–name condition, since white head and black body are additive facts that do not require models specifying perspectives.

Whither Metalinguistic Awareness?

There is one consequence of this new explanation that David Olson might not like. It renders the original finding useless as evidence for metalinguistic awareness in any strict sense. Martin Doherty and I had argued that if the "synonyms" task does require an understanding of synonyms being different forms of a symbolic medium with the same meaning then our results show an early onset of metalinguistic awareness. And the evidence that our task does tap such metalinguistic understanding lay in its good correlations with the false belief task predicted by RUM. In that case, we argued, 4-year-old children have truly metalinguistic awareness (in Gombert's, 1992, sense) and not just an epilinguistic ability. Unfortunately, with the switch from RUM to PUM as an explanation for the correlation between belief tasks and the synonyms task, there is little evidence left of any strictly metalinguistic awareness.

The metalinguistic abilities that we thought to have uncovered might, however, be demonstrated in other tasks. In particular, Doherty (1998) and Clements et al. (1998, 1999) have used a homonyms task modeled after the original synonyms task in which four pictures are presented, one of them showing, for instance, the animal *bat* and another a baseball *bat*. In the judgment version the child is asked to point to the bat. If the child chooses to point to the baseball bat, then the puppet should point to the other kind of bat, that is the animal bat, but sometimes makes an error

Table 13.2 Correlations between Homonyms Task, Synonyms Task, and False Belief Task

| | *Correlations between* | | |
	homonyms × belief	synonyms × belief	homonyms × synonyms
Doherty (1998)			
Exp. 1	.55**	.71**	.67**
Exp. 2 (production)	.73**	—	—
Clements et al. (1998)			
Exp. 1	.68**	—	—
Exp. 2	.55**	—	—
Exp. 3	—	.75**	—
Clements et al. (1999)	.73**	—	—

**$p < .01$

and points to the same bat as the child or a totally incorrect item. Children's ability to judge the puppet's pointing correlated almost as strongly with the false belief task as did the synonyms task (Table 13.2).

In this task it is a matter of understanding that the same linguistic form "bat" is used to denote quite different kinds of entities: animal and sports equipment. Children's ability to master the homonyms task does, therefore, reflect a truly metalinguistic awareness and its correlation with the false belief task can be explained by the fact that an understanding of perspective (PUM) brings with it an understanding of representation (RUM).

Another task that points to the emergence of such metalinguistic awareness at the age of 3 to 5 years is the one developed by Ellen Bialystok (1991, in press) who finds that in that period children start to appreciate that a verbal label, for example "duck" placed below a picture of a duck does *not* change its meaning when it is moved to a different picture. Martin Doherty had a quick brush with trying to relate performance on this task to performance on the false belief task but with little success. Children found his version much too easy because it involved an exchange of name tags between themselves and the experimenter. Even the youngest who failed false belief understood that the label with their name on it when attached to the experimenter was still their name. People's names, as Bialystok reports, are a particularly easy version of this task. Since people have names (that belong to them in some sense) children may construe the task not (as intended) in terms of the label's meaning but in terms of possession. If you have my name tag then it is still my name in the same sense as when you are wearing my hat it still remains mine. In contrast, the label "duck" is not something that belongs to a particular duck. This standard task, therefore, is more likely to tap an understanding of written forms having a fixed meaning, and this understanding might emerge with an understanding of false belief.

Conclusion

The correlation between the false belief task and the synonyms task reported by Doherty and Perner (1998) is impressively high. This provided strong support for the theory that gave rise to this investigation, namely that both tasks require an understanding of representation (RUM). More recent results (Perner & Stummer, 1998) have, however, made this explanation untenable. Attempts to establish an account in terms of executive control were only partially successful. An overarching explanation can be given with the insight that individuation of objects through different sortals leads to a difference in perspective and that the synonyms task and other say-something-different tasks require understanding of different perspectives. Moreover, it is necessary to conceptually separate the simultaneously developing achievements indexed by the mastery of the false belief task, namely the representational understanding of mind (RUM) from the perspectival understanding of mind (PUM). With this separation one can see that the common intellectual achievement required for the false belief task and the synonyms task is the understanding of perspective.

Acknowledgments

I thank George Botterill, Johannes Brandl, Peter Carruthers, Bob Gordon, Alan Leslie, and Gabriel Segal for steering me to a clearer position on the relationship among various theoretical terms, and Susan Carey for imprinting on me the critical difference between sortals and other predicates.

References

Arthur, T. (1985). *An investigation into children's use of pragmatics in ambiguous situations and the effect of children's belief about knowledge states on question interpretation.* 3rd year project, Laboratory of Experimental Psychology, unpublished manuscript, University of Sussex.

Astington, J. W., Harris, P. L., & Olson, D. R. (Eds.) (1988). *Developing theories of mind.* New York: Cambridge University Press.

Bialystok, E. (1991). Letters, sounds, and symbols: Changes in children's understanding of written language. *Applied Psycholinguistics, 12,* 75–89.

Bialystok, E. (in press). Symbolic representation across domains in preschool children. *Journal of Experimental Child Psychology.*

Clark, H. H., & Marshall, C. R. (1981). Definite reference and mutual knowledge. In A. K. Joshi, I. Sag, & B. Webber (Eds.), *Linguistic structure and discourse setting* (pp. 10–63).

Cambridge, UK: Cambridge University Press.

Clements, W. A., Heider, A., Brooks, J., & Garnham, A. (1998). *From synonyms to homonyms: Exploring the role of metarepresentation in language understanding.* Unpublished manuscript, University of Sussex.

Clements, W. A., Kvarv, M., & Garnham, A. (1999). *Syntax, inhibition and false belief: Why language matters in assessing metarepresentational ability.* Unpublished manuscript, University of Sussex.

Doherty, M. (1994). *Metalinguistic understanding and theory of mind.* Unpublished doctoral dissertation, Laboratory of Experimental Psychology, University of Sussex.

Doherty, M. (1998). *Children's understanding of homonymy: Metalinguistic awareness and theory of mind.* Unpublished manuscript, University of Stirling.

Doherty, M. J., & Perner, J. (1998). Metalinguistic awareness and theory of mind: Just two words for the same thing? *Cognitive Development, 13,* 279–305.

Donaldson, M. (1978). *Children's minds.* London: Fontana.

Fauconnier, G. (1985). *Mental spaces: Aspects of meaning construction in natural language.* Cambridge, MA: MIT Press.

Flavell, J. H. (1988). The development of children's knowledge about the mind: from cognitive connections to mental representations. In J. W. Astington, P. L. Harris, & D. R. Olson (Eds.), *Developing theories of mind* (pp. 244–67). New York: Cambridge University Press.

Flavell, J. H., Everett, B. A., Croft, K., & Flavell, E. R. (1981). Young children's knowledge about visual perception: Further evidence for the Level 1–Level 2 distinction. *Developmental Psychology, 17,* 99–103.

Flavell, J. H., Flavell, E. R., & Green, F. L. (1983). Development of the appearance-reality distinction. *Cognitive Psychology, 15,* 95–120.

Garnham, A., & Perner, J. (1990). Does manifestness solve problems of mutuality? (Commentary on Sperber & Wilson, *Relevance,* 1986). *Behavior and Brain Sciences, 13,* 178–9.

Gombert, J. E. (1992). *Metalinguistic development.* London: Harvester Wheatsheaf.

Goodman, N. (1976). *Languages of art.* Indianapolis, IN: Hackett Publishing Co.

Gopnik, A., & Astington, J. W. (1988). Children's understanding of representational change and its relation to the understanding of false belief and the appearance-reality distinction. *Child Development, 59,* 26–37.

Gopnik, A., & Rosati, A. (1998). *Duck or rabbit? Reversing ambiguous figures and understanding ambiguous representations.* Unpublished manuscript, University of California at Berkeley.

Hirsch, E. (1982). *The concept of identity.* Oxford, UK: Oxford University Press.

Jastrow, J. (1900). *Fact and fable in psychology.* Boston, MA: Houghton-Mifflin.

Johnson-Laird, P. N. (1983). *Mental models.* Cambridge, UK: Cambridge University Press.

Leslie, A. M. (1988). Some implications of pretense for mechanisms underlying the child's theory of mind. In J. W. Astington, P. L. Harris, & D. R. Olson (Eds.), *Developing theories of mind* (pp. 19–46). New York: Cambridge University Press.

Lewis, D. K. (1969). *Convention: a philosophical study.* Cambridge, MA: Harvard University Press.

Markman, E. M. (1989). *Categorization and naming in children: Problems of induction.* Cambridge, MA: MIT Press/A Bradford Book.

Masangkay, Z. S., McCluskey, K. A., McIntyre, C. W., Sims-Knight, J., Vaughn, B. E., & Flavell, J. H. (1974). The early development of inferences about the visual percepts of others. *Child Development, 45,* 357–66.

Olson, D. R. (1970). Language and thought: aspects of a cognitive theroy of semantics. *Psychological Review, 77,* 257–73.

Parkin, L. J. (1994). *Children's understanding of misrepresentation.* Unpublished doctoral dissertation. University of Sussex.

Parkin, L. J., & Perner, J. (1996). *Wrong directions in children's theory of mind: What it means to understand belief as representation.* Unpublished manuscript, University of Sussex.

Perner, J. (1988). Developing semantics for theories of mind: From propositional attitudes to mental representation. In J. W. Astington, P. L. Harris, & D. R. Olson (Eds.), *Developing theories of mind* (pp. 141–72). New York: Cambridge University Press.

Perner, J. (1991). *Understanding the representational mind.* Cambridge, MA: MIT Press/A Bradford book.

Perner, J., & Garnham, A. (1988). Conditions for mutuality. *Journal of Semantics, 6,* 369–85.

Perner, J., & Howes, D. (1992). "He thinks he knows"; and more developmental evidence against the simulation (role-taking) theory. *Mind & Language, 7,* 72–86.

Perner, J., & Lang, B. (2000). Theory of mind and executive function: Is there a developmental relationship? In S. Baron-Cohen, H. Tager-Flusberg, & D. Cohen (Eds.), *Understanding other minds: Perspectives from developmental cognitive neuroscience* (2nd ed., pp. 150–81). Oxford, UK: Oxford University Press.

Perner, J., Leekam, S., and Wimmer, H. (1984). *The insincerity of conservation questions: Children's growing sensitivity to experimenter's epistemic intentions.* Poster presented at the APA Convention in Toronto, August 1984, and at the British Psychological Society—Developmental Section Annual Conference in Lancaster, September 1984.

Perner, J., Leekam, S. R., & Wimmer, H. (1987). Three-year olds' difficulty with false belief: The case for a conceptual deficit. *British Journal of Developmental Psychology, 5,* 125–37.

Perner, J., & Stummer, S. (1998). *Say something different – ToM! Metalinguistic awareness, embedded conditionals or executive function?* Unpublished manuscript, University of Salzburg.

Perner, J., Stummer, S., & Lang, B. (1999). Executive functions and theory of mind: Cognitive complexity or functional dependence? In P. D. Zelazo, J. W. Astington, & D. R. Olson (Eds.), *Developing theories of intention: Social understanding and self-contol* (pp. 133–52). Mahwah, NJ: Erlbaum.

Robinson, E., Goelman, H., & Olson, D. R. (1983). Children's understanding of the relation between expressions (what was said) and intentions (what was meant). *British Journal of Developmental Psychology, 1,* 75–86.

Rock, I., Gopnik, A., & Hall, S. (1994). Do young children reverse ambiguous figures? *Perception, 23,* 635–44.

Schiffer, S. (1972). *Meaning.* Oxford, UK: Oxford University Press.

Sperber, D., & Wilson, D. (1986). *Relevance: Communication and cognition.* Oxford, UK: Blackwell.

Waldhör, E. (1996). *Entwicklung eines metalinguistischen Bewußtseins und einer* "Theory of Mind" (Development of metalinguistic awareness and a theory of mind). Unpublished Masters Thesis, University of Salzburg.

Wiggins, D. (1980). *Sameness and substance.* Oxford, UK: Blackwell.

Wimmer, H., Hogrefe, J., & Sodian, B. (1988). A second stage in children's conception of mental life: Understanding sources of information. In J.W.Astington, P.L. Harris, &

D.R.Olson (Eds.), *Developing theories of mind* (pp. 173–92). New York: Cambridge University Press.

Wimmer, H., & Perner, J. (1983). Beliefs about beliefs: Representation and constraining function of wrong beliefs in young children's understanding of deception. *Cognition, 13,* 103–28.

14

Mind, Memory, and Metacognition: The Role of Memory Span in Children's Developing Understanding of the Mind

Thomas Keenan

My introduction to David's ideas on the role of working memory in the child's development of a theory of mind came from a rather cryptic remark he made to me early in my graduate career at OISE. While we were engaged in a discussion of theory-of-mind research, he suddenly interjected with the statement, "I've been thinking about counting things." I paused, but he didn't go on to elaborate. Given David's work on ambiguity in speech and the distinction between what is said and what is meant by a speaker, I inferred that there was more to this remark. In fact, I have to admit that given that my own PhD thesis was on children's comprehension of sarcasm, I tried to decide whether his remark might have been directed to me in some other way. Shortly after this curious event, David began to circulate drafts of his presidential address to the Canadian Psychological Association (Olson, 1989), and his remark finally made sense to me. Somewhat later, David asked me if I would work with him on an empirical test of his working memory hypothesis.

Introduction: The Working Memory Hypothesis

In his 1989 presidential address to the Canadian Psychological Association, Olson essentially proposed a new theory of representational development which had implications for the child's development of a theory of mind. He proposed that the child's theory of mind might instead be thought of as the organization of behavioral schemas into propositions, which can be represented as *true* or *false*. This organization was brought about by increases in the number of "mental elements" which could be held in mind. In a revised version of the theory (Olson, 1993), he suggested that increasing computational resources, namely working memory, played a role in this increasing combination of mental elements into the structures which made an understanding of false belief (and other aspects of a theory of mind) a possibility.

Prior to our studies on working memory and theory of mind, there was relatively little in the way of research which addressed the question of how children develop a theory of mind; that is, what mechanisms underlie children's developing theory of mind and how are they responsible for the regularity of its expression in preschool children? As I understood his thinking, Olson had been largely unsatisfied with other accounts of the development of theory of mind and was keenly aware that this was an important question for researchers in the field. Olson's theory of representational development attempts to provide an answer to this question. According to him, previous theories have generated important evidence regarding the nature and growth of the child's developing theory of mind (see Astington & Gopnik, 1991), yet not one of them answers the critical question as to *why* children's understanding of false belief appears with such regularity around age 4. As he argued, previous theories ultimately appealed to the conceptual complexity of the achievement in order to explain the shift observed at age 4, however, this answer is not entirely satisfactory. On Olson's account, none of these theories provided a particularly complete or accurate explanation for why children showed a shift in their understanding of mental representation at age 4.

Olson's theory of representational development, and ultimately, his answer to why false belief understanding develops with such regularity around age 4, builds on the well-documented phenomenon that as children develop, their capacity to process information increases. As they mature, children have an increasing capacity to "hold in mind" or mentally represent information to themselves (e.g., Case, 1985; Halford, 1993). In other words, the capacity of their working memory seems to increase (although there is some debate as to whether this increase in working memory capacity represents a biological increase in finite capacity or an increase due to the increased efficiency with which resources are used). Olson (1989, 1993) invoked this increase in working memory as a factor which played a role in the development of representations, and thus, the child's conceptions of the mind. Increases in capacity allow children to construct more complex mental models of the physical and social worlds, models which guide children's understanding. Thus like Halford (1993), Olson saw the increases in processing capacity afforded by increases in the child's working memory as leading to the construction of the concepts themselves and not simply as a factor which limits children's expression of innate concepts. Simply put, Olson argued that as children's capacity to hold information in mind increases, they are able to form more complex mental representations out of basic schemata and thus move from simply using symbols to understanding how one's representations of the world relate to reality.

In his theory, Olson specifically relates the development of the logical structures which support an understanding of false belief to the information processing requirements or number of elements which children must "hold in mind." He shows how the development of this capacity gives rise to new and more powerful concepts such as *belief*, which can be held as being "true" or "false" in relation to the world. In his more recent work (Gordon & Olson, 1998), he suggests that the concept of *false belief* is not actually the construction of a new concept, but rather comes about as children learn to negate previous concepts such as *self*, *true*, and *real*. False belief understanding comes about when the child has the computational resources to: (1) hold in mind a previously created representation; (2) to compare it against a new representation created by the freeing up of the perceptual system; and (3) accommodate the conflicting representations by assigning them to different people and marking one representation as *not true* or as *not real*. The construction of *false belief* depends upon the acquisition of more basic concepts such as *self* and *true*. However, the co-ordination of these earlier concepts involves the requisite computational resources, namely working memory, which allows children to "hold in mind" the various representations for comparison.

Olson's contention that increasing processing resources play a role in the child's developing theory of mind has garnered empirical support in a number of studies (Davis & Pratt, 1995; Frye, Zelazo, & Palfai, 1995; Gordon & Olson, 1998; Hughes, 1998a; Keenan, 1998, 1999; Keenan, Marini, & Olson, 1993; Keenan, Olson, & Marini, 1998). Moreover, the theory seems to be increasingly influential in research on children's theory of mind. Olson's assertions regarding the role of working memory in the child's theory of mind clearly preceded much of the current interest in domain general developmental influences on theory of mind, and more specifically, the recent interest in the relation between *executive functions* and children's theory of mind (e.g., Frye et al., 1995; Hughes, 1998; Keenan, 1999; Perner, 1998; Russell, 1996; Zelazo, Frye, & Rapus, 1996).

While the claim being made in this paper is that working memory is related to children's understanding of false belief, it is important to stress that the argument is *not* that working memory is the sole determinant of false belief task performance. In my own view, working memory is one of a number of factors which allow the child to acquire a representational understanding of concepts such as *belief*. Working memory would seem to be a candidate for a domain general developmental process which has an impact on the development of the child's theory of mind and many other developmental achievements. Other domain general developmental processes such as inhibitory capacity are also likely to play a role (e.g., Carlson, 1997). However, these processes cannot produce an understanding of false belief in isolation. The child requires experience within the wider culture which employs mental state talk and attributions in its day-to-day workings. A number of studies have shown a clear relation between the parental use of mental state language in the home and the child's acquisition of a theory of mind (Brown & Dunn, 1991; Dunn, Brown, Slomkowski, Tesla, & Youngblade, 1991; Ruffman, Slade, Clements, & Import, 1998). Clearly, social factors are a powerful determinant of individual differences in the child's acquisition of a theory of mind. While the data described in the following section suggests an association between theory-of-mind understanding and working memory capacity, much work remains to be done in sorting out exactly how changes in capacity interact with social variables, such as talk about mental states, to produce an understanding of concepts like false belief.

Additionally, it is also important to remind the reader that these data are correlational and thus, do not speak to the issues of causal direction among the variables under study. While a number of researchers have claimed executive functioning measures predict theory-of-mind performance (Hughes, 1998b), the opposite argument – that developments in the child's theory of mind may produce changes in executive functioning – is a possibility (Perner, 1998; Perner & Lang, 2000). Theory of mind and executive functioning may also be related in a more complex, reciprocal fashion. Further work is required in order to sort out these issues. The studies reported here are only a first step in beginning to examine these possibilities.

Research on Working Memory and Theory of Mind

To date, there has been relatively little research which explicitly tests the relation between children's working memory capacity and their developing understanding of the mind. This section will provide a brief summary of the work done in my own lab as well as a survey of other studies which have examined this question.

What evidence is there that information-processing capacity such as working memory might play a role in the development of a theory of mind? Empirical evidence regarding the hypothesis that increases in children's working memory capacity support the development of an understanding of mind is divided. Jenkins and Astington (1996) gave a sample of 3- to 5-year-old children a series of false belief tasks and administered measures of general language ability (the Test of Early Language Development (TELD), Hresko, Reid, & Hammill, 1981) and nonverbal memory (using the Stanford–Binet bead memory measure). They found evidence of a significant correlation between memory and performance on the false belief tasks ($r = .49$), however, this correlation was reduced to nonsignificant ($r = .18$) when the effects of age were statistically removed. In contrast, general language ability did remain significantly associated with false belief when the effects due to age were partialled out. The authors conclude that their data provide no support for the association of false belief understanding and memory.

Evidence supporting an association between false belief understanding and children's working memory has recently been generated by Davis and Pratt (1995) and Keenan (1998; Keenan et al., 1993, 1998). Davis and Pratt demonstrated that working memory capacity was positively associated with performance on theory-of-mind tasks in preschool children. They administered 3- to 5-year-old children two false belief tasks, two false photograph tasks (Zaitchik, 1990), a language measure (the Peabody Picture Vocabulary Test Revised, Dunn & Dunn, 1981) and two measures of memory capacity: a backwards digit span (BDS) task and a forwards digit span (FDS) task. Davis and Pratt found that children's performance on the BDS predicted their performance on the false belief task when controlling for both age and language. Memory span, as measured by the BDS task accounted for approximately 6% of the variance in children's false belief scores, contrasting sharply with the findings of Jenkins and Astington (1996). Working memory also accounted for a significant amount of the variance on the false photograph task, leading the authors to conclude that, since the false belief and false photograph tasks were only weakly correlated, working memory capacity determines performance on the two tasks.

Although the findings of Davis and Pratt are suggestive of a role of working memory in theory-of-mind development, this conclusion is limited by problems with their measure of working memory. Most children experienced considerable difficulty with the BDS task, being unable to recall two numbers in reverse order. To overcome the problems associated with the distribution of children's BDS scores, Davis and Pratt created a dichotomous variable, where a score of 0 reflected an inability to recall two numbers in reverse order and a score of 1 showed that they could do so. While the rationale for creating this dichotomous variable from a continuous score is presented by the authors, the problems associated with doing so are clear (Cohen, 1990). This procedure has the effect of discarding information about the relations among the variables under study which may effectively reduce the correlation of the altered variable with other variables.

Based on our pilot work in this area (Keenan et al., 1993), David Olson, Zopito Marini, and I (Keenan et al., 1998) attempted to resolve the question of whether or not working memory does indeed predict children's performance on the false belief task. We gave a sample of 100 children, aged 3, 4 and 5 years, a test of working memory based on a counting span task designed by Case, Kurland, and Goldberg (1982) and a number of false belief tasks. Unlike simple memory span measures such as a forwards digit span (FDS) task, which involves no executive component, our counting span task requires concurrent processing and storage (Daneman & Carpenter, 1980). Children are required to carry out an operation (in this case counting a small series of dots), store the product of that operation, carry out another operation, store the result and then output the products in the correct order. Children must also inhibit the tendency to count the distractor items. The argument presented here is that the counting span task directly involves the central executive and therefore is a stringent test of children's working memory capacity. Davis and Pratt (1995) make a similar distinction between backwards digit span (BDS) tasks and forwards digit span (FDS) tasks. Whereas BDS involves concurrent processing and storage and thus, is closer to being a true working memory task, FDS requires children only to output a series of digits held in the articulatory loop which incurs no involvement by the central executive.

The counting span task consisted of three levels, with each level being composed of three sets of items. First, the child was given a set of practice trials. There were three cartoon characters, each covered by a small number of red dots ranging in number from 2 to 5, which the child was asked to count. In addition to the red dots (the target items), there were also a number of distracter dots (blue, yellow, and green in color). The Level 1 task consisted of one drawing of each character. The Level 2 task used two of the drawings for each trial and the Level 3 task used all three drawings in the same order for each trial. For all levels, children were asked to look at the picture, to count only the red spots, and to point to each spot while counting aloud. This procedure was designed to eliminate any form of rehearsal the children might spontaneously use. The task ended when children failed two consecutive trials at a given level.

For Level 1 of the counting span task, the child was told "I'm going to show you some pictures and I want you to count the red spots on their face, only the red spots. Then I'm going to turn the picture over and I'm going to ask you to tell me how many red spots there were on (name of character)". The child was then presented with a picture and was asked to count the red spots. After the child counted the red spots, the picture was flipped over and the child was asked, "How many red spots were there on (name of character)?" After the child answered, the next trial was given. When the child completed the items making up Level 1, testing moved to Level 2. If they failed two consecutive trials, the task was ended.

At the beginning of Level 2, children were told, "Now we're going to make the game a little harder. I'm going to show you two pictures in a row. I'll show you one picture and you count only the red dots and remember how many there are. Then I'll show you another picture and you count the dots on that one too, and try to remember how many dots were on it. Then I'm going to ask you how many dots were on (name of Character 1) and then how many dots were on (name of Character 2)." The child then was presented with the first picture and asked to count the spots, it was turned over and the process was repeated for the second picture. (The experimenter attempted to ensure that the pictures were presented with a delay of two to three seconds). The child was then asked "How many red spots were there on (character 1)?" and again, "How many red spots were there on (character 2)?" For Level 3, the instructions were the same. The same process used in Level 2 was employed, with the addition of a third question for each trial.

As mentioned earlier, two versions of the false belief task were given, the smarties task and a standard false belief story task, both based on Perner, Leekam, and Wimmer (1987). The smarties false belief task was identical to the version used by Gopnik and Astington (1988) and included a question about the child's own prior belief. Thus, children were asked three false belief questions in total.

Scoring for the two tasks was performed as follows: for the counting span task, children were given a score of 1 for each trial they answered correctly (range = 0–9), and they were given a score of 1 for each of the three false belief questions answered correctly (range = 0–3).

Children's performance on the false belief tasks reflected a variety of levels of competence and was not simply an all or none phenomenon. Overall, 48% of the sample correctly answered all three questions, 13% failed all three false belief questions, while the remaining 39% answered one or two questions correctly. On the counting span task there was a steady increase in performance with age, with mean scores of 2.75 for the 3-year-olds ($SD = 1.06$), 3.88 for the 4-year-olds ($SD = 0.94$), and 4.75 for the 5-year-olds ($SD = 1.97$). A one-way analysis of variance conducted using the counting span score as the dependent variable and age group as an independent variable revealed a significant difference between groups ($F(2, 97) = 18.7$, $p < .001$). Post hoc testing using Tukey's Honestly Significant Differences test revealed that the 4-year-olds were significantly different from the 3-year-olds and furthermore, that the 5-year-olds were significantly different from each of the two younger groups.

Each of the zero-order correlations among false belief scores, counting span task scores, and age in months is significant (false belief x counting span, $r = .54$, $p < .001$; false belief x age, $r = .55$, $p < .001$; counting span x age, $r = .56$, $p < .001$). In order to test the hypothesis that children's working memory capacity predicts their understanding of false belief, we conducted a hierarchical regression analysis. The false belief score was used as the criterion variable and the child's age in months entered first, followed by their score on the counting span task. When age alone was entered the regression equation explained 30% of the variance in false belief understanding ($R^2 = .30$, $F(1, 98) = 42.05$, $p < .001$). When counting span task scores were added, the resulting equation explained an additional 8% of the variance ($R^2 = .38$, F Change $(1, 97) = 11.5$, $p < .001$). Since age and counting span strongly covary ($r = .56$), much of the age-related variance in false belief will be shared with counting span. Conducting a second hierarchical analysis with the false belief score as the criterion variable and entering counting span, followed by age, revealed that counting span accounts for 28.5% of the variance in false belief, while age uniquely accounts for a further 8.8% of the variance. Thus, counting span does not account for all of the age-related variance in false belief. Of particular interest is the fact that the unique variance in false belief understanding accounted for by our working memory measure, 8%, is very close to that reported by Davis and Pratt (1995), who found that their backwards digit span (BDS) score accounted for 6% of the variance in false belief understanding.

In line with the previous findings of Davis and Pratt (1995), our data are indicative of a fairly robust and stable contribution of working memory to children's performance on the false belief tasks. The work reported here supports the argument made by Olson (1989, 1993) that general processing capacity is associated with children's development of a theory of mind. This study indicates that increases in children's computational resources, in particular, working memory, contribute to children's acquisition of a theory of mind. On almost any theory, such resources are considered to be relevant, if not to the construction of the requisite concepts, at least to children's performance on the tasks.

The results of the present study provide a strong replication of Davis and Pratt's (1995) findings on the role of information processing capacity in children's understanding of false belief. In addition, they build on these findings through the use of another memory measure and a larger set of false belief tasks. Even with these changes, the amount of variance uniquely predicted by the working memory measures in the two studies (6% in their study and 8% in the present study) is remarkably similar. This suggests that the memory measures used in these two studies tap some common relation with children's understanding of false belief. Unlike the memory task employed by Jenkins and Astington (1996), the backwards digit span (BDS) task used by Davis and Pratt and the counting span task used in the present study both required children to hold one number in mind while performing an operation on another. We argue that such tasks place a heavier demand on the central executive (Baddeley, 1986), and it is this element which differentiates these tasks from tasks such as the bead memory measure used by Jenkins and Astington or the forwards digit span (FDS) used by Davis and Pratt.

Language, Working Memory and Theory of Mind

One problem with the findings of our study was that a language measure was not included in the original study. Based on the working memory literature, one might reasonably expect working memory and general language ability to be highly correlated, and indeed, Jenkins and Astington showed this to be the case. This oversight in our original study seemed an important one to rectify as individual differences in language ability might potentially provide a reasonable "third variable" explanation for the relation between working memory and false belief. A number of accounts of how language, working memory, and false belief understanding might be tied together have been put forward in the literature.

First, the suggestion has been made that language might act as a "scaffold" for developing representational systems like those which might underlie a child's folk psychological understanding of the mind (Astington & Jenkins, 1999; Plaut & Karmiloff-Smith, 1993). Language may organize the system of developing representations which comprise a theory of mind. Second, research by de Villiers (de Villiers, 1995; de Villiers & Pyers, 1997) has suggested that children's understanding of false belief is dependent on their mastery of the syntactic construction of object complementation. Tager-Flusberg and Sullivan (1994) make a similar point, arguing that the core competence at the heart of theory-of-mind tasks may be syntactic ability. Third, in their work on cognitive and family factors associated with theory of mind, Jenkins and Astington (1996) showed a relation between false belief understanding and performance on the Test of Early Language Development (TELD, Hresko et al., 1981). Their results showed that in order to pass false belief tasks, children need to reach a linguistic performance threshold on the TELD (a raw score of 14 or better), suggesting a strong relation between linguistic ability and false belief performance. In summary, each of these arguments would suggest a connection between language ability and false belief understanding, a relation that may explain the correlation between working memory and false belief demonstrated by Keenan et al.

In a second study (Keenan, 1998), I addressed one of the major limitations of our initial research on working memory and theory of mind: the failure to include a language measure. In order to test the hypothesis that children's linguistic ability might serve as a "third variable" which explains the relation between false belief understanding and working memory, 60 children aged 4 and 5 years were given a measure of working memory (the counting span task used by Keenan et al., 1998), a measure of general language ability (the TELD, Hresko et al., 1981), and a number of standard false belief tasks. The prediction made in the present study was that the working memory measure should account for a significant amount of variance in children's false belief scores when controlling for language performance and age.

The procedures for the counting span task were almost identical to those used in Keenan et al. (1998) and scores again could range from a minimum of 0 to a maximum of 9. Children's scores on the false belief tasks were summed to form a composite score which could range from 0 to 3. The mean for the counting span (4.65, $SD = 1.35$) task was very similar to the performance of the 5-year-olds observed in Keenan et al. (4.75 in the previous study). Children's performance on the TELD (a mean raw score of 20.1, $SD = 4.44$) was slightly higher than the sample (mean age of 4 years) reported in Jenkins and Astington (1996). In the false belief task children averaged at least two out of three correct (mean = 2.42, $SD = 0.81$). Scores on false belief ranged from 1 to the maximum of 3: a full 60% of the sample (36 children) achieved a perfect score on the false belief tasks whereas 25% (15 children) answered two out of three correctly, and 15% (9 children) only managed to get one correct answer.

Table 14.1 gives the correlations between children's age in months, and TELD, counting span, and false belief scores. All variables were significantly and positively correlated with each other. Of particular interest are the correlations of the counting span and TELD scores with false belief. The observed relation of false belief and TELD scores ($r = .30$) was somewhat smaller than the $r = .64$ reported by Jenkins and Astington, presumably due to the restricted age range and the near ceiling effect observed on the false belief measure. When the effect due to age was partialled out, each of these correlations remained significant, except for that be-

Table 14.1 Pearson Product Moment Correlations of TELD, False Belief Scores, Counting Span Task Scores, and Children's Age in Months from Keenan (1998)

	Counting span task	TELD	False belief
TELD	.40**		
False belief	.59**	.30*	
Age in months	.34**	.36**	.34**

Partial Correlations Controlling for Age in Months

	Counting span task	TELD
TELD	.31*	
False belief	.53**	.20

Note. *$p < .05$, **$p < .01$

tween false belief and TELD scores. While age clearly accounts for some of the variance in these measures, the pattern of correlations remains similar when the effect of age is removed. However, it would seem that the observed relation between language and false belief understanding in this sample is largely explained by the child's age.

A hierarchical multiple regression analysis was conducted to test the hypothesis that working memory predicts false belief understanding when controlling for both age and language ability. Whereas TELD scores did not result in a significant change in the amount of variance accounted for, adding the counting span scores accounted for significant additional variance in false belief scores, variance not accounted for by the child's age or language scores.

The current findings replicate and extend previous research, demonstrating that the relation between working memory and false belief scores is not simply accounted for by general language ability. Again, these data reveal a significant contribution of working memory to children's performance on false belief tasks. The finding of a significant relation between working memory and false belief in these three studies and in other work (Gordon & Olson, 1998; Hughes, 1998; Keenan, 1999) goes some way toward eliminating explanations based on some particular artefact such as the nature of the memory task. They present a picture which clearly suggests a relation between children's false belief understanding and developmental increases in working memory. The work reported here also adds further support to Olson's argument that general processing capacity is a significant factor in children's development of a theory of mind (Olson, 1989, 1993).

The Relation of Working Memory and Inhibitory Control to False Belief Understanding

In a number of recent studies, inhibitory control has been suggested as an important factor in the child's development of a theory of mind. For example, Carlson, Moses, and Hix (1998) showed that when the inhibitory control requirements of a deception task were removed, children were able to demonstrate a much earlier understanding of deception. In another study, Carlson (1997) showed that children who performed well on a battery of inhibitory control tasks also performed well on a set of theory-of-mind measures. According to Carlson, inhibitory control is critical to children's ability to express their conceptual knowledge in action. However, the conclusion that inhibitory control is a necessary component of performance on all theory-of-mind tasks may be premature. First, Carlson (1997) reported correlations between an aggregate measure of theory of mind (composed of false belief, deception, and appearance-reality tasks) and a battery of inhibitory control tasks. While the use of such aggregate measures is a powerful method for observing such relations, it may obscure the relation between children's performance on individual tasks such as inhibitory control and false belief. Second, Carlson controlled for children's general language ability using the Peabody Picture Vocabulary Test

(PPVT). As Ruffman et al. (1998) have argued, this test is suspect as a measure of children's general language competence and furthermore, only measures receptive vocabulary, not expressive language skills (but see Happé, 1995). Finally, Carlson included no control for the possibility that the observed association between inhibitory control and theory of mind was the result of changes in general cognitive ability.

I recently (Keenan, 1999) presented a group of fifty-four 3- and 4-year-old children with measures of inhibitory control, false belief understanding, a dual task (the counting and labeling task, Gordon & Olson, 1998), general language ability, and speed of processing. Speed of processing was included as a control for measures of general processing ability (Kail & Salthouse, 1994) and was measured using two "cross out" tasks. Inhibitory control was measured using an aggregate of children's performance on a modified Stroop task and a version of Kochanska, Murray, Jacques, Koenig, and Vandegeest's (1996) "Bear-Dragon Task" (a variant of the common "Simon Says" game) while working memory was an aggregate of children's performance on the counting span task and a new task – the spatial span task. False belief understanding was measured using two variants of the task: the smarties task and a standard false belief story task (e.g., Perner et al., 1987).

The results showed significant zero-order correlations of the inhibitory control and working memory measures with children's false belief performance ($r = .32$ and .48, respectively). In contrast, the counting and labeling performance was not significantly associated with false belief performance ($r = .05$). However, when children's age and performance on the language and speed of processing measures were controlled for, working memory remained significantly associated with false belief understanding ($pr = .30$) but inhibitory control did not. Moreover, when controlling for inhibitory control scores in addition to these other variables, the association between working memory and false belief performance remained significant ($pr = .32$).

The findings of this study add further support to the claim that working memory capacity is associated with performance on false belief tasks. More importantly, these results run counter to Carlson's (Carlson & Moses, 1999) claim that inhibitory control is necessary for performance on theory-of-mind tasks whereas working memory is not. There are at least two explanations for this discrepancy. First, Carlson (1997) controlled for verbal intelligence using the PPVT. As noted earlier, the PPVT may not adequately measure children's language ability (Ruffman et al., 1998). Therefore, it remains a possibility that Carlson's study captures a relation between language ability (the child's primary means of inhibitory control) and theory of mind, not a relation between inhibitory control and theory of mind. In our study, the use of the TELD provided a more comprehensive control for general language ability.

A second possibility is that because I (Keenan, 1999) did not employ as diverse an array of theory-of-mind tasks as did Carlson (1997; Carlson & Moses, 1999), the relation between inhibitory control and theory of mind was not observed. In particular, it may be that inhibitory control is particularly related to performance on the deception task. This suggestion is supported by Hughes' (1998) finding that inhibitory control was only related to performance on a deception task (controlling for age and nonverbal ability). Given the suggestion that theory of mind is a concept with many components, the present finding of no relation between inhibitory control and false belief understanding may underestimate the true relation between inhibitory control and theory of mind in general.

Gordon and Olson (1998) have argued that strict measures of memory span or capacity do not get at the heart of the relation between working memory and theory-of-mind development postulated in Olson's (1993) theory. Their argument is that strict span measures do not require executive functioning and fail to test the child's ability to "hold in mind" some information while allowing the perceptual system to update this information based on changes in the environment. Gordon and Olson argue that it may be the case that existing memory span measures are too "crude" to get at this relation; measures like Keenan et al.'s (1998) counting span task simply tap the capacity of working memory but fail to utilize executive function and therefore do not allow for a test of whether the child can hold one set of information in mind and then establish a relation between a new state of affairs in the world and this information already represented in mind. The results of Keenan (1999) suggest otherwise. Performance on the counting and labeling task was not associated with false belief understanding in this sample whereas performance on the working memory measure was. Given that the counting and labeling task was significantly correlated with the inhibitory control measures ($r = .44$), the suggestion made here is that the Gordon and Olson task may tap inhibitory control more so than it taps working memory.

My own view of Gordon and Olson's (1998) analysis of the counting span task used by Keenan et al. (1998) is that it is not entirely convincing. First, as I illustrated earlier, our working memory task – the counting span task – is a true dual task. As Morris, Craik, and Gick (1990, p. 67) argue, "Working memory tasks are those in which the person must hold a small amount of material in mind for a short time while simultaneously carrying out further cognitive operations, either on the material held or on other incoming material." This description would seem to describe the counting span task to a tee. Second, contrary to Gordon and Olson's claim that the counting span task does not involve an executive component, I would suggest that the task requires the involvement of the central executive in at least two ways. First, attention must be allocated between the storage and active information gathering in the task. That is, the child must count and store a number repeatedly. In Baddeley's (1986) model, the allocation of attention is clearly a function of the central executive. Secondly, children are faced with both target items which they are required to count and distractor items which they must refrain from counting. This constraint clearly requires some degree of inhibitory control, again, clearly an executive function. Thus, on the account presented here, Gordon and Olson's suggestion that the counting span task does not require an executive component is misleading.

Limitations of the Present Research

A limitation of our findings on the association between working memory and false belief understanding which still needs to be addressed is whether the association of these two factors is explained by variables other than language. One clear candidate for a domain general change which predicts working memory development is speed of processing (e.g., Kail & Salthouse, 1994). The speed with which children can carry out elementary cognitive operations has been shown to correlate with working memory. I (Keenan, 1999) used an aggregate measure of speed of processing to control for changes in general cognitive ability which might be invoked as an even more fundamental explanation for the association between theory-of-mind development and working memory. Working memory predicted false belief task performance, controlling for speed of processing. While it is unlikely that theory-of-mind development is simply a matter of increases in the speed of children's processing, we would not discount the fact that domain general changes such as increasing speed of processing play a role in the onset of a representational theory of mind in the preschool years.

Another issue which remains to be addressed has to do with Perner's (1998) contention that developments in the child's theory of mind might drive related changes in children's executive functioning. Perner has argued that in order to carry out executive functions such as planning or inhibiting stereotypical response patterns, children must be able to represent their intentions to themselves. In other words, the child requires the ability to engage in metarepresentation. Although Hughes (1998b) found no evidence for such a relation, the suggestion made here is that to effectively evaluate Perner's claim a longitudinal study which measures executive function and theory-of-mind development at two different time points is required. We (Keenan & White, 1999) have recently undertaken such a study and hope to be able to examine Perner's claim in the near future.

Conclusions

Our findings, taken together with those of other researchers (Davis & Pratt, 1995; Gordon & Olson, 1998; Hughes, 1998) demonstrate that working memory shows both a robust and consistent association with children's acquisition of an understanding of false belief. However, it is also clear that the present data do not permit one to go much beyond claiming that working memory is relevant to performance on these tasks. Two claims as to how working memory influences theory-of-mind development have been put forward. First, as Fodor (1992) and others have suggested, increases in processing capacity may allow children to express concepts for which they did not previously have the resources, reducing their need to rely on heuristics which might lead to errors in predicting others' mental states. However, findings by Wimmer and Weichbold (1994) have challenged this view. Second, congruent with Olson's work (1989, 1993), working memory might also play a role in the very development of theory-of-mind concepts such as *belief, desire,* and *intention,* the linguistic constructions which support these concepts, and finally, the system of inferences which relates them to one another. This second suggestion in particular is at odds with recent arguments by Gopnik (1996; Gopnik & Meltzoff, 1996) who explicitly disavows the role of working memory in the acquisition of a theory of mind in favor of the "theory theory." However, the data from our studies would suggest that the development of a theory of mind is not simply the result of domain specific changes in the child's theories, although this is certainly an important aspect of its development. Rather, domain general changes in processing capacity lead to changes in the formation of the concepts which make up one's theory of mind. Further work is required to sort out what role (or roles) developmental changes in working memory might play in children's acquisition of a theory of mind, whether changes in capacity parallel changes in the child's theories, and how exactly changes in memory span might lead to an understanding of false belief.

The fact remains, however, that once children recognize the possibility of someone holding a false belief, they still must integrate this understanding into their theory of mind. In some areas, this process may take some time. For example, as Ruffman and Keenan (1996) demonstrated, children's understanding of surprise seems to lag behind their understanding of false belief, as children integrate their concept of false belief into their understanding of emotion, developing a belief-based concept of surprise. Such findings suggest that even though capacity increases might allow for the possibility of concepts such as false belief, these concepts still need to be integrated into children's previous theories.

In my own view, a comprehensive developmental account of the child's theory of mind is likely to be multifactorial (Astington & Gopnik, 1991). In regard to the child's acquisition of a theory of mind, development is likely to be governed by a multiplicity of factors including biological constraints, developing cognitive resources like working memory, aspects of the child's social ecology such as parental talk about mental states, sibling interactions, and family structure, as well as by the child's construction of increasingly adequate theories (Gopnik & Meltzoff, 1996).

To reiterate, working memory is *not* the sole determinant of a child's acquisition of a theory of mind, but one of several factors which has a role in the child's developing understanding of the mind. Developing an understanding of mind is not simply a memory problem: certain concepts (e.g., belief, desire, and intention) must also be in place. However, it is likely that working memory has some role in the developing ability to form and to express those concepts, as it does in many other areas of cognitive development. These findings present a challenge to the "theory theory" and suggest that a reasonable addition to the theory, on the basis of the available evidence, would be the inclusion of developmental changes in working memory as a factor in children's development of increasingly sophisticated theories of mind.

As a graduate student, David presented me with an opportunity to carry out some research with him on his suggestion of an association between working memory and the child's developing theory of mind. That he entrusted me to work with him on our original project was a privilege. While our work on this subject has demonstrated some interesting relations between information processing capacity and the child's developing understanding of mind, it is clear that much work remains to be done on the topic, both theoretically and empirically. In my view, it is a testament to his influence as a scholar and as a PhD advisor that I have continued to remain interested in and working on these same questions today.

References

Astington, J. W., & Gopnik, A. (1991). Theoretical explanations of children's understanding of the mind. *British Journal of Developmental Psychology, 9,* 7–31.

Astington, J. W., & Jenkins, J. M. (1999). A longitudinal study of the relation between language and theory-of-mind development. *Developmental Psychology, 35,* 1311–20.

Baddeley, A. (1986). *Working memory.* Oxford, UK: Clarendon.

Brown, J. R., & Dunn, J. (1991). "You can cry, mum": The social and developmental implications of talk about internal states. *British Journal of Developmental Psychology, 9,* 237–56.

Carlson, S. (1997, April). *Individual differences in inhibitory control and children's theory of mind.* Poster presented at the Biennial Meeting of the Society for Research in Child Development, Washington, DC.

Carlson, S., & Moses, L (1999, April). *How specific is the relation between executive function and theory of mind?* Paper presented at the Biennial Meeting of the Society for Research in Child Development, Albuquerque, NM.

Carlson, S., Moses, L., & Hix, H. (1998). The role of inhibitory processes in young children's difficulties with deception and false belief. *Child Development, 69,* 672–91.

Case, R. (1985). *Intellectual development: Birth to adulthood.* New York: Academic Press.

Case, R., Kurland, M., & Goldberg, J. (1982). Operational efficiency and the growth of short-term memory. *Journal of Experimental Child Psychology, 33,* 386–404.

Cohen, J. (1990). Things I have learned (so far). *American Psychologist, 45,* 1304–12.

Daneman, M., & Carpenter, P. A. (1980). Individual differences in working memory and reading. *Journal of Verbal Learning and Verbal Behavior, 19,* 450–66.

Davis, H., & Pratt, C. (1995). The development of children's theory of mind: The working memory explanation. *Australian Journal of Psychology, 47,* 25–31.

de Villiers, J. (1995, April). *Steps in the mastery of sentence complements.* Paper presented at the Biennial Meeting of the Society for Research in Child Development, Indianapolis, IN.

de Villiers, J., & Pyers, J. (1997, April). *On reading minds and predicting action.* Paper presented at the Biennial Meeting of the Society for Research in Child Development, Washington, DC.

Dunn, J., Brown, J., Slomkowski, C., Tesla, C., & Youngblade, L. (1991). Young children's understanding of other people's feelings and beliefs: Individual differences and their antecedents. *Child Development, 62,* 1352–66.

Dunn, L. M., & Dunn, L. M. (1981). *Peabody Picture Vocabulary Test – Revised manual for forms L and M.* Circle Pines, MN: American Guidance Service.

Fodor, J. A. (1992). A theory of the child's theory of mind. *Cognition, 44,* 283–96.

Frye, D., Zelazo, P. D., & Palfai, T. (1995). Theory of mind and rule-based reasoning.

Cognitive Development, 10, 483–527.

Gopnik, A. (1996). Theories and modules: Creation myths, developmental realities and Neurath's boat. In P. Carruthers & P. K. Smith (Eds.), *Theories of theories of mind.* (pp.169–183). Cambridge, UK: Cambridge University Press.

Gopnik, A., & Astington, J. W. (1988). Children's understanding of representational change and its relation to the understanding of false belief and the appearance-reality distinction. *Child Development, 59,* 26–37.

Gopnik, A., & Meltzoff, A. (1996). *Words, thoughts, and theories.* Cambridge, MA: MIT Press.

Gordon, A. C. L., & Olson, D. R. (1998). The relation between acquisition of a theory of mind and the capacity to hold in mind. *Journal of Experimental Child Psychology, 68,* 70–83.

Halford, G. S. (1993). *Children's understanding: The development of mental models.* Hillsdale, NJ: Erlbaum.

Happé, F. G. E. (1995). The role of age and verbal ability in the theory of mind task performance of subjects with autism. *Child Development, 66,* 843–55.

Hresko, W., Reid, D., & Hammill, D. (1981). *The Test of Early Language Development (TELD).* Austin, TX: Pro-Ed.

Hughes, C. (1998a). Executive function in preschoolers: Links with theory of mind and verbal ability. *British Journal of Developmental Psychology, 16,* 233–53.

Hughes, C. (1998b). Finding you marbles: Does preschoolers' strategic behavior predict later understanding of mind? *Developmental Psychology, 34,* 1326–39.

Jenkins, J., & Astington, J. W. (1996). Cognitive factors and family structure associated with theory of mind development in young children. *Developmental Psychology, 32,* 70–8.

Kail, R., & Salthouse, T. (1994). Processing speed as a mental capacity. *Acta Psychologia, 86,* 199–225.

Keenan, T. (1998). Memory span as a predictor of false belief understanding. *New Zealand Journal of Psychology, 27,* 36–43.

Keenan, T. (1999, April). *The role of working memory and inhibitory control in children's understanding of false belief.* Poster presented at the Biennial Meeting of the Society for Research in Child Development, Albuquerque, NM.

Keenan, T., Marini, Z., & Olson, D. R. (1993, April). *Memory span and its relation to children's performance on a set of false belief tasks.* Presented at the Biennial Meeting of the Society for Research in Child Development, New Orleans, LA.

Keenan, T., Olson, D. R., & Marini, Z. (1998). Working memory and children's developing understanding of mind. *Australian Journal of Psychology, 50,* 76–82.

Keenan, T., & White, S. (1999). *Age-specific relations between executive functions and the child's theory of mind.* Unpublished manuscript, University of Canterbury.

Kochanska, G., Murray, K., Jacques, T., Koenig, A., & Vandegeest, K. (1996). Inhibitory control in young children and its role in emerging internalization. *Child Development, 67,* 490–507.

Morris, R. G., Craik, F. I. M., & Gick, M. L. (1990). Age differences in working memory tasks: The role of secondary memory and the central executive system. *The Quarterly Journal of Experimental Psychology, 42A,* 67–86.

Olson, D. R. (1989). Making up your mind. *Canadian Psychology, 30,* 617–27.

Olson, D. R. (1993). The development of mental representations: The origins of mental life. *Canadian Psychology, 34,* 293–306.

Perner, J. (1998). The meta-intentional nature of executive functions and theory of mind. In

P. Carruthers & J. Boucher (Eds.), *Language and thought.* (pp. 270–83). Cambridge, UK: Cambridge University Press.

Perner, J., & Lang, B. (2000). Theory of mind and executive function: Is there a developmental relationship? In S. Baron-Cohen, H. Tager-Flusberg, & D. Cohen (Eds.), *Understanding other minds: Perspectives from developmental cognitive neuroscience* (2nd ed., pp. 150–81). Oxford, UK: Oxford University Press.

Perner, J., Leekam, S., & Wimmer, H. (1987). Three-year-olds' difficulty with false belief: The case for a conceptual deficit. *British Journal of Developmental Psychology, 5,* 125–37.

Plaut, D. C., & Karmiloff-Smith, A. (1993). Representational development and theory of mind computations. *Behavioral and Brain Sciences, 16,* 70–1.

Ruffman, T., & Keenan, T. (1996). The belief-based emotion of surprise: The case for a lag in understanding relative to false belief. *Developmental Psychology, 32,* 40–9.

Ruffman, T., Slade, L., Clements, W., & Import, A. (1998). *How language is related to verbal and nonverbal theory of mind.* Unpublished manuscript, University of Sussex.

Russell, J. (1996). Development and evolution of the symbolic function: The role of working memory. In P. Mellars & K. Gibson (Eds.), *Modelling the early human mind* (pp. 159–70). Cambridge, UK: McDonald Institute Monographs.

Tager-Flusberg, H., & Sullivan, K. (1994). Predicting and explaining behavior: A comparison of autistic, mentally retarded and normal children. *Journal of Child Psychology and Psychiatry, 35,* 1059–75.

Wimmer, H., & Weichbold, V. (1994). Children's theory of mind: Fodor's heuristics examined. *Cognition, 53,* 45–57.

Zaitchik, D. (1990). When representations conflict with reality: The preschooler's problem with false beliefs and "false" photographs. *Cognition, 35,* 41–68.

Zelazo, P. D., Frye, D., & Rapus, T. (1996). An age-related dissociation between knowing rules and using them. *Cognitive Development, 11,* 37–63.

15

Nonverbal Theory of Mind: Is it Important, is it Implicit, is it Simulation, is it Relevant to Autism?

Ted Ruffman

I came to OISE in 1986 as a Master's student in clinical psychology. Clinical psychology has just about nothing in common with theory-of-mind (ToM) research but I had a research assistantship to help a professor carry out an empirical study. All I knew was that I wanted to work with children and there were two projects on offer. I talked with both supervisors, the second being David Olson. I knew nothing about either area or about either professor but I asked to work on David's project simply because I liked him.

I remember a few things from my first year at OISE. I worked on a project examining the relation between seeing and knowing, building on a study that Heinz Wimmer, Jürgen Hogrefe, and Josef Perner (1988) had carried out. To my surprise (given my lack of experience in this whole area) and to David's credit, we ended up publishing that study (Ruffman & Olson, 1989). I also remember research groups at OISE. We had a great group. Janet Astington was fresh (exhausted?) from organizing the Developing Theories of Mind conference and was editing the volume that came from it. Robin Campbell was a visiting professor and I remember research groups being considerably enlivened by his frequent outbursts of laughter. I also remember David's never-ending enthusiasm, patience, and encouragement about our research and any meagre comment I managed to make in research groups. It was these qualities and my admiration for David's work that got me hooked on the puzzles in experimental psychology and ToM, and took me completely away from my initial direction. I feel extremely fortunate that I just happened to find David and his research project.

In this chapter I present some data and ideas that build on those early days. I begin with the question of whether nonverbal measures of ToM are important.

Are Nonverbal or Implicit Indices of ToM Important?

Psychologists tend to fixate on certain issues. A good example over the last 15 years has been false belief understanding. Wimmer and Perner's (1983) seminal study of false belief was a great work and many subsequent articles have provided invaluable insights. False belief task performance is an unambiguous marker of children's understanding of representation and mental states and is important in its own right. Yet I can't help but think that the majority of ToM research that has involved variations on false belief tasks has been too narrow in its focus. Over the last few years we have tried to take stock and have become interested in nonverbal and implicit ToM. We have also become interested in aspects of social understanding that have until now received little attention. In particular, I think that there has been an unnecessary fixation on whether children understand that *mental states* guide behavior and whether they understand *representation*. Of course it all depends on one's purpose, but there is much more to social sensitivity than metarepresentation and understanding mental states.

Consider, for instance, the 12-month-old infant who when on a visual cliff and uncertain of whether to proceed, looks to its mother. If the mother looks fearful the infant stops and if she looks happy the infant proceeds (Sorce, Emde, Campos, & Klinnert, 1985). This shows that 12-month-olds can successfully interpret (i.e., react appropriately to) the significance of their mother's emotional expression of fear or happiness. Perner (1991) pointed out that infants need not understand the mental states that underlie the mother's emotional expression. They need only react appropriately to her behavioral expression of emotion. That much seems clear. It is equally clear that infants cannot verbalize their understanding (i.e., label their mother's emotion or the situation as dangerous), and it is at least an open question whether they are even conscious of how their mother feels (or of anything for that matter).

It is perhaps for these reasons that with only a few exceptions, ToM researchers have generally steered clear of tasks such as the visual cliff. Relatively few have used behavioral measures of any sort although there is an increasing trend in this direction (e.g., Carpenter, Akhtar, & Tomasello, 1998; Clements & Perner, 1994; O'Neill, 1996; Repacholi, 1998; Repacholi & Gopnik, 1996). Instead, researchers (myself included) have focused mainly on insights that require the child to understand that the mind mediates between events in the world and behavior. False belief, and to a lesser extent desire, have been the primary targets. Research has centered on the age at which children understand such mental states, and more recently, on the correlates of belief or desire understanding. Such research has been informative.

Yet I wish to highlight that the understanding needed for successful performance on the visual cliff – even though it need not involve insight into mental states and may even be unconscious – is absolutely essential to the infant's very survival. In this respect there could not be a better measure of social understanding. Moreover, whereas the need to understand false belief is relatively rare (Perner, 1991), the need to understand the significance of others' emotional expressions is positively rife, as is the need to understand how others are likely to react. Further still, my intuition is that nonverbal measures will often be more central to social sensitivity because in real social interactions one is not usually called upon to comment on another person's beliefs, desires, or actions. Although it is true that conscious verbal understanding enables a certain degree of flexibility in utilizing knowledge, in real life social interactions one need only have some inkling of how another will react and this understanding may often be nonverbal or even unconscious. This is particularly true with young children for two reasons. First, they have impoverished verbal skills. Second, they are relative novices in ToM. Many ToM concepts will undergo much development and cognitive development can likely be characterized by a pattern of implicit knowledge before explicit knowledge (Karmiloff-Smith, 1992). Such realizations have led me to re-evaluate the issues that we want our research to address. If one's interest is even partially in children's social abilities, then insights that are non-metarepresentational, nonmental state, nonverbal, and even nonconscious, may nevertheless be very important.

Does Nonverbal Understanding of Belief Index Unconscious Knowledge?

Our own efforts in this area build on those of Clements and Perner (1994). They found that from the age of about 2 years, 11 months, children look to the correct location when anticipating a story character's return in a false belief task even when they answer the verbal question incorrectly. They suggested that children develop an *implicit* or *unconscious* understanding of false belief before they develop an explicit or conscious understanding. Yet they acknowledged that such claims were only speculation. Perhaps children were aware of the knowledge conveyed in eye movements but lacked confidence in this answer and so provided a different verbal answer. Below I outline our studies aimed at determining whether anticipatory looking in a false belief task indexes truly unconscious knowledge (Ruffman, Clements, Import, & Connolly, 1998).

We tested this idea in two experiments using the basic paradigm of Clements and Perner (1994). The apparatus we used included two locations, each with a different slide by it (see Figure 15.1). Children were shown that Ed (the story character) used the left slide to obtain the object in the left box, and the right slide to obtain the object in the right box. Ed then hid the object in the left-hand location, went away, and a second character moved it to the right-hand location. Just before Ed returned, the child heard a prompt: the narrator of the story (recorded on audiotape) announced that the story character was about to return and then wondered aloud, "I wonder which slide Ed will come down?" This was the *eye gaze prompt*. It was not a direct question to the child regarding where Ed would look (i.e., no child answered verbally), but rather, a means of determining whether the child anticipated Ed returning to the left location where he had placed the object or the right location where the object had been moved to. The child was also given a standard *explicit question*: "Which slide will Ed come down?" In addition, in a true belief condition, Ed (or a different story character to that used in the false belief task) saw the object moved from the left box to the right box. This condition helps rule out various alternative explanations of the eye direction effect, for example children

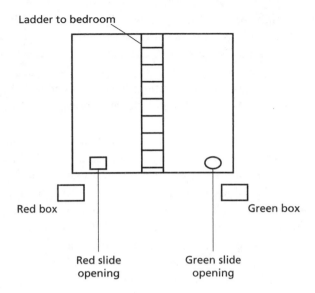

Ladder to bedroom

Red box

Green box

Red slide
opening

Green slide
opening

Figure 15.1 Apparatus used in betting experiments.

simply retrace the story events and look to the left location because this is where the character first placed the object. If children look to the right box in the true belief condition then this kind of explanation could not be correct because Ed first placed the object in the left box in the true belief task as well.

To measure certainty in their answer we asked children to place plastic counters at the location where they thought the story character would appear ("Put your counters next to the slide where Ed will come down. If you don't know where Ed will come down put counters next to both slides. You can put the same number next to both slides or a different number"). We refer to this technique as the "betting" procedure, though we did not use this term with children. In the literature on implicit learning (e.g., Berry & Dienes, 1993), betting is taken as a marker of explicit knowledge because the individual is asked to make an explicit commitment to a given answer. In the false belief task, if children bet confidently on the answer consistent with their eye movements (character will go to left location) rather than their verbal answer (character will go to right location), then there would be *no* evidence for the suggestion that eye movements reveal implicit knowledge. By betting on the answer consistent with their eye movements, children would have shown some degree of explicit awareness that the character would look in the left location. Such a pattern could be explained by positing that these children are in a transitional stage in their understanding of belief. Their eye movements show some explicit understanding of belief but they are not yet confident enough of this answer to give it when asked where the character will look. Such children would be aware that their verbal answer could be wrong. In contrast, it may be that children who show correct eye movements in the false belief task but an incorrect verbal answer bet highly on the right-hand location (consistent with their verbal answer). This pattern would provide evidence for the idea that eye direction reveals implicit knowledge because children would show no awareness of the knowledge conveyed through their eyes.

In addition we included control conditions in the form of probabilities tasks, also narrated on audiotape. For instance, children were shown a bag containing 10 red objects that could go down the red slide but not the green one (10–0). They were asked to bet counters on which slide they thought the object would come down, and to make similar predictions for a bag containing 10 green objects (0–10), and for a bag with nine red objects and one green object (9–1). The key difference was between betting in the 10–0 and 0–10 conditions relative to the 9–1 condition. The question was whether children would bet differently when they had complete confidence in the result in contrast to when a relatively small element of uncertainty was introduced. If children did bet differently this would show that betting is a sensitive measure of even slight changes in certainty. Children's betting in the false belief condition could then be examined knowing that heavy betting on one location should decrease when a child has even slight uncertainty about where the story character will look for the object.

We conducted two experiments that included seventy-nine 3- to 5-year-olds. Children were given a true and a false belief task, and three probabilities tasks (in a counterbalanced order). For each trial the child was given 10 new counters to bet. For the belief and probabilities tasks children were videotaped as they watched the stories unfold. Videotapes of the child's eye movements for the 4-second period following the prompt were later analyzed to determine how long children looked to the left and right containers when anticipating Ed's return.

Children were counted as passing the implicit measure if over the 4-second time window, they looked mainly to the right location in the true belief task and mainly to the left location in the false belief task. They were counted as failing for all other patterns. They were counted as passing the explicit measure if they answered the explicit question correctly in both tasks (see above), and otherwise as failing.

Like Clements and Perner (1994), we found that children showed correct eye movements before they gave correct verbal answers. Thirteen children failed both the implicit and explicit measures, 35 passed the implicit but not the explicit measure, 5 passed the explicit but not the implicit measure, and 26 passed both measures. Our main interest was in the 35 children who passed only the implicit measure, and the 26 who passed both measures. We were curious whether certainty would increase or potentially even decrease as children came to pass the explicit measure. Indeed, data from this experiment have the potential to provide insights into the transition between incorrect and correct verbal performance. To examine this we assumed that younger children would, by and large, be further from fully understanding false belief than older children. Thus, we divided the data to give four groups: the 18 younger children who passed the implicit but not the explicit measure, the 17 older children who did this, the 13 younger children who passed both measures, and the 13 older children who did this.

In the false belief task betting was analyzed as a function of verbal answer. For children who said the character would return to the left location, we looked at the number of counters bet on the left location. For children who said the character would return to the right location, we looked at the number of counters bet on the right location. In addition, we examined betting on the right location in the true belief task, the red location in the 10–0 task, the green location in the 0–10 task, and the most probable (red) location in the 9–1 task.

Figure 15.2 shows how children in the four groups bet in the different tasks. It reveals two clear trends. First, certainty tends to be lower in all groups in the 9–1 task. Second, certainty in the false belief task tends to drop steadily to a low among the younger passers, and then recovers somewhat in the older passers. To understand these trends better we conducted pairwise t tests between the betting of the four groups, first in the false belief task, and then in the remaining four tasks. In the false belief task, the younger failers were significantly more certain than the older failers, $p < .02$, the younger passers, $p < .001$, and the older passers, $p < .01$. No other differences were significant in any of the other tasks. These data are particularly striking in that they reveal differences in certainty amongst children who when classified on the standard explicit question have the same level of false belief understanding.

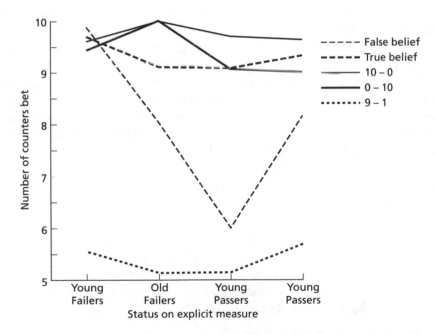

Figure 15.2 Mean number of counters bet in different tasks of betting experiments.

We then used t tests to check whether there were differences in certainty within each group's betting on the false belief task relative to the 9–1 task. The younger failers, $p < .001$, and the older failers, $p < .02$, were more certain on the false belief task.

The results are consistent with the idea that children who show correct eye movements but who give incorrect verbal answers are genuinely unaware of the knowledge conveyed by their anticipatory gaze (i.e., the knowledge is unconscious). If such children were aware of the possibility that Ed would go to the left container then they should have bet some counters on this location. Yet by and large they did not. Further, betting was a sensitive measure of certainty because the children who failed the explicit measure bet more confidently in the false belief task relative to the 9–1 task. Particularly intriguing was that for children who showed correct eye movements but an incorrect verbal answer, there was no difference between betting in the false and true belief tasks despite the fact that children's verbal answers were correct in the true belief task but incorrect in the false belief task. Our findings contradict claims by Zelazo, Frye and Rapus (1996) who suggested that eye movements in false belief tasks might index conscious knowledge.

The trends in Figure 15.2 suggest that 3-year-olds are initially very certain even though they are incorrect, they then begin to doubt this incorrect answer yet still verbally yield to it, they then shift to a new verbal answer but are still uncertain, and at some point later become more certain again about their correct verbal answer. These trends must remain speculative because not all differences between groups were significantly different. Presumably this could be because of the relatively small numbers of children in each group and because age is an imperfect means of identifying developmental level. Nevertheless, the differences in certainty help make sense of findings that indicate some variability in false belief performance over time (e.g., Mayes, Klin, Tercyak Jr., Cicchetti & Cohen, 1996). Children in the Mayes et al. study may have been caught in the transitional stage. The data also provide good evidence for Siegler's (1996) claims that conceptual development is accompanied by periods of transition in which children use different strategies, and that it is technically incorrect (though it has some practical use as a simplifying statement) to make claims about when children "understand" or "do not understand" a particular concept.

The results are inconsistent with claims that syntactic abilities, and in particular, children's understanding of sentential complements are at the heart of false belief understanding (Tager-Flusberg & Sullivan, 1994). They argued that false belief tasks tap the understanding that "John thinks that the chocolate is in the left box," where the content of the belief is an embedded clause. Our true belief task has the same sort of embedding, yet nearly all children were correct on this task. (See Astington & Jenkins, 1999, for other arguments that sentential complements are not at the heart of false belief understanding.)

Other Social Insights

At the outset I argued that social referencing on the visual cliff is a crucially important ability even if it does not entail an understanding of mental states or representation. In this section I examine children's understanding of someone's behavioral response in a situation analogous to the visual cliff (Ruffman, Clements, Import, & Crowe, 1999). We called this measure the emotion-behavior task and we tested 39 children in two experimental tasks, obtaining both a verbal and a nonverbal response. Figure 15.3 illustrates the experimental set-up. In each task there were two rooms (e.g., red and green) and two associated windows, a boy, and a father. When the boy entered the red room he would appear in the red window and when he entered the green room he would appear in the green window. The boy knew that one of the rooms wasn't safe and asked the father whether the red room was safe to enter. In one task the father smiled and in the other he looked fearful. The child then heard a prompt narrated on audiotape to elicit anticipatory eye gaze ("I wonder which window Sam will go to?"), and we videotaped their anticipatory eye movements for 4 seconds. We were interested in which room the children expected the boy to enter (i.e., which window did they look to?). The children were then asked the explicit question ("Which window will Sam go to?"). In a between-participants design, 20 children were given two control tasks that were identical except that Dad said either, "Yes," or, "No," when asked if the red room was safe. The experimental tasks required children to understand the link between emotion and behavior, the control tasks, the link between verbal statements and behavior.

To be counted as passing the nonverbal tasks the child had to do the following over the 4-second period following the prompt. When Dad said "No" to the question about whether the target room was safe and when he looked afraid, the child had to look more to the opposite room when anticipating the boy's return than to the room the boy had asked about. When Dad said "Yes" and when he looked happy, the child had to look more to the room the boy had asked about. To be counted as passing the verbal tasks the child had to point to or name the appropriate room.

Of the 39 children in the experimental group there were seven 2-year-olds, twenty-two 3-year-olds, and ten 4-year-olds. In the control condition there were nine 3-year-olds and eleven 4-year-olds. Children's performance on the different tasks is

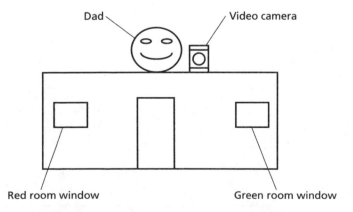

Figure 15.3 Apparatus used in the emotion-behavior experiment.

shown in Table 15.1. A child who was guessing would be expected to get one out of two (happy and fear) tasks correct. Scores were evaluated against chance using *t* tests. Children did very well on the verbal and nonverbal measures of the control tasks. In the experimental tasks, they did well on the nonverbal measure but only 4-year-olds were above chance on the verbal measure. We compared performance in the experimental condition to that in the control condition for each age group. Because both 3-year-olds and 4-year-olds were slightly older in the control condition, we treated age as a covariate. The 3-year-olds in the control condition were significantly better than those in the experimental condition on the verbal measure, *p* < .05, but there was no difference on the nonverbal measure. The 4-year-olds in the control condition were as good as those in the experimental condition on the verbal measure, and on the nonverbal measure. In the experimental group, children were significantly better on the nonverbal measure than the verbal measure, *p* < .001. In the control group there was no difference between the two measures.

In sum, whereas only 4-year-olds passed the verbal question in the experimental condition, even older 2-year-olds did well on the nonverbal measure, and 3-year-olds and 4-year-olds did well on both measures of the control condition. This result

Table 15.1 Mean Number of Tasks Correct in the Emotion-Behavior Task

	Mean number of tasks correct (Maximum = 2)	
Experimental task: (*n* = 39)		
Verbal		
2-year-olds	0.86	(.38)
3-year-olds	0.77	(.87)
4-year-olds	1.60*	(.70)
Overall mean	1.00	(.83)
Nonverbal		
2-year-olds	1.71**	(.49)
3-year-olds	1.73***	(.55)
4-year-olds	1.90***	(.32)
Overall mean	1.77	(.49)
Control task: (*n* = 20)		
Verbal		
3-year-olds	1.78*	(.67)
4-year-olds	1.73***	(.47)
Overall mean	1.75	(.55)
Nonverbal		
3-year-olds	1.89***	(.33)
4-year-olds	2.00***	(0)
Overall mean	1.95	(.22)

Notes. Standard deviations are in parentheses

Performance above chance: **p* < .05, ***p* < .01, ****p* < .001.

provides another example, in addition to false belief, where eye gaze precedes verbal understanding.

Our results were also inconsistent with inhibition accounts of ToM development (e.g., Hughes, 1998; Russell, Mauthner, Sharpe, & Tidswell, 1991). In a false belief task children must inhibit their own knowledge of where the object is. However, in the emotion-behavior task their own belief about which room is safe should be the same as the story character's, but children still find this task as difficult as false belief. Nor was there a significant tendency for children to err on any one emotion-behavior task (e.g., when the father looked fearful) which could be interpreted as, for instance, a bias to always name the room the boy asked about, and that would have to be inhibited. In short, inhibitory deficiencies did not seem to be at the heart of emotion-behavior performance.

In the past, numerous researchers have found correlations between false belief tasks, appearance-reality tasks, and representational change tasks (Gopnik & Astington, 1988; Gordon & Olson, 1998; Moore, Pure, & Furrow, 1990), and between false belief tasks and synonyms tasks (Doherty & Perner, 1998; Perner, this volume, Chapter 13). Perner (1988, 1991) argues that these correlations exist because the tasks tap a common insight into representation. Yet in another experiment we found that there was a significant correlation between verbal performance on the two emotion-behavior tasks and performance on two belief tasks (true and false belief), $r = .45$, $p < .05$. Correct performance on the emotion-behavior task does not require insight into either mental states or representation. The common age of onset in understanding makes me wonder whether what develops at age 4 and accounts for false belief understanding is really representation per se as Perner (1991) has so eloquently argued, but rather simply verbal *social* knowledge. Again, it makes me think that there are a host of important social insights that are as yet untapped and that there has been an inordinate amount of attention devoted to false belief and representation in ToM research. Below, we consider in more detail why performance on the emotion-behavior and false belief tasks may correlate.

Are Verbal and Nonverbal Insights Derived by Similar Means?

One's social understanding could be based on a theory (loosely, a coherent body of knowledge) or simulation (imagining yourself in another person's circumstances). Perner (1996) suggested that whereas verbal answers in a false belief task are derived by means of a theory, eye gaze could reflect the initial stages of simulation in that they indicate empathic identification with the story character.

Our data looking at emotion-behavior understanding could be interpreted as offering support for the idea that explicit and implicit indices are based on different processes. To understand why, however, it is first necessary to consider how performance on ToM tasks correlates with language. It is well established that performance on explicit ToM measures, such as false belief, correlates with general language abilities (e.g., Astington & Jenkins, 1999; Happé, 1995). It is not known, however, whether performance on implicit indices such as eye gaze correlates with general language ability. One might conjecture that answers both to the explicit question and eye gaze would correlate with language because children who engage in more social interactions will foster both their linguistic abilities and their general social understanding. Each of these skills will then facilitate future social interactions. If so, language should correlate with both explicit performance and eye gaze because both measures tap social insight.

In contrast, Astington and Jenkins (1999) argued that language enables the child to keep track of the story character's representation (to metarepresent) when the object is moved from the first location to the second. The key for Astington and Jenkins is that the child can keep track of the story character's representation in the face of a conflicting reality (i.e., the object is in the right, not the left container). Further, they argue that syntactic abilities are "crucial" here to represent the spatial arrangement of the hiding places and the object's whereabouts. The emotion-behavior task does not require an understanding of representation and children could egocentrically attribute their own mental state to the story character (i.e., use the father's emotion to infer which location is safe and attribute this inference to the character). Because emotion-behavior performance does not require an understanding of representation, it seems a fair assumption that it should not correlate with language on Astington and Jenkins' account.

Yet a third possibility is that language correlates only with answers to explicit questions. This may be, for instance, because explicit measures are tapping conscious knowledge whereas eye gaze in the absence of explicit insight is tapping mostly implicit or unconscious knowledge. Explicit understanding may be more theory driven whereas implicit understanding may be either largely simulation based (Perner, 1996), or based on something akin to the prototheories described by Carey (1985). To think about and refine the explicit postulates of theories, advanced language will be a helpful tool. Eye gaze need only reflect very vague intuitions not so closely dependent on an explicit ability to articulate or understand explicit theoretical principles and language (beyond simply understanding language well enough to make sense of ToM tasks). In general, one might conjecture that as knowledge becomes more explicit there will be a move away from processes of simulation. It is much simpler to form a general theory – an interrelated body of knowledge for predicting social outcomes – than to laboriously conduct a simulation afresh each time. Language will help one to consider and form such a rule.

We examined how eye gaze and answers to the explicit question correlate with language ability. Children who received the emotion-behavior task were given three language tests: two subtests of the Clinical Evaluation of Language Fundamentals – Preschool (Sentence Structure and Linguistic Concepts); and the Information subtest of the Weschler Primary and Preschool Scale of Intelligence. These tests tap a range of syntactic and semantic language skills, as well as expressive and receptive language. To create an eye-gaze measure with plenty of variance, we used a continuous measure: (time spent looking at the correct location) – (time spent looking at the incorrect location) over the happy and fear tasks. The range on this measure was

−2.2 seconds to +8.0 seconds with a mean of 3.0 seconds and a standard deviation of 2.2 seconds. This measure assumes that children who looked longer at the correct location would have a more robust understanding of the emotion-behavior link. This is plausible in that children who had a very weak understanding might look back and forth between the rooms. Further, the continuous measure was validated in that it correlated well with age, $r = .34$, $p < .05$, which was comparable to the correlation between the verbal measure with age, $r = .37$, $p < .05$, and better than the dichotomous eye gaze measure and age, $r = .26$, ns.

Performance on the three language tests did not correlate with eye gaze (either individually, or together, $r = .10$, ns) For the explicit measure, two children were eliminated from the analyses because of experimenter error which made us unable to determine whether they pointed or answered verbally. Of the remaining 37 children, there were 24 who pointed on the explicit measure in the fear condition and the same number who did so in the happy condition. There were 13 children who answered verbally in each condition. Pointers were about 4 months younger and tended to do worse on the explicit questions. On both the fear and happy conditions pointers were correct 42% of the time. On the fear condition children who answered verbally were correct 62% of the time, and on the happy condition they were correct 77% of the time. General language was more clearly associated with verbal success than it was with pointing success. Performance on five of six language tests correlated significantly with whether verbal answers were correct over the fear and happy conditions. The correlations between the composite language measure and verbal success were $r = .56$ and $r = .57$ on the happy and fear tasks (both $p < .01$). One language measure correlated significantly with pointing performance, one correlation was marginally significant, and all correlations were positive and of mainly moderate magnitude, including the composite language measure ($r = .27$ and .30 with success on fear and happy tasks). Thus, there was a continuum in the extent to which measures related to language. Eye gaze did not relate, pointing in response to an explicit question related moderately, and verbal answers to the explicit question were highly related.

These data have an interesting interpretation. There is no clear reason for thinking that verbal answers to the explicit question are any more *conscious* than answers based on pointing. Thus, it does not seem to be consciousness per se which leads to correlations with language. It is also intriguing that one nonverbal answer – pointing – correlates significantly with language whereas the other nonverbal answer – eye gaze – does not. It seems pretty clear that all children had the ability to identify a location verbally rather than just point, so the ability to verbalize an answer seems an unlikely reason for why pointing is less related to general language ability than verbal answers (although I should acknowledge that the differences between the correlations are not significant).

The data lead me to wonder whether children's social understanding becomes increasingly theoretical as they grow older. The youngest children showed correct eye gaze but eye gaze did not correlate with language. This is perhaps because eye gaze is based on simulation or loose, not very well-specified prototheories, both of which are not intimately related to language ability. What about children who answered the explicit question by pointing? These children were on average 4 months younger than children who answered verbally. Because pointers were younger, one can propose that pointers were at a less advanced stage in their theory building than children who answered verbally. Indeed, pointers may have been less confident of (though equally conscious of) their answer because they had had less time and less in the way of language skills to work out their theory, and this is why they pointed.

Overall, the data suggest that language may not correlate with core social insights, but with explicit understanding, particularly verbal understanding. The core social insight may be manifest in eye gaze which then gets built on with age (i.e., becomes increasingly well specified and theoretical). The data are not consistent with the idea that language correlates with ToM measures because of the representational component in the ToM measure. Emotion-behavior success does not necessitate representational insights yet verbal performance correlated highly with language ability. Nor are they consistent with the idea that language correlates with all core social insights because it facilitates communication that in turn facilitates social understanding.

Explaining Autism

The ToM hypothesis applied to autism contends that the symptoms of children with autism can be explained at least partially by their ToM deficits (e.g., Frith & Happé, 1994). Children with autism are typically compared to children with mental handicap (MH) because both groups have low IQ but only the autistic children show the characteristic social impairments. Two problems with the ToM hypothesis are that: (a) autistic children do not show deficits on all ToM tasks relative to MH children; and (b) previous studies have used a limited range of ToM tasks and may have missed genuine differences (e.g., the emotion-behavior task may reveal important real-life social insights).

Recently we have been exploring whether previous researchers' exclusive reliance on verbal measures has masked differences between autistic and MH children, based on the idea that nonverbal understanding as indexed by eye gaze may sometimes be more central to social abilities than verbal understanding. For the 16 autistic children tested thus far, we have found no consistent sign of correct eye gaze, unlike normal 3-year-olds. We are currently expanding our study to include an additional 40 autistic children and 40 MH children. Our hypothesis is that despite the sometimes equal verbal ToM performance of autistic and MH children, MH children have more in the way of implicit understanding, which accounts for their better social skills.

One intriguing possibility that follows from the theory-simulation debate is that the ToM understanding which the gifted group of autistic children possess is strictly verbal and based on theoretical processes of induction or teaching. The nonverbal understanding that they might lack may be based on more spontaneous processes (and perhaps, simulation). For instance, theoretical processes might be incapable of producing true empathy. One could have an intellectual understanding of a person's predicament and what they might do. Yet this would not produce empathy unless one could use the predicament to envision how one would feel oneself. Thus, nonverbal insights that are arrived at spontaneously and possibly through simulation might account for differences between MH and autistic children.

Indeed, the same kinds of things might be true of normal children. Perhaps some children's insights into ToM are based on more theoretical means than other children who have more intuitive and spontaneous insights (possibly based on simulation). These latter children may be more socially sensitive because they can immediately imagine how they would feel if they were in another person's shoes. The results of a recent study we carried out can be interpreted within this framework (Ruffman, Perner, & Parkin, 1999). We asked mothers how they would react to various disciplinary situations and found that mothers who said they would ask their child how he would feel if someone did "X" to him or her, had children with more advanced false belief understanding. Such parenting techniques invite the child to engage in simulation and may facilitate such skills or at least increase the likelihood of simulation.[1]

Conclusions

I have argued that behavioral measures such as eye gaze may index important social abilities, may be implicit, and may be based on rudimentary prototheories or as Perner (1996) suggests, on processes of simulation. I also argued that autistic children's key deficit may be in implicitly grasping social insights rather than explicit understanding, and that general language ability may not correlate with core social insights, but instead with explicit verbal understanding. Finally, I argued for expanding the classic range of ToM tasks to tasks that do not necessarily tap metarepresentation or understanding of mental states. The emotion-behavior task represents one such example. In general, my feeling is that the vast majority of ToM research has made the probably unwarranted assumption that mental state understanding will necessarily be of special relevance to the child's social well being in contrast to general social knowledge not predicated on mental state insights. Perhaps a more appropriate name for the field would be "children's social understanding." Finally, I speculated that the primary difference between autistic and MH children may be rooted in nonverbal understanding rather than verbal understanding, and perhaps in simulation abilities. Many of these ideas await full empirical validation.

In thinking about David and his influence I was struck by a realization. A few years ago I published a paper in which I used an amibiguity task (among others) to examine whether belief ascriptions stem from a theory or from simulation (Ruffman, 1996). Ambiguity tasks have been at the center of some of my work with David and of a good deal of David's own work. Yet when I developed this task I had no awareness of how it related to ambiguity or to claims we made in an earlier paper. We claimed that ambiguity tasks tap false belief understanding; one doesn't know what an ambiguous stimulus is because one could hold a false belief about the stimulus (Ruffman, Olson, & Astington, 1991). Although I didn't connect the work on simulation with the work on ambiguity at the time, I now realize that the simulation work supports our earlier claims about ambiguity. At 4 years of age, around the time children come to understand false belief, they also tend to attribute false beliefs to a person who has access to an ambiguous stimulus. I wonder what other ways my research and thinking continues to be implicitly and explicitly influenced by my years with David at OISE.

Acknowledgments

Thanks to Pete Clifton for supplying the software to analyze looking time; Lance Slade, Wendy Clements, and Arlina Import for helpful discussion of these issues; and to the Economic and Social Research Council (Award #: R000237322 and R000237071) for financial support.

Note

1   I thank Paul Harris for the suggestion that "how would you feel?" responses may facilitate simulation skills.

References

Astington, J. W., & Jenkins, J. M. (1999). A longitudinal study of the relation between language and theory-of-mind development. *Developmental Psychology, 35*, 1311–20.

Berry, D. C., & Dienes, Z. (1993). *Implicit learning: Theoretical and empirical issues*. Hove, UK: Erlbaum.

Carey, S. (1985). *Conceptual change in childhood*. Cambridge, MA: MIT Press.

Carpenter, M., Akhtar, V., & Tomasello, M. (1998). Fourteen- through 18-month-old infants differentially imitate intentional and accidental actions. *Infant Behavior and Development, 21*, 315–30.

Clements, W. A., & Perner, J. (1994). Implicit understanding of belief. *Cognitive Development, 9*, 377–95.

Doherty, M. D., & Perner, J. (1998). Metalinguistic awareness and theory of mind: Just two words for the same thing? *Cognitive Development, 13*, 279–305.

Frith, U., & Happé, F. (1994). Autism: Beyond "theory of mind". *Cognition, 50*, 115–32.

Gopnik, A., & Astington, J. W. (1988). Children's understanding of representational change and its relation to the understanding of false belief and the appearance-reality distinction. *Child Development, 59*, 26–37.

Gordon, A. C., & Olson, D. R. (1998). The relation between acquisition of a theory of mind and the capacity to hold in mind. *Journal of Experimental Child Psychology, 68,* 70–83.

Happé, F. (1995). The role of age and verbal ability in the theory of mind task performance of subjects with autism. *Child Development, 66,* 843–55.

Hughes, C. (1998). Executive function in preschoolers: Links with theory of mind and verbal ability. *British Journal of Developmental Psychology, 16,* 233–53.

Karmiloff-Smith, A. (1992). *Beyond modularity: a developmental perspective on cognitive science.* Cambridge, MA: MIT Press.

Mayes, L. C., Klin, A., Tercyak Jr., K. P., Cicchetti, D. V., & Cohen, D. J. (1996). Test-retest reliability for false-belief tasks. *Journal of Child Psychology and Psychiatry, 37,* 313–19.

Moore, C., Pure, K., & Furrow, D. (1990). Children's understanding of the modal expression of speaker certainty and uncertainty and its relation to the development of a representational theory of mind. *Child Development, 61,* 722–30.

O'Neill, D. K. (1996). Two-year-old children's sensitivity to a parent's knowledge state when making requests. *Child Development, 67,* 659–677.

Perner, J. (1988). Developing semantics for theories of mind: From propositional attitudes to mental representation. In J. W. Astington, P. L. Harris, & D. R. Olson (Eds.), *Developing theories of mind* (pp. 141–72). New York: Cambridge University Press.

Perner, J. (1991). *Understanding the representational mind.* Cambridge, MA: MIT Press.

Perner, J. (1996). Simulation as explicitation of predicate-explicit knowledge about the mind: Arguments for a simulation-theory mix. In P. Carruthers & P. K. Smith (Eds.), *Theories of theories of mind* (pp. 90–104). Cambridge, UK: Cambridge University Press.

Repacholi, B. M. (1998). Infants' use of attentional cues to identify the referent of another person's emotional expression. *Developmental Psychology, 34,* 1017–25.

Repacholi, B. M., & Gopnik, A. (1996). Early reasoning about desires: Evidence from 14- and 18-month-olds. *Developmental Psychology, 33,* 12–21.

Ruffman, T. (1996). Do children understand the mind by means of simulation or a theory? Evidence from their understanding of inference. *Mind & Language, 11,* 388–414.

Ruffman, T., Clements, W., Import, A., & Connolly, D. (1998). *Does eye direction indicate implicit sensitivity to false belief?* Unpublished manuscript, University of Sussex, Brighton.

Ruffman, T., Clements, W., Import, A., & Crowe, E. (1999). *Verbal and nonverbal social knowledge: Understanding the link between emotions and behavior.* Unpublished manuscript, University of Sussex, Brighton.

Ruffman, T., & Olson, D. R. (1989). Children's ascription of knowledge to others. *Developmental Psychology, 25,* 601–6.

Ruffman, T., Olson, D. R., & Astington, J. W. (1991). Children's understanding of visual ambiguity. *British Journal of Developmental Psychology, 9,* 89–102.

Ruffman, T., Perner, J., & Parkin, L. (1999). Parenting style and its relation to false belief understanding. *Social Development, 8,* 395–411.

Russell, J., Mauthner, N., Sharpe, S., & Tidswell, T. (1991). The 'windows task' as a measure of strategic deception in preschoolers and autistic subjects. *British Journal of Developmental Psychology, 9,* 331–49.

Siegler, R. S. (1996). *Emerging minds: The process of change in children's thinking.* New York: Oxford University Press.

Sorce, J. F., Emde, R. N., Campos, J., & Klinnert, M. D. (1985). Maternal emotional signalling: Its effect on the visual cliff behavior of 1-year-olds. *Developmental Psychology, 21,* 195–200.

Tager-Flusberg, H., & Sullivan, K. (1994). Predicting and explaining behavior: A comparison of autistic, mentally retarded and normal children. *Journal of Child Psychology and Psychiatry, 35,* 1059–75.

Wimmer, H., Hogrefe, J., & Perner, J. (1988). Children's understanding of informational access as source of knowledge. *Child Development, 59,* 386–96.

Wimmer, H., & Perner, J. (1983). Beliefs about beliefs: Representation and constraining function of wrong beliefs in young children's understanding of deception. *Cognition, 13,* 103–28.

Zelazo, P. D., Frye, D., & Rapus, T. (1996). An age-related dissociation between knowing rules and using them. *Cognitive Development, 11,* 37–63.

16

Language and Metalanguage in Children's Understanding of Mind

Janet Wilde Astington

Much of my academic career has been spent in fruitful conversation with David Olson, talking about texts and thoughts. Most of our collaborative work has investigated children's understanding and use of the metalinguistic and metacognitive terms that refer to text and thought. One question which repeatedly arises in our discussions is this: Why do these terms matter, that is, what difference do they make to the child's understanding of texts and thoughts? David's answer is always clear and forthright: "In western cultures, the acquisition of an understanding of beliefs, desires, and intentions is completely tied up with the acquisition of a mentalistic language for talking about these events" (Olson, 1994, p. 251); "it is the acquisition of this metalanguage that, I suggest, is central to the development of a theory of mind" (Olson, 1988, p. 424). I am less convinced. Although I believe that children's understanding of mind depends on language, such that linguistic development promotes the development of a theory of mind (Astington & Jenkins, 1999), it seems to me still to be an open question whether this effect is due to particular vocabulary items in contrast to general linguistic competence. That is the issue I explore in this chapter.

Language and Thought

In the spring of 1980 I was completing an undergraduate degree in Psychology at the University of Toronto and wanted to go on to graduate studies in cognitive and linguistic development. My advisor told me to go and talk to David Olson at OISE – just up the road from the Psychology Department but a world apart in other ways (indeed, another professor tried to persuade me not to make the move, although conceding that David Olson was a great theoretician, as I subsequently discovered). I talked with David and made plans to enter OISE's MA program in September. Meanwhile, he told me to spend the summer reading Piaget's (1945/1962) *Play, Dreams, and Imitation in Childhood*, and Vygotsky's (1931/1962) *Thought and Language*. Looking back, I understand why.

Piagetian and Vygotskian ideas on the development of mind are often portrayed as contrastive, at least in undergraduate textbooks, where the issue is often debated in terms of the relation between language and thought. Piaget's position is usually characterized as "language is dependent on thought" and Vygotsky's as its seeming opposite "thought is dependent on language". Olson made me realize that "which comes first?" is an unproductive "chicken or egg?" sort of question. Language and thought are interdependent, and Piaget's and Vygotsky's viewpoints should be seen as complementary rather than opposed, as indeed, they themselves saw them. Language simultaneously serves two functions; it is a system that both represents and communicates (Olson, 1980b). Piaget's focus on the representational, logical aspects of language led to his argument that children come to know language through their knowledge of the world, while Vygotsky's focus on language's communicative, social function led to his argument that children come to know the world through language. It would be a mistake to try to argue that either one of these perspectives provides a more satisfactory explanation of cognitive growth than does the other. "Cognition rests as much on a cultural foundation as it does on a biological one" (Olson, 1980a, p. 3). Easily said, perhaps, and leaving open almost as many questions as it answers, but none the less a good beginning for a research career in cognitive development.

When I arrived at OISE in the fall of 1980 the say/mean distinction was high on Olson's research group agenda, emanating from two crucial papers from the previous decade (Olson, 1970; 1977 – both of which later became citation classics). In the 1970 paper Olson argued against the then prevalent view in linguistics, that meaning is a property of words, and for a more psychological view, that meaning is a property of the intentions of speakers. This distinction reflects that between language as a representational system and language as a communicational system. Olson argued that representation, though providing symbols for thinking, does not in itself restructure thought, although communication may, at least for the listener. He suggested that language is used to indicate intended referents, which though known to the speaker, may be unknown to the listener and so may influence his or her thinking. Objections to the claims made in this paper led Olson (1977) to distinguish between meaning in spoken dialogue, where the focus is on intentions, and meaning in written text, where the focus is on words. Writing, Olson argued, fixes the verbal form and allows for the distinction between words – what is said – and intentions – what is meant. Written text has a literal meaning, which is in the text itself. In some ways, this was out of the frying pan and into the fire; that is to say, this later argument met with even more opposition than the earlier one. In particular, Olson's idea of autonomous texts, which mean no more nor less than what they say, was strongly opposed by those who argued that meaning is constructed by the reader. Indeed, on more than one occasion David has said, in a typical self-deprecating way, that these two papers became citation classics because they had to be cited so often in order to be so soundly disputed.

World and Mind

Be that as it may, the say/mean distinction, generated by the idea of autonomous text, proved fruitful in many ways. Once established, it could be applied to speech as well as writing, and used to investigate, for example, children's understanding of indirect requests, metaphor, and sarcasm – where what is said and what is meant do not coincide – and children's understanding of ambiguity – where what is said may be interpreted in more than one way (Olson & Hildyard, 1983; Olson & Torrance, 1983; Robinson, Goelman, & Olson, 1983). The say/mean distinction is based on seeing a difference between something in the world and something in the mind. What is in the world is the utterance – the actual words that the speaker says and the listener hears. What is in the mind is the speaker's intention and the listener's interpretation. Thus, thinking about intentions and interpretations, distinguished from utterances and expressions, is one aspect of thinking about the distinction between mind and world.

My own work at this time, in my MA thesis, addressed children's understanding of a related distinction – that between intention and action (Astington, 1981; 1986). Again, intention is what is represented in mind; the action is what is seen in the world. Up to this point much of the work on children's recognition of intentional and unintentional action had been conducted in the context of their moral judgments, whereas my focus was on children's understanding of the linguistic terms used to mark the distinction between actions performed deliberately and what happens by accident, terms such as *intend, mean, plan, on purpose*. I remember David saying, when I began this work, "Wouldn't it be nice if psycholinguistics could explain moral development?" This was perhaps my first exposure to his confidence in the power of semantic development, subsequently revealed in many ways.

Olson spent 1983–84 as a Fellow at the Center for Advanced Study in the Behavioral Sciences at Stanford, and became a regular participant in John Flavell's research group meetings in the Psychology Department at Stanford University. In the fall of 1984 he returned to our research group at OISE, excited by Flavell's work on children's ability to distinguish between appearance and reality (e.g., Flavell, Flavell & Green, 1983). When young children were shown trick objects, such as a sponge painted to look like a rock, they had difficulty acknowledging that although it looked liked one thing (a rock), it was really something else (a sponge). We saw this as another aspect of young children's inability to think separately about world and mind, in this case the real object in the world and its appearance in the mind, and it led to our experiments on children's ability to distinguish between what is seen and what is known (Olson & Astington, 1987).

I remember receiving a letter from David just before he went to Stanford (Olson, pers. comm., June 9, 1983). He wrote that he had been thinking about children's knowledge of "other minds" in light of my suggestion that children may not be aware of others' intentions until they have a concept of intention. He continued, "Now, I'd like to push that back to other mental states, thinking and wanting. Kids at an early age attribute desires: the dog wants to bite me, the kitty is thirsty, etc. But what about others' thoughts? Suppose a kid saw or heard that X put an object in one location L and left the room. Y moved the object to a new location L' and the kid saw both. If X returns to the room where will the kid think X will look for the object. At that age when they're learning Hide & Seek they should expect X to look where *it is* not where X *thinks* it is." In reply I sent him a photocopy of an article that I had just come across in the OISE library, the now well-known first study of young children's inability to recognize false beliefs (Wimmer & Perner, 1983). Children's understanding of false belief has since come to epitomize their understanding of the distinction between mind and world. That is to say, when children respond appropriately in false belief tasks, for example by predicting that a person will look for an object where he or she last saw it and not where they themselves know it was subsequently moved to, they show that they understand that people represent the world in mind, and act on the basis of that representation even when it misrepresents the actual situation in the world.

The say/mean distinction thus was part of, and indeed helped generate, a lively new area of study that took shape at this time – children's theory of mind. By 1985 Olson was co-director of the McLuhan Program in Culture and Technology at the University of Toronto where he formed a research group with Alison Gopnik from Psychology, Lynd Forguson from Philosophy, and me. The four of us frequently discussed and were impressed by the variety of ways in which young children grapple with the distinction between world and mind – distinguishing between reality and belief, reality and appearance, action and intention, utterance and interpretation – and also the variety of ways in which researchers were investigating this understanding. We organized an international conference at the McLuhan Program to see if there was a common body of ideas among the disparate scholars, and indeed there was. The conference in the spring of 1986 and resulting publication (Astington, Harris & Olson, 1988) helped establish children's theory of mind as an important area of research in cognitive development, one which has burgeoned over the past decade and a half.

Theory of Mind and Language

Nowadays the term "theory of mind" is interpreted in a variety of ways (Astington, 1998), from being broadly taken to mean something like "social understanding" to being narrowly equated with the ability to pass false belief tasks. My own view occupies some middle ground: children's theory of mind underlies their ability to attribute beliefs, desires, intentions, and emotions to the self and others in order to explain and predict behavior. Its development begins in infancy in joint attention and shared reference; by 18 months of age children clearly show an understanding of a person's attentional focus and referential intent (Baldwin & Moses, 1994). This early theory continues to develop through the toddler years as children acquire an understanding of emotion, desire, and perception (Gopnik, Slaughter, & Meltzoff,

1994; Meltzoff, Gopnik, & Repacholi, 1999). Then toward the end of the preschool period the core abilities that are taken to indicate the possession of a representational theory of mind develop: that is, the ability to attribute false beliefs to the self and others, and to distinguish between appearance and reality (Flavell et al., 1983; Gopnik & Astington, 1988; Wimmer & Perner, 1983).

In the main, it is these later abilities that have been assessed in relation to language development. Happé, (1995), using data pooled from a number of studies, showed that 3- to 4-year-olds' verbal ability measured by the British Picture Vocabulary Scale (BPVS; Dunn, Dunn, Whetton & Pintilie, 1982) was correlated with their false belief task performance ($r(68) = .55$, $p < .01$), making a significant contribution to variability in false belief scores independent of age. Jenny Jenkins and I (Jenkins & Astington, 1996) found correlations between 3- to 5-year-olds' scores on standard false belief tests and standard measures of general language ability such as the Test of Early Language Development (Hresko, Reid, & Hammill, 1981) and the sentence memory subtest of the Stanford Binet (with age controlled, $pr(65) = .33–.35$, $p < .01$). Cutting and Dunn (1999) showed that children's aggregate performance on a range of false belief tasks correlated with their scores on the BPVS and with scores on a test of narrative speech (the Bus Story; Renfrew, 1991), even when age and family background were accounted for ($pr(118) = .33–.50$, $p < .01$). Hughes (1998) showed that verbal ability measured by a composite of receptive vocabulary, narrative speech, mean length of utterance, and grammatical complexity, makes a significant contribution, independent of age, to variability in false belief understanding measured by prediction, explanation, and deception tasks. Thus, a number of studies using a range of theory-of-mind and language measures has shown a relation between the two.

Moreover, it is not just that language and theory of mind develop concurrently. I believe that there is a causal relation involved, such that general language ability plays an important role in theory-of-mind development (Astington & Jenkins, 1999). We tested 3-year-olds three times over a period of seven months, assessing their language competence using a standardized measure of early language development (Hresko et al., 1981) and assessing theory of mind using false belief tasks and appearance-reality tasks. We found that changes in children's theory of mind were predicted by their language competence, but there was no reciprocal relation, that is to say, language development was not predicted by the theory-of-mind test scores. These findings are consistent with the argument that linguistic development promotes theory-of-mind development. It is true that the false belief and appearance-reality tasks we used are verbal tests, requiring some linguistic ability for successful performance. It is also true that false belief tasks are easier if they require less linguistic ability; for example, children can act out a search better than they can make a verbal prediction of where a character will look for an object that has been moved (Freeman, Lewis, & Doherty, 1991). However, as Cutting and Dunn (1999, p. 854) point out, "correlations between language ability and theory-of-mind performance have now been established . . . for a wide range of theory-of-mind measures, some less verbal than others, so the linguistic demands of standard tasks are unlikely to account fully for correlations between language ability and performance on theory-of-mind tests."

Furthermore, although one can simplify the false belief task by simplifying its linguistic demands, omitting language altogether is not helpful. Completely non-verbal tasks are at least as difficult (Call & Tomasello, 1999) and may be more difficult (Plaut & Karmiloff-Smith, 1993) than the standard tasks. These findings support the argument that theory of mind depends on language, such that linguistic development supports theory-of-mind development. From this point of view, it is not that linguistic immaturity masks children's underlying competence, but rather, theory-of-mind development and language development are themselves fundamentally related and interdependent.

Thus, it is well established that in normal development there is a strong and quite possibly causal relation between language and theory-of-mind development. Further evidence for a causal link is provided by studies of deaf children whose language development is delayed although their nonverbal intelligence and social adjustment are within normal levels. When these children are tested on standard false belief tasks, adapted to their mode of communication, they frequently fail the tasks, although responding correctly to control questions (de Villiers & de Villiers, in press; Peterson & Siegal, 1995). More strikingly, the de Villiers and their colleagues have shown that such children find nonverbal theory-of-mind tasks just as difficult. Moreover, deaf children's performance on the nonverbal tasks is predicted by their level of language development. Further, children with autism generally fail theory-of-mind tasks and have lower levels of general language ability than normal children (Tager-Flusberg, 1997). Importantly, verbal ability appears to be the crucial factor for those children with autism who do pass false belief tasks (Happé, 1995). These findings from different populations support the idea that language development precedes and promotes theory-of-mind development.

Theory of Mind and Metalanguage

The studies discussed so far support the argument that general language ability is related to and may foster theory-of-mind development. Olson's (1988, 1994) argument is more specific, however. He argues that theory-of-mind development is dependent on the acquisition of the metacognitive and metalinguistic terms that are used to refer to mental states and speech acts. In support of this argument, Moore, Pure, and Furrow (1990) found significant correlations between children's scores on theory-of-mind tasks and a task assessing their comprehension of the terms *think* and *know*, although they did not measure the children's general linguistic competence which may explain the relation found. Indeed, Hughes and Dunn (1997), who measured frequency of metacognitive talk in pretend play, showed that both general verbal ability and frequency of metacognitive talk are correlated with theory-of-mind task performance, but the relation between metacognitive talk and theory of mind was not independent of general verbal ability. However, Hughes and Dunn (1998) showed that frequency of metacognitive talk did predict children's theory-of-mind task performance one year later, independent of general verbal ability, thus providing some support for Olson's argument.

In order to use metacognitive verbs to contrast mind and world one has to report an agent's attitude to the propositional content of the mental state. Thus, mental state reports are of the form: [agent]-[attitude]-[proposition]. For example, "Maxi thinks the chocolate is in the cupboard" and "I thought there were Smarties in the box." This requires a complex construction consisting of a main sentence with another sentence embedded in it. The embedded sentence, "the chocolate is in the cupboard," or "Smarties are in the box" forms a subordinate clause that acts as the grammatical object of the verb *think* in the main sentence. In linguistics such clauses are called *object complements*. They allow the report of false beliefs; that is, the whole construction may be true even though the embedded sentence is false. Thus, I can truthfully say, "Maxi thinks the chocolate is in the cupboard," even if it is actually in the drawer and I know that. Likewise I can truthfully say, "I thought there were Smarties in the box," even though I now know it contains only pencils. De Villiers and de Villiers (in press) argue that it is acquisition of the syntax of complementation toward the end of the preschool years that provides the representational format needed for false belief understanding. They show that children's mastery of complement syntax, assessed by comprehension of complex wh-questions and production of complements in spontaneous speech, predicts false belief task scores at a later time, but the reverse is not the case, that is, earlier false belief scores do not predict later syntax scores. In addition, for deaf children, verbal and nonverbal theory-of-mind task performance is predicted by complement production scores. The de Villiers argue that although language and theory-of-mind development in general may be interdependent, the crucial acquisition of false belief understanding is fundamentally dependent on mastery of the syntax of complementation.

A major problem, to my mind, is that it is not clear that a distinction can be made between the de Villiers' and Olson's hypotheses. That is to say, both semantics and syntax are implicated in mental state reports. The de Villiers argue that verbs of communication also involve object complements and so provide a contrasting case to the metacognitive verbs in their experiments ("Maxi says that the chocolate is in the cupboard"). That is, children's use of verbs of communication, like *say*, as well as metacognitive verbs, like *think*, is assessed in the de Villiers' comprehension and production tasks. However, verbs of communication are metalinguistic and are just as much a part of the metalanguage as metacognitive verbs. It may well be that we cannot separate semantics and syntax in this regard. Having a full semantic understanding of any term involves understanding the syntactic constructions in which the term appears. In her study of children's understanding of the metalinguistic verbs *ask*, *tell*, and *promise*, Chomsky (1969) said that children knew the meaning of these terms quite some time before they understood all of the syntactic structures in which the terms appeared. However, I agree with Nelson (1996) who argues that the full meaning of metacognitive terms is only gradually acquired. Comprehending object complementation is part of understanding the meaning of metacognitive terms.

General mastery of object complementation may be less important than the precise metacognitive or metalinguistic term involved. Custer (1996) found that 3-year-olds can respond correctly in a picture choice task when the test scenario includes the sentence [person]-[is pretending]-[that x] (e.g., "He is pretending that his puppy is outside") but not, in exactly the same task, when the sentence is [person]-[thinks]-[that x] (e.g., "He thinks that his puppy is outside"). Both types of sentence include the same object complement, yet children pass the task when *pretend* is used, and fail when *think* is used. This finding supports Olson's argument that it is semantics that is important. Even though *pretend* and *think* appear in the same constructions, their meaning is different, and children comprehend one before the other.

I turn now to some recent empirical studies that I have conducted with my colleagues Jenny Jenkins and Janette Pelletier, investigating relations among theory of mind, language, and metalanguage.

Theory-of-Mind Task Performance and Spontaneous Use of Metacognitive Language

Twenty three-year-olds, making up one cohort of those involved in the study mentioned above (Astington & Jenkins, 1999) whose language and theory-of-mind development were followed over a period of 7 months, were also videotaped at each test time during 10 minutes of pretend play with a peer, and the videotapes were transcribed and coded. In addition, parents of nine of these children kept a diary for one month around each of the three test points. Parents were told that we were studying the period when children start to recognize that they and other people have thoughts about things in the world. Parents were asked to record any examples in which their child talked about his or her own thoughts or about other people's thoughts. They were given a number of examples where a child contrasts someone's belief with reality, or contrasts his or her own belief with that of another person, or recognizes that he or she made a mistake, or tells a lie, or plays a trick on another person. We asked parents to watch out for incidents like the examples, and to record the details as instructed, especially to note the exact words the child used.

We coded the mental verbs used during pretend play into three categories: cognition (*think, know, guess, remember, forget, guess, trick, mean*); desire (*want, need, like, love*); and perception (*look, see, show, watch*). We divided the pretend play transcripts into speaker turns, defined as one child's utterance bounded by another child's utterances, and counted the number of turns in which a particular mental verb was used. Table 16.1 shows the mean number of total turns, and of turns containing mental verbs in each category, for the three time points. Then we examined the relation between children's theory-of-mind scores and their use of mental verbs, as we did with their general language scores. Again, we were interested in the pattern of relations from an earlier time point to a later one. Only the correlations

Table 16.1 Mean Number of Total Turns, and Mental Verb Turns, at Three Time Points

	Time-1	*Time-2*	*Time-3*
Total turns	16.35	42.45	46.28
Mental verb turns			
Cognition	.60	1.25	1.67
Desire	1.75	2.85	5.39
Perception	.75	1.00	1.39

Note. $N = 20$ at Time-1 and Time-2; $N = 18$ at Time-3.

between theory-of-mind scores and cognitive verb use show any pattern of significant relations. However, the relation was not in one direction only, from the language to the theory-of-mind measure, as it was for general linguistic competence. Children's use of cognitive verbs at Time-1 predicts their theory-of-mind task performance at Time-2. Similarly and reciprocally, theory-of-mind task performance at Time-1 predicts use of cognitive verbs at Time-2, perhaps providing evidence of mutual boosting between theory of mind and language.

Be that as it may, it is certainly the case that children use cognitive verbs before they can perform successfully on theory-of-mind tasks. Table 16.2 shows the number of children using cognitive verbs compared with their performance on the theory-of-mind tasks. As can be seen, at each time period five children who score low on the theory-of-mind tasks use one or more cognitive verbs. One can also see that

Table 16.2 Number of Children Using Cognitive Verbs Compared with their Theory-of-Mind (ToM) Task Performance, at Three Time Points

Time-1, N = 20	*ToM score 0–2*	*ToM score 3–6*
No verbs	10	4
1 or more verbs	5	1

Time-2, N = 20	*ToM score 0–2*	*ToM score 3–6*
No verbs	3	5
1 or more verbs	5	7

Time-3, N = 18	*ToM score 0–2*	*ToM score 3–6*
No verbs	1	2
1 or more verbs	5	10

some children, who performed better on the theory-of-mind tasks, used no cognitive verbs in their pretend play (four children at Time-1, five at Time-2, and two at Time-3). This may indicate that they could not use them, but probably just indicates that they happened not to use them in the 10 minutes of play while they were videotaped.

The children who scored low on the theory-of-mind tasks but who used cognitive verbs during pretend play used them appropriately. A striking example comes from the Time-2 transcripts:

> *Child-A*:　I'll trick, I'll trick her. When she comes back, she'll think I'm a real person, but I'm. . . .
> *Child-B*:　Yah, I'm gonna put my umbrella up and you squirt me.
> (9 turns intervene)
> *Child-A*:　She'll still think I'm a real person and I'm not a real person. I'll be not a real person.

At this time Child-A was 3 years, 5 months old and his score on the theory-of-mind tests was only 2 out of 6 correct.

We found a similar pattern in the parents' observations. That is to say, parents recorded examples of their child's spontaneous reference to his or her own thoughts or another person's thoughts during time periods when the child was failing a majority of theory-of-mind tasks in the lab. For example, at Time-1, Child-C, aged 2 years, 10 months, scored 2 out of 6 on the theory-of-mind tasks. One day she was in the kitchen with her mother and was worried by the noise of the washing machine. It reminded her of her bedtime fear of monsters. She said to her mother, "After I was in bed I heard a clump, clump, clump. I thought it was a monster coming up the stairs but it wasn't." Another day in the same time period she said to her mother who had been calling her, "I thought you were a monster so I didn't come. But you're not a monster you're my mom."

Child-A, aged 3 years, 1 month at Time-1, scored zero on the theory-of-mind tasks. One bedtime his father read him a story from *The Wind in the Willows*, where Toad disguises himself as a washerwoman to escape from jail and then, still in disguise, gets a train engineer to give him a free ride. The child said to his father, "He [the engineer] doesn't know it's Toad." A few days later the child got upset at breakfast because he thought there was no oatmeal left. His mother showed him the pot and he said, "I thought the oatmeal was gone but I was wrong." It is important to note that these examples are just like those recorded from children who passed a majority of the theory-of-mind tasks.

How can we explain the fact that children can talk about mental states in an appropriate way in a naturalistic setting yet fail the theory-of-mind tasks? Successful performance on the experimental tasks seems to depend on comprehension of the semantic terms and syntactic constructions the children themselves spontaneously produce. Olson or the de Villiers might argue that children's naturalistic use of the term *think* (with object complement) comes in first and leads to false belief understanding, but the force of this argument is lost if the time lag is too great – as it was in some of these cases. For example, Child-A, quoted above using mental verbs and object complements at Time-1 when his theory-of-mind score was zero, and at Time-2 when he scored 2 out of 6 on theory of mind, still scored only 3 out of 6 in the final test period.

In this section I have compared children's performance on theory-of-mind tasks with their spontaneous use of metalanguage. The fact that spontaneous use of metacognitive verbs precedes successful test performance could be due to differences between the experimental and naturalistic situations. Donaldson (1992) suggests that in production children are carried along by their own motivation and involvement in the situation. I should note that these children were comfortable and co-operative in the test situation and answered the control questions correctly. However, in the next section I will make a more even-handed comparison and examine children's performance on theory-of-mind experimental tests and their performance on experimental tests of metalanguage production and comprehension.

Theory-of-Mind and Metalanguage Test Performance

Recently Janette Pelletier and I have followed 107 children during their transition to school (Astington & Pelletier, 1999). The aim of the study is to describe the pattern of relations among children's theory of mind, metacognitive language abilities, and school performance, controlling for general language competence and family background, in order to determine whether children's understanding of mind makes a difference to their success in school. The children were tested once each term over two years, that is, six times in all. Here I refer to some of the first-year data in order to compare performance on theory-of-mind tasks and metalanguage tasks.

At the start of the year the mean age of the younger group was 4 years, 4 months, and the older group 5 years, 4 months. The children came from a number of different schools and a variety of home backgrounds; 23% spoke another language at home in addition to English, but their English language competence was sufficient for them to participate comfortably in the testing. All the children were tested on first-order false belief tasks at the start of the year, and those who did not reach ceiling were tested again (using similar but not identical tasks) at the end of the year. Four standard tasks were used: two Maxi-like story tasks, in one of which children were asked to predict where a character with a false belief would look for an object and in the other, where the character would think the object was; and two Smarties-like tasks involving something unexpected, in which children were asked to predict their friend's false belief in the situation. We also tested children's general language competence at the start of the year, using the Test of Early Language Development (Hresko et al., 1981).

In the middle of the year children's metalanguage production was tested in a story retelling task. The experimenter told children a story from a wordless picture book and then they retold it to the experimenter. The story was 233 words long, including 14 tokens of 5 types of metacognitive terms; for example, part of the story ran thus: " . . . Scott *knows* that Grey Squirrel will be sad because he won't *know* where his nut is. Scott *decides* to play a *trick* on Brown Squirrel. He *decides* to take the nut from the flower pot. He puts the nut back under the bush. Scott *knows* that Grey Squirrel will look for the nut under the bush because he *thinks* that's where it is. Scott *knows* that Brown Squirrel will look for the nut in the flower pot because he *thinks* that's where it is . . . "

Some children, although they followed the story, retold the action plot without using any metalanguage, for example: ". . . They're running back. And he . . . the squirrel's checking where it is. He's, the squirrel's checking where it is in the pot. The squirrel gots it back. . . ." However, other children's retelling did use metalanguage, perhaps in imitation of the experimenter, although sometimes different metalanguage terms were used; for example: ". . . Then Grey Squirrel comes back. And Scott knows that Grey Squirrel will look under the bush cause he thinks it's there. And that Brown Squirrel will try in the flower pot because he thinks it's there."

At the end of the year children's metalanguage comprehension was tested with a newly developed vocabulary test, consisting of six metacognitive verbs (*know, guess, remember, forget, wonder, figure out*). The experimenter told a story with pictures and at times during the story the child was asked to make a choice between two different metacognitive terms. For example: ". . . Dad comes into the room and says, 'Time for bed. If it's sunny tomorrow, we'll go to the park.' In the morning John gets out of bed and looks out the window. He sees the rain pouring down. 'Oh no,' says John, 'Look at that! We won't be going to the park today.' Tell me: Does John *know* it's raining or does John *remember* it's raining?" Another example, later in the story: ". . . Tomorrow it will be John's birthday. John looks in the closet and sees a birthday present all wrapped up with his name on it. John says, 'Maybe this present is a new baseball glove, or maybe it's a football, or maybe it's a new toy truck.' Tell me: Does John *wonder* what the present is or does John *forget* what the present is?" Each verb was used twice in the test questions, once as the correct choice and once as the incorrect choice; the child had to get both right to get credit for that verb.

Table 16.3 shows the mean scores, standard deviations, and range on the false belief, language, and metalanguage tasks. Table 16.4 shows correlations among the measures. Scores on false belief, language, and both metalanguage tasks are all significantly correlated. Of more interest, when age and general language are accounted for, the metalanguage measures are still significantly correlated with false belief understanding: for production of types, $pr(103) = .23$, $p < .05$; and of tokens, $pr(103) = .31$, $p < .01$; and for comprehension, $pr(103) = .21$, $p < .05$. Similarly, controlling for age and metalanguage (in one composite measure) general language is still significantly correlated with false belief understanding: $pr(103) = .55$, $p < .001$. Thus, general language and metacognitive language make independent contributions to variability in children's understanding of false belief.

Table 16.3   Mean Scores, Standard Deviations, and Range on Theory-of-Mind and Language Measures (N = 107)

Test	Test Period	Mean	SD	Range
1st-order False Belief	start year	2.9	1.5	0–4
General Language (TELD)	start year	20.8	6.2	1–32
Metalanguage Production: Types	mid year	2.1	1.2	0–5
Metalanguage Production: Tokens	mid year	3.5	2.3	0–10
Metalanguage Comprehension	end year	3.2	1.7	0–6
Age in months	start year	58.6	6.7	46–69

Table 16.4   Pearson Correlations of False Belief, General Language, Metalanguage, and Age (N = 107)

	Age	FB	Lang	Type	Token
FB	.22*				
Lang	.40***	.61***			
Type	.32**	.40***	.38***		
Token	.26**	.40***	.27**	.78***	
Comp	.40***	.28**	.22*	.32**	.32**

Legend
FB   1st-order False Belief
Lang   General Language (TELD)
Type   Metalanguage Production: Types
Token   Metalanguage Production: Tokens
Comp   Metalanguage Comprehension
* $p < .05$, ** $p < .01$, *** $p < .001$

One might argue that these findings are not surprising, given that the false belief tasks are linguistic tasks that use metalanguage in the test questions. However, it is worth noting that *think* is the only metaterm used in the false belief testing whereas a range of terms was produced and comprehended in the metalanguage tasks. Moreover, one of the first-order false belief tasks did not use any metalanguage; children were asked where the story character who held a false belief would look for the object that had been moved. All children were given this task at the start of the year and 45 of them received the task at the end of the year (those who had not yet reached ceiling, as explained above). At each test time there was no difference between children's responses to the story that asked where the character would *look* for the object and the story that asked where the character would *think* the object was. In other words, there is no indication that children's false belief understanding was dependent on their comprehension of the term *think* in contrast to the term *look*.

Language and Metalanguage: Biology and Culture

Where does this leave us? Are Olson and I any closer to resolving our argument about the contribution of language and metalanguage to theory-of-mind development? On my view, general language development is crucial because language provides a means of coding perceptual reality (e.g., "chocolate is in cupboard") and holding on to it when the visual display changes (e.g., the chocolate is moved to the drawer – "chocolate was in cupboard"). The child can also code the fact that Maxi was present when the chocolate was put in the cupboard and absent when it was moved to the drawer. In order to predict where Maxi will look for the chocolate when he returns, the child has to recognize that there is a mismatch between what is now the real state of the world and what was the state when Maxi was last on the scene. The child's linguistic ability is crucial because it allows the child to represent the past situation, in the face of the conflicting situation in the visual display. As Plaut and Karmiloff-Smith (1993, p. 70) say: "We believe the developmental results [of false belief tasks] are best interpreted in terms of increasing capability in using and generating symbolic representations that are sufficiently well elaborated to override the otherwise compelling interpretations generated by direct experience. Furthermore, language is central to theory-of-mind processes precisely because it provides particularly effective 'scaffolding' for symbolic representations."

When the child successfully predicts that Maxi will look in the cupboard we say that she understands Maxi's false belief – she knows that Maxi thinks that the chocolate is in the cupboard. But perhaps not. Is it possible for the child to follow the story and make the necessary causal connections without the embedded representation "Maxi thinks that the chocolate is in the cupboard"? Could the child predict that Maxi will look in the cupboard because that is where he put the chocolate before he went out? Perner (1988) denies this possibility and argues that the child has to recognize that Maxi currently represents the past situation ("chocolate in cupboard") and acts according to it, even though it misrepresents the current situation. But perhaps language provides the cognitive capability to model Maxi's representation and understand it as a misrepresentation of the perceived situation, without construing it in terms of "Maxi *thinks* that . . . "

Language is a biological universal. Whatever cultural differences exist in conceptualizing social interaction (Vinden & Astington, 2000) it is likely that people everywhere understand someone's search for a misplaced object, and understand misleading appearances, tricks, and so on. However, not all cultures talk about these things using metacognitive terms (Vinden, 1996). It is language itself that allows for a contrast between mind and world, even if it is not construed in terms of "mind" – there is still the contrast between the linguistic and the perceptual representations (Plaut & Karmiloff-Smith, 1993).

It is here that the moral from my Piaget and Vygotsky reading comes into play. To repeat: "Cognition rests as much on a cultural foundation as it does on a biological one" (Olson, 1980a, p. 3). In our culture this contrast between mind and world, between the linguistic representation and the perceptual display, is mapped onto metacognitive terms and object complements. That is, I can contrast what Maxi thinks is the case and what I see is the case by representing it as [Maxi]-[thinks]-[chocolate in cupboard] and [I]-[see]-[chocolate in drawer]. Furthermore, the acquisition of different metacognitive terms allows a variety of contrasts to be made, for example, "I *see* the chocolate in the drawer but I *remember* the chocolate was in the cupboard," "My friend *thinks* there are Smarties in the box but I *know* it's pencils," and so on.

I would argue that both language and metalanguage are involved in theory-of-mind development in western children. Language is a biological universal that allows for representation of a false belief in contradistinction to the evidence provided in the visual display. Metalanguage provides children with our culture's way of making this distinction explicit. False beliefs – indeed, mental states generally, such as believing, remembering, inferring, guessing, and so on – are not directly perceived, although we may see their effects in people's actions in the world. Young children may have some understanding of these actions and effects. However, importantly, children can reflect on and articulate this understanding when the unobservable mental phenomena are brought to their attention by the adult's use of metacognitive terms to talk about the actions and effects. The acquisition of metacognitive terms is a cultural acquisition that helps children to conceptualize the contrast between the world and the mind. Thus, Olson and I can agree that language and metalanguage are both of importance in the development of children's theory of mind.

Acknowledgments

I am very grateful to Jenny Jenkins and Janette Pelletier for our research collaborations and for their permission to cite data produced in our work together. I would also like to thank Janette Pelletier, Philip D. Zelazo, Joan Peskin, and Deepthi Kamawar for their helpful comments on this chapter, and the Natural Sciences and Engineering Research Council of Canada and the Social Sciences and Humanities Research Council of Canada for financial support.

References

Astington, J. W. (1981). *Children's understanding of verbal expressions of intention*. MA thesis, University of Toronto (OISE).

Astington, J. W. (1986). Children's comprehension of expressions of intention. *British Journal of Developmental Psychology, 4*, 43–9.

Astington, J. W. (1998). Theory of mind, Humpty Dumpty, and the icebox. *Human Development, 41*, 30–9.

Astington, J. W., Harris, P. L., & Olson, D. R. (Eds.). (1988). *Developing theories of mind*. New York: Cambridge University Press.

Astington, J. W., & Jenkins, J. M. (1999). A longitudinal study of the relation between language and theory-of-mind development. *Developmental Psychology, 35*, 1311–20.

Astington, J. W., & Pelletier, J. (1999). *Young children's theory of mind and its relation to their success in school.* Unpublished manuscript, University of Toronto.

Baldwin, D. A., & Moses, L. J. (1994). Early understanding of referential intent and attentional focus: Evidence from language and emotion. In C. Lewis & P. Mitchell (Eds.), *Children's early understanding of mind* (pp. 133–56). Hove, UK: Erlbaum.

Call, J., & Tomasello, M. (1999). A nonverbal false belief task: The performance of children and great apes. *Child Development, 70*, 381–95.

Chomsky, C. (1969). *The acquisition of syntax in children from 5 to 10.* Cambridge, MA: MIT Press.

Custer, W. (1996). A comparison of young children's understanding of contradictory representations in pretense, memory, and belief. *Child Development, 67*, 678–88.

Cutting, A. L., & Dunn, J. (1999). Theory of mind, emotion understanding, language and family background: Individual differences and interrelations. *Child Development, 70*, 853–65.

de Villiers, J. G., & de Villiers, P. A. (in press). Linguistic determinism and the understanding of false beliefs. In P. Mitchell & K. Riggs (Eds.), *Children's reasoning and the mind.* Hove, UK: Psychology Press.

Donaldson, M. (1992). *Human minds.* Harmondsworth, UK: Penguin.

Dunn, L. M., Dunn, L. M., Whetton, C., & Pintilie, D. (1982). *British Picture Vobulary Scale.* Windsor, UK: NFER-Nelson.

Flavell, J. H., Flavell, E. R., & Green, F. L. (1983). Development of the appearance-reality distinction. *Cognitive Psychology, 15*, 95–120.

Freeman, N. H., Lewis, C., & Doherty, M. J. (1991). Preschoolers' grasp of a desire for knowledge in false-belief prediction: Practical intelligence and verbal report. *British Journal of Developmental Psychology, 9*, 139–57.

Gopnik, A., & Astington, J. W. (1988). Children's understanding of representational change and its relation to the understanding of false belief and the appearance-reality distinction. *Child Development, 59*, 26–37.

Gopnik, A., Slaughter, V., & Meltzoff, A. (1994). Changing your views: How understanding visual perception can lead to a new theory of mind. In C. Lewis & P. Mitchell (Eds.), *Children's early understanding of mind* (pp. 157–81). Hove, UK: Erlbaum.

Happé, F. G. E. (1995). The role of age and verbal ability in the theory of mind task performance of subjects with autism. *Child Development, 66*, 843–55.

Hresko, W. P., Reid, D. K., & Hammill, D. D. (1981). *The Test of Early Language Development (TELD).* Austin, TX: Pro-Ed.

Hughes, C. (1998). Executive function in preschoolers: Links with theory of mind and verbal ability. *British Journal of Developmental Psychology, 16*, 233–53.

Hughes, C., & Dunn, J. (1997). "Pretend you didn't know": Young children's talk about mental states in pretend play. *Cognitive Development, 12*, 477–99.

Hughes, C., & Dunn, J. (1998). Understanding mind and emotion: Longitudinal associations with mental-state talk between young friends. *Developmental Psychology, 34*, 1026–37.

Jenkins, J. M., & Astington, J. W. (1996). Cognitive factors and family structure associated with theory of mind development in young children. *Developmental Psychology, 32*, 70–8.

Meltzoff, A. N., Gopnik, A., & Repacholi, B. M. (1999). Toddlers' understanding of intentions, desires, and emotions: Explorations of the Dark Ages. In P. D. Zelazo, J. W. Astington, & D. R. Olson (Eds.), *Developing theories of intention: Social understanding and self con-*

trol (pp. 17–41). Mahwah, NJ: Erlbaum.

Moore, C., Pure, K., & Furrow, D. (1990). Children's understanding of the modal expressions of speaker certainty and uncertainty and its relation to the development of a representational theory of mind. *Child Development, 61*, 722–30.

Nelson, K. (1996). *Language in cognitive development.* New York: Cambridge University Press.

Olson, D. R. (1970). Language and thought: Aspects of a cognitive theory of semantics. *Psychological Review, 77*, 257–73.

Olson, D. R. (1977). From utterance to text: The bias of language in speech and writing. *Harvard Educational Review, 47*, 257–81.

Olson, D. R. (1980a). Introduction. In D. R. Olson (Ed.), *The social foundations of language and thought* (pp. 1–15). New York: Norton.

Olson, D. R. (1980b). Some social aspects of meaning in oral and written language. In D. R. Olson (Ed.), *The social foundations of language and thought* (pp. 90–108). New York: Norton.

Olson, D. R. (1988). On the origins of beliefs and other intentional states in children. In J. W. Astington, P. L. Harris, & D. R. Olson (Eds.), *Developing theories of mind* (pp. 414–26). New York: Cambridge University Press.

Olson, D. R. (1994). *The world on paper.* Cambridge, UK: Cambridge University Press.

Olson, D. R., & Astington, J. W. (1987). Seeing and knowing: On the ascription of mental states to young children. *Canadian Journal of Psychology, 41*, 399–411.

Olson, D. R., & Hildyard, A. (1983). Literacy and the comprehension and expression of literal meaning. In F. Coulmas & K. Ehlich (Eds.), *Writing in focus* (pp. 291–325). New York: Mouton.

Olson, D. R. & Torrance, N. G. (1983). Literacy and cognitive development. In S. Meadows (Ed.), *Developing thinking: Approaches to childhood cognitive development* (pp. 142–60). London: Methuen.

Perner, J. (1988). Developing semantics for theories of mind: From propositional attitudes to mental representation. In J. W. Astington, P. L. Harris, & D. R. Olson (Eds.), *Developing theories of mind* (pp. 141–72). New York: Cambridge University Press.

Peterson, C. C., & Siegal, M. (1995). Deafness, conversation and theory of mind. *Journal of Child Psychology and Psychiatry, 36*, 459–74.

Piaget, J. (1962). *Play, dreams and imitation in childhood.* New York: Norton. (Original work published 1945)

Plaut, D. C., & Karmiloff-Smith, A. (1993). Representational development and theory-of-mind computations. *Behavioral and Brain Sciences, 16*, 70–1.

Renfrew, C. E. (1991). *The Bus Story: A test of narrative speech.* Oxford, UK: Winslow Press.

Robinson, E., Goelman, H., & Olson, D. R. (1983). Children's understanding of the relation between expressions (what was said) and intentions (what was meant). *British Journal of Developmental Psychology, 1*, 75–86.

Tager-Flusberg, H. (1997). Language acquisition and theory of mind: Contributions from the study of autism. In L. B. Adamson & M. A. Romski (Eds.), *Communication and language acquisition: Discoveries from atypical development* (pp. 135–60). Baltimore, MD: Paul Brookes Publishing.

Vinden, P. G. (1996). Junín Quechua children's understanding of mind. *Child Development, 67*, 1707–16.

Vinden, P. G., & Astington, J. W. (2000). Culture and understanding other minds. In S. Baron-Cohen, H. Tager-Flusberg, & D. Cohen (Eds.), *Understanding other minds: Per-*

spectives from developmental cognitive neuroscience (2nd ed., pp. 503–19). Oxford, UK: Oxford University Press.

Vygotsky, L. S. (1962). *Thought and language*. Cambridge, MA: MIT Press. (Original work published 1931)

Wimmer, H., & Perner, J. (1983). Beliefs about beliefs: Representation and constraining function of wrong beliefs in young children's understanding of deception. *Cognition, 13,* 103–28.

Afterword

Angela Hildyard and Nancy Torrance

Unlike the other authors in this celebratory volume, we have shared a unique relationship with David. Specifically, we have both worked full time *for* David as research assistants and full time *with* David as research associates/collaborators. Together we span almost 30 years of productive, academic relationship. Angela was hired as David's research assistant back in 1970. Nancy came to work for him in 1973 (after Angela had become one of his graduate students). We worked as a three-person collaborative team from 1976 to 1983 and then Angela drifted off into administration, leaving Nancy to hold the fort – a position that she held until 1998.

Life in the early days was always eventful. David was usually surrounded by eager and bright young doctoral students – many desperate to prove themselves. We recall the early lunchtime research group meetings, which could be quite cut-throat in nature! Much to the chagrin of many of these students, we, of course, had the inside edge with essentially unlimited access to David's office, David's time, and David's attention. With the passage of time, as students became more comfortable with David's relaxed style and his genuine enthusiasm for their ideas, research meetings evolved into more collaborative and more constructive forums for the sharing and testing of ideas. As we refined our own ideas for the future directions of our various projects, we watched David's graduate students developing an expertise in the design and implementation of their own experiments, a constructively critical eye when they looked at their own and others' work, and increasingly a level of comfort when discussing research in a group setting.

Departmental monthly research seminars during the 1970s were attended by such notables as Carl Bereiter, Robbie Case, Peter Lindsay, Frank Smith, and Josef Perner (then a student), with occasional visits from University of Toronto's Bob Lockhart and Gus Craik, and every once in a while Jerry Bruner, providing all of us with the opportunity to enjoy academic colleagues engaging in polite but extremely pointed debate. In those golden days when research funding was more generous than is now the case, we, along with various students, were often able to travel with David to conferences. David was always good at, even insistent on, introducing students and us to key people in the field, routinely asking to have students in attendance at closed conferences and workshops. Under David's direction, we have hosted many such events at OISE and the University of Toronto to the mutual benefit of colleagues, students, and ourselves.

The early years were also characterized by some innovative graduate co-teaching. David loved to be challenged by his colleagues, thriving on the intellectual debate while offering a tremendous learning experience to students. Angela recalls one unforgettable course David offered with Peter Lindsay and Frank Smith in the early 1970s, the first of many co-taught with OISE colleagues and visitors.

Reading the various chapters in this book has reminded us of the hours that we would spend with David, dreaming up experiments and developing experimental materials. Nancy's renditions of the Peanuts characters became one of her trade-marks! As we both became moms, our children were often the guinea pigs, al-though they quickly became wise to that and demanded one "real" story for each experimental one we told them!

Back in the 1970s data analysis involved developing computer programs, key-punching the data, and being quite expert – and persistent – at disentangling the numbers which emerged. Many of our original experiments involved collecting re-action time data. In his foreword, Jerry Bruner reminds us of David's enduring interest in diagonal lines. We both recall spending hours trying to disentangle and make sense of the milliseconds it took for experimental subjects to verify that an arrow pointed up to the right versus down to the left and so on. We also collected verification data on such seminal statements as *The car hit the truck* and *The truck was hit by the car* – even *John hit Mary* and *Mary was hit by John*, because in those days we weren't concerned about the political correctness or the social appropriate-ness of our various experimental materials! Nancy recalls the struggle in the late 1980s to develop the methodology for a children's verification task involving coun-terfactual statements, a study that was going to advance our knowledge of chil-dren's theory of mind and literal versus intended meaning. The study died (mercifully) when we realized that even adults didn't know what to make of the question, *If John knows that 2 and 2 is 5, is it true that 2 and 2 is 5?*

Several of David's colleagues have commented on the key role that he has played in helping to describe how we make sense of our worlds and communicate that sense or meaning to others. In retrospect, it seems surprising that we would initially have devoted so much time and energy to exploring cognitive development through techniques which divorced the testing situation from the world as the child knows it. One of David's talents, though, has always been his ability to listen to descrip-tions of everyday activities and events involving children making sense of their worlds and to relate those descriptions to theory. Many insights came over coffee as David made sense of his interactions with one or other of his five young children. Nancy recalls an early, highly productive proposal-writing session in David's office with David's rapid-fire typing (before any of us had a computer) amid three young chil-dren who were alternately hanging off the back of his chair, climbing the desk to hang their artwork, and drawing or writing at his feet, all cheerfully conversing with him as he calmly planned the next year's work. Nowadays his anecdotal evidence comes largely from his grandchildren who have inspired much of his recent work on early conceptions of negation and language.

We see in the chapters of this volume a certain familiarity to the topics and writing, recognizing some themes as recurring even, for Angela, some 16 years later. Andrew Ortony once remarked that one thing he and David had in common was that they would take a problem and work it to death, coming at it over and over again from different perspectives until they were satisfied that they understood every aspect. David once quipped that one really good idea was enough for a lifetime and Nancy often noted parts of that really good idea resurfacing in much the same form every 10 years more or less. This, we think, is also part of David's legacy to his students, encouraging a desire to look, and look again, at a problem or a piece of data, not only in the fine detail but also always as part of the larger picture. As Jerry Bruner puts it – David's incurable interest in the particular and his devotion to Large Ideas.

While David has been celebrated as a marvelous supervisor and colleague, we have been privileged to experience his support and assistance in other areas of our professional lives. Like many of his students, we both benefited greatly from working through the issues of oral and written language, becoming much more focused on the written word and more careful to make our own writing clear and logical. In particular, Angela notes how this style of writing has benefited her work as a university administrator, especially in the area of labor relations where the explicit written word is paramount. Nancy has applied this standard not only to her own writing but also to the many editing tasks undertaken in the past decade.

Although David was highly supportive of his colleagues and students, we remember that his opinion of administrators wasn't nearly so good. We recall expensive lunches with a bemused David and a particular government official, in David's view the prototypical bureaucrat, who insisted on verbal progress reports delivered over a martini or two. One of us also experienced first hand David's indifference at best, and negativism at worst, toward administration and administrators. He became quite respectful though when Angela became his boss, proudly taking credit for discovering her talents early on.

As we ponder David's legacy, we note that he is the first of OISE's faculty to be made a University Professor, an acknowledgement not only of his distinguished contributions to the study of representations of language and thought but also of the growing importance of the field of education within the research-intensive University of Toronto. Other laurels include honorary degrees from the University of Saskatchewan and Götenberg, the prestigious Whitworth Award from the Canadian Educational Association and Fellowship in the Royal Society of Canada.

Throughout much of the past 30 years, David has maintained that he wasn't interested in the application of his theory to applied settings, a job he was willing to leave to other people. We know, however, that his theories have had a great impact, especially on those classroom teachers and educational practitioners who have studied with him. He has often returned from his graduate class with some new insight that developed during a discussion based on a teacher's observations and insights about his or her classroom students. These primary and secondary school educators provided David with some of the raw data for his thinking. They also took away from his classes a new perspective on the learning processes of students which could be applied in their own classroom settings. More recently, David has taken on a more applied role, first, in the broader field of cognitive development through editing the *Handbook of Education and Human Development: New Models of Learning, Teaching and Schooling* (1996) which considers recent theoretical work in cognitive science and applications to the more practical issues of classroom learning; and second, the July 1997 workshop, Literacy and Social Development, sponsored by UNESCO and DSE (German Foundation for International Development) in which David co-organized a meeting of literacy scholars and field workers from developing countries who worked together to formulate concrete recommendations for developing literate societies.

Notwithstanding David's notable contributions to education and cognitive science and his great accomplishments as an educator, the greatest gifts that David has given us have been his patient ear, his (usually) sound advice and his enduring friendship. He is leaving a wonderful legacy – and we look forward to our continuing relationships.

Reference

Olson, D. R., & Torrance, N. (Eds.) (1996), *The handbook of education and human development: New models of learning, teaching and schooling.* Oxford, UK: Blackwell.

Names Index

Page numbers in italics indicate reference list items

Subject Index